Paul Damian

Getting Clients, Keeping Clients

The *Wiley Financial Advisor* Series

Tax-Deferred Investing: Wealth-Building and Wealth-Transfer Strategies
Cory C. Grant and Andrew D. Westhem

Getting Clients, Keeping Clients: The Essential Guide for Tomorrow's Financial Adviser
Dan Richards

Managing Family Trusts: Taking Control of Inherited Wealth
Robert A. Rikoon and Larry Waschka

Advising the 60+ Investor: Tax and Financial Planning Strategies
Darlene Smith, Dale Pulliam, and Holland Toles

Tax-Smart Investing: Maximizing Your Client's Profits
Andrew D. Westhem and Stewart Weissman

GETTING CLIENTS KEEPING CLIENTS

THE ESSENTIAL GUIDE FOR TOMORROW'S FINANCIAL ADVISER

DAN RICHARDS

A Marketplace Book

John Wiley & Sons, Inc.
New York • Chichester • Weinheim • Brisbane • Singapore • Toronto

This book is printed on acid-free paper. ♾

Published by John Wiley & Sons, Inc.
Published simultaneously in Canada.

Library of Congress Cataloging-in-Publication Data:
Richards, Dan, 1950–
Getting clients, keeping clients : the essential guide for tomorrow's financial adviser / Dan Richards.
p. cm.—(The Wiley financial advisor series)
Includes index.
ISBN 0-471-36329-4 (cloth)
1. Financial planners. I. Title. II. Series.
HG179.5.R53 2000
332.024'0068'8—dc21 99-046498

Printed in the United States of America.

10 9 8 7 6 5 4 3 2 1

Dedication

This book is lovingly dedicated to my daughters, Alys and Laura, who have without complaint sacrificed so much of their father's time and attention to make this book possible.

One of my fondest hopes is that one day soon they'll understand what it is exactly that their dad does at the office all day—just as soon as I've figured it out myself.

ACKNOWLEDGMENTS

THIS BOOK SYNTHESIZES EVERYTHING I'VE LEARNED IN NEARLY A DECADE OF research about the things a financial adviser needs to do to become and to stay successful.

Undertaking a task of this magnitude would have been unthinkable without extraordinary good fortune in the support which I have received over the past nine years since founding Marketing Solutions. As I read the final draft of this book one final time before it goes to press, there are four distinct groups that I'd like to thank.

The first are the financial advisers across Canada who have been so remarkably generous in sharing their insights and experiences. I'd like to especially salute the 250 financial advisers who took 90 minutes to participate in a research study on the habits of top performing advisers and the more than 100 financial advisers from across Canada and the United States who have unsparingly given of their time to speak at the Top Performers Conferences, which I have hosted annually since 1994. The practical, real world experiences which are documented in this book would not have been possible without their candor and generosity of spirit.

Secondly, I would like to recognize my colleagues at Marketing Solutions. I can't imagine any entrepreneur being blessed with a management team more patient and dedicated than the one that I have been lucky enough to be surrounded by. It continues to be a privilege to work with them. This book would not have been possible without their commitment.

I wish, thirdly, to recognize my collaborators in translating the concept of this book into reality. In particular, a huge thank you to Harvey Schachter, who took on the prodigious task of taking my random musings into a tape recorder and making them coherent, but also to

Jackie Young of INK Design who shaped Harvey's words into a visual product which is a pleasure to read, and Rosanne Johnstone who co-ordinated the process in its later stages. This book would not have happened without their efforts.

And finally, acknowledgment must go to the many clients who have supported my efforts and those of Marketing Solutions over the last nine years. Neither Marketing Solutions nor this book would have been possible without them.

D. R.

CONTENTS

"Innovation is the single act of
entrepreneurs which most endows them with
new capacity to create wealth."

PETER DRUCKER
Innovation and Entrepreneurship, 1986

"To be successful in this world,
you have to bring something to the table
besides your appetite."

JESSE JACKSON
(as recounted by Dodee Frost Crockett)

"People don't care how much you know
until they know how much you care."

UNKNOWN

Getting Clients, Keeping Clients

INTRODUCTION

Attaining Liftoff

EVERY YEAR I HOST A TOP PERFORMERS CONFERENCE AT WHICH SOME OF our industry's leading lights share the secrets of their success. A few years ago, Dodee Frost Crockett, from Merrill Lynch's Dallas office, related an anecdote that would startle anyone who still considers a financial adviser somebody who simply sells investment instruments through a mixture of glib sales patter and shrewd economic insights.

Dodee builds deep relationships with clients. She informs them that she has resided in Dallas all of her life, knows lots of people, and if they ever confront a problem in which they're stuck for a solution—even if it has nothing to do with money—they should contact her. "That's what I'm here for," she says.

Clients take advantage of her open-ended offer. Some appeal for assistance when they need a good plumber or carpenter. Others have contacted her because they couldn't enroll their child in a private school and hoped she knew an influential alumnus or board member. Once she received a frantic call when the photographer for a client's wedding tumbled down some stairs on the momentous day and broke a leg. "Dodee, can you find me a photographer?" was the plea.

Dodee recites an anecdote about a distraught client telephoning one Tuesday morning with the news he had been diagnosed with cancer and advised to have an operation by Friday. The client said: "I was told, however, that if I wanted a second opinion I could certainly get one—but not before Friday. I've been calling around and around and, frankly, I've been unable to get through to anybody to arrange a second opinion. Then my wife reminded me that you said if I ever needed help with anything I should contact you. I know it's a long shot, but I'm calling to see if you might be able to assist."

Dodee commiserated with the client and promised to act immediately. After hanging up, she considered who might assist. As it happens, another of her clients is on staff at a local teaching hospital. She dialed him but the receptionist took the call, advising he was in a meeting. "Tell him it's his broker and it's important," Dodee replied.

When he got on the line, she informed him about the problem and reminded him of her pledge to clients. "Now tell me, Joe: If this was your dad, who would you send him to?" she asked.

"That's easy," he replied. "I'd have him see the head of oncology here at the hospital."

But it was Tuesday, Dodee pointed out, and the surgery was Friday. "Listen, I know the guy well. We play golf every Saturday," her client said. "Let me head down the hall and see what I can do."

Ten minutes later, Dodee's phone rang. "Your client has an appointment for 4:30 today," her physician-client advised. As it turned out, the surgery was necessary and, in fact, her client liked the doctor who provided the second opinion so much he chose him to perform the operation. The tumor was benign; the client fully recovered. And Dodee Frost Crockett now has an ecstatic client who is convinced his broker saved his life—and is eagerly referring everybody he knows to her for financial advice.

Marketing is the component of success for financial advisers that has received the least attention.

The Four Secrets of Success

Like Dodee Frost Crockett, every financial adviser develops an imaginative formula for success. They all bring their own special flare to the business but four crucial building blocks are necessary for success (Figure I.1).

First, the adviser needs to develop self-management skills, including goal orientation, self-discipline, and time-management. Stephen Covey, among others, has written extensively in this area. It's wise to seek continuous improvement on this aspect of our lives.

The second crucial component is a positive mental attitude. In any sales role, endless opportunities arise for discouragement. The adviser constantly needs to beat back the temptation to succumb to dejection or even to abandon this field. A positive mental outlook is critical, particularly when building your business. It's perhaps less important when you've established a solid client base, but all financial advisers experience frustrating rebuffs and rejections that test their willpower. Again, this domain is well-documented, dating from Napoleon Hill's *Think and Grow Rich* to the latest popular exponent, Anthony Robbins.

Figure I.1

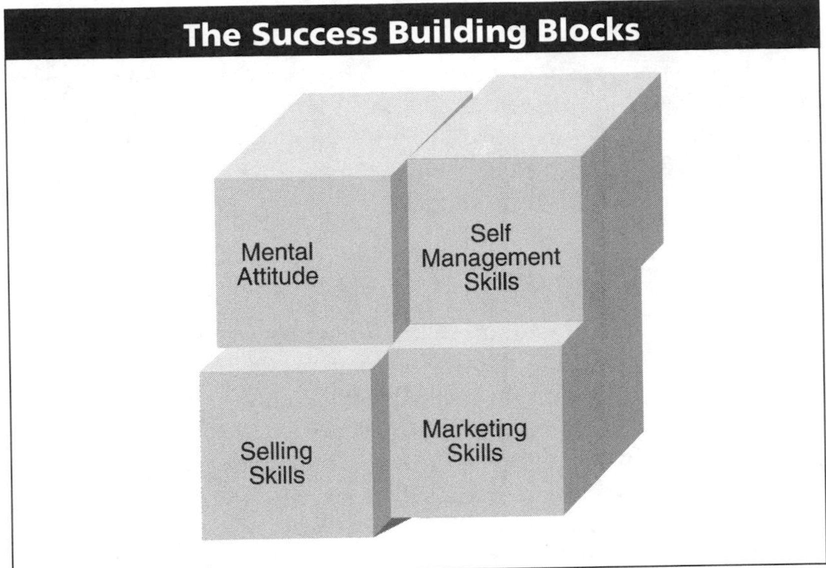

The third element, obviously, is selling skills. When talking to prospects or clients, we need to establish empathy: determine their interests, and formulate recommendations they can and will act upon. That's essentially a persuasive process of convincing your clients that your recommendation is indeed in their best interest. And again, literature, audio tapes and videos abound on sharpening selling skills.

Marketing vs. Selling

The fourth component for success is marketing skill. Marketing has generally acquired less attention than the other elements and has been greatly undervalued. Indeed, many people remain confused about the difference between marketing and selling. An excellent way to distinguish is this: Selling involves convincing somebody you have what they want; marketing is making sure that you have what somebody wants.

Those are two entirely different propositions. No matter how persuasive you are as a salesperson, if you're trying to sell Edsels, you won't achieve much success. Or, to take a more recent example, if you're running a music store that sells only records in this age of CDs, no matter how magnificent your sales skills, you are unlikely to flourish.

There's another handy way for financial advisers to distinguish between selling and marketing. Selling is basically what happens when you are face to face with the prospect or client. It's an interaction. Marketing, on the other hand, is everything that happens prior to—and after—that interaction called selling.

Salespeople spend a phenomenal amount of energy and effort ensuring they have the maximum likelihood of success in the all-important sales interaction. And that's logical. But they don't tend to put much attention on what transpires—or what ideally should transpire—before and after that crucial encounter. Yet a little dose of marketing savvy prior to the meeting can dramatically increase your probability of success. Similarly, nurturing the client after the sale can profoundly increase your chances of future success.

A Marketing Focus

This book will concentrate on marketing: How to maximize success by positioning yourself as the type of financial adviser a prospect or a client wants to work with. In particular the book will repeatedly focus on the need to pay paramount consideration to our client's needs rather than our own. It's easy in the tumult of our everyday lives to ignore the client's words and needs as we struggle to promote our own interests. Easy, but dangerous.

Operating our business in the client's interest is the pivotal element in a successful marketing strategy. Marketing, in turn, is a mandatory investment in your business. It pays dividends immediately and in the long term. It will carry you to liftoff—a dramatic surge in your business.

Liftoff is a thrilling word we generally associate with NASA, not financial advice. It's that climactic moment when a rocket's explosive drive begins to propel the astronauts into their marvelous ascent. Nobody can help but being awed by that stunning sight.

Although liftoff seems sudden, it only comes after the confluence of many forces that are invisible to the casual observer. It takes meticulous planning, both short and long term. For NASA's scientists, liftoff involves subordinating their own personal concerns to the over-arching needs of their clients, the astronauts. Liftoff involves trust. It also requires patience.

For your business, liftoff requires the same formula. You must focus on the client's needs rather than your own. You must exercise discipline and patience. You must also invest in your business. That constellation of marketing activities will build trust with clients and add value for them, allowing you to forge sturdy relationships. It will also help you to differentiate yourself from other advisers. Together, that dynamic will ignite liftoff.

Liftoff for your business is timed quite differently from the Cape Canaveral version. It doesn't take place in a single instant. As you apply intelligent marketing ideas to your business, you'll start to notice gradual rewards. And as you invest more and more in these techniques, you will eventually achieve liftoff: Your sales, like a spacecraft, will soar exponentially. But let me caution you that it takes time. The big rewards are not immediate (Figure I.2).

Getting Clients, Keeping Clients

In its broadest sense, our business involves two elements. We have to get clients. And then, we have to keep clients. This book will address those challenges, preparing you for liftoff.

We'll spend a lot of time—the biggest section of the book—on getting clients, because that's where our challenge begins. We'll look at everything from making the initial contact, to using the media, to automating your prospecting process, to the increasingly important approach of target marketing.

Once you have those clients, you want to keep them. The surest way to attain that is having clients feel ecstatic about your performance. So we'll look at a variety of techniques to build long-lasting, deep relationships. That will include improving listening skills, implementing a sensible program for feedback, and learning to sometimes suspend your self-interest in order to persuade the client that you truly care.

The closing section of the book will focus on implementation, building a foundation so that these activities can be introduced to your practice in a manageable fashion. I'll provide specific ideas to improve the functioning of your office so that the many ideas in this book don't become pipe dreams but are achievable.

In that vein this book contains some elements of a workbook. At times you'll be asked to fill out questionnaires while you're reading. So, for example, when I explain how to improve your chances of gaining testimonials from those ecstatic clients, you'll find the script and

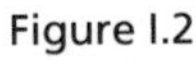
Figure I.2

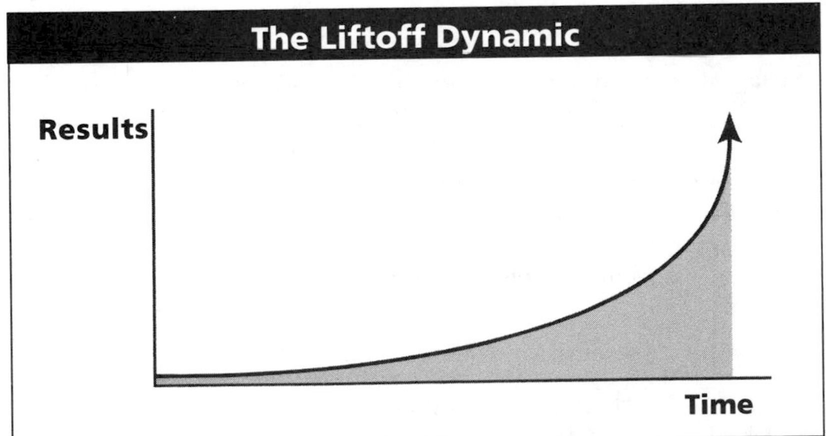

letters you'll need to implement my suggestions. In many cases, all you have to do is place our sample letters on your letterhead, add your signature, and you have a new tool to increase your effectiveness.

The advice gathered in this book is practical. The book isn't littered with fuzzy intellectual exercises. It offers concrete, tangible ideas—suggestions you can put in place relatively easily. In the vast majority of cases those suggestions will also be quite simple. That's because I've learned the complicated ideas usually don't work. It's the simple stuff that tends to have the biggest impact.

The $5 Solution

Consider, for example, the effort you typically expend in setting up a meeting with a prospective client. Once it's arranged, three results can flow from that work—and unfortunately only one is positive:

- The session can transpire exactly as you want: You establish empathy, encourage the client to open up, and wind up either with the client starting an actual account or, at least, agreeing to a further meeting to carry the process along. Success!
- The opposite can also happen. You may discover that you don't relate to the client—he or she is not very open or receptive to your ideas. The meeting is a bust.
- The third possibility is that the meeting never even takes place. And that happens far too often. You receive a message from the client—the day before the meeting, a few hours before the session, or just as you're heading out the door—that she is unable to attend. She has changed her mind, or something else has come up. Maybe you're able to re-schedule the meeting, maybe you're not; but such missed opportunities are enormously frustrating.

Suppose you could invest $5 to reduce significantly the possibility of that meeting being canceled and, indeed, to increase the chances of a positive outcome from the session. Just $5. No doubt like most financial advisers your reaction would be, "Absolutely. Where do I sign?" Given the difficulty of arranging the meeting and the stakes involved, $5 is a small investment to help ensure it happens.

Here's the solution: After booking the meeting, send out a confirmation letter to the prospective client. Attach some information about yourself, your firm, and some financial-related matters that the client might find of value. Simple, right? But our company's research has found that modest confirmation package substantially increases the likelihood of the client following through on the meeting and offering a positive response to your recommendations.

Notice that technique has nothing directly to do with what transpires in the meeting. It has everything to do with what happens prior to the meeting. It's marketing. It helps to condition a positive response from that particular client.

Trust and Patience

Many themes recur over and over throughout this book. One is the critical role of building trust, which must pervade everything we do. Another is the need to learn patience. That may seem odd because, historically, patience has been the antithesis of what was sought in successful financial advisers. Traditionally, success seemed based on an action orientation—fire in the belly, the conviction to make things happen.

If as recently as ten years ago you'd asked a manager in charge of recruiting at any of the major firms how important patience was in a new adviser, the answer would have been "it's not important at all." In fact, patience was considered a negative. Someone who was patient didn't possess sufficient get-up-and-go, lacked the absolute determination to make things happen.

Financial advisers today obviously still need zeal and a pronounced goal orientation. But those qualities must be tempered with a degree of discipline and patience that hasn't been required until now. We need to take a longer-term view of the returns from our marketplace activities.

Let me offer an example. You may decide to approach your local newspaper's editor as a result of reading later comments in this book about the credibility that an association with the media can bestow on financial advisers. The editor gives you the go-ahead to write an article on the importance of financial planning. After a considerable amount of effort researching, writing, and fine-tuning the article, you complete it, submit it for publication, and are told it will run on Monday morning.

Confident in the boost this will give your business—anticipating imminent liftoff—you cancel all your Monday appointments and arrange for an extra phone line to be installed, because you don't want to miss any of those urgent calls from prospective clients who, after reading your column, grab the phone to find out where to send their checks. Monday arrives, you're prepped—and you wait, and wait, and wait. Nothing happens. So you decide, "That was a waste of time. Clearly, the effort wasn't worthwhile."

In the short term—on that particular day—the article didn't furnish any obvious returns. But in the mid term and certainly in the long term, that column could prove to be one of the best investments of time and energy you could make. It's the liftoff dynamic. The column has positioned you as a trusted, credible financial adviser in the minds of prospective clients—and not just among those reading the paper that day, but with all the prospects who will see the article when you show it to them as part of your future marketing activities.

So that's an example of adopting the longer view in how we spend our time. We still must generate short-term activity that provides short-term results. But we have to balance that pursuit with some patient activities that pay off in the future.

The Ideas That Work

At the end of the day, the measure of success for the time and money you invest in this book will be whether you implement the ideas. You may turn the last page thinking, "That was one of the most phenomenal books I've read! What wonderful ideas!" But if six months from now—or a year from now—you aren't operating differently, despite the time, effort, and money allotted to the book, then you will not have received any return. It will only be a successful investment if you change your routines and move toward liftoff.

With that in mind, the ideas are presented in a manner that allows ready implementation and action. Throughout the book I discuss how to carve out time for the new approaches I outline and how to structure those ideas into your existing practice. But at the end of the day, it's only a commitment from you as a financial adviser to follow through that will catapult you to success.

It's worth mentioning that a lot of legend pervades this business about the things that work—the ingredients needed for success. Much of that lore is rooted in activities that worked in the past (although some, I'm fairly confident, never even worked then). But over the years the myths have been dutifully woven, expanded, and exaggerated until they are now widely viewed as prerequisites to success.

I take a different approach. After hearing an idea, I evaluate it: Does the approach make sense, based on everything I know? Sometimes it does; sometimes it doesn't. But if it does—if the idea might work—I then take the nugget to the next logical stage. I test it.

Marketing Solutions, the company that I founded in 1988, works with financial advisers across North America to improve their performance. One of our hallmarks is a strong commitment to original research. We talk extensively to advisers and clients. We test different options. We separate the fanciful from fact.

The ideas in this book work. They aren't myth or fantasy. They have been tested in the marketplace against the ultimate critic—the consumer. The result of that research has been a barrage of successful ideas which are outlined in succeeding chapters.

Some of those ideas I hope you'll consider of great value to your business. Others, no doubt, you'll view as completely out to lunch. Please don't let an idea that's unsuitable for your operation tarnish your judgment of the other recommendations. Simply say, "Doesn't work for me. Might work for somebody else." Because the next idea, the one you rave over and start to implement tomorrow, might be considered flaky by some other financial adviser. As well, if you were to love every single idea contained in the book, it would be impossible to implement even 10 percent of them. So pick and choose wisely.

The Top Performers

It's worth stressing that when you successfully implement those ideas, much of the credit belongs to financial advisers who in some cases originated the ideas and in other instances agreed to test them in the field, with real prospects and real clients. A highlight for me of that sharing is our annual Top Performers Conference, a two-day event in which fifteen to twenty successful financial advisers from across the continent—people like Dodee Frost Crockett—show us what differentiates them from others in the field. Given the diversity of markets and the variety of styles in this business, the conference presents a broad set of approaches and philosophies.

But those top performers display three virtually universal characteristics:

- The first is a strong client focus. Almost all of the top performers establish deep client relationships and go above and beyond what clients might consider the call of duty. Dodee Frost Crockett scrambling to locate a doctor for her client is just one example.
- The second characteristic they share is a strong commitment to investing in their business. They have generally hired strong teams to assist them. They thoroughly commit themselves to investments in technology, offices, and other infrastructure, as well as to potent marketing programs.
- Thirdly, they almost always have established a well-defined approach to their business and have prepared written business plans setting out their objectives and methods for achieving those goals.

It is my hope that as you work through this book you will be inspired to emulate those top performers and increase your client focus, invest in your business, and end up with a structured, well-conceived business strategy that will smooth the path to a magnificent liftoff.

Snapshots

✔ *Four ingredients are crucial to operating successfully as a financial adviser: self-management skills, a positive mental attitude, selling skills, and marketing savvy.*

- ✔ *Marketing, which has traditionally been undervalued, will be this book's focus. Marketing is everything that takes place before and after the crucial meeting at which you sell.*
- ✔ *To attain liftoff, financial advisers need careful planning, both short term and long term. You must subordinate your own personal concerns to the over-arching concerns of your clients.*
- ✔ *After you book a meeting, increase your chances of success by sending out a confirmation letter to the prospective client with some information attached about yourself, your firm, and some financial-related matters the client might find of value.*
- ✔ *Trust and patience are crucial skills for a financial adviser. In the past, patience was viewed as a negative. In the future, it will be mandatory.*
- ✔ *The ideas in this book aren't myth or fantasy; they have been tested in the marketplace against the ultimate critic—the consumer.*
- ✔ *The top performers share three characteristics: a fervent client focus; a strong commitment to investing in their business; and a well-defined approach to their business, including the preparation of business plans.*

Section I
The Changing Environment

CHAPTER 1

Understanding the Evolving Consumer

THE INVESTMENT BUSINESS, AS WITH MOST BUSINESSES, IS CHANGING FASTER than at any time in history. Four fundamental forces are driving that transformation: an evolving consumer, intensified competition, changing technology, and the increasingly important role played by the media.

All of those forces are important of course, but the most critical is the dramatically more knowledgeable, dramatically more demanding, dramatically more assertive, and dramatically more value-conscious consumer. Occasionally a financial adviser will tell me, "I do a good job. I put my clients' interests first. Then I sit down to talk to a client and I'll be subjected to all of this skepticism and cynicism. It seems as if they don't trust me! It's not fair."

It isn't fair. But that's the way of the world. And the skepticism we encounter is not just hammering our industry. All professionals are finding they are no longer placed on a pedestal, their acumen and empathy taken for granted by clients.

A physician friend of mine echoed those concerns recently in describing his changing interactions with his patients. When he first opened his practice about 15 years ago, he says, after a patient came into his office he would complete a diagnosis and then offer a prescription—an expert solution to the patient's problem. If he was pressed for time with other patients waiting, he wouldn't take long to explain the nature of the problem. The patient would grab the prescription, thank him profusely, and be out the door in five minutes.

Today, after he presents his diagnosis, the deluge of questions begins. "Tell me more, doctor. How serious is it? How sure are you? What else could it be? What could this lead to?" It's like Twenty Questions. And when he offers the prescription, another flood of queries washes over him. "What are the side effects? Are there options? Did you see the item on this problem on CNN last week? What happens if I do nothing?" No more doctor on a pedestal.

Indeed, one recent experience with a patient exemplified today's changed consumer. The woman visited his office with a young infant in considerable distress. The doctor soon determined that the child was suffering from an ear infection that could be dealt with swiftly through antibiotics. He explained the problem, handed out the prescription, and the woman left, thanking him.

Advisers must prepare themselves to stay abreast, or preferably ahead, of accelerating change.

Forty-five minutes later his nurse informed him the woman was on the phone, eager to talk. "Doctor, sorry to bother you," she began, "but before I went to fill the prescription, out of curiosity I looked up the problem on our CD-ROM medical dictionary. I found a little discrepancy between what it says and what you told me. I just wanted to get a clarification."

Doctors have historically enjoyed the greatest trust from their clients of any profession. But they too are exposed to a more knowledgeable, more demanding, more assertive, more value-conscious consumer. It's not just us. It's everybody. Client relationships are being transformed in category after category.

And it won't suddenly ease up. The pace of change heightened in the late 1980s, propelled by a more aggressive, competitive attitude and the tougher economic environment. And what is happening to that pace of change today? Is it slowing down? Is it leveling off? Of course not—it's accelerating. And you will likely experience the same magnitude of change in the next five years that you've encountered in the last ten.

Staying Ahead of Shifting Consumer Values

Consider for a moment successful financial advisers from a decade ago who haven't adjusted to these profound transformations in our environment. They're still operating in the same manner today as ten years ago. What are the chances that they are equally successful today? The answer is: slim to none.

That decline in their effectiveness has nothing to do with them. They still remain as talented as ever. But if they haven't kept pace with the evolving, maturing consumer, their business has inevitably suffered.

Indeed, it won't be enough in the future to simply keep pace with the ever-changing consumer. One of the critical issues financial advisers will face is to stay ahead of those shifting consumer attitudes and values. The real winners will be those who anticipate where clients are going to be in three to five years and get there first. The winners will be those who embrace changes and opportunities rather than resisting them as a threat. Advisers need to identify how to reorient themselves and then do so enthusiastically before they are forced to.

The second propellant of change will be intensified competition. That will hit us on two levels. We'll undoubtedly see some significant new entrants into the marketplace. We'll also observe existing competitors become considerably more aggressive. That scenario should not be treated as a *maybe,* a prediction that perhaps could prove true. It's guaranteed, rock-solid certain that you will face more aggressive, harder-running competition in the future for those evolving consumers.

Technology is the third wave of change affecting our business. We've just scratched the surface so far, opening up broad accessibility of information and new options for tracking and reporting on performance. In the near future clients will have the opportunity to conduct transactions directly. In fact, the real competitors we should be worried about might well be Microsoft and Intuit, with their impressive consumer software capacity and aggressive hunt for new markets.

The media are the fourth force driving change. The media have driven the growth of the investment business, particularly the mutual fund side, over the last decade. Financial advisers can thank the media for improving the level of awareness around investing: the realization by clients of the need to take responsibility for their financial futures and to pay much more attention to how they manage their money, rather than continuing with the traditional routes.

We can applaud the media for that. But the price we pay, as we have seen and will continue to experience, is that the media are increasingly critical. In the United States, some media columnists play a powerful role in shaping attitudes and values. That will not only persist; it will spread further afield. The skeptical consumer will become more so in future.

Those four forces of change—the evolving consumer, more aggressive competition, rapidly changing technology, and a more influential and critical media—will continue at the forefront of accelerating change in the future (Figure 1.1). We don't have any control over those four forces. They are givens. The issue is not whether change will occur, because it will. The issue, rather, is how to prepare ourselves to stay abreast, or preferably ahead, of those changes.

Figure 1.1

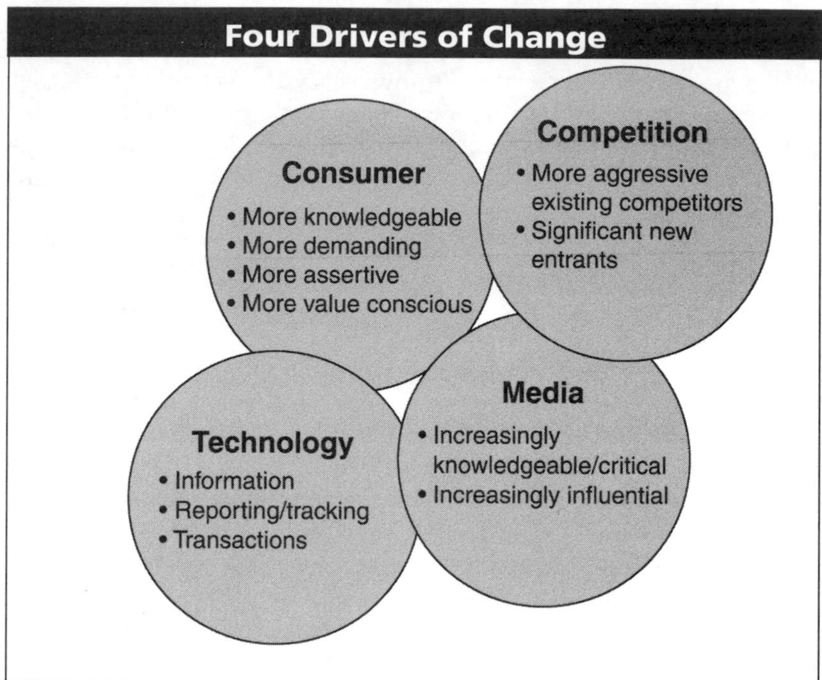
Four Drivers of Change
Consumer
• More knowledgeable
• More demanding
• More assertive
• More value conscious
Competition
• More aggressive existing competitors
• Significant new entrants
Technology
• Information
• Reporting/tracking
• Transactions
Media
• Increasingly knowledgeable/critical
• Increasingly influential

The Implications of Changing Consumers

Let's delve more deeply into the nature of the new consumer. Remember the characteristics: more knowledgeable, more skeptical, more value-driven. Less trusting, less loyal, less resistant to change. And those attributes, remember, apply to customers of my physician-friend, General Motors, IBM, the corner store, and the education system. Everybody is under assault from more knowledgeable, more demanding, more assertive, and more value-driven consumers.

What are the implications? First, as Figure 1.2 shows, knowledgeable consumers demand access to the best products. If you're dealing with a client who is not terribly aware or educated and you recommend an investment, a new issue or mutual fund that isn't among the best, the chances are still solid that you'll clinch the sale because the client doesn't know any better. When you're facing a knowledgeable consumer, you can't risk that approach. You may still get away with a substandard recommendation once or twice, but over the long term, if you don't provide access to the best products, you won't retain that particular client. I could cite case after case of organizations, for example, that have traditionally sold in-house

Figure 1.2

More Knowledgeable Consumers Require

- ❑ Access to the best products
- ❑ Focus on insight vs. information
- ❑ Greater emphasis on "total picture"
- ❑ Greater commitment to communication and education
- ❑ Higher standard of client satisfaction
- ❑ Clear focus on value

products—captive items—but have now been forced to sell externally managed funds. In the process they had to replace their management fee with a much smaller trailer, under pressure from the more demanding, discerning consumer.

A second implication is the need for financial advisers to place greater emphasis on the total picture. Historically, many advisers have conducted business without putting into place an in-depth financial plan: a complete picture of the client's circumstances, needs and objectives. That lapse won't continue because clients won't accept it. In-depth plans will be a mandatory cost of doing business in the future. We will have to invest time at the beginning of the process to gather all the relevant information and identify the client's direction.

The first question such plans address is: Where do the clients need to be today financially, given the age at which they wish to retire and the lifestyle they want to enjoy then? Next, based on current savings and the rate of saving, where are the clients likely to end up? That leads to the third question: What kind of gap, if any, exists between future financial needs and likely financial capacity? Will they hit their target? If not, we have to answer the most important question: How will they close the gap?

One possibility is that they'll reduce the standards of their post-retirement lifestyle. But of course most clients don't welcome that proposition. Will they consider working longer? Many clients are accepting that as a possibility, albeit with some reluctance. Can they save more? In some instances, that's a reasonable option. Or do they intend to change their asset mix? Will they adopt a different investment pattern to hit their retirement objective, even if they may subject themselves to some greater degree of volatility along the way?

Only by undertaking that information-gathering and objective-setting process at the start of your relationship with the client will you both understand the total plan. And both adviser and client will need to understand the total plan—need to be in harmony—if you are to operate in the client's interest and continue to serve the evolving consumer. I remember reading that Merrill Lynch sold 150,000 financial plans a few years ago at $150 apiece. That points to the importance they place on this element of our work.

Satisfactory Isn't Satisfactory

The third implication of dealing with increasingly sophisticated clients is that we will be forced to make an enhanced commitment to communication and education. Clients will demand it. If we don't deliver, they will move on.

Another factor is pushing us into that educational role. Ten years ago clients invariably turned to their financial adviser as the sole source of investment information and financial advice. Today clients pick up financial information and advice from everywhere. They soak it up from television, radio, newspapers, friends, people they encounter at parties, and co-workers. Your clients are absorbing a wide range of information on financial matters. The only question is: Are they receiving sufficient information from you to maintain your prime position in that galaxy of advice? The existence of more knowledgeable clients necessitates a much-intensified commitment to client communication and education.

A fourth implication of serving these more informed clients is that advisers will have to achieve a much higher standard of client satisfaction. This is a central focus of the book, discussed in detail later; but for now let me make the point that the traditional standards of customer service aspired to by all businesses, while once appropriate for the time, are no longer sufficient. The objective financial advisers have tended to set, for example, was simply to maintain client satisfaction. Keep them satisfied, they would remain loyal, and you would scoop up more of their money and more referrals.

Sounds fine, until you switch to today and place yourself in the customer's chair. Imagine you dine out on Saturday evening. The next morning, your neighbor asks, "How did you enjoy that new restaurant?" And you respond, "I was satisfied."

How stirring is that recommendation? How compelling for your neighbor will the proposition of visiting that restaurant be after your recommendation? And how high will that restaurant be on your list next time you're dining out? Not very.

After all, what does "satisfaction" mean? It conveys the impression that the experience was okay. It wasn't terrible. It wasn't so bad that you walked out. In short, the pain of staying was less than the pain of leaving.

With less critical clients, that was once an adequate standard. But no longer. What's the response today's restaurateur must evoke in patrons? Not "I was satisfied." Not "It was okay." Rather, that restaurateur needs to earn an inspiring recommendation. "It was fabulous." "It was terrific." "I was thrilled." "I was delighted."

And we need to arouse those same responses in our clients, when friends, associates, or neighbors ask how they enjoy dealing with their financial adviser. If the best your client manages is "I am satisfied," then you probably won't win that potential referral. Worse, you're vulnerable to that client deserting you someday for a competitor who appears better than merely satisfactory. If the only reason for continuing to be your client is that the pain of leaving is greater than the pain of staying, at some point the client will encounter somebody who reduces the pain of leaving.

This highlights a crucial shift in the mindset of clients. Ten years ago the client's view toward us was, "I'm going to stay unless you give me a reason to leave. It may not be that easy to attract me as a client in the first place, but once I'm your client, I'm yours—for life—unless you do something to antagonize me." Today, that proposition has reversed. Today, increasingly, the attitude is, "I'm going to leave unless you give me a reason to stay." Again, it's nothing we provoked. We haven't changed that dramatically. It's entirely a function of the more demanding, more discriminating, more discerning client, who has remolded the environment in which we operate.

Going Beyond the Five Es

The final area of change is the necessity to focus on value. Traditionally, dealing with relatively unknowledgeable clients who were driven by emotion, financial advisers simply needed the four Es to succeed: enthusiasm, empathy, effort, and some expertise. You needed to know more than your client which, given the state of client knowledge, wasn't particularly challenging. In fact, for some advisers such expertise consisted entirely of a fifth E, equities—knowing that those were a sensible recommendation.

Today, clients are comparatively knowledgeable and although still driven somewhat by emotion, they increasingly depend on reason. Advisers still need enthusiasm, empathy, effort, and expertise, but the level of expertise demanded has risen considerably. With your clients more knowledgeable, you in turn have to be more knowledgeable. The death knell for an adviser is when the client knows more than you.

But you need something extra for today's client: You need to add value. Clients must feel that they are receiving clear and distinct value from you. That value can take many different forms, but it must be present, and visible to the clients.

One form it can take is the financial plan, the foundation for work with the client and the framework for the client to evaluate whether he or she is on track, relative to future goals. Value can also flow from the advice crafted for clients. As we move forward, clients will be seeking more sophisticated advice. The standards we've accepted historically, in some cases fairly sophisticated but in many more cases relatively simplistic, are not sufficient for the future. We'll have to tackle more refined asset allocation, more complex portfolio construction, and more frequent rebalancing. We'll have to offer fully competitive products.

Reporting can also provide value to clients. We must communicate regularly to our clients how they stand—ideally on the basis they prefer for the communication. I can visualize a scenario in the not-too-distant future when you sit down with a new account who has just made the first purchase and announce:

"Mr./Ms. Client, let me show you the alternatives available for our reports on your portfolio. Here are five options, with a range of detail and complexity. Most of my clients prefer the middle option, number three, because they find that the best balance, but depending on your needs we can be more or less detailed. Which do you prefer?

"And by the way, how frequently will you want those reports? Most of my clients prefer quarterly reports, but if you like less constant reporting, I can slow that down to every six months or even every year. If you want more frequent reports, that can be provided as well; it might involve a modest cost, but the option exists.

"So we can report to you in the fashion that you prefer, at the frequency you want, and also in the manner you find most convenient. Would you like the statements mailed to you? Should we fax them? E-mail them? Provide them by disk? Or would you want them downloaded into your computer automatically?"

That may seem daunting now, but it will soon be standard customer service. Reporting is one area where we can easily add value. In fact, currently it's a prime source of complaints from customers. Some clients are convinced a conspiracy by the investment industry is afoot to obfuscate and confuse customers in reporting performance. If it wasn't a deliberate strategy, they figure, you couldn't possibly end up with the disorganized, difficult-to-comprehend statements the industry churns out. It must be part of a master plan.

Communication is another area to add value and differentiate you from competitors. Our company's research shows that the number one cause of client defections is not poor performance, administrative screw-ups, or even your client's daughter marrying somebody in the business who then snatches the account away from you. The prime reason for defection is simply: "I did not hear from my adviser frequently enough." Given the evolving marketplace, that complaint will become increasingly common unless we respond. A principal source of value will be frequent contact with the client.

A final area of value that advisers must ponder is a commitment to education. Clients are taking their finances—and financial futures—more seriously. They will be looking for your commitment to help them become more knowledgeable about those investments.

The challenge for investment advisers in the future will be to not only touch all those bases but also provide superior value in at least some of them. That's a tall order. But these are tumultuous and unforgiving times. In our own lives as consumers we expect superior service from the businesses we patronize. And our clients have similarly exacting standards. If we don't provide superior value—if we merely aim for satisfactory—somebody else will provide our clients with a reason to leave.

Snapshots

- ✔ *Four forces are reshaping the environment in which we operate: an evolving consumer, increased competition, changing technology, and the increasingly important role played by the media.*
- ✔ *Of those four forces, the most critical is the dramatically more knowledgeable, dramatically more demanding, dramatically more assertive, and dramatically more value-conscious consumer.*
- ✔ *It won't be sufficient in the future to simply keep pace with the evolving consumer. Financial advisers must stay ahead of shifting consumer attitudes and values.*
- ✔ *Satisfactory won't be satisfactory anymore. We must aim for superior service or somebody else in this highly competitive environment will give our clients a reason to leave.*
- ✔ *Today's knowledgeable consumers demand sophisticated advice and access to the best products.*
- ✔ *In-depth financial plans will be mandatory in the future.*
- ✔ *The prime reason for client defection is "I did not hear from my adviser frequently enough."*
- ✔ *Financial advisers will need to provide a menu of reporting options to meet individual client needs.*

CHAPTER 2

Strategies That Attract Clients Today

RECENTLY WE WERE COMMISSIONED BY ONE OF OUR CLIENTS, TALVEST FUND Management Inc., to study the all-important process by which clients select a financial adviser. Specifically, we were intent on investigating a crucial question for today's financial adviser: What leads clients to shift from one adviser to another?

We studied how many clients initiate new relationships with advisers each year, how they decide to switch, what determines the new advisers they will consider for their business, and what hot buttons lead them to prefer one adviser over another. Most importantly, we tried to determine the implications for financial advisers of client migration, a growing phenomenon. How can advisers minimize their own client losses and be more successful in winning new clients?

We began by talking with advisers, developing fifteen preliminary hypotheses based on their sense of the new-client process (Figure 2.1). When we collected data and tested those hypotheses, however, we learned to our shock that every single one was wrong to some extent or other.

The study focused on households with a minimum of $50,000 in investments and insurance savings, drawn from a larger pool of 15,000 households we surveyed. We found that only about three in ten households fell into our preferred financial bracket. The majority of households—56 percent—actually have under $25,000 in investable assets. If you want to know why so many people are pessimistic about their financial future, you don't have to look any further than that statistic.

Making up the 31 percent of households falling into our target group were the 12 percent of the population with $50,000 to $100,000 in investable assets, 10 percent with $100,000 to $200,000, and 9 percent with over $200,000 (Figure 2.2).

Figure 2.1

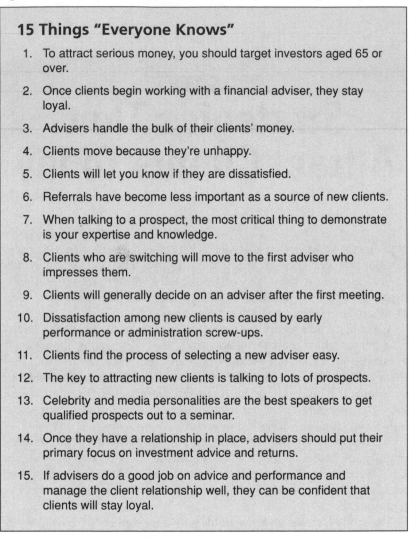

15 Things "Everyone Knows"

1. To attract serious money, you should target investors aged 65 or over.
2. Once clients begin working with a financial adviser, they stay loyal.
3. Advisers handle the bulk of their clients' money.
4. Clients move because they're unhappy.
5. Clients will let you know if they are dissatisfied.
6. Referrals have become less important as a source of new clients.
7. When talking to a prospect, the most critical thing to demonstrate is your expertise and knowledge.
8. Clients who are switching will move to the first adviser who impresses them.
9. Clients will generally decide on an adviser after the first meeting.
10. Dissatisfaction among new clients is caused by early performance or administration screw-ups.
11. Clients find the process of selecting a new adviser easy.
12. The key to attracting new clients is talking to lots of prospects.
13. Celebrity and media personalities are the best speakers to get qualified prospects out to a seminar.
14. Once they have a relationship in place, advisers should put their primary focus on investment advice and returns.
15. If advisers do a good job on advice and performance and manage the client relationship well, they can be confident that clients will stay loyal.

Financial advisers assume that to find serious money it's best to target households with people over age sixty-five. Generally, those folks have accumulated savings throughout their lives and are considered to offer the brightest investment possibilities. While they are admirable prospects, our data revealed that they are not the only prospects with significant financial resources.

In fact, 24 percent of households with people aged between thirty-five and forty-four surpass our $50,000 threshold, as do 37 percent of households with people aged forty-five to fifty-four. Those are intrigu-

Figure 2.2

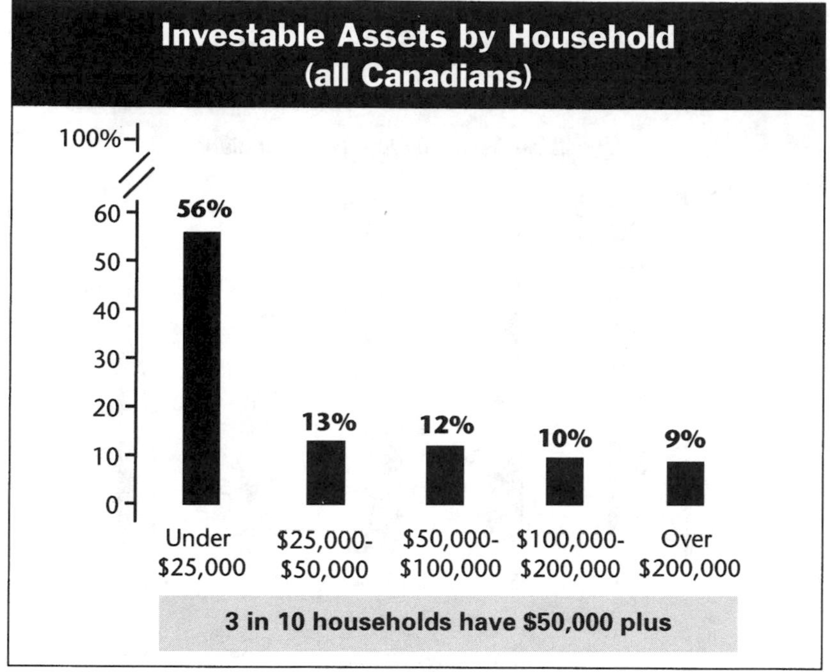

ing statistics, but obviously these age groups are not yet prime targets for investment advisers. More enticing, however, is the fact that 50 percent of households in the fifty-five to sixty-four age bracket transcend our threshold—almost the same percentage as the 51 percent in the sixty-five plus bracket with such funds (Figure 2.3).

Expanding Our Age Horizons

So that shatters our first myth. We shouldn't be assuming age sixty-five is the magic cutoff. The fifty-five to sixty-four year olds are a highly attractive target. Indeed, when you consider some crucial psychological predispositions, this age group becomes even more lustrous. Because they are younger, they are often less set in their ways than the sixty-five plus investors. They also have a longer life span to be concerned about, making financial planning critical for them. And in most cases they are still squarely in the acquisition phase, adding to their assets rather than depleting them.

This age group's importance to financial advisers can be shown from a different angle: looking at what percentage of households with our preferred assets fall into each age bracket. The sixty-five-plus group contains about a quarter of the households with the requisite savings. That's

Figure 2.3

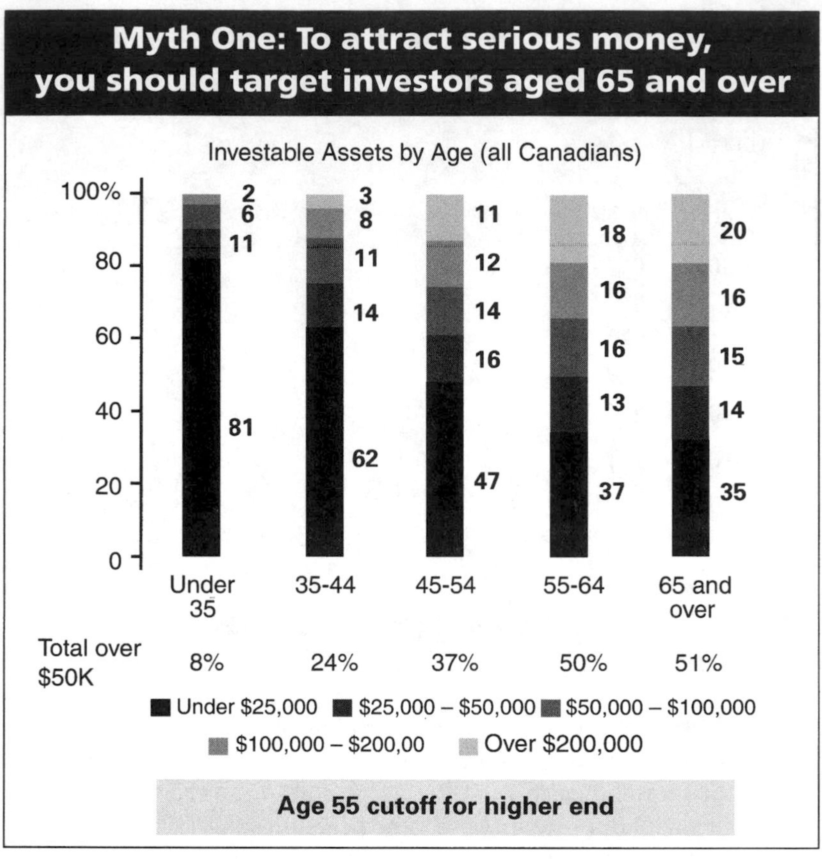

an attractive target. But adding fifty-five to sixty-four-year-olds opens up a combined target of 43 percent of the households with serious money.

That combination is even more dynamic at higher asset levels. Targeting the two groups will point financial advisers at 56 percent of households with investable assets of between $100,000 and $200,000 and 70 percent of households with over $200,000 (Figure 2.4). Clearly, the fifty-five to sixty-four age group merits special attention. That is a critically important finding, challenging a prominent myth.

Another myth advisers share is that the bulk of households with significant money still keep their funds in banks, basically uncared for and therefore prime picking for advisers. In fact, over the past five years a significant movement occurred from financial institutions to independent financial advisers, driven to a large extent by low interest rates. Annual savings are no longer plunked automatically into government investment certificates. Low interest rates pushed families into alternative investments. Today investment advisers have been

Figure 2.4

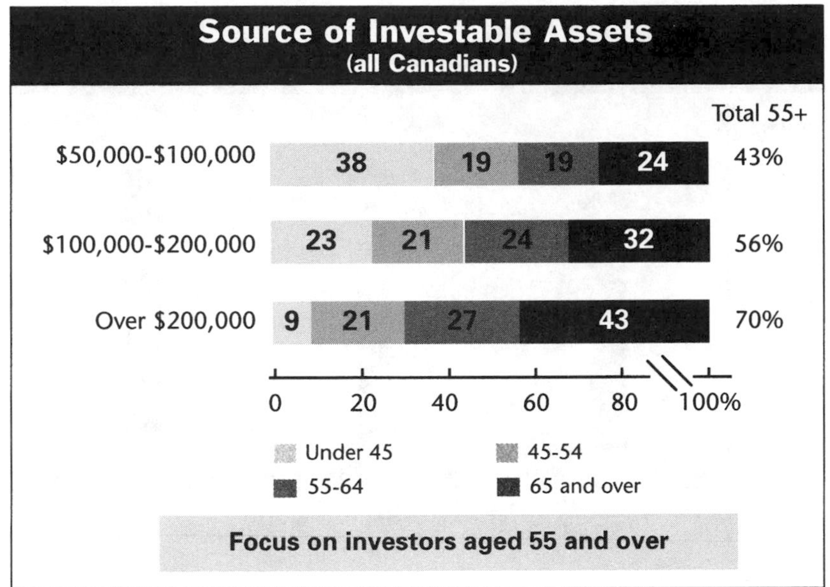

employed by about 75 percent of households with investable assets of over $50,000 (Figure 2.5).

Of those households, 32 percent have always used the same financial adviser. On the other hand, 35 percent have changed financial investors at some point. Again, this contradicts prevailing belief. Advisers generally assume that once investors have edged away from a bank and experienced the joys and benefits of working with a financial adviser, they will stay loyal to that adviser. Not so: one in three have jumped ship (Figure 2.6).

When we eliminated those investors who only started working with their financial adviser in the previous eighteen months, we found that half the clients had actually changed advisers at some point. And that increased by asset level: six in ten investors with more than $200,000 in investable assets had switched at some point (Figure 2.7).

The Competition for Clients' Money

Another myth financial advisers hold is that they know where all their clients' savings are invested and have been the sole counsel in determining those investments. In actuality, nine in ten clients hold assets outside their advisers' purview. Even if we discount that finding somewhat—assuming the second investment institution is their bank—we still have to confront the fact that six in ten households invest with three or more firms. It's a competitive world for our clients' money (Figure 2.8).

Figure 2.5

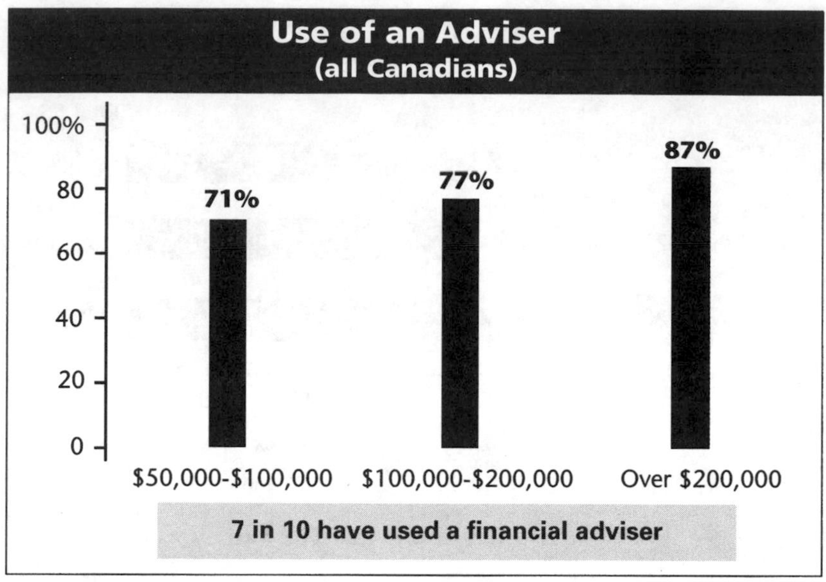

Figure 2.6

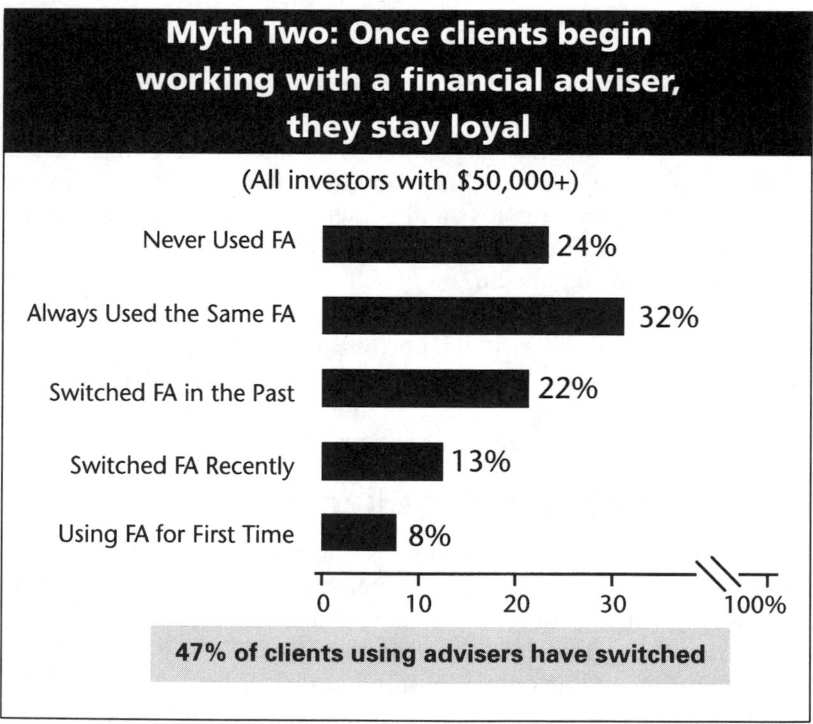

Figure 2.7

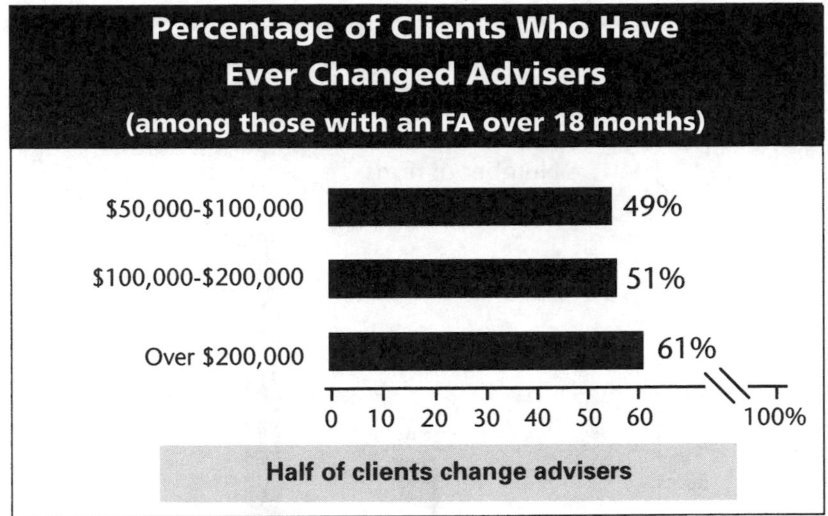

Our survey found that households opting for a financial adviser had often been relying on a financial institution before for advice: 44 percent fell into that category. That's no surprise. But 30 percent had no source of investment advice previously. They relied on themselves. As complexity increases, more and more individuals are seeking a higher level of advice (Figure 2.9).

Naturally, advisers assume that those people who switched their source of investment advice were unhappy with the previous source. In fact, only 16 percent were unhappy before the shift. More surprisingly, 24 percent—nearly a quarter—say they were happy with the previous source of advice (while 60 percent were neither satisfied nor dissatisfied). If in the past clients left financial advisers because they were dissatisfied, today they leave because they are not satisfied enough (Figure 2.10).

Most advisers believe that clients will let them know when they are dissatisfied. Wrong. Advisers were given a clear warning in only 8 percent of the conversions. A further 18 percent of the time, clients offered hints. Three out of four, however, gave no warning (Figure 2.11). Unless advisers ask clients about their satisfaction level—in a manner comfortable enough for the client to respond honestly—they are unlikely to learn when a breach is near. Later in this book we'll study some strategies that encourage clients to share their discomfort early in the relationship when you can still react rather than leaving it until they speak with their feet by leaving.

Another myth pertains to the role of referrals in the selection of new financial advisers. Most advisers recognize that referrals play an

Figure 2.8

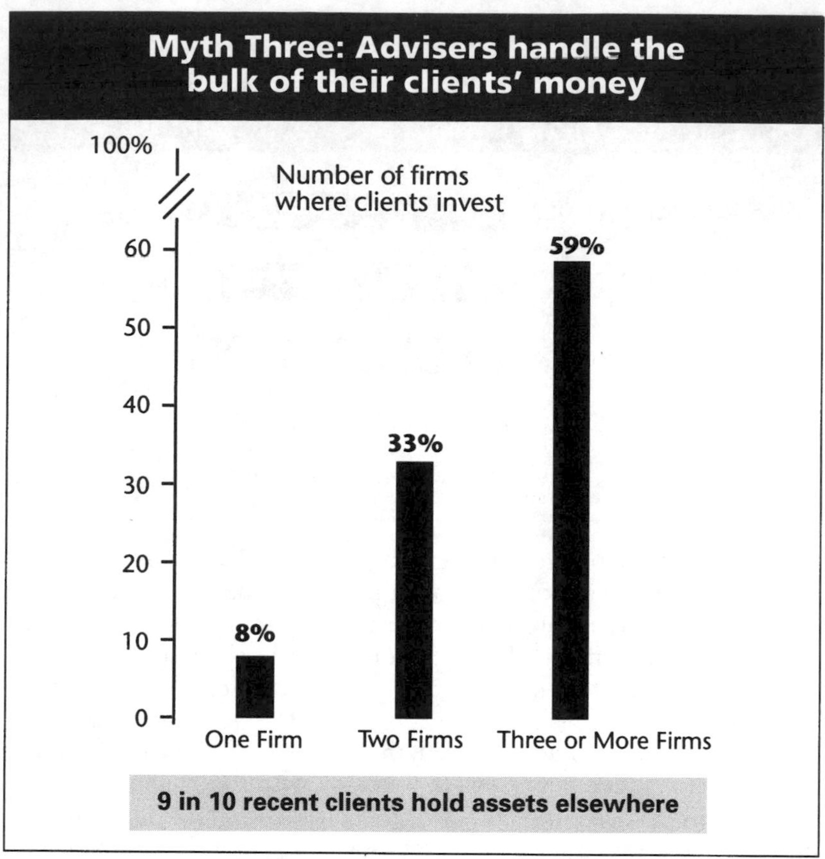

important part in that process. But a body of thought contends that referrals have become less important than in the past, because of new techniques on the scene like database marketing, advertising, and prospecting at large seminars.

That's not true either. In 1990 a Toronto Stock Exchange study found that when choosing a financial adviser about 61 percent of clients received a referral from family friends or colleagues, while another 12 percent received referrals from people they trusted, such as an accountant, lawyer or bank manager (Figure 2.12). In total, seven out of ten relied on a referral in picking an adviser. Fast forward through the decade and our study came up with the same seven-in-ten finding. The portion relying on family, friends, or colleagues dipped from 61 percent to 49 percent, while 16 percent acted upon a bank branch referral and 5 percent on an accountant or lawyer. But seven in ten clients still reacted to a referral when choosing a new financial adviser

Figure 2.9

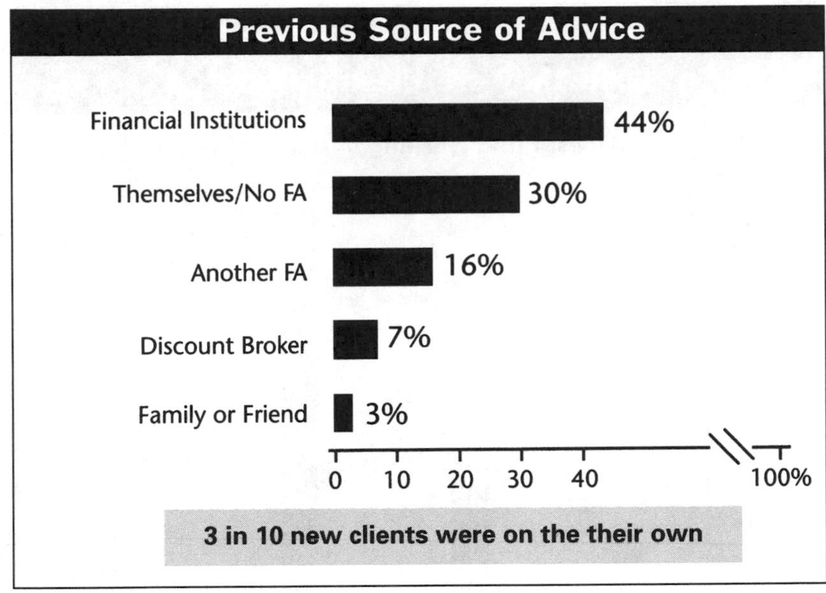
Previous Source of Advice
Financial Institutions
44%
Themselves/No FA
30%
Another FA
16%
Discount Broker
7%
Family or Friend
3%
0
10
20
30
40
100%
3 in 10 new clients were on the their own

Figure 2.10

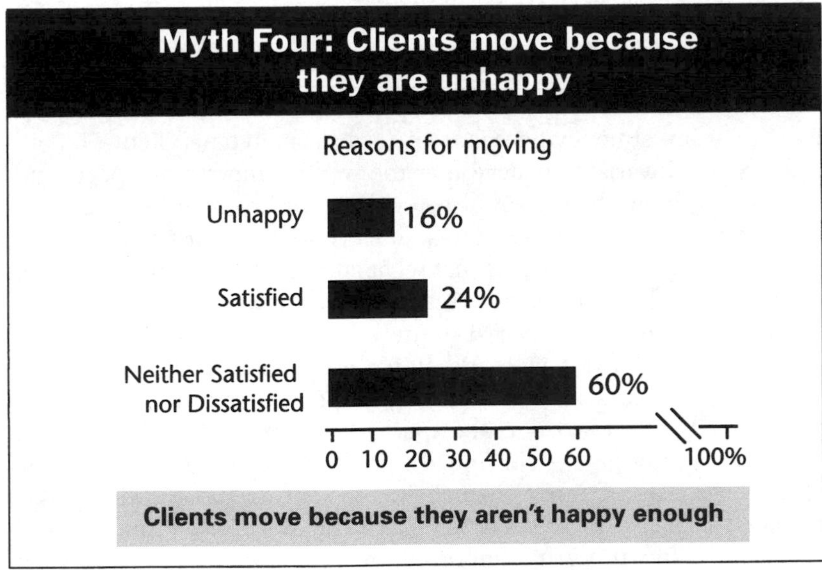
Myth Four: Clients move because they are unhappy
Reasons for moving
Unhappy
16%
Satisfied
24%
Neither Satisfied nor Dissatisfied
60%
0 10 20 30 40 50 60
100%
Clients move because they aren't happy enough

Figure 2.11

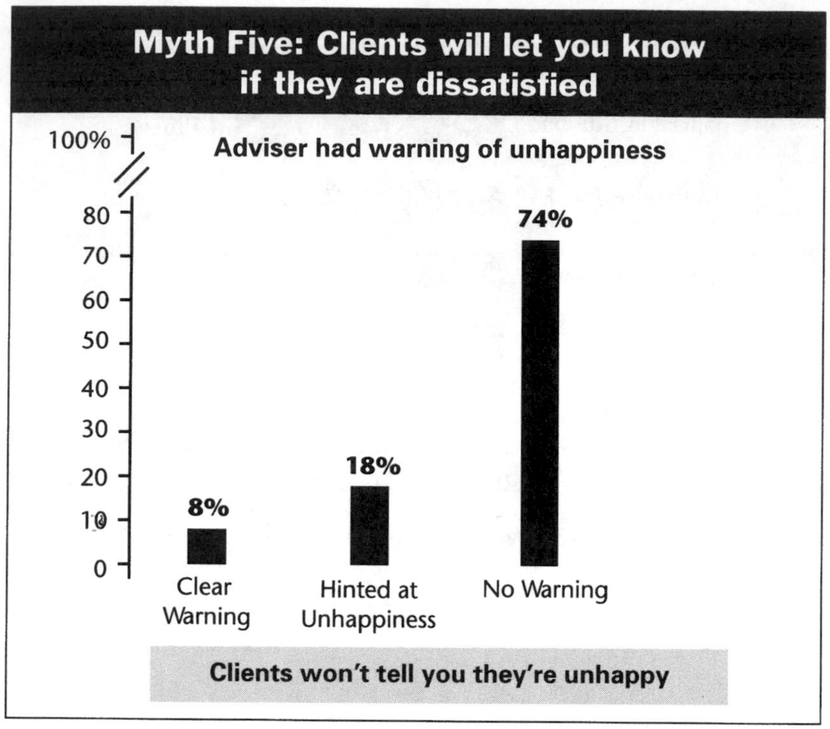

(Figure 2.13). Not recognizing the sustained importance of these referrals hampers financial advisers in their work.

Communication Counts

Advisers are also misled by the widespread misconception that the quality of their investment advice is what attracts and retains clients. Financial advisers invariably believe that the way to impress prospects and clients is to blow them away with evidence of financial expertise. Yet every piece of research I've seen—and I've seen at least twenty solid studies on this issue—stresses that what attracts clients is trust. Lack of trust, on the other hand, sends them scurrying away (Figure 2.14).

All the research has been absolutely consistent on this score. And our own study didn't deviate. When we asked clients the most important thing they seek in a new adviser, 60 percent said trust—twice as many as cited performance or expertise (Figure 2.15). That meshes with our finding on the continued importance of referrals. Referrals, after all, are a transference of trust: Somebody who has faith in a given financial adviser is recommending that a friend can trust this adviser.

At the same time, it's important to recognize that the referral

Figure 2.12

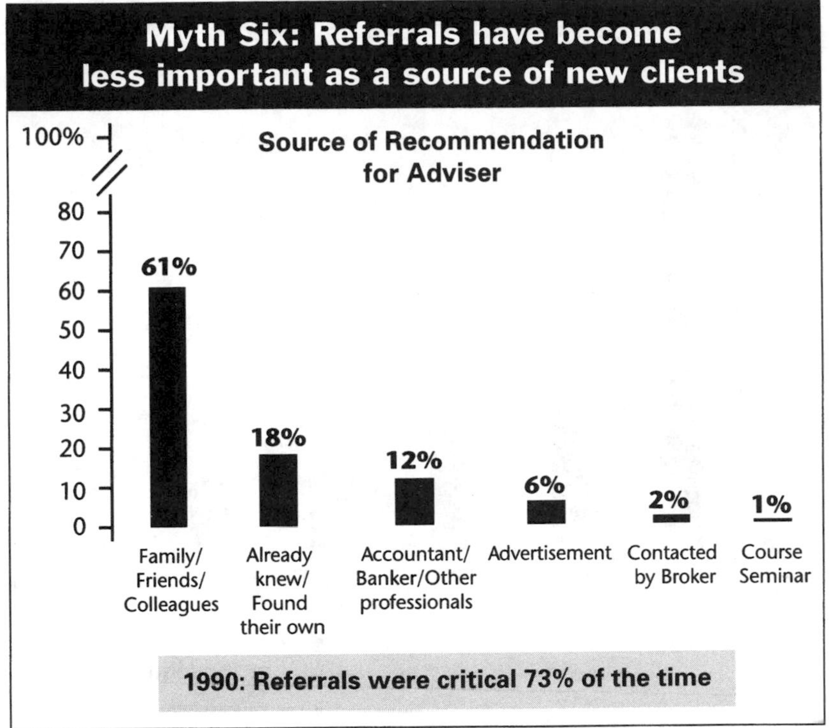

process is changing in not commonly recognized ways. In the past if you received a referral from a good client, it was a slam dunk to turn that prospect into a new client. The chances of not ending up with a new client were virtually nil. Today, clients are shopping around more. We found that 55 percent of clients talked to two or more advisers before making their choice (Figure 2.16).

In the past, referrals handed you a client. Today, referrals grant you the right to compete for clients. Prospects are obtaining multiple referrals and then systematically interviewing advisers before deciding. In two out of three cases, selecting an adviser requires multiple meetings often with multiple advisers (Figure 2.17). Indeed, the more money that prospects have to invest the more likely it is they will interview multiple advisers (Figure 2.18).

Nearly half of the decisions on selecting an adviser took over a month. Twenty-five percent of our sample took one to three months, 15 percent took three months to a year, and 5 percent took over a year (Figure 2.19). That means advisers need to establish a process to continue communications with prospects at a reasonable pace throughout the decision-making period, whatever its length. You also need a strat-

Figure 2.13

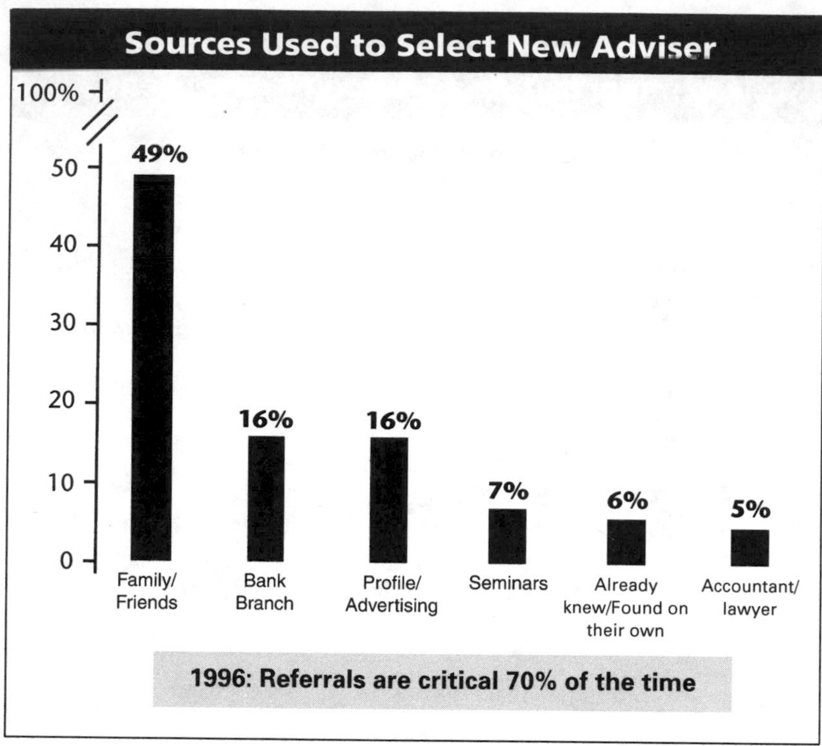

egy to differentiate yourself from the competing financial advisers. Just being referred is not enough in today's environment.

I was impressed by the zeal with which one speaker at our Top Performers Conference responds to a referral. He begins by immediately calling to arrange a meeting. Then he sends a confirming note, along with a free copy of a $30 book on financial planning that he coauthored with a professional writer. A couple of days before the scheduled meeting, either he or his assistant—depending on the importance of the prospect—calls and says, "Mr. Prospect, I'm just phoning to confirm our meeting on Thursday at 5 P.M. You should know that sometimes the parking lot in our building gets congested, so when you arrive look for the parking spot with your name on it." Sure enough, when the prospect pulls into the parking lot, he finds a spot reserved for him.

That, by the way, is not a comprehensive list of that adviser's courtship techniques; it's just some of the opening steps. He keeps track of his record on referrals. He won eighteen of the last twenty—and he's still upset about the two he missed. Financial advisers have to recognize this new paradigm: You are competing for client business even when it's referred to you. You must differentiate yourself by developing strategies

Figure 2.14

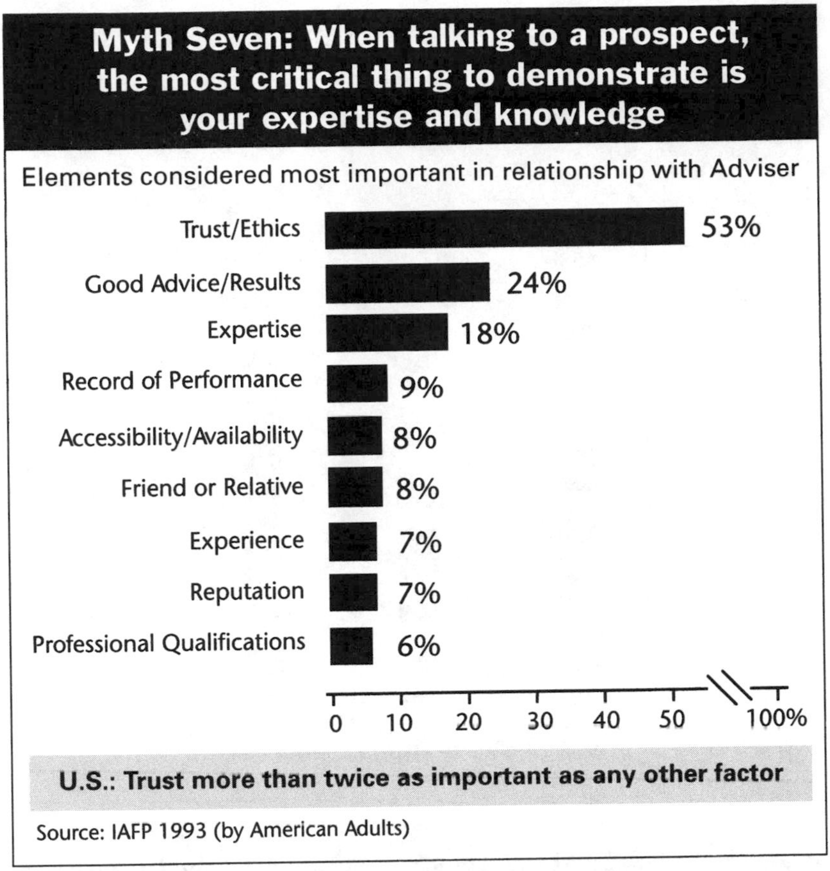

Myth Seven: When talking to a prospect, the most critical thing to demonstrate is your expertise and knowledge

Elements considered most important in relationship with Adviser

Trust/Ethics	53%
Good Advice/Results	24%
Expertise	18%
Record of Performance	9%
Accessibility/Availability	8%
Friend or Relative	8%
Experience	7%
Reputation	7%
Professional Qualifications	6%

0 10 20 30 40 50 100%

U.S.: Trust more than twice as important as any other factor

Source: IAFP 1993 (by American Adults)

Figure 2.15

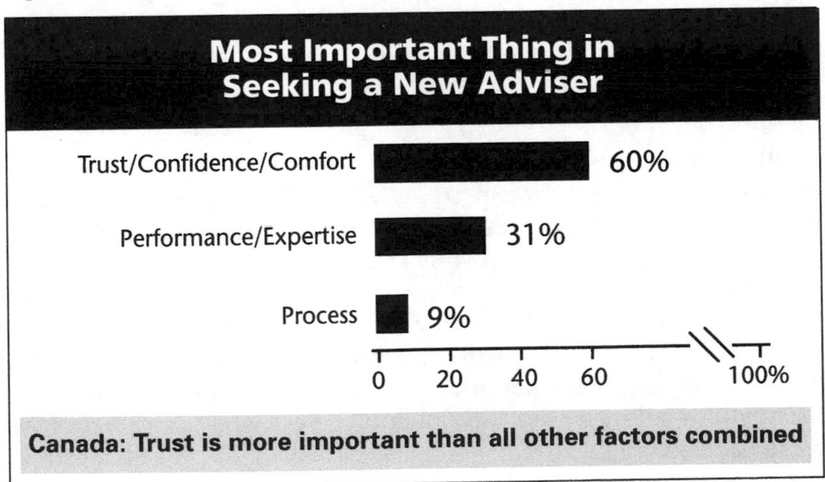

Figure 2.16

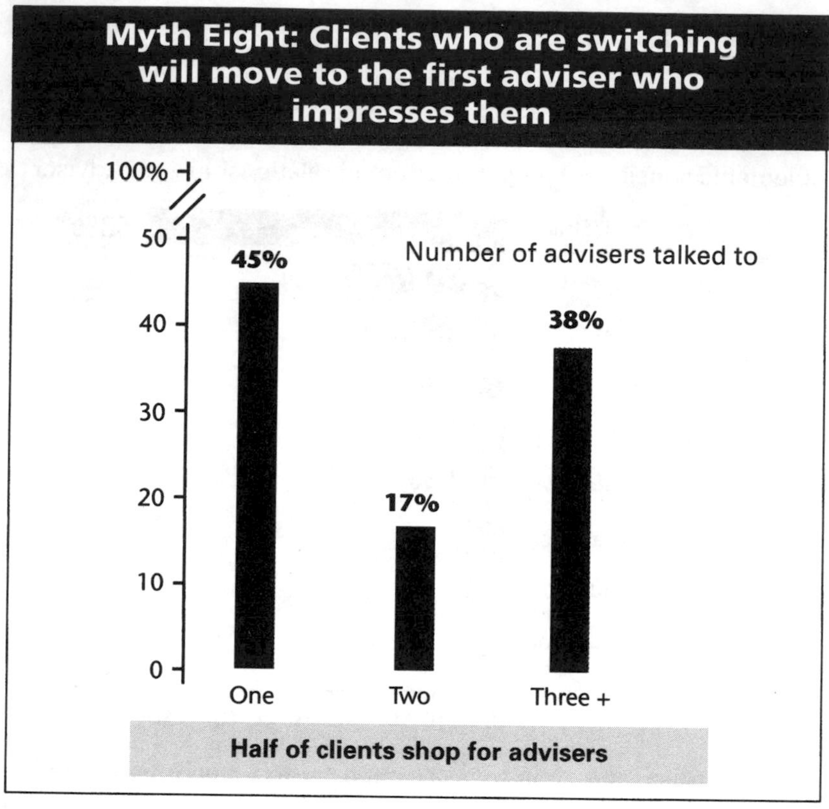

and techniques to build trust. Vince Lombardi, the legendary coach of the Green Bay Packers, once said, "Winning isn't everything, it's the only thing." For a financial adviser courting a prospect, creating a sense of trust isn't everything, it's the only thing.

Expectations and Reality

Another area we tested was whether the adviser performed better or worse than the new client expected. Here the findings were encouraging: In 87 percent of cases the adviser performed either better than expected or as well as expected (Figure 2.20). It's interesting, however, to check those other situations where performance fell below expectation. Was it because the financial results were lackluster? No. Was it because of administrative hassles moving the new money in? No. The number one reason for performance falling below expectations was the adviser's failure to keep in touch (Figure 2.21). Lack of contact creates a cancer of dissatisfaction that eventually kills the relationship.

Figure 2.17

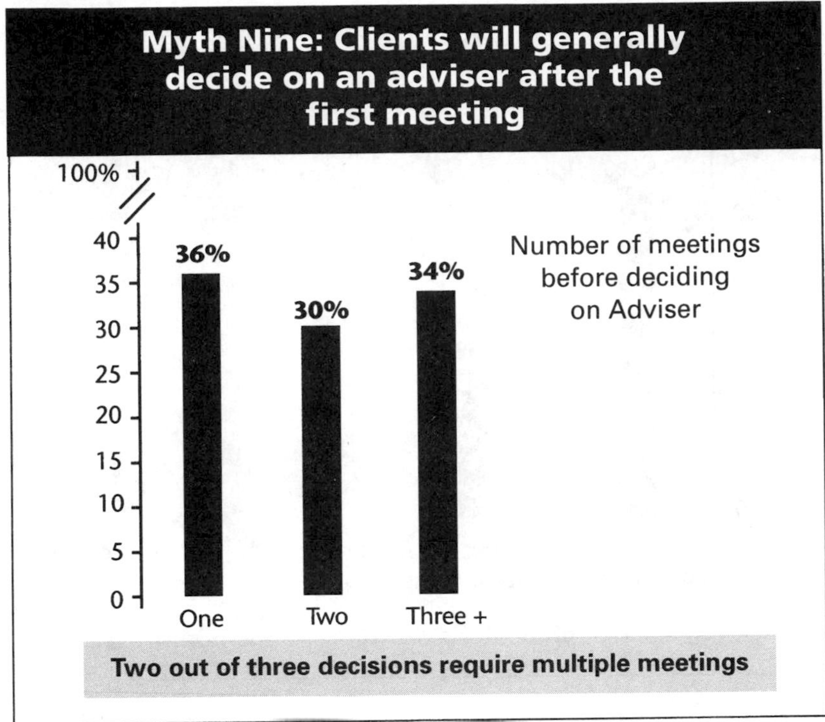
Myth Nine: Clients will generally decide on an adviser after the first meeting
100%
40
35
30
25
20
15
10
5
0
36%
30%
34%
One
Two
Three +
Number of meetings before deciding on Adviser
Two out of three decisions require multiple meetings

Figure 2.18

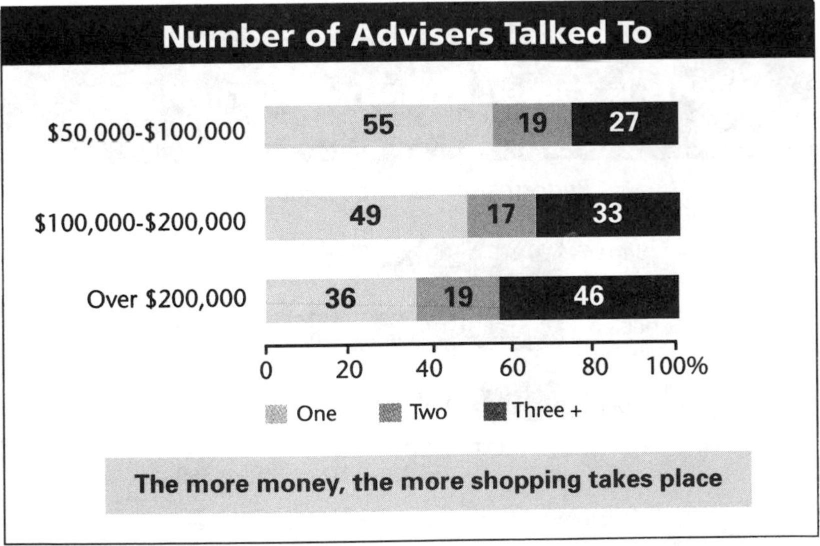
Number of Advisers Talked To
$50,000-$100,000
55
19
27
$100,000-$200,000
49
17
33
Over $200,000
36
19
46
0
20
40
60
80
100%
One
Two
Three +
The more money, the more shopping takes place

Figure 2.19

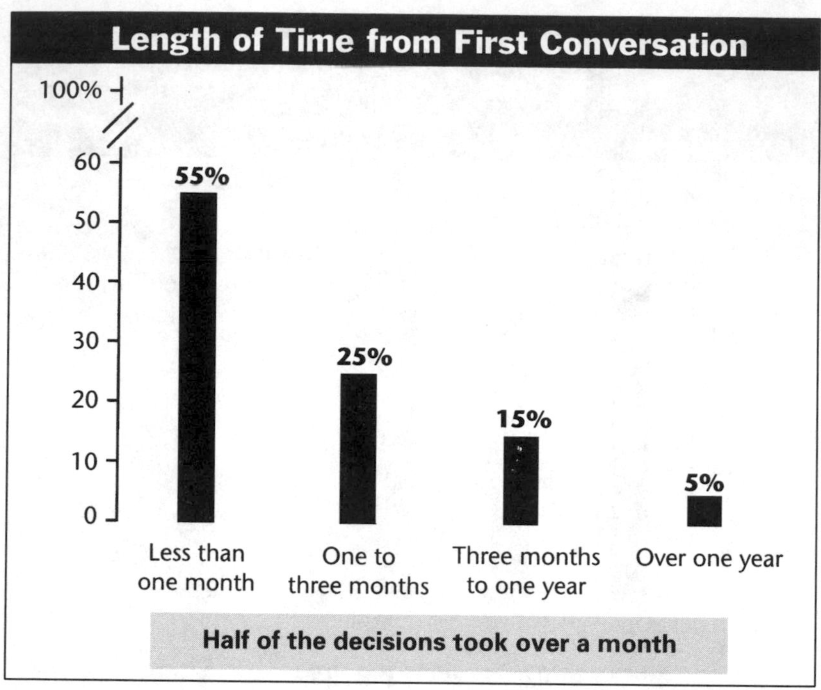
Length of Time from First Conversation
100%
60
50
40
30
20
10
0
55%
25%
15%
5%
Less than one month
One to three months
Three months to one year
Over one year
Half of the decisions took over a month

Figure 2.20

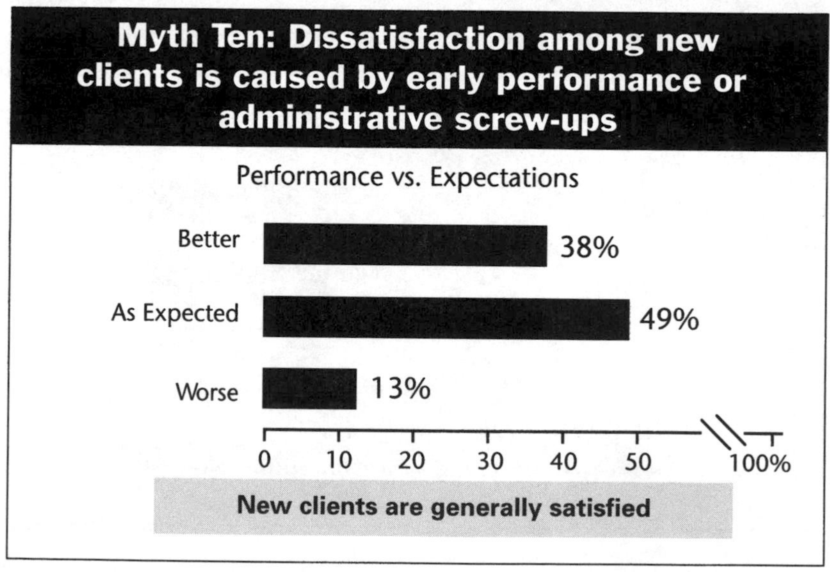
Myth Ten: Dissatisfaction among new clients is caused by early performance or administrative screw-ups
Performance vs. Expectations
Better
38%
As Expected
49%
Worse
13%
0
10
20
30
40
50
100%
New clients are generally satisfied

Figure 2.21

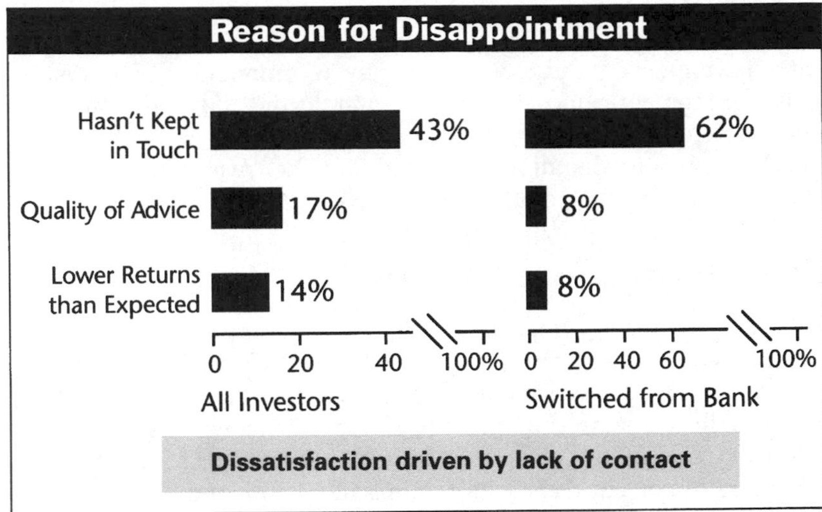

With so many financial advisers in enthusiastic pursuit of new prospects, you might expect that those prospects found the process of selecting a financial adviser easy. Quite the contrary: half of them considered it a difficult process (Figure 2.22). That's not because the advisers weren't keen, enthusiastic, and capable. The problem was that the prospects would talk to several advisers and find them *all* keen, enthusiastic, and capable. It was hard to choose the best.

Figure 2.22

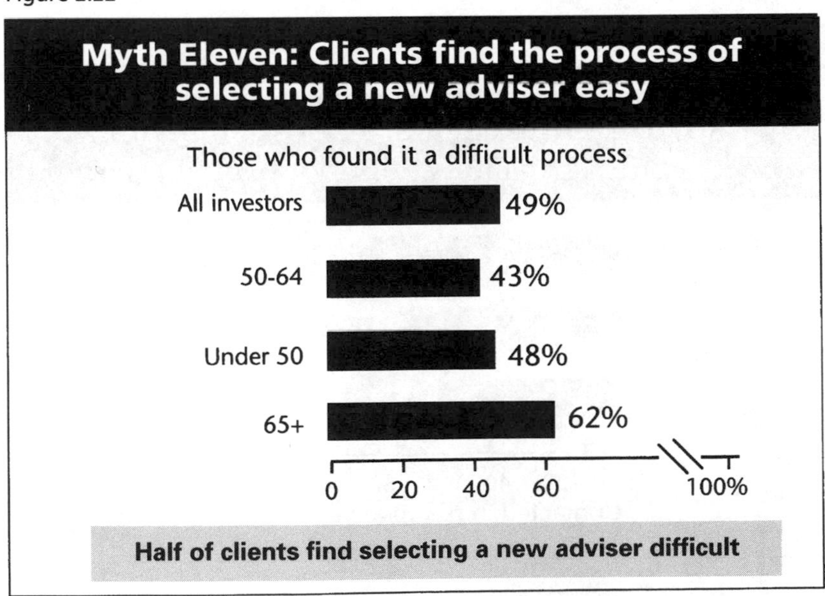

In the search for ways to differentiate yourself, this is an area of opportunity. Make the process easy for your prospective clients by developing some technique that sets you apart. One client recalled interviewing several advisers, all highly recommended. The distinguishing moment came when one adviser, at the end of the meeting, volunteered the names of some of his clients that she could call to check up on him. She didn't even call, but she trusted him more because of that unsolicited offer.

Sinking Response Rates

It used to be that if a financial adviser worked hard, he or she would be successful. Now, given the increased competition, that's no longer the case. Clients are constantly being wooed by competing financial advisers. In our sample, 61 percent of respondents with assets of over $200,000 received a cold call from a financial adviser seeking their business, 78 percent received a seminar invitation, and 83 percent received an investment newsletter (Figure 2.23). The average high-end client was contacted fourteen times over a two-year period through everything from seminar invitations to social encounters (Figures 2.24, 2.25).

As a result the response rate to the classic prospecting techniques has plummeted. The effort that would have led to 400 people attending a seminar two years ago will elicit only 150 to 250 guests. One of my clients recalls that a decade ago, when trainees were just finishing their program, they would mail a postcard to about 1,000 households

Figure 2.23

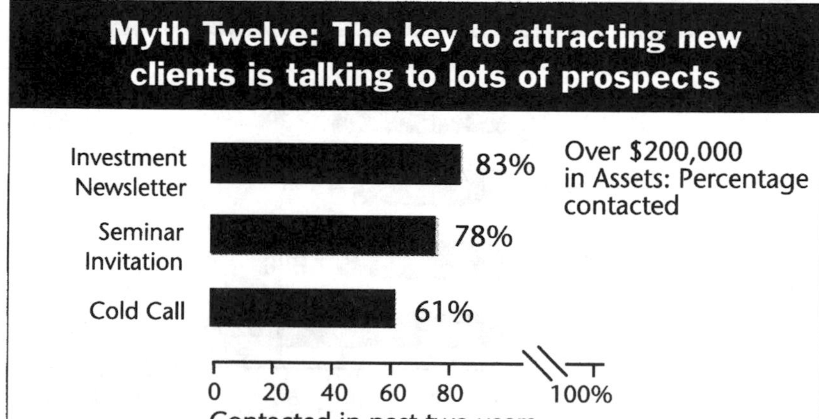

Figure 2.24

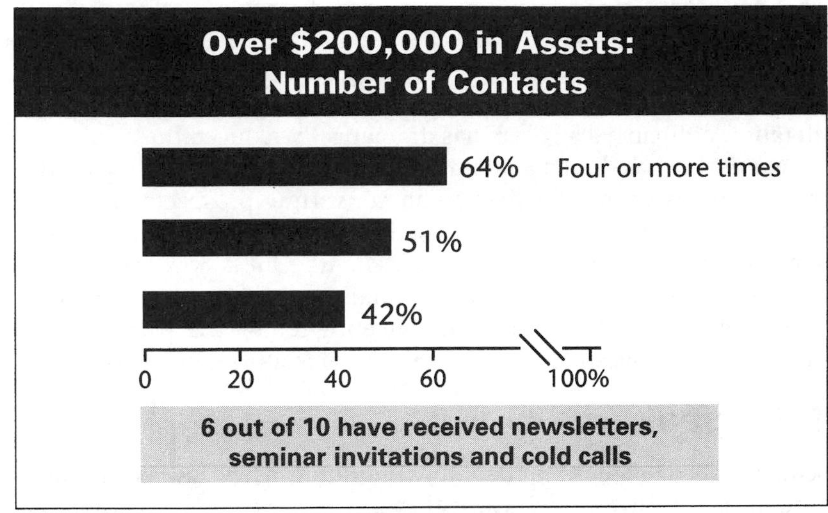
Over $200,000 in Assets:
Number of Contacts
64%
Four or more times
51%
42%
0
20
40
60
100%
6 out of 10 have received newsletters, seminar invitations and cold calls

Figure 2.25

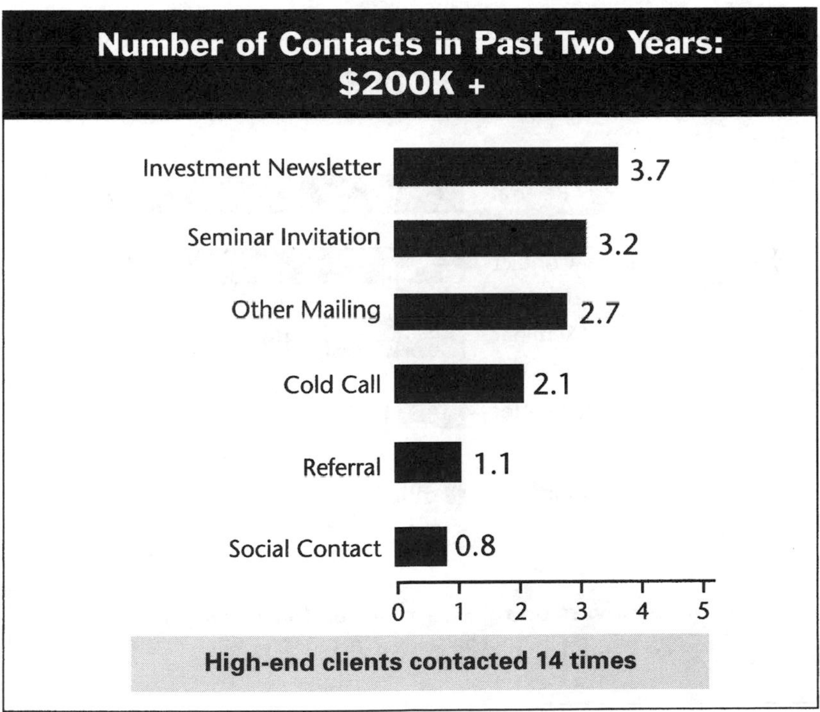
Number of Contacts in Past Two Years: $200K +
Investment Newsletter
3.7
Seminar Invitation
3.2
Other Mailing
2.7
Cold Call
2.1
Referral
1.1
Social Contact
0.8
0
1
2
3
4
5
High-end clients contacted 14 times

offering a free meeting and receive 120 to 150 affirmative responses. That gave that trainee a running start into the business. Today, forget the postcard. That's been replaced with a slick, elaborate brochure, targeted specifically to homes with the appropriate income level, from which the trainee might pull in five to ten signals of interest. The proliferation of financial advisers has dramatically reduced the results.

Again, that has placed a premium on building trust. The higher the trust, the greater the effectiveness in converting prospects to clients. Financial advisers must therefore institute techniques that will engender more trust and produce more new clients. Our survey showed, for example, that referrals and social contacts, which have a high trust residue, are more likely to lead to a meeting than lower-trust vehicles like a seminar, investment newsletter, or cold call (Figure 2.26).

The Speakers Game

Seminars are a middle ground in this continuum. They have been widely used in the past five years because they are quite appealing to prospects. Seminars address the thirst for objective information on financial affairs that's widespread today. They also offer safety: The prospect knows another 100 to 200 people will be in the room and can therefore take comfort in not being one-on-one with the adviser at this early stage.

Figure 2.26

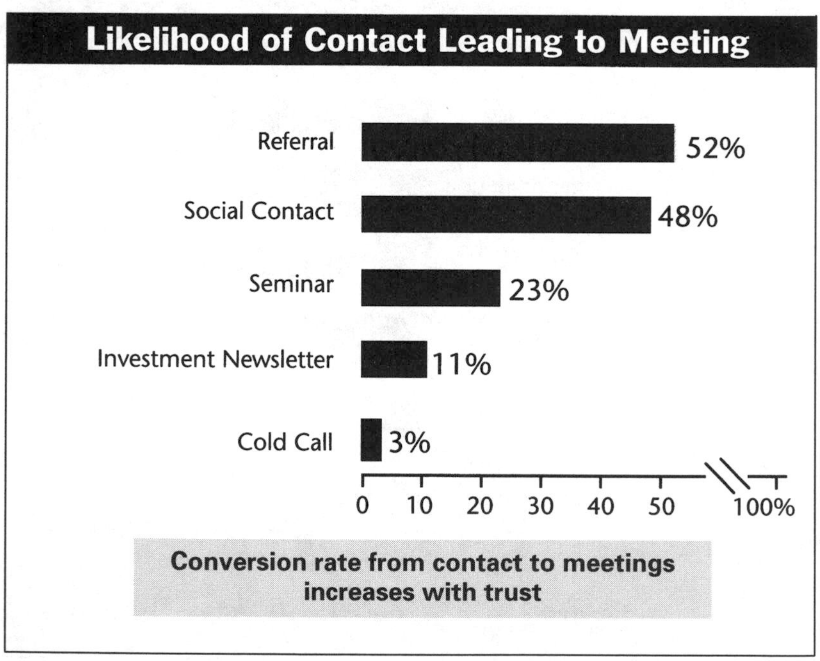

In many cases advisers have been spending big bucks on prominent media commentators to headline these events. Fees range as high as $25,000 a seminar. But our study cast some doubt on this approach. When we asked our sample of clients and prospects which of three types of speakers they would prefer, 41 percent picked a radio or newspaper commentator, not that far ahead of the 36 percent who chose an accountant speaking on tax savings (Figure 2.27). A lawyer talking on estate planning was favored by 22 percent. Interestingly, when we isolate the results by age, the accountant is more attractive than the media commentator for people over age fifty, while the lawyer talking on estate planning narrows the gap, particularly with over sixty-fives (Figure 2.28).

In probing how to secure the all-important initial meeting, we again found a somewhat surprising result. Forty-eight percent of respondents said they would probably agree to a meeting after a referral from an accountant or lawyer—the most effective of fifteen possibilities we tested. But the second-best option wasn't what you might expect: a referral from a friend or a bank. Both were edged out by the promise from the financial adviser of a customized report as a part of their service (Figure 2.29).

That illustrates the importance of adding value—for prospects as well as clients. Advisers can no longer get away with the minimum. They must ensure they are providing value. That's why this will be a constant theme in this book.

Figure 2.27

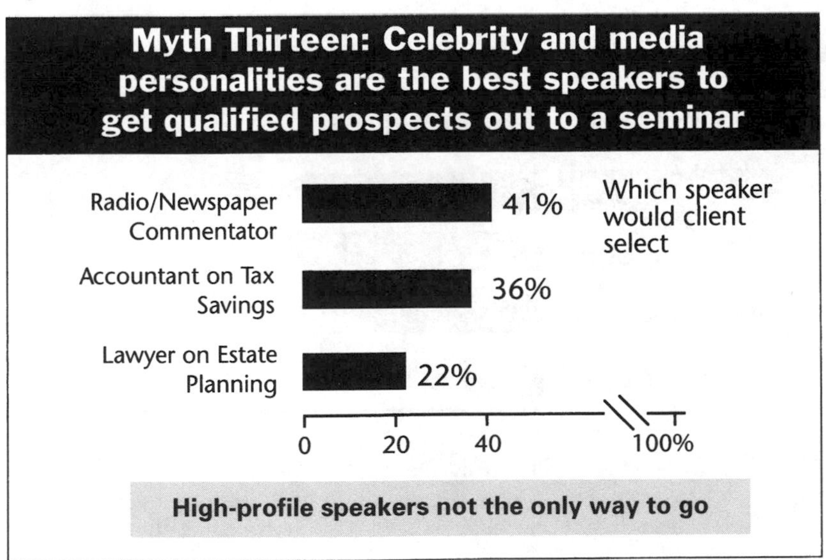

Figure 2.28

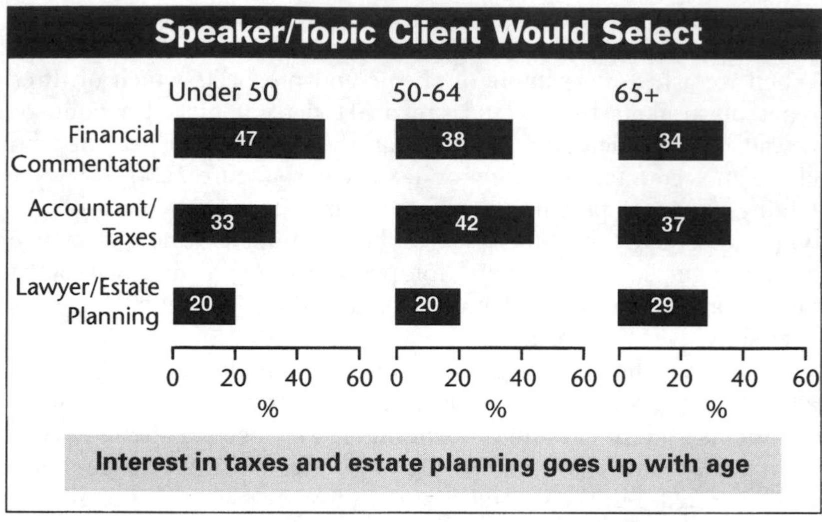
Speaker/Topic Client Would Select
Under 50
50-64
65+
Financial Commentator
47
38
34
Accountant/ Taxes
33
42
37
Lawyer/Estate Planning
20
20
29
0 20 40 60
%
Interest in taxes and estate planning goes up with age

Figure 2.29

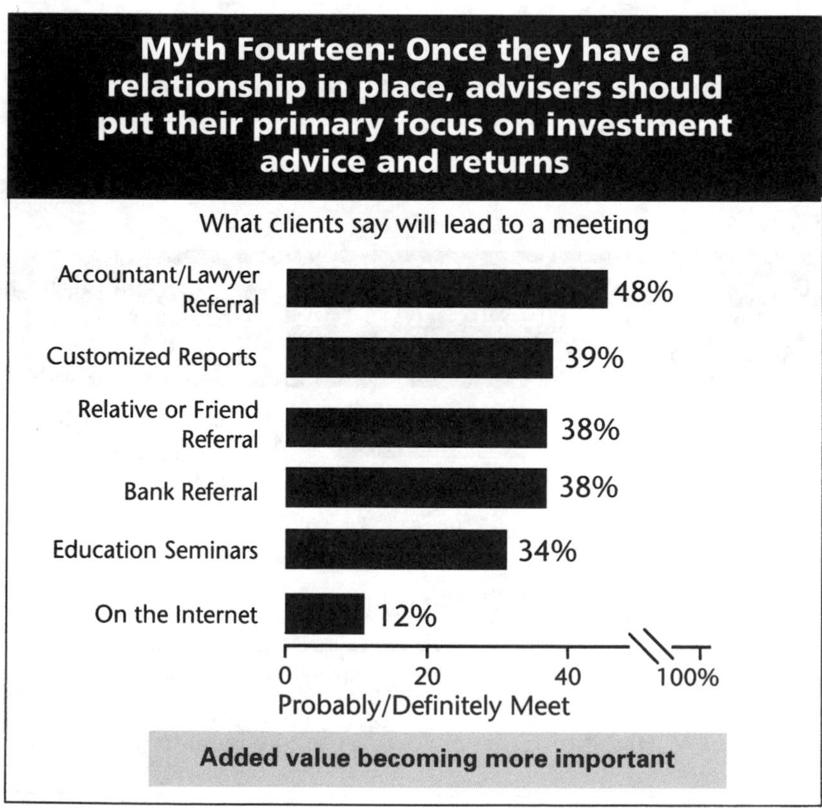
Myth Fourteen: Once they have a relationship in place, advisers should put their primary focus on investment advice and returns
What clients say will lead to a meeting
Accountant/Lawyer Referral
48%
Customized Reports
39%
Relative or Friend Referral
38%
Bank Referral
38%
Education Seminars
34%
On the Internet
12%
0
20
40
100%
Probably/Definitely Meet
Added value becoming more important

A few years ago, in another study, we asked investors with significant assets to rank the appeal of five possible approaches by a previously unknown financial adviser. The least likely to lead to a meeting was the opportunity to invest in a biotech company: Only 8 percent of our sample were interested. The chance to discuss new investment ideas with the adviser wasn't much more attractive: Only 11 percent indicated it would lead to a meeting. The best motivation was the chance to sit down with the adviser and listen to an analysis of retirement needs: Nearly one in three respondents said that would spark a meeting. Next best was a similar review of their tax savings, with 28 percent inclined to meet. Also effective was the promise of a second opinion on the individual's portfolio without any cost obligation, with 21 percent of prospects inclined to meet (Figure 2.30). Those approaches represent added value in this day and age. They are the kinds of methods advisers must employ in the increasingly competitive climate.

The Importance of Goal Setting

Our final question was based on the conviction most financial advisers have that if they communicate with the client effectively, set expectations realistically, and provide competitive returns, they can be confident that their clients will stay their clients. As it turns out, that is unequivocally the case, providing interest rates stay low. However,

Figure 2.30

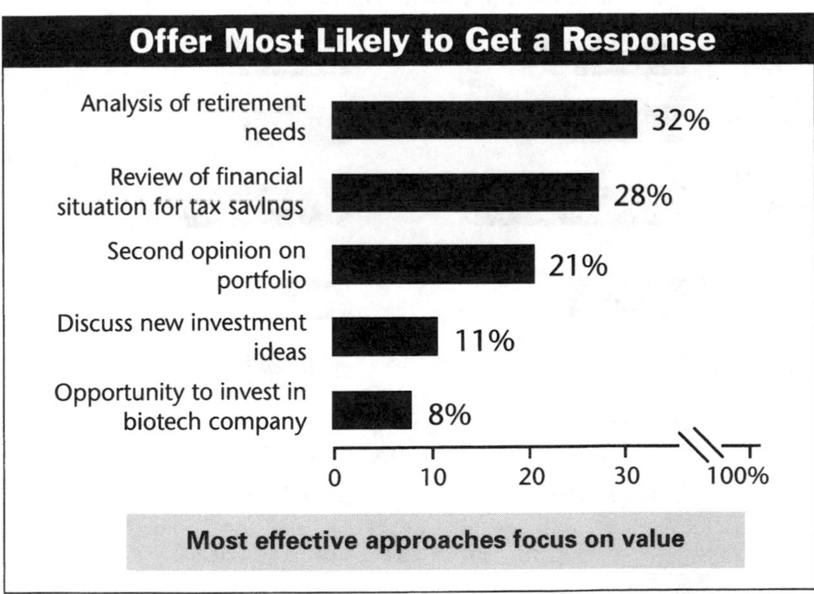

when we asked our sample what they would do if they could receive an 8 percent return on a fixed-term investment such as a government certificate, half indicated they would march as quickly as possible to their nearest bank branch and grab that opportunity. And that instinct holds —in fact, it grows—for our plum prospects and clients, people with over $200,000 in investable assets (Figure 2.31).

That's both fascinating and frightening. Half of clients would defect from their financial adviser for a guaranteed 8 percent return, even though from our research we know that the average client needs more like 10 to 12 percent returns, and in some cases even higher, to reach financial goals. Why is that 8 percent return so attractive to so many people? The answer is that 80 percent of clients, according to research, don't even know what percentage return they need to hit their retirement goals. Too many financial advisers have not worked through that calculation with clients—or if they have, often the advisers have not made the point sufficiently clearly and sufficiently fre-

Figure 2.31

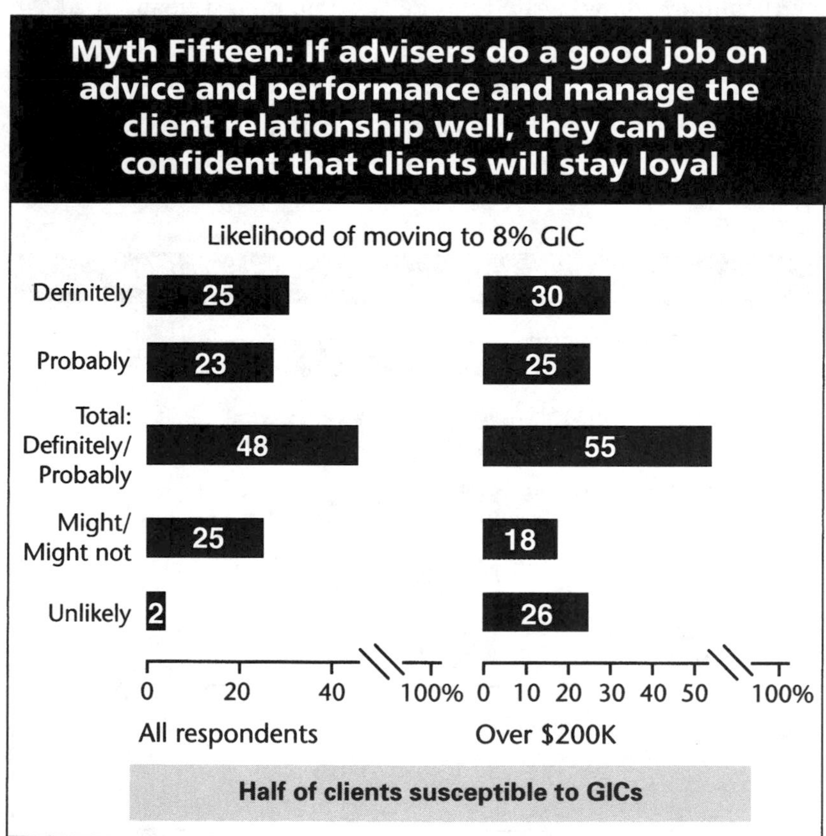

quently so that it's properly assimilated. That failure in understanding, obviously, is not the client's fault. It's the financial adviser's responsibility to educate clients on this critical issue.

That lapse, like most of the myth-debunking facts our recent research unearthed, reveals a trend and offers an opportunity. The client environment has changed—and is continuing to change—rapidly. This book will help advisers to turn those changes to their advantage.

In the book we will be identifying four critical strategies for the period ahead—strategies that will help you with *Getting Clients, Keeping Clients*. First of all, advisers must develop strategies for providing value. The '90s have been called the Value Decade. Advisers must ensure they are providing added value to their clients.

Second, advisers must create a strategy for building trust. Trust isn't everything; it's the *only* thing, as we stressed earlier. And trust does not happen by accident. Trust is earned. To be successful, financial advisers must form well-defined, explicit strategies to earn trust.

Third, advisers must shape strategies for building deep client relationships. Times have changed, and what it takes to keep a client has changed as well. A client no longer stays with an adviser unless that adviser gives him or her a reason to go. Today, more and more, clients are operating on the premise that they are going to leave unless the adviser gives a reason to stay. That's a fundamental shift in the rules, and advisers operating on the old basis will increasingly encounter trouble (Figure 2.32).

Finally, advisers require a strategy to generate referrals. Referrals are the best way to win new clients. This book will devote a lot of attention to ideas for generating more referrals for your practice.

Those four strategies will be crucial in determining success for all financial advisers. Naturally, every adviser will execute those strategies differently. No two advisers will have the same tactics and activities in place to provide value, build trust, nurture lasting client relationships, and maximize referrals. The specific program will depend on the specific talents, inclinations, and energy of each adviser. But each adviser must have some activities in place to carry out those four key strategies.

Figure 2.32

1988: "I'll stay unless you give me a reason to go."

1998: "I'll go unless you give me a reason to stay."

Snapshots

- ✔ *When we studied fifteen common beliefs of financial advisers, we found that all were wrong to some extent or another.*
- ✔ *To find serious money, it's best to expand our horizons beyond the over sixty-fives. The fifty-five to sixty-four-year-olds offer considerable promise. Targeting the two groups will point financial advisers at 56 percent of households with investable assets of between $100,000 to $200,000 and 70 percent of households with over $200,000.*
- ✔ *Over the past five years a significant migration has occurred from financial institutions to independent financial advisers, driven to a large extent by low interest rates. Today, investment advisers have been employed by about 75 percent of people with investable assets of over $50,000.*
- ✔ *Of those households, 35 percent have changed financial investors at some point. When we eliminated those investors who only started working with their financial adviser in the last eighteen months, we found that half the clients had changed advisers at some point.*
- ✔ *It's a myth that financial advisers know where all their clients' savings are invested and have been the sole counsel in determining those investments.*
- ✔ *Only 16 percent of people switching financial advisers were unhappy before the shift. If in the past clients left financial advisers because they were dissatisfied, today they leave because they are not satisfied enough.*
- ✔ *Clients rarely signal their dissatisfaction before leaving. Advisers, therefore, need strategies to find out how their clients feel about their service.*
- ✔ *Referrals continue to play an important role in the selection of new financial advisers.*
- ✔ *Research repeatedly shows that what attracts clients is trust rather than the adviser's financial expertise. Lack of trust, on the other hand, sends prospects and clients scurrying away.*
- ✔ *In the past, referrals handed you a client. Today, referrals grant you the right to compete for clients.*
- ✔ *Advisers need to establish a process to continue communications with prospects at a reasonable pace throughout the decision-making period,*

whatever its length. You also need a strategy to differentiate yourself from the competing financial advisers.

- ✔ *The number-one reason for performance falling below client expectations is the adviser's failure to keep in touch. Lack of contact creates a growing dissatisfaction that eventually kills the relationship.*
- ✔ *Prospects find it difficult to choose between the many capable financial advisers vying for their portfolio. Figure out ways to make the decision easy for them.*
- ✔ *The response rate to the classic prospecting techniques has plummeted in the past three to five years. Again, this places a premium on building trust. The higher the trust, the greater the effectiveness in converting prospects to clients.*
- ✔ *Popular media commentators are not necessarily the best people to headline a seminar.*
- ✔ *Remember the importance of a customized report as a lure for the first meeting with a client.*
- ✔ *Today's financial adviser must provide value—to prospects as well as clients. Advisers can no longer get away with the minimum.*
- ✔ *The best motivator for an initial meeting, according to our survey, was the promise to sit down and discuss retirement needs. Next was a similar review of tax savings. Also effective was the promise of a second opinion on the individual's portfolio without any cost obligation.*
- ✔ *Half of clients would defect from a financial adviser for a guaranteed 8 percent return even though from our research we know that the average client needs more like 10 to 12 percent returns, and in some cases even higher, to reach financial goals. This occurs because too many financial advisers have not worked through that calculation with clients.*
- ✔ *Four strategies are needed to help you with* Getting Clients, Keeping Clients*: a strategy for adding value, a strategy for building trust, a strategy for nurturing deep client relationships, and a strategy for obtaining referrals.*

Section II
Getting Clients

CHAPTER 3

Making the Initial Contact

FIVE BASIC STEPS ARE REQUIRED FOR AN ADVISER TO DEVELOP A CLIENT relationship (Figure 3.1).

Step 1: The process begins with making the initial contact. It's important that the initial contact occurs in a manner that predisposes a positive reaction so that client development opens on a solid footing.

Step 2: Having established contact, you build your level of trust with that prospective client.

Step 3: As trust is built, you must create the motivation to meet. It's not enough to simply establish contact; you must persuade the prospective client to invest the time to sit and talk with you. And time, of course, is not the real impediment. The substantive concern is the client's fear of an unpleasant experience—being pressured to purchase something he or she doesn't want to buy.

Step 4: Once you've met with the client, the next stage is closing the sale. The meeting must be turned into a transaction.

Step 5: Finally, you must convert that transaction into a relationship, making the customer a long-term client.

Figure 3.1

Developing a New Client

Step One:	Making the initial contact
Step Two:	Building your trust level
Step Three:	Creating the motivation to meet
Step Four:	Closing the sale
Step Five:	Converting a transaction into a relationship

Most advisers realize that to be successful they must get all five steps right. Four out of five is not enough. All five steps must be in place. But ask yourself: Which one or two steps are the most difficult? Which one or two steps require the most effort? Which pose the greatest hurdle for most financial advisers?

The answer, clearly, is the initial two steps: making the initial contact with prospective clients in a way that predisposes a positive response, and building your trust level. Handling those two steps effectively does not guarantee the remainder of the process will be automatic. But creating the motivation to meet, closing the sale, and converting the transaction into a long-term business relationship flow naturally out of those first two steps.

A strong correlation exists between how much a prospect trusts an adviser and the likelihood that they will become a client.

This section, Getting Clients, will focus on those two steps. We'll develop strategies to place you in front of prospects in a manner that's likely to trigger a positive rather than negative response. We'll also concentrate on building your trust level. Later in the book we'll concentrate on how to convert the transaction that develops into a long-term relationship.

Establishing Contact

Let's begin by examining the first step, establishing contact. Almost as many alternatives exist for making contact with clients as there are financial advisers.

Some advisers prefer mass marketing techniques: advertising, widely publicized seminars, and direct mail. Others concentrate on cold calling. Still others focus on a variation of cold calling dubbed cold knocking: They visit industrial parks at 7:30 A.M. and introduce themselves to the only person typically present at that hour, the owner, and begin cultivating a relationship.

Some advisers focus on offering seminars to companies in their community, as a channel to meet the employees. Other alternatives they try include developing referral networks with accountants and lawyers in the community, networking among the people they know, or deliberately raising their visibility and prominence through activity on boards or charitable organizations. Finally, some advisers rely on raising their media profile in the community. They write for the local newspaper, seek out opportunities to appear on the local radio or television station, and perhaps even host a call-in show on finances.

As you read that list, inevitably you wonder which is the best prospecting method. So it's important to state at the outset that there isn't one. All of those prospecting methods are effective for different advisers, depending on their personalities, philosophies, and the development stage of their practice. You have to determine which prospecting approaches make most sense for you at this time.

Financial advisers commonly use four criteria to evaluate which prospecting alternative to use. The first is the response they elicit: the immediate gratification from that prospecting method. Second is the comfort level: how comfortable they feel using a particular method. A third consideration is the difficulty: how much effort it requires. The fourth concern is cost (Figure 3.2).

Evaluating Prospecting Methods

Interestingly, all four of those criteria are essentially short term in orientation. The response is short term. Your comfort is short term. The effort is short term. The cost is short term. Yet advisers seek a long-term result: clients who will bond to us for the long haul.

Given that dichotomy, I'd like to suggest a better method for evaluating prospecting methods. To do so, I want to set out ten of the most common prospecting alternatives:

- accountants/lawyers referral network
- advertising
- client newsletter/market letter
- cold calls
- community involvement
- direct mail
- referrals
- seminars
- speaking to a group as an invited guest speaker
- trade shows/booths

Imagine you show up at the office on Monday morning and are told that in order to keep your position with the firm you have to spend that entire day prospecting—and you have to employ each of those methods. I'd like you to consider your comfort level with each of those methods

Figure 3.2

Criteria in Selecting a Prospecting Approach

1. Response
2. Comfort Level
3. Effort
4. Cost

and mark it on Figure 3.3 in the left-hand column, with 10 signifying a very high comfort level and 1 indicating a very low comfort level. If you're not terribly comfortable nor terribly uncomfortable, call it a 5.

Now imagine that ten advisers in the community who are identical in every respect each spend that same Monday morning using one of those prospecting methods on clients. How do you suppose the clients rate those prospecting methods, on the basis of the all-important trust created in the initial contact? Return to our chart and in the right-hand column take a stab at measuring that trust, from the client's perspective, again employing our 1-to-10 scale.

My company investigated this concept with clients and through that research developed what we call the Trust Spectrum (Figure 3.4). The high-trust activities are professional referrals, client referrals, serving as a guest speaker, knowing somebody through community involvement, and meeting people through giving a seminar. At the low end of the trust scale—from the client's perspective, let me remind you—are the mass marketing techniques: direct mail, advertisements, and cold calling.

The reason the trust spectrum is an effective means of evaluating prospecting methods is that our research revealed a direct correlation between the level of trust an adviser evokes in a prospect and the likelihood of that person becoming a client. The higher the level of trust, the more likely the individual is to become a client. Conversely, the lower the level of trust, the less likely he or she is to become a client.

Moreover, our research shows that in the early stages of cultivating a prospect, nothing shapes the level of trust that a prospect experiences toward you as much as how the initial contact was made. The prospecting method you select, in effect, drives the level of trust that

Figure 3.3

Evaluating Prospecting Alternatives

	Your Comfort	Client's Trust
1. Accountants/lawyers	______	______
2. Advertising	______	______
3. Client newsletter/market letter	______	______
4. Cold calls	______	______
5. Community involvement	______	______
6. Direct mail	______	______
7. Referrals	______	______
8. Seminars	______	______
9. Speaking to groups as an invited guest speaker	______	______
10. Trade shows/booths	______	______

Figure 3.4

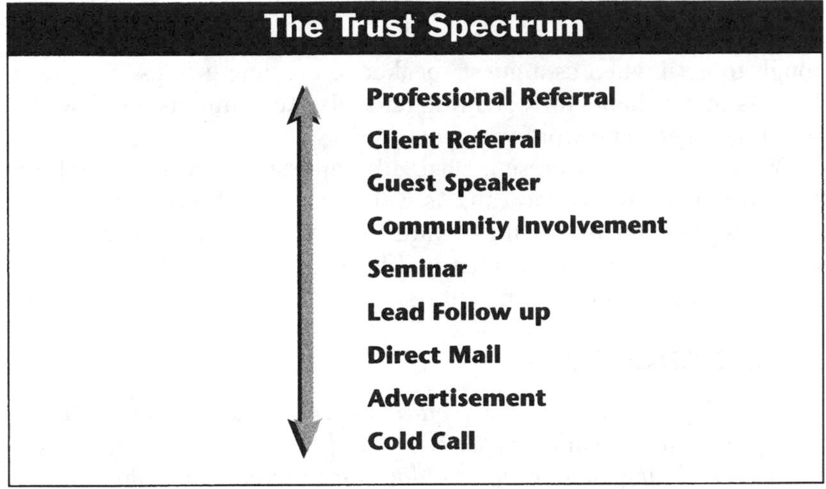

prospective clients feel toward you in that all-important early stage of developing a relationship.

That doesn't mean, by the way, that you can't successfully employ one of the mass marketing techniques: advertising, direct mail, or cold calling. You can. But they're harder. Because mass marketing reaches more people, it will connect you to a larger number of prospects. But the level of trust those prospects develop toward you will be lower and the hurdles you must overcome will consequently be higher.

The Formula for Success

Those findings led us to develop a formula to identify the long-term effectiveness of different prospecting approaches:

T + P + U + E = Success.

The level of *trust* that a prospecting method evokes, plus the extent to which it positions you as a *professional* in the mind of a prospect, combined with its level of *uniqueness,* along with, finally, your *effectiveness* in using that particular prospecting method, will determine success.

As you consider what prospecting methods to employ, you'll want to consider that research. Evaluate how much you're succumbing to short-term considerations in your current prospecting: short-term response, effort, comfort, and cost. Figure out how much you're being driven by long-term considerations: trust, professionalism, uniqueness, and effectiveness. Obviously, for long-term effectiveness, you'll want to shift up the trust spectrum and accentuate the accelerants of success in our formula.

It may be impossible to shift immediately, given the stage of your business. If you're just starting out or have only been in the business awhile, it's difficult to operate at the top of the trust spectrum. It's tough to get invited as a guest speaker to credible groups. You don't have as many clients for obtaining referrals. Accountants and lawyers won't be eager to network with you.

But whatever your present stage, it's important to work as high up the trust spectrum as you can. As well, you should have a mid-term business objective of moving toward the top of the trust spectrum as quickly as you can. That's what will lead to greater success and productivity in your prospecting efforts.

Snapshots

✔ *Attracting clients is a five-step process: making initial contact in an effective manner, building trust with the client, creating the motivation to meet, closing the sale, and building a long-term relationship.*

✔ *The first two steps are the most difficult: making the initial contact with prospective clients in a way that predisposes a positive response and building your trust level.*

✔ *In evaluating prospecting methods, advisers wrongly tend to use short-term criteria such as the immediate gratification, the comfort level, the difficulty, and the cost.*

✔ *The trust spectrum shows clients award highest trust through initial contacts made via professional referrals, client referrals, serving as a guest speaker, knowing somebody through community involvement, and meeting people through giving seminars. At the low end of the trust scale are the mass-marketing techniques: direct mail, advertisements, and cold calling.*

✔ *A direct correlation exists between the level of trust an adviser evokes in a prospect and the likelihood of that person becoming a client. Moreover, in the early stages of cultivating a prospect, nothing shapes that level of trust as much as the prospecting method chosen for the initial contact. So the prospecting method drives the level of trust, which in turn helps to determine the likelihood of a successful outcome.*

✔ *Remember the formula: T + P + U + E = Success. The level of trust from a prospecting method, plus the extent to which it positions you as a professional, plus its uniqueness, plus your effectiveness in using that particular prospecting method = Success.*

CHAPTER 4

Operating from the Client's 99

IMAGINE THAT YOU RECEIVE A PHONE CALL ONE MORNING FROM YOUR FIRM'S human resources department. The caller tells you that after an extensive evaluation of employee records, you have been selected as the most qualified person to choose the new computer system that will carry your company into the next century.

You are the buyer. And imagine that I'm the seller, talking to you about my company's services and the splendid solutions we can provide for your needs. As we're talking, what proportion of your focus and energy is devoted to your needs as the buyer and what proportion is devoted to my needs as a seller?

Obviously, very little of your attention is on my needs. In fact, even after I show you the pictures I carry of my daughters and elderly mother, if you're like most people the best you can muster in such a situation is to dig deep within yourself and find it in your heart to allocate 1 percent of your concern to the other guy. Ninety-nine percent of your focus and energy is aimed at your own needs. That's your priority.

Now turn the tables. What about the prospects and clients you deal with every day as a financial adviser? What proportion of their focus and energy is targeted at their needs and what proportion at your needs? The answer is the same. Ninety-nine percent of their focus and energy is directed at their priorities—as it should be.

If we're going to be successful, then, whose 99 do we have to operate from? Ours—or our client's? Clearly the answer is our client's. For success, we have to operate—continually—from our Client's 99.

Adopting the Client's 99

Now imagine this scenario: On the same day, you deal with two clients with distinctive needs and sell them two different packages.

Fast-forward six months: One of those investments has climbed by 25 percent, while the other has plummeted by 25 percent. Both clients pop up on your computer screen as due for contact, but you only have time to telephone one. Who are you going to call?

The vast majority of financial advisers would pick the client who is up. After all, a pleasant conversation seems guaranteed. So if you're operating from your 99, you'll phone the client who made money.

Advisers must ensure that they are operating from the client's point of view—the Client's 99.

But who do you need to call? Undoubtedly the client whose investment improved would love to hear from you. But the client who needs to hear from you is the person who has lost money. If you're operating from the Client's 99, that's the person you would automatically call.

Now some advisers might counter that if that client has any questions or is unhappy, he or she would call. But it's the rare client that actually does, as our recent research confirmed. The majority of unhappy clients simply sit there, lose sleep, and simmer over their misfortune. They don't call you. But they will pick up the phone for those who call them, one of whom might be a competing adviser. The next time you hear from that client may be via a transfer form shifting the account to another adviser.

A few years ago when the markets were generally dim, I spoke to one financial adviser who knew a flood of statements containing less-than-enthusiastic news was being mailed out to clients. He took a day out of his schedule, stayed home, and phoned those clients. His message was simple: "Mr. Client/Ms. Client, in the next few days you'll receive your statement for this quarter, and if you've been following the performance of the markets, you'll know they have been disappointing. Unfortunately it's one of those periods that we knew would come along, when the market has underperformed. But I'm calling to let you know that our firm's research director has conducted a comprehensive review of market conditions and has reiterated that we have reason to be positive on the mid-term prospects. Even though you're down in the short term, you don't really have to be concerned. You are well positioned in terms of where you need to be for the future."

What kind of response do you think that adviser received from that batch of calls? Do you figure his clients were livid—yelling and cursing? Not at all. In fact, the clients thanked him for calling. One client said, "Listen, I really appreciate you taking the time to call. You know, I was talking to someone who is unhappy with her existing adviser and I'd like to phone her in the next few days and suggest you contact her."

So the adviser called his clients with bad news and ended up receiving a referral. The issue isn't that you're passing along bad news. Your clients probably know that. If they don't, they will certainly learn the truth pretty soon. The issue is that you're operating from the Client's 99. Clients want to know they have an adviser who is watching out for their interests—who is thinking about them, and is prepared to take the time and effort to call them, even when the news is sour.

Now some advisers might second-guess taking a whole day to make those calls. On the surface it seems a considerable commitment of time and loss of productivity. But how many calls do you think that adviser received for elaboration or for queries on performance after the clients received their statements? The answer, of course, is none. He was going to have to spend some time with his clients regardless. By spending it before they received their statements rather than after, he turned what could have been a fairly negative experience into a positive one. And he communicated with the close-lipped clients, those who are dissatisfied but who don't bother to call, remaining prey for a competitor's advances.

I'm not suggesting you immediately scan your client list for underperforming investments that will give you an opportunity to call clients with bad news. In the normal course of events over an extended period of time, those opportunities will unfortunately arise. But when it happens, you have to remember to operate from the Client's 99.

Clients expect you to call when the news is good. If you want to show them you really care, call them as well when the news is bad. That's an example of operating from the Client's 99.

The Two-Meeting Principle

Another example comes at an initial meeting with a prospect when after 45 minutes of detailing her financial situation she asks, "What do you think?" Most advisers would take that as a signal to begin framing recommendations: "On balance, I think you're in pretty good shape, but there are some areas that can be improved upon. Here they are. . . . "

But how does the prospective client subconsciously feel as you begin your spiel? How much thought does she figure you have given her situation—which from her perspective is unique? Although she has invited those recommendations, by providing them you are indicating you haven't given her circumstances the maximum possible thought. You haven't operated by her 99 as much as by rote.

An alternative is to respond to the client's query with a request for more time to properly consider her situation. "If you're really anxious, I could give you some off-the-cuff reactions. But I would prefer to think about what you've told me, perhaps carry out some further research, and then sit down with you in a week's time and review your portfolio in more detail. At that point I'll have some detailed recommendations."

It's highly unlikely after proposing that course of action that the prospect would demand to know immediately what you recommend. She will be quite content to wait the week, knowing she is getting careful attention to her needs. Even if the ultimate recommendations are the same as you would have offered immediately, she will react more positively because from the Client's 99 you have taken time to reflect and research her unique situation. You have sent a positive signal that you operate not by a smash-and-grab-a-client approach but by a professional, individualized approach.

That style is not unlike the large accounting firms. No matter how simple your tax return, you won't find a large accounting firm offering to provide it in less than three days. Does it really take three days to handle every tax return? Of course not. But part of the accounting firm's message is that if you want quick and cheap, H&R Block is just down the street. If you want quality and attention to detail, that will take more time and cost a little extra.

The difference in both cases is not the product. It's not the investment recommendations or the tax returns. The difference is communicating to the Client's 99 that you will take the time to provide a top-quality job.

The two-meeting principle is a very effective method of providing assurance to the prospective client that he or she is dealing with an adviser who is professional and concerned about putting the client's interest before making a quick sale. Like calling the client with bad news, it signals that the client's interest is at the top of our agenda. In everything we do, we must learn to focus on the client's point of view and operate from the Client's 99.

Snapshots

✔ *For advisers to be successful, they continually have to take the client's point of view and operate from the Client's 99.*

✔ *When you have bad news for clients, don't hide and hope they won't notice. Give them a personal call and cement the relationship by adopting their 99.*

✔ *Consider the two-meeting principle—a first meeting to listen to the client and a second meeting to outline proposals—as a way of signaling your professional approach and determination to abide by the Client's 99.*

CHAPTER 5

Building Trust

MANY ADVISERS ASSUME THE PRIME REASON THAT CLIENTS WORK WITH US IS financial performance. After all, that's what our firms pay us to provide. But that supposition badly misreads our clients. The elixir that clients search for in their financial adviser is trust. And that's why it's critical for financial advisers to build trust, with prospects as well as clients.

In 1993, for example, the International Association for Financial Planning asked a sample of American adults what elements they considered most important in their relationship with a financial adviser. The respondents did consider returns and performance important: those were selected 24 percent of the time. Expertise, which is related, was also picked 18 percent of the time. But the single most important factor was trust, cited 53 percent of the time. One in two Americans consider trust the most important element in their relationship with a financial adviser (Figure 5.1).

That corresponds with studies which our firm and others have carried out. It also fits with some intriguing research our firm conducted on why investors persist in dealing with banks even though financial advisers are easily accessible and thought to provide higher quality advice.

We opened by asking a sample of investors to rank the knowledge level of six possible sources of financial advice: fee-based financial planners, commission-based financial planners, stock brokers, accountants, bank managers, and insurance agents. The investors used a 10-point scale to rate this aspect of their confidence in each adviser. The highest ranked was the fee-based financial planner, followed by the commission-based financial planner and stock broker. Accountants and bank managers finished below them, with insurance agents lagging well behind (Figure 5.2).

The bank manager ranked more than 10 percent behind the fee-

Figure 5.1

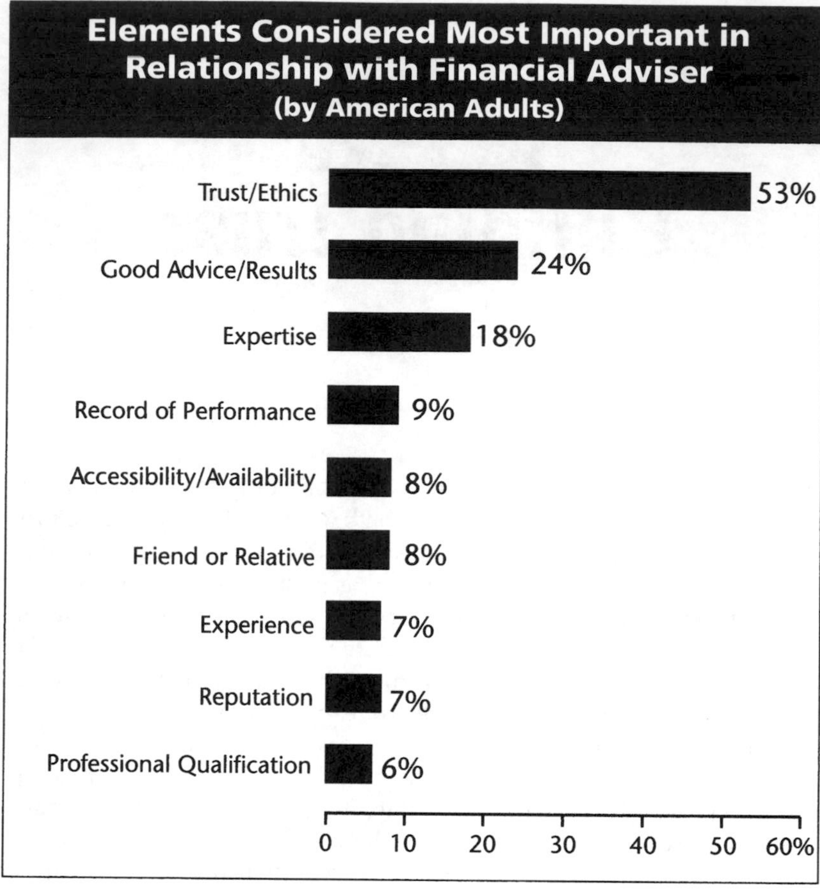

based financial planner on the rating scale. But our second question provided a quite different ranking. This time we looked at confidence from another perspective: We asked respondents to calculate their confidence that the financial advice offered by those sources would be in the client's best interest. The accountant and bank manager now jumped to the top, followed by the fee-based financial planner. The stock broker and commission-based financial planner fell well behind, with the insurance agent again languishing at the bottom of the pack (Figure 5.3).

Let's imagine that a prospective client has the opportunity of dealing with two financial advisers. The prospect has absolute confidence in the knowledge of the first adviser, but only moderate confidence in that adviser's integrity. With the second adviser, the situation is reversed: The prospective client only has moderate confi-

Figure 5.2

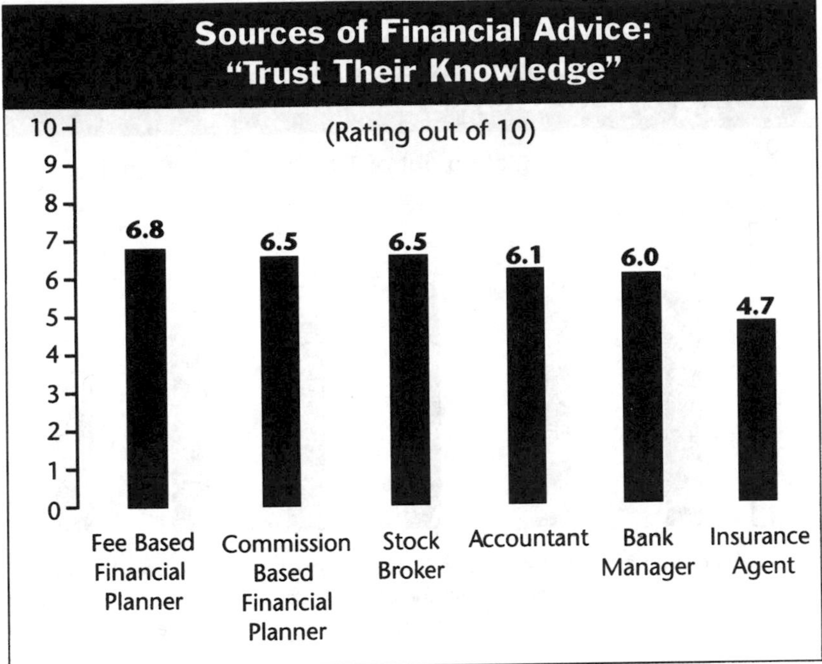

dence in the adviser's knowledge but absolute confidence in the adviser's integrity. Which will he choose? Clients opt for integrity almost every time.

The Need for a Trust-Building Strategy

The challenge for financial advisers, then, is to establish a high level of trust with prospective clients, bearing in mind that the single biggest obstacle to developing that confidence is the fact consumers know we're paid on commission. They recognize that anyone who is reimbursed in this way inherently has a potential conflict. How do we cultivate the same level of trust as a bank manager, when we are viewed as handicapped by this conflict of interest?

In essence, that's our main challenge in the prospecting process. Every prospecting activity must be designed to increase consumers' confidence in our professionalism and integrity. They must trust that our advice is developed in their best interest.

Interestingly, financial advisers will often have well-refined strategies for prospecting, communication, raising profile, selling, and product presentation. But how many financial advisers have constructed as part of their marketing plan a trust-building strategy? How

Figure 5.3

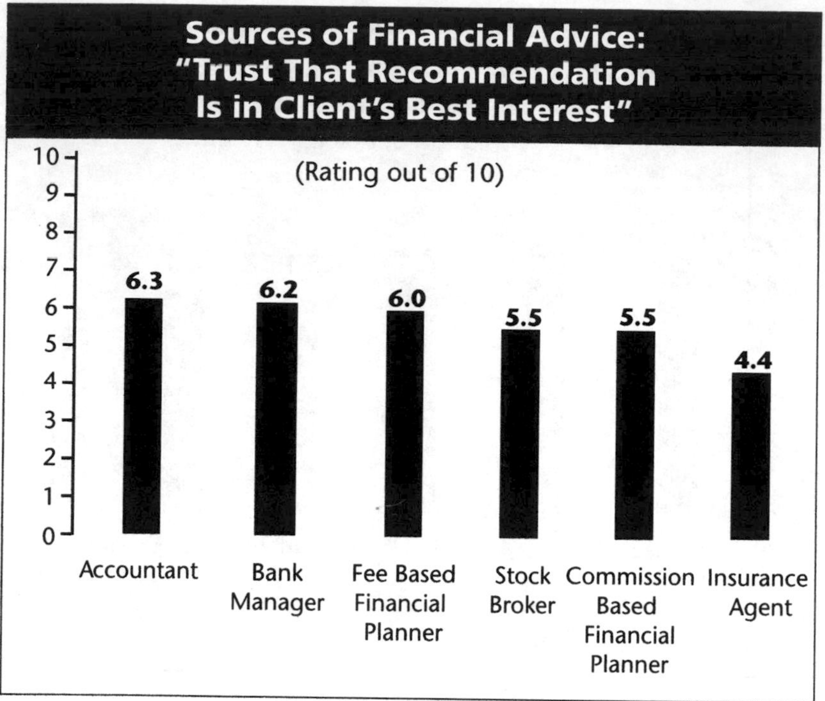

many financial advisers have explicit plans in place to develop trust in the minds of their prospects and clients?

Remember: trust is the paramount issue. More than anything else, trust determines whether a prospect will engage in business with you. Your knowledge, your staff, and the quality of your advice are secondary considerations; it's your integrity that is primary. It follows, therefore, that to be highly successful you must craft a strategy to assure prospects they can trust you.

Four pillars form the foundation of a trust-building strategy (Figure 5.4), and we'll explore them in detail in the next chapters.

1. The first pillar is the Banker's Rule (to be discussed in the next chapter), which involves assuming the reassuring persona and practices of a banker.
2. Next is borrowing credibility: recognizing that since we may not be innately credible ourselves, we have to carefully associate ourselves with identified sources of credibility from which we can borrow trust.
3. We also have to build our profile in a trustworthy fashion.
4. Finally, we have to earn trust through demonstrated patience.

Figure 5.4

Four Pillars of Trust Building

1. The Banker's Rule
2. Borrowing credibility
3. Building profile in a trustworthy fashion
4. Demonstrating patience

That may seem like a lot of unnecessary work, and some advisers might be tempted to skip the process. After all, they figure, if solid financial returns are provided, clients won't stray and new prospects will be suitably impressed. But that justification flows from the Adviser's 99, not the Client's 99. The client's chief concern, all the studies warn us, is not financial returns. It is: Can I trust my adviser?

For most clients, performance is simply a threshold issue. They have a minimum level of performance that they consider acceptable, and they expect their adviser to satisfy that standard. Comfort, enthusiasm, and loyalty are built when the adviser meets that minimum threshold of performance and generates trust by reassuring the client that his or her interest comes first.

Imagine two clients dealing with different financial advisers. The first client has only attained that performance threshold but has developed a very high level of confidence in the adviser's integrity. The second client has received an extraordinarily high investment return and is thrilled about performance but is only moderately satisfied about the relationship with the adviser. Perhaps the client feels pressured in meetings, doesn't get enough contact, or feels questions aren't properly answered.

In the short term, both advisers will retain their client. But imagine the markets dip and performance suffers. For the first adviser, the solid relationship buys time—often quite a bit of time—to allow performance to rebound to acceptable limits. But the second client, now with poor results and a poor relationship with the adviser, is probably very open to advances from another adviser. High performance was the glue that kept client and adviser together. Now it has disappeared. The adviser without the proper trust-building strategy is vulnerable.

We can all learn a lesson from Dodee Frost Crockett on trust. That's what she builds with her pledge to help clients with anything—and her subsequent delivery on the promise. Obviously she wouldn't have landed her clients without the ability to give reliable investment advice. They didn't come to her, originally, in case they might someday need a plumber or doctor. But driving the enthusiasm of that client who had cancer is the sense he can absolutely trust his adviser—she really cares. In the future, it's that sense of trust which will make us successful.

Snapshots

- ✔ *Surveys show trust to be the most important element in the relationship of clients with their financial adviser.*
- ✔ *Many investors choose to deal with a bank manager, even though they don't rate the quality of financial advice from that source as highly as that received from a financial planner. Why? They believe a bank manager is more likely to offer advice in the client's best interest.*
- ✔ *The challenge for financial advisers is to establish a high level of trust with prospective clients, bearing in mind that the single biggest obstacle to developing such trust is that consumers know we're paid on commission.*
- ✔ *The four pillars of a trust-building strategy—to be discussed in detail in the next chapters—are the Banker's Rule, borrowing credibility, building our profile in a trustworthy fashion, and earning trust through demonstrated patience.*

CHAPTER 6

Practicing the Banker's Rule

FOR FINANCIAL ADVICE, PEOPLE PREFER TO DEAL WITH SOMEONE WHO LOOKS, sounds, and feels conservative. Somebody safe—like their banker or accountant. Even entrepreneurs, who are risk-takers by nature, prefer people handling their money who are safe, conservative and, yes, low risk.

That leads to what I call the Banker's Rule: When we're dealing with prospective clients, we must communicate that we're as safe to deal with as their banker. That involves examining the signals we send, directly and indirectly, through our clothes, our appearance, the amount of jewelry we wear, how our office looks, our letterhead style, and even the magazines we leave out for browsing in the reception area. All should be selected to nurture an impression of safe, low-key conservatism.

It might appear silly to worry about such seemingly superficial matters when prospective clients are presumably searching for financial acumen. But people often respond to us on an emotional, seemingly irrational basis. You should influence those crucial filters, when you can.

Start with those magazines. You could pick *Reader's Digest* and *National Geographic,* and your clients might figure they stumbled into a dentist's office by mistake. Or you could spread out publications such as *Fortune, Forbes,* and the *Wall Street Journal.* They send a clear-cut message about what your office—and you—are about. *Time* and *Newsweek,* those staples of innumerable waiting rooms, won't necessarily hurt you. But they won't send as focused and as powerful a message as *Fortune, Forbes,* and their ilk.

Let me stress that the magazines don't have to be exclusively financial. But generally you want business-oriented or financially oriented publications, because they convey the right message. And everything else in your office should as well. Tomorrow, when you arrive at your workplace, evaluate it from the Client's 99. Ponder the sign on the door, examine the reception area, consider the decorations on the walls, study your personal office. Do they signal this adviser is someone a client can be absolutely confident in trusting, like a banker?

Our car sends an important message to clients. That doesn't decree you should borrow your friend's Mercedes to impress prospects. But it does mean that if the prospect hears you pull up in a 1984 rusted-out Pinto, you will have a significant hurdle to overcome in building trust and delivering the message that you are safety and conservatism personified.

Advisers must look as conservative and safe to deal with as a banker or accountant.

Hold the Photo

I'm often asked by advisers about the advisability of putting their photograph on their business card. "It will cost more," the adviser will suggest, "but I figure the visual impact will make it worthwhile." But that decision, in reality, doesn't revolve around cost. When you think about business cards with pictures, what occupations come to mind? The answer: life insurance, real estate, and used cars. When you hand a prospective client a business card with your picture on it, that's the link you're unconsciously making. And it's the wrong link.

You want a conservative business card, just like the client's accountant, lawyer, and banker. The best investment is not adding your photograph to business cards and letterheads but spending some extra money to climb to a higher quality paper stock, or, alternatively, to engrave or raise the name and the logo. The cards and letterhead should resemble material from J.P. Morgan or Morgan Stanley, not the used car dealer down the road.

A financial adviser approached me some time ago, enthusiastic about the mass-marketing technique he was concocting for his small community of about 5,000 households. He had ordered fridge magnets, which he intended to deliver to every door in the town. I remember him saying the cost paled beside the advantages of having his name and face (the magnet had his picture on it as well) on every fridge in every kitchen in the area. I had a vision of all those refrigerators with his magnet indeed attached, but on one side would be the local pizza delivery outlet and on the other side would be the local real estate agent.

Another example of the importance of the Banker's Rule stems from some of my client research. I was talking to a very successful business owner who had been called by a financial adviser referred to him by a good friend. "Frankly, I wasn't hugely unhappy with my existing broker," the business owner admitted, "but a couple of niggling concerns bugged me. I figured, maybe I should at least listen to what this new guy had to say."

The business owner agreed to a-thirty-minute get-acquainted session. "When we finally met, he seemed like a pretty reasonable guy, so we began chatting, and about ten minutes into our conversation he asked if I minded if he takes notes," the business owner recalls. "I told him, 'No, go ahead' and he pulled out this 19-cent pen with the name of a local restaurant on it. Maybe it's not reasonable or rational on my part, but my visceral reaction was that if this guy can't afford his own pen then he's not the right kind of financial adviser for me."

That doesn't mean you should rush out and buy a $300 Mont Blanc pen and some $2,000 suits, because you can carry this approach too far. Looking too flashy, too expensive, can hurt you as well. But invest in a solid $10 pen—the kind a banker would use—and similarly sensible clothes. Adopt a sensible hairstyle that complements the image.

To some extent, tailor your approach to the client you're dealing with. You should dress differently for the CEO of the biggest company in town than for the fellow running a pig farm. But in general, find the middle line: You want to look successful but at the same time conservative, safe, and understated. Just like a banker.

Snapshots

- ✔ *Abide by the Banker's Rule: When you're dealing with prospective clients, tacitly communicate that you're as safe to deal with as their banker.*
- ✔ *Evaluate your office by the Banker's Rule. Are the magazines business or financially oriented? Do the signage, reception area, pictures on the wall, and the inside of your own office inspire confidence?*
- ✔ *Business cards, letterheads, your car, your clothes and even your pen should abide by the Banker's Rule. And forget those fridge magnets.*

CHAPTER 7

Borrowing Trust

ENCOUNTERING NEW CLIENTS, WE DON'T INHERENTLY CARRY A LOT OF TRUST with us—even when we're cloaked in banker's garb and toting the latest issue of *Forbes*. We may have gained some trust through a referral or a mutual association with the prospect on some board. But potential clients know that we're motivated by the money we can generate through the investments they might place, and they therefore begin the relationship with some—or even a lot—of skepticism toward us.

Since we don't carry a lot of trust ourselves, one valuable strategy is to compensate by borrowing it from other sources. Most people, for example, trust educational institutions. So if you're talking to a prospect and mention you teach personal finance at the local university or community college, it inspires trust in you, borrowed from the educational institution. If you teach, you must be an expert.

In today's society the media are both trusted and distrusted but still possess sufficient elements of trust that financial advisers can profitably borrow. Ideally you'd like to inform new prospects, "I periodically write articles on investment for the local newspaper, and here are a couple that may be of interest." It doesn't have to be a newspaper. It would be equally beneficial to be able to say, "One of the things I do from time to time is appear on local television as an expert on financial news," or, "I host a monthly radio call-in show on financial issues." Again the prospect assumes that if you're in the newspaper or on TV or radio, you must be an expert.

This habit of borrowing trust applies to the sources of information we send clients. Our company's research shows investors want to deal with advisers who are professional. One way to communicate that impression is to mail clients or prospective clients copies of articles conveying solid information from a newspaper or magazine. Those articles shouldn't be focused on the latest hot stock, but offer more substantive insights.

Interestingly, not all publications are created equal. We tested how prospects would feel receiving the same article from an assortment of publications and found a clear hierarchy. The most credible information source is the *Wall Street Journal,* followed by *Fortune, Business Week, Barron's,* and then a marked drop to your local newspaper.

Operating High Up the Trust Spectrum

A ten-cent photocopy of a newspaper article creates more trust than a four-color brochure from head office.

You want to operate as high up that trust spectrum as possible when selecting articles to pass out to your clients, because you are borrowing the publication's credibility and, as with the Banker's Rule, what you read indicates something about your abilities. Sending an article from the local newspaper won't hurt, but it won't transmit as strong a statement about your professionalism and commitment as an article from a more sophisticated, less accessible publication.

Consider the selection from your Prospective Client's 99. After meeting you once, she receives a note (Figure 7.1) with an accompanying article from the local newspaper. Is that client going to be surprised that you read the local newspaper? Of course not. She expects that. But when you send her a *Wall Street Journal* clipping, she concludes that you probably read that top-rated financial newspaper regularly or, at least, from time to time. It sends a message about your expertise, intelligence, and the access to information and insight that you will bring to the relationship.

We also asked our test sample to rate the same article if submitted from a newsletter published by the adviser's firm. That option winds up close to the bottom of the list—above the *National Enquirer,* but not much higher. The reason is simple. When prospective clients see an article from the *Wall Street Journal,* it's real—an impartial authority is conferring credibility. When they see the same article in a slickly produced, four-color newsletter from an investment firm, they figure, "Hey, am I being sold?"

While some head offices invest millions of dollars in producing glossy prospecting and marketing material, often advisers would be wiser to invest in ten-cent photocopies. You convey a stronger statement of your credibility and trust level with that ten-cent photocopy from *Forbes* than with the fancy newsletter or research report from your company.

Figure 7.1

Date

Dear __________,

It has never been more essential for investors to stay abreast of change in the financial marketplace.

Over the next while, I will be sending important articles on investment developments to a select group of people who may find this kind of information of particular value. The attached article from the *Wall Street Journal,* dealing with the impact of global diversification on investment return, touches on some especially interesting developments.

I hope that you find these and future articles of interest. Please feel free to call if you have any questions or if I can be of assistance.

Best regards,

That's not to claim material from your firm isn't important. It is, especially with existing clients. Those existing clients have developed trust and want quality information; having it emanate from your firm is absolutely appropriate. But with prospects, your number-one priority is building trust, and you should focus on borrowing it from the best sources available.

Snapshots

✔ *Since we don't inherently carry a lot of trust ourselves, financial advisers must borrow credibility from other sources of trust.*

✔ *Educational institutions and the media are excellent sources for borrowing trust.*

✔ *When sending out informative articles from publications, remember the trust spectrum. The most credible information source is the* Wall Street Journal, *followed by* Fortune, Business Week, *and* Forbes, *with a rather steep drop to your local newspaper.*

✔ *Company newsletters have a role to play with existing clients but don't carry much credibility with prospects.*

CHAPTER 8

Using the Media

NOT LONG AGO I RECEIVED A CALL FROM A FINANCIAL ADVISER IN A MID-sized community who was facing an imminent disaster. He had booked a well-known financial commentator and media personality to visit his community and deliver a seminar. The fee was $5,000 and it cost another $2,000 to fly in the speaker and reimburse his expenses. The adviser had spent $1,000 to book a room and provide light refreshments, and $5,000 to advertise the seminar. He was in the hole $13,000, it was Tuesday morning with the seminar scheduled for the next evening, and only 100 people had registered to attend. How could he salvage the event in the next thirty-six hours?

In discussing alternatives, he mentioned a popular open-line radio show in the community. Since the speaker was arriving the night before the seminar, he would be available to appear on that program. The financial adviser shot down to the radio station to sweet-talk them into putting his speaker on air, only to call me with another dilemma. The station was amenable, as long as the adviser agreed to fork over a further $2,000 in advertising over the next few months.

Since the adviser had already invested $13,000, we decided the additional $2,000 was unavoidable. The guest speaker wowed listeners for three hours the morning of the seminar, drawing plenty of calls and managing to slip in several tantalizing promos for the evening event at which he assured everyone he would be elaborating on his radio remarks. That night, 700 people flooded the seminar.

Why did the seminar skyrocket from 100 registrants to 700 attenders in the one day? The catalyst was the radio show's credibility. Since the financial commentator appeared on that radio program, he must be an expert. The seminar immediately became more attractive. A second factor was getting noticed. Large companies that can afford full-page newspaper advertisements generally punch their message through. The financial adviser, on the other hand, was naturally taking small ads and couldn't cut through the advertising clutter effectively. By shifting the appeal from advertising to the news side through the talk show, the speaker and the seminar were more likely to be noticed.

In many communities the media are the most credible sources for borrowing trust. Achieving that can be intimidating initially, but the media are often surprisingly accessible. However, just as converting prospects to clients requires an understanding of the Prospect's 99, building credibility through the media requires that you heed the Media's 99.

The media often offer the most credible sources for borrowed trust.

If you're dealing with the local newspaper's business editor, the community paper's publisher or editor, or the radio station's manager, two criteria dominate. First, they're interested in producing information of general interest to their reading or listening audience. It doesn't matter how much they like you: they need to be assured their audience will like you. Secondly, they have to be confident that they won't be embarrassed. When they put you on the air or print your column, they are implicitly endorsing you as a financial adviser. They have to be confident that decision won't backfire.

Approaching Radio Stations

Many advisers have met those criteria and built credibility and visibility through local radio stations. Let's assume the station doesn't have anybody providing stock market updates. Offer to fill the gap: "Would you be interested in a daily or weekly market report? It could happen at the end of the day, or in the morning to recap the previous day's performance, or at the end of the week to review what transpired over that longer period."

That approach opens a lot of options, allowing the report to be contoured to the Station's 99. But it's conveniently narrowed in on your 99, assuming regularity and frequency. You don't want to be slotted as an occasional voice on air, when the station feels moved to discuss financial affairs. You want prominence through regularity.

For credibility, quantity is actually more important than quality. You're better off winning a one-minute spot for 365 days a year than hosting a one-hour or two-hour segment once a year. Persistent day-in-day-out visibility nourishes credibility.

It probably won't be difficult to persuade the station manager that many listeners would find the information of value. Given the investment boom, most station managers recognize the thirst for such news. If the station already receives a syndicated national report, stress the advantages of a local version. Radio stations like to be seen as community focused, listeners prefer local personalities, and you can shape your reports to the community's particular interests, mentioning local firms.

The bigger hurdle is convincing the station manager it's not a high-risk proposition to put you on air. You'll find it helpful, therefore, to prepare a demo tape. That can be recorded in your office or at the local community college if it has a journalism, broadcasting, or advertising program. As well as offering samples of the proposed broadcasts, you can ease the station manager's qualms by initially proposing a trial period of several weeks.

You could also appeal to the Station Manager's 99 by volunteering to find a sponsor for the report, perhaps your own firm or a fund company that you can approach. Even if you can't pledge to sell the advertising personally, you should still point out to the station manager the item's attractiveness for many advertisers, given the upscale demographics of its target listeners.

Some advisers have talked radio stations into a regular call-in show. That grants the adviser a longer period of exposure. It provides more flexibility than those daily, tightly scripted sixty-second spots (and possibly less work because it is less scripted). It's helpful for such shows to arrange for some guests to call in regularly and be interviewed by you on air—an analyst from your firm, an economist, business executives, or marketing representatives from the fund companies.

Of course, orchestrating that line-up and performing well can entail significant effort—and if you find you don't perform well on air, it's not worth attempting, as the last thing you want is to embarrass yourself or spotlight your shortcomings. But if you can manage such a program effectively, it's probably worth the effort. Advisers who introduced call-in shows in their communities found it had a fundamental impact on their visibility and credibility. While that doesn't necessarily happen overnight, over time the impact is certainly felt.

Getting on Screen or into Print

It's harder to appear on television than radio because television stations are less plentiful than radio stations and their news component tends to be smaller. But if your community has a television station that doesn't currently broadcast a regular financial report, an opportunity may exist to redress that on a once-a-week basis, with a one- or two-minute update for viewers. Those appearances would nicely position you as an expert in your community. You should also investigate whether you can gain access to the local cable station's community channel if one exists.

Radio and television exposure is highly visible, transmits personality well, and potentially offers a high degree of exposure. The disadvantage is that when your spot is over, the opportunity to extract ongoing benefits from the segment is limited; people either heard or saw your report, or they did not. For those who did not, it's as if your item (and all your hard work) never existed.

Newspapers, on the other hand, offer a much longer shelf life. Some advisers I know are still taking advantage of columns they wrote for newspapers a decade ago. The material is still timely, and in the course of photocopying over the years the publication date conveniently tends to get lost, so the piece doesn't appear outdated. The point is you may still be able to recycle an article years afterward, unlike a daily radio market report or a call-in show.

So let's examine the 99 of your local newspaper editor or financial editor. They seek copy that people will want to read—material that meets their audience's needs. They want it to be credible, easy to read, and available by the agreed deadline without any hassles.

Again, you have to scout the opportunities for such material. Is somebody already providing such a regular column? Large newspapers typically print such material, so it's extremely difficult to squeeze in yourself. But it's easier in smaller communities. Many advisers in larger centers have successfully approached their local community paper, where often a key element of the Editor's 99 is how to fill space. If you can provide useful information, on an ongoing basis, on deadline, then you're rendering some attractive value to the editor.

Let's say you're signed on for a regular stint (with no signing bonus, probably no payment, and no written contract, I should add). Where do you find the material? Some advisers can research and write it themselves. But that may be daunting for you so an option is to borrow material from other sources. Your head office, perhaps, has articles that you can quickly adapt. Many of the mutual fund companies can provide access to sources of information.

In one case, half a dozen advisers from the same firm in different communities pooled their resources to write for their weekly paper. Each wrote columns for a month, which their colleagues altered and adapted to their own preferences and then furnished under their own name to their community's paper. Under that arrangement, every six months an adviser had to allocate the time to research and write four columns, but then he or she was essentially off the hook for another five months.

Writing for Newspapers

While the notion of writing a column can be intimidating, the typical size is 750 words—three double-spaced pages—and most of us, if we focus, have the ability to generate that length. The paper is not expecting a dazzling literary spectacle. It wants a clearly presented exposition, which most of us have the ability to produce.

One adviser had the ideas but suffered from writer's block. He posted a notice at the local journalism school seeking a student for some writing. The student interviewed him each week on the topic at hand and transformed the notes into a column. The adviser then reviewed and refined the article before handing it in to the paper. He ended up with a weekly column for an investment of less than an hour and the $50 payment to the student, something most advisers would consider a wonderful bargain. Alternatively, you may find writing that column the highlight of your week, something you look forward to as an opportunity for crystallizing your thinking.

When you spot a paper with a gap in its financial coverage, don't rush in to tell the editor, "I'd like to appear in your paper, so give me a chance." From his 99, that's high risk with low payback. Instead, tell him: "I think your readers would benefit from some ongoing perspectives on the market. I'd like to talk to you about writing a column on a regular basis, with a schedule that meets your needs. Here are three or four sample columns I've written that give a flavor of the approach I would take and the kind of information readers would receive." That reduces the risk and smooths the path to a positive decision by the editor (Figure 8.1).

With community papers, remember that often the decision-maker will be the owner, who has two agendas. One is editorial content; the other is the bottom line. For the column to run, you may have to be prepared to buy advertising with the paper or obtain it elsewhere by tapping into your relationships. The publisher may insist on that quid pro quo.

Advisers generally would love the bottom of their column to resemble an advertisement, with their own name, their firm's name, key phone numbers, and maybe even a few other tidbits to attract customers. While

Figure 8.1

Steps to "Getting Published"

1. Research the publication.
2. Come up with a short list of two or three "ideas."
3. Contact the editor with a proposed column.

you can try for such promotional fireworks, it's important to recognize that newspapers view the tag line, as it's known, as serving their ends rather than your promotional needs. It should affirm your expertise to be published on this topic. (Just as you borrow their credibility, they are borrowing yours.) Newspapers also don't like news material to appear to be serving commercial interests (Figure 8.2).

They will generally allow your firm's name to appear but hardly ever include your phone number. Interestingly, there's now a certain cachet in providing a writer's e-mail address, because it increases the paper's interactivity, so you might be able to include that. Ultimately, the phone number (and even the firm's name) are not critical. While you would love immediate response—people seeing your phone number and calling—what you're actually after is the long-term exposure.

Some advisers neglect to extend their column's reach. Yes, it appears weekly or bi-weekly in the community paper. But the benefit doesn't end when somebody reads (or chooses not to read) your piece. You can include photocopies of columns as part of your ongoing trust portfolio for prospects and clients. Often newspapers have monthly in-depth sections on investments, so you have an opportunity to collect something you've written for a smaller market and try to persuade the larger-circulation daily to include it in the special supplement.

Being Quoted as an Expert

A final component to building trust through the media is arranging to be quoted as an expert authority in your community. Every media outlet from time to time needs somebody to call for information or an opinion on investment issues. You want that somebody to be you.

Often that involves nothing more complicated than identifying the media outlet's personal finance writer or editor and picking up the phone to let that person know of your availability. "I'm a financial adviser with XYZ firm here in the community, and recently I've been

Figure 8.2

Writing an Article

- The title is critical
- Stick to one idea
- The first paragraph is key
- Be concrete/specific
- Use examples
- Keep it simple
- Don't try to say too much
- Don't try for perfection
- Don't expect your phone to ring

spending a lot of time talking to my clients about some of the issues that concern them," you say. "I've noticed two or three common threads that I thought you might find of interest, and I wonder if you might be willing to have a coffee some day and talk about what I'm seeing happening in the community." It's remarkable how few calls like that financial editors receive. Chances are if you take that low-key approach, they'll say yes. Journalists can be cynical and suspicious, but from their 99, they need stories. If you can provide interesting content, you're offering them irresistible value and they will be intrigued.

Use that initial encounter to build trust with the journalist, as with a client. Don't be too aggressive. But at some point, you'll want to mention casually, "By the way, if you're ever looking for someone to give you some information or a comment on what's happening in this field, I'd be happy to do that." Some firms have compliance issues or other policies that might restrict you. But in many cases you have flexibility as an adviser to provide comments on market events.

The key element to remember when you receive such a call is that the Reporter's 99—be it for a newspaper, radio, or TV—is tied to a deadline. She needs information fast. So respond to that call immediately. If she knows she can rely on you for a quick comment, you'll be high on her list of people to call next time.

She'll also want a quote that's pithy and to the point. You'll have to develop the discipline of responding in bite-sized chunks rather than rambling on and on. There's a knack to doing this. Some financial advisers have taken advantage of journalism schools to learn the technique, arranging for students to interview them in practice sessions that help both the adviser and the student journalist learn their respective interview skills.

It's important to remember that a reporter considers everything you say from the start of a phone call or meeting to be on the record and capable of being used in a story. You can't withdraw a comment after it has been uttered. Some reporters don't mind if you give them information just for their own background or as a lead for them to investigate. But you have to agree on the terms of such information-sharing before—not after—you serve it up. The key point to remember is that from the Reporter's 99, anything you pass along that they can't use is exactly that: useless. Just as we want to gain a sale when we meet with new prospects, they want to gain a detailed story.

While it's important that you accommodate the media's framework—speed and lively comments—it's also important that the quality of the insights offered be high. If a question is asked that you're not confident about, nothing is lost by telling the journalist, "Look, I'm tied up now. I'll call you right back in five minutes." That period allows you to collect your thoughts, jot down a few notes, carry out some quick research and call her back better prepared for the immediate, punchy response she's looking for.

Once you meet a Reporter's 99 a few times, chances are she'll call you on a regular basis. Think of your own work style: You tend to continue using the courier, printer, or florist who served you well in the past; you don't search out new ones each time. Journalists are no different, once they have found reliable suppliers of news. And for an adviser, few things beat the credibility of appearing as an expert on financial matters in your community on a regular basis—the quoted expert on what's happening in financial affairs.

Snapshots

- ✔ *The media is often the most credible source from which you can borrow trust. And the media can be surprisingly accessible, if you understand their 99.*
- ✔ *Editors, station managers, and media owners are interested in information that will be of general interest to their readership or audience. They also must be confident they won't be embarrassed by giving you access to that audience.*
- ✔ *Quantity is actually more important than quality for granting credibility. You're better off winning a one-minute spot for 365 days a year than hosting a one or two-hour segment once a year.*
- ✔ *Consider preparing a demo tape if you're seeking a radio stock-market report, to assure the station manager of your broadcast skills.*
- ✔ *You might want to offer to find a sponsor for a stock-market report, perhaps your own firm or a fund company that you can approach.*
- ✔ *Advisers who introduce or host call-in shows find it helps their visibility and credibility.*
- ✔ *It's harder to get on television than radio because there are fewer television stations, but if your community has a television station that doesn't present a regular financial report it's worth proposing a one-or two-minute update once a week.*
- ✔ *The advantage to radio and television exposure is that it's highly visible, transmits personality well, and potentially offers a high degree of exposure if the show has a large audience. Newspapers, on the other hand, offer a longer shelf life.*
- ✔ *Many advisers in larger centers have volunteered to write a column for their local community paper, meeting one of the key issues in the Editor's 99, the need to fill space. Preparing three or four sample*

columns will help persuade the editor that you know what you're doing and that the risk is minimal. A final component to building trust through the media is to arrange to be quoted as an expert authority in your community. That often involves nothing more complicated than identifying the personal finance writer or editor for the media outlet and informing that person of your availability.

✔ *Remember that journalists need information fast. Return their calls promptly. And discipline yourself to provide short, punchy comments.*

CHAPTER 9

The Two-Minute Rule

RECENTLY AN ADVISER TOLD ME THAT SHE HAD SOME GOOD NEWS AND some bad news after implementing prospecting ideas from my seminar. The good news was that the techniques had increased the number of appointments she gained with prospective clients. The bad news was that she was suffering a significant cancellation rate on those appointments, around 15 percent, and when she met with prospects she wasn't successful as often as she wished.

The issue as we defined it was two-fold: how to increase the likelihood of the appointment taking place, and how to increase the likelihood of a successful outcome. I was reminded of an article in *Psychology Today* discussing some California research on sales. It monitored salespeople from a broad range of fields—from computers to real estate—on their introductory sales calls with prospects. The researchers tracked the ultimate outcome that flowed from those initial encounters, sometimes after several months of follow-up, to determine whether the original contact was successful or not. Then they interviewed the prospective client to unravel the decision-making process.

They concluded that over half the time the prospective clients decided within the first two minutes whether this was the kind of salesperson they wanted to work with. That assessment doesn't take place at a rational level. It's an emotional, visceral reaction. But it's a powerful one.

Think about it: You're just getting warmed up in those two minutes, preparing for the next hour, not having touched on any of your major themes or proposals, and the prospect has already effectively reached a conclusion. The prospect has decided, on emotional grounds, whether you are knowledgeable, professional, and trustworthy—whether you are the kind of person he or she wants to deal with.

That doesn't mean that if you're successful in the first two minutes you can whip out the account operating form and point to the appropriate places to sign. You still have to cultivate and nurture the prospect and the process. Nor does it mean that if you're unsuccessful in the first two minutes you should pack up your things and leave. You can recover—although it's tough.

But the fact is that those first two minutes are critical in shaping the prospect's perceptions of you and, particularly, the extent to which he or she can trust your knowledge, integrity, and professionalism. So our goal is to work as hard as possible on creating a positive initial impression.

Instead of just piling on the benefits of doing business, advisers must pay more attention to reducing the risks.

The Risk-Benefit Teeter-Totter

As usual, in considering how to do that, it's helpful to look at the process from the Client's 99. Whenever we ask the prospect to do something—meet with us, share information, answer questions, provide more information to open an account—that prospect is weighing the benefits of the activity against the risks. It's a teeter-totter: risk vs. benefit (Figure 9.1).

Advisers are marvelously adept at demonstrating to prospects the benefits of doing business—of taking the process to the next step. When the prospect balks, we instinctively figure we haven't shown enough benefits yet. So we throw more benefits at the prospect. And if that doesn't work, we display even more. We keep piling on the benefits.

That's one method of bringing the prospect on-side. But another route is available to you. Instead of increasing the benefits, you can at-

Figure 9.1

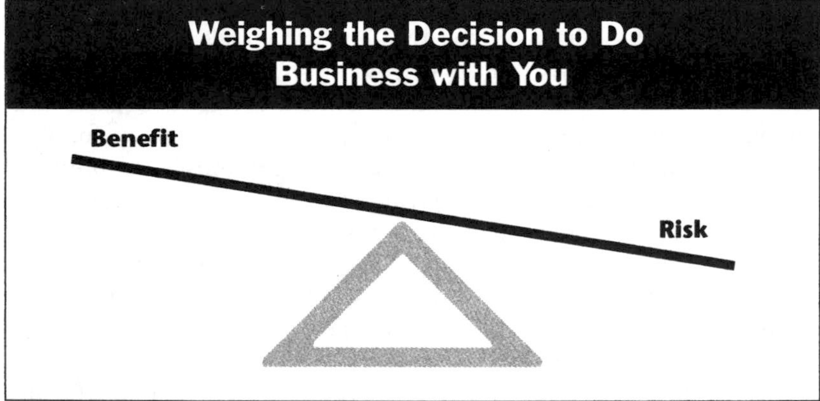

tack the other side of the teeter-totter by reducing the risks. Often, reducing the risks of doing business with you is a far easier and more productive manner of persuading the prospect to come on board than showcasing still more benefits.

With the above adviser who was experiencing difficulty, we looked at reducing the risks of meeting with her, in order to prevent meetings from being canceled and to increase the likelihood of prospects feeling comfortable enough in those meetings to do business. It came down to increasing her trust level, because that's at the core of both the two-minute problem and the teeter-totter of risk vs. benefit.

Whenever she arranged an appointment, she would send a two-sentence follow-up note confirming the meeting (Figure 9.2). Attached to the note would be a folder with the firm's name printed on the cover and a few carefully chosen informational elements inside. One page cataloged key points about her firm, such as years in business, number of clients, and asset levels. Another highlighted her own background, credentials, experience, and education. A third page was a photocopy of an article she had written some time before for a local community paper, but the topic was still current and appropriate. As

Figure 9.2

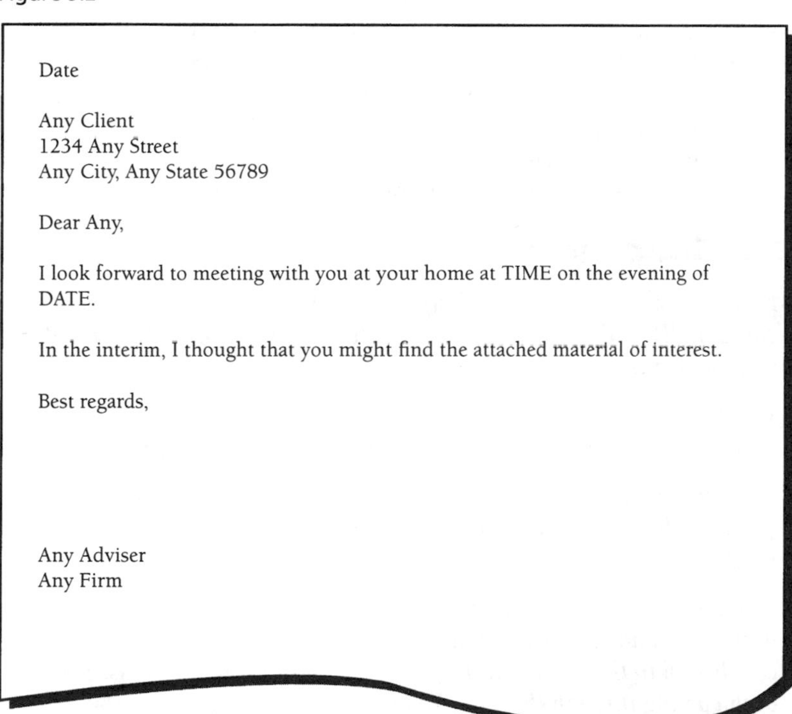

Date

Any Client
1234 Any Street
Any City, Any State 56789

Dear Any,

I look forward to meeting with you at your home at TIME on the evening of DATE.

In the interim, I thought that you might find the attached material of interest.

Best regards,

Any Adviser
Any Firm

well, she inserted a couple of articles from high-trust publications, in this case *Fortune* and the *Wall Street Journal,* that would interest prospects. Finally, she threw in some client testimonials: one sheet with four clients quoted on the positive experience of dealing with her.

Her cancellation rate plummeted from 15 percent before the confirmation letter and pre-meeting package to just under 1 percent. Prospects occasionally cancel for legitimate reasons having nothing specifically to do with us: another issue or meeting arises that is more pressing or unavoidable. But most prospects cancel because they have cold feet. They agreed to the appointment under duress, or they've had second thoughts. They're worried about the risk—having a bad experience, wasting time, or being pressured to buy something they don't really want. They don't have sufficient trust in the financial adviser, and so to avoid the risk of a negative experience they pull out. The pre-meeting package addressed that concern.

Significantly, the adviser not only reduced her cancellation rate to near zero but also increased the percentage of times that the meeting was successful, either leading to the immediate opening of an account or at least propelling the process along the road toward that conclusion. The reason lies in the two-minute rule. If the number-one objective in the first two minutes of a meeting is to raise your trust level to provide reassurance, this financial adviser had built up a considerable amount of trust before she even came though the door.

She positioned herself as a trusted source of financial advice, someone who operated in a professional fashion and was appropriately backed by a solid firm. She marketed herself beforehand, making the selling that much easier. She's now on the winning side of the two-minute rule.

Snapshots

✔ *Research indicates that over half the time prospective clients decide emotionally within the first two minutes whether this is the kind of salesperson they want to work with.*

✔ *Whenever we ask the prospect to do something, that person weighs the benefits of that action against the risks. It's a teeter-totter: risk vs. benefit.*

✔ *Advisers are adept at demonstrating the benefits of doing business. But you can also attack the other side of the teeter-totter by reducing the risks.*

✔ *To reduce the risk of doing business, develop a pre-meeting package. It decreases cancellations and increases the chances of a successful conclusion to the initial meeting, because you've built up trust before even coming through the door. You're on the winning side of the two-minute rule.*

CHAPTER 10

The Elements of a Pre-Meeting Package

In building your pre-meeting package, always keep the purpose in mind. It's not an excuse to provide a reminder of the upcoming meeting—your secretary could simply call the prospect the day before the session to accomplish that. It's not a contest to show how many pieces of financial information you can shove into a folder. It's a trust-building exercise that must be judiciously designed to be effective (Figure 10.1).

After the covering letter, the next element in the package is background on your firm. While prospects don't typically select advisers because of the company, they are reassured if the adviser represents a reputable, professional firm. They won't generally work with you because of your firm, but they might decide not to choose you if they aren't comfortable with its institutional profile.

If your company has high visibility and prominence in the community, a pathway has already been cleared for you. But it's important to remember that while you and other advisers are acutely aware of the various landmarks on the financial services terrain,

Figure 10.1

Pre-Meeting Package

- Letter
- One page on your firm
- A credible third-party article
- A personal profile
- Client testimonials
- Folder to hold information

most prospects aren't as informed about the firms. Even if you represent Merrill Lynch, which has turned itself into a household name, you'll benefit from providing some brief background about the firm.

You might want to highlight when the firm was established, the number of clients, assets overseen, the range of products and investments, and any external evidence of its institutional strength, such as awards won for its research capacity. Don't overwhelm prospects with pages and pages of prose. You want four to six key points that the prospect can scan and quickly conclude, "These people are safe."

Any adviser can get testimonials if they ask the right way.

Your own personal profile should be similarly framed: a few key items, on a single page, reassuring prospects about your capability. You might relate how long you've been in the business and relevant previous experience (if you flipped hamburgers in a past life, you might want to flip by that credential). Indicate if your clients fit a certain pattern or

Figure 10.2

Sample Personal Profile

Pat Williams, B.A., C.F.P.

A financial adviser with the XYZ firm since 1991; previously had a career in account management with a leading computer manufacturer.

Specialize in the unique financial needs of individuals who are approaching and in retirement.

Currently Program Chairman, London Chapter of Canadian Association of Financial Planners.

Possess a Bachelor of Arts from Queen's University and am certified as a Chartered Financial Planner (CFP), among the highest designations available to financial advisers.

Have taught Personal Finance at Fanshawe College and have contributed articles on financial issues to leading business publications.

Currently serve on the Board of Directors of Big Sisters of London and on the Executive of the Oakridge Ratepayers Association.

you serve special needs. Also worth highlighting are associations, positions of responsibility, and certification. Finally, mention any of the trust-building credentials I've discussed previously—teaching, writing, radio or television exposure—as well as community activity, which can enhance credibility (Figure 10.2).

Most of those elements, you'll notice, depend upon borrowing credibility from trustworthy sources. If you've been in the business for five years, worked previously in a financial capacity, belong to some industry and community organizations, have 300 clients, and write or teach, the client invariably suspends disbelief and trusts your degree of knowledge and professionalism.

Enhancing Your Trust Credentials

The form we've developed for trust-building credentials (Figure 10.3) serves as a useful guide. Most advisers won't mark something in every category, but you should be able to focus on two or three areas. If you end up with a blank or nearly blank sheet, you should consider investing in your trust-building credentials. It won't happen serendipitously, so give it some planning. It will pay off in the long term.

Figure 10.3

Trust Building Credentials

1. Education ______________________________
2. Professional designation ______________________________
3. Time in business ______________________________
4. Previous career ______________________________
5. Community involvement ______________________________
6. Writing ______________________________
7. Teaching ______________________________
8. Other ______________________________

Don't be intimidated. After all, how many personal finance courses do you have to teach to be able to say, "I have taught personal finance at the community college?" The answer is one. You may discover that you actually enjoy the teaching and wish to continue. Some advisers have built practices based on members of the community who take such courses, are impressed with the adviser, nurture a relationship, and eventually turn to him or her to manage their portfolio. But again I stress that just as when you write an article for the local paper you shouldn't expect an immediate payback, when you teach a course you shouldn't expect an immediate return. If it happens, that's a bonus. The effort, however, is aimed at building up your trust-building credentials for the long haul.

As for associations, generally those are easy to add to your trust portfolio. How difficult is it to be named program chair of the local investment advisers' association? How hard-fought is the election? That's right: Whoever puts up his or her hand often gets the nod. And how big is the budget, how arduous the responsibility? Certainly some effort is involved, and you don't want to embarrass yourself or disadvantage your colleagues by not following through on

Figure 10.4

Your Philosophy

What Can I Expect from You?

"As a conservative investor, you should expect three things from your financial adviser. First, a financial plan which is tailored to your specific objectives and circumstances. Second, an investment strategy which provides long-term growth with emphasis on preservation of capital. Third, consistent and regular communication. That's what I aim to deliver."

What Kind of Investments Do You Recommend?

"Just as every client is different, so every investment strategy will vary—until I know your situation, I won't know what's right for you. In general, however, I favor conservative investments which allow me and my clients to sleep soundly, tempered with some investments to provide higher growth."

How Often Will I Hear from You?

"Every client receives a quarterly statement and regular newsletters. If we haven't talked recently, you'll also get a telephone call from me or my assistant every six months; where appropriate, I also meet with clients periodically to update and review their situation."

What If a Client Has a Question for You?

"I have a policy that I or one of my staff return every call the same business day so clients are never left hanging with unanswered questions."

your promise. But the burden is not unreasonable; as with teaching, it might also prove enjoyable; and the payoff—in terms of being able to say, "I have a credible role in the industry"—can be considerable.

In some small or mid-sized communities, no local association may exist. That's a wonderful opening. If you approach the national or regional association to establish a local chapter, guess what: you're the chair. And now you can tell prospects you chair the local association of financial advisers. Your credentials are noticeably enhanced.

Outlining Your Philosophy

If you're still building trust credentials and don't yet have much to display, another less direct avenue to achieve the same purpose in the pre-meeting package is to devote some space to discussing your philosophy (Figure 10.4). Such statements should answer the ten prominent questions from clients shown in Figure 10.5.

It's not an exhaustive list, of course, but those ten questions are frequently on the mind of prospects. If you deal with them in the pre-meeting package, even before the two minutes begin you're a step ahead. To help you along, Figure 10.6 shows some possible answers to common questions from prospects. Those responses aren't intended for dutiful copying but for demonstrating style and provoking your own ideas. To be effective, the dialogue you present must reflect your own personality and philosophy.

Another element of the pre-meeting package would ideally be a financial article you have contributed to some credible publication. If you haven't yet managed that, send out a feature you have read in one of the better publications on our trust hierarchy. It hints at the professionalism you bring to a client's affairs.

Figure 10.5

Questions Which Clients Are Concerned About

1. What can I expect from you?
2. What types of investments do you recommend?
3. How often will I hear from you?
4. What if I have a question and you're not there?
5. What is your philosophy toward investing?
6. How do you arrive at your recommendations?
7. How do I know if a particular investment is right for me?
8. How can I be sure that I'll be able to retire comfortably?
9. What kinds of clients do you work with?
10. How much do I need to invest with you?

Figure 10.6

What My Clients Can Expect

1. My relationship with my clients starts with the development of a comprehensive financial plan to achieve their long-term financial goals. As part of this plan, we cover the investment, insurance, tax and estate planning aspects of each client's situation.
2. I strive to serve as my clients' chief financial adviser. As part of this role, I coordinate the activities of existing professional advisers such as tax accountants and estate lawyers. If required, I also tap into my own network of professional advisers.
3. My investment philosophy is essentially conservative in nature. Operating within each client's risk profile, an investment portfolio is structured which will achieve long-term growth without undue risk. As a result, both my clients and I sleep soundly at night.
4. Tax planning and minimization is a key component of the financial plan for most clients. As part of the overall plan, strategies such as income splitting, prudent use of leverage and family trusts are evaluated.
5. Every three months, all clients receive a summary of performance. The information is presented as clearly as possible. In addition, the format of the report is reviewed with all new clients at the outset of each relationship, to minimize confusion or misunderstanding about how to read the results.
6. Each client's account is monitored on an ongoing basis to take advantage of opportunities created by changing circumstances. In addition, each plan is reviewed annually and appropriate adjustments made.
7. I make myself as accessible to clients as possible. All telephone calls are returned the same business day, either personally or by my assistant.
8. I believe that my best client is the one who is fully informed. As a result, I have a strong commitment to client communication through a regular newsletter, regular workshops for clients on market updates and guest speakers. In addition, I maintain a library of some of the very best books on personal finance, available for loan to all my clients.

The Value of Testimonials

The final element of the pre-meeting package is testimonials. Advisers, as it turns out, are more cynical about these than clients. When I show a sample like those in Figure 10.7, some advisers sneer, "It would insult my clients if I implied they were stupid enough to believe those. No prospect accepts that a page of testimonials is honest or representative—that it will include, say, the views of the last two clients who fired me. They'll know it's cherry-picked and treat it as phony—a pitch."

While some clients may espouse that sour view, when we tested testimonials with clients we actually found a positive response. Prospects find it reassuring to view real comments from real people talking about their experience with an adviser. It builds trust.

Just one caution: Sometimes I come across effusive testimonials

Figure 10.7

What Clients Say About Pat Williams

"Pat doesn't just wait for me to call her. She's in regular contact, to ensure that my circumstances haven't changed and that any questions are answered; whenever I do call, she's always quick to respond."

Andrea Davidson
Royal LePage
Client since 1991

"We've asked Pat many questions over the years. She always takes the time to come back with well researched and complete answers."

Robert and Lily Desaulniers
Retired
Clients since 1991

"Pat spent a lot of time listening to our views and helped us develop an approach to investing and saving which exactly fits our needs."

John and Linda Moore
Pharmacists, Courtesy Drug Mart
Clients since 1992

"For the first time, I really know where I'm going financially and have a plan in place to get there."

Richard Winters
President, Lawton Graphics
Client since 1993

and at the bottom it notes, cryptically, "S.R." Those will indeed inspire doubt. If you want credible testimonials, initials don't work. You must provide the full name and ideally some elaboration, such as professional status or community lived in. If the person is a business owner, president of an ethnic association, lawyer, or retired, put that in. If he has been a client for a few years, indicate that: "Client since '91." Such longevity encourages prospects.

Nowhere in the sample testimonials in Figure 10.7 does it exult that "this adviser doubled my money." Nowhere does it trumpet that as a result of working with this adviser I retired at age thirty-seven. The message, instead, is that my adviser is in contact, answers my questions, listens to my needs, helps me to understand where I am financially. Simple, straightforward stuff. Indeed, you might wonder, what's so special about those declarations? It's the minimum clients should expect. While that's true, in fact it's still reassuring for prospects to see real clients testifying to those attributes about their adviser.

Most advisers can visualize the benefit of testimonials in prospecting. But the barrier is how to obtain those testimonials in a fashion that's comfortable for both you and the clients. The last thing an adviser wants is to procure the testimonials and in the process place clients under pressure or, worse, antagonize them. That would be too great a sacrifice.

We've found, however, that if you ask properly, 90 percent of clients satisfied with an adviser's work are more than willing to provide testimonials. The key is whom you ask and how.

How to Ask for Testimonials

In selecting the right source for testimonials, four considerations emerge (Figure 10.8). Obviously the client has to be fairly well satisfied. That's a given. Next, your comfort level is vital. Ironically, the impediment blocking advisers from obtaining client testimonials is not refusals by the client but the refusal of advisers to ask. So identify the clients you would feel comfortable asking.

Third, ideally the clients you solicit should have outgoing personalities. Overly cautious accountants, for example, don't tend to be productive sources of testimonials. You want individuals who are enthusiastic by nature. Finally, it's helpful if they bring some credibil-

Figure 10.8

Criteria for Soliciting Testimonials

- Your comfort level
- Satisfaction level
- Personality
- Credibility/credentials

ity and credentials. The testimonials will clearly be more effective if they are from the president of a local company, well known in the community, or the chair of some significant community association.

In workshops we ask advisers to think of clients who fit that criteria. Most readily summon up four or five clients. Next, you have to ask in a manner that is low in stress for both you and the client. You don't want to jeopardize the special relationship with the client that led you to consider this appeal.

Begin the conversation, "John, I'm calling to ask a small favor. One of my goals this year is to add more clients like you to my practice." How does the client feel at this point? You've asked for a favor and most people love to help people they know and like. You've also talked about adding more people like him to your practice. That's quite flattering.

Of course, the client is also probably somewhat apprehensive, wondering what's next. So you answer that immediately: "To help me, I'm developing a written summary of very brief comments from some of my existing clients, talking about their experience with me. I'm calling to check if you could help me out with a short comment that I might use, along with those from some of my other clients."

If the client relationship is indeed sound, that's not a tough request. In fact, most clients are probably relieved that you aren't calling to ask for the names of their friends, relatives, and neighbors. They quickly agree to help.

At that point don't fall into the trap that snares many advisers. Relieved that the client assented and promised to send a testimonial over after giving it some thought, you jubilantly hang up the phone, figuring, "Wow, that's over! I have a testimonial!" You don't have a testimonial. You have an agreement to provide a testimonial, which can be a giant step from a testimonial.

In fact, three outcomes are possible at this juncture, and only one is positive. The client may send over a well-worded testimonial in a few days that is perfect for your needs. On the other hand, the client may procrastinate—clients procrastinate, just as we do—and since you don't want to hound him, you start avoiding him, and he, feeling guilty, starts avoiding you. A sweet client relationship has turned sour—exactly what you wanted to avoid. The worst possibility, however, is that the client does pass along a testimonial but it's unusable. And it's then difficult to pick up the phone, call him, and say, "John, nice try, but could you write another one and get it right this time?"

To avoid that pitfall, when the client promises to write something and pop it in the mail, you have to politely but firmly block him. "John, that's terrific. Listen, I really appreciate your help on this. But if I could get one more minute of your time—suppose that you had a next-door neighbor who asked what your experience had been working with me: How would you answer that question?"

Now sit back and listen. Almost every time, in the next fifteen to thirty seconds you'll hear exactly the message you want to transmit to prospects: "My adviser listens . . . my adviser returns my calls . . . my adviser answers my questions . . . my adviser provides advice." Remember, this is not a forty-page testimonial. You want about five to ten key words that can be combined into a short, punchy statement. Make a note of the key words and then advise the client, "What you've told me would be perfect. Let me tell you what I just heard you say: 'My adviser does a great job of listening to my needs and then making sure those needs are met.' Could I Use that?" Naturally, he'll agree. It's what he believes—and he's off the hook! He has completed the favor. And you have a testimonial (Figure 10.9).

At one workshop, I covered this particular component just before the break. After coffee, I noticed that one of the participants who had been sitting in the middle of the front row hadn't returned. That happens from time to time, and I've learned to steel myself to the disappointment. But about twenty minutes later he came back into the

Figure 10.9

Asking for Testimonials: Sample Script

John, hi, it's Pat Williams. Do you have a minute?

(Response)

John, I'm calling to ask a favor. One of my goals for this year is to add more people like yourself to my practice.

To help me do that, I'm developing a written summary of very brief comments from some of my existing clients, talking about their experience working with me. I'm calling to see if you might be able to help me out with a short comment that I could use, along with those from some of my other clients.

(Response)

John, that's great, I really appreciate your help on this. If I could take just one more minute, suppose someone you knew asked you about your experience working with me, how would you answer that question?

(Response)

You know, what you just said would be perfect. Could I use that comment right there?

room waving a piece of paper. He'd rushed to a phone booth, called four clients, and in that short period elicited four testimonials.

I'm not suggesting you stop reading and dash to the phone, because you probably need to give some thought to whom you're going to ask and exactly how. You need to feel comfortable posing the question. Generally it's helpful to practice the script you intend to use four or five times—try it with your spouse or a colleague—until you feel relaxed asking the question. But that anecdote illustrates that getting testimonials need not be intimidating if you take it step by step, operating from the Client's 99.

Other Testimonial Options

Some advisers don't feel comfortable calling the client right out of the blue to ask for a testimonial. They prefer to send a letter first, smoothing the pathway. That's perfectly acceptable. An advantage is that you can note, as in our firm's sample version of such a letter, that you are including some examples of comments from other clients who have agreed to help (Figure 10.10).

Some advisers, starting their practice, worry about approaching a client prematurely. And that's sensible: you don't want to pop the question a few months after taking somebody on as a client. But after a year, if the client is really happy and meets the other criteria—a good comfort level, outgoing, and has credibility—it's not unreasonable to ask.

If you're a newcomer to the business, it's also possible to seek testimonials from people who aren't clients. You could approach past employers and customers, or people you've worked with, and ask them to attest to skills that would be attractive to prospects in this new endeavor (Figure 10.11). The testimonials, after all, don't focus on your investment acumen. They focus on your service orientation, which you have probably displayed previously.

If somebody gives you a testimonial, I think it's appropriate to recognize or thank her for helping you out. You could write a short thank-you note, which is certainly sufficient. Some advisers send over a bottle of wine, or a book, or make a small donation—say $20—to the client's favorite charity. You don't want the client to feel bribed, but you do want her to feel acknowledged and appreciated. The client had done you a favor, by offering the testimonial, but if you acknowledge and thank her, she ends up feeling better about the relationship.

Once you've arranged the testimonials, you don't have to limit their use to the pre-meeting package. I know one adviser who ends his meetings with prospective clients by presenting testimonials. This adviser has invested some effort in testimonials, gathering more than thirty, which he has broken down into different categories. He has a

Figure 10.10

Date

Any Client
1234 Any Street
Any City, Any State 56789

Dear Any,

One of my goals in the period ahead is to add more people like yourself to my practice. I am writing to ask for your help as one of my most valued clients.

In talking to prospective clients, it's been suggested to me that it would be useful to have a page of candid comments from existing clients about the experience they've had working with me and the service I've provided.

I'm currently in the early stages of putting this page together—it will be titled "What Clients Say About Any Adviser." I'm hoping that you might be able to assist me with a short comment that I could include along with those from five to six other clients.

I will give you a call next week to answer any questions and to talk about this further.

Thank you in advance for your help on this.

Best regards,

Any Adviser

P.S. For your information, I'm attaching sample comments from a couple of other clients who've already agreed to help me out.

set for professionals, for business owners, for widows, for retirees, and a general collection as well. Each is on a single sheet—remember, you don't need pages and pages of these—and he fits the testimonials he hands out to the prospect he's dealing with.

"Mr. Prospect/Ms. Prospect, I've really enjoyed talking to you and from everything you said, I really think we operate very much on the same wavelength and will work together effectively," he says. "But I recognize that this is a big decision for you and an important one. So what I'd like to do is leave you with a list of names and phone numbers of some of my clients whose circumstances might be similar to yours. They've indicated that should you be interested in contacting

Figure 10.11

New Entrants to the Investment Business: Asking for Testimonials

John, hi, it's Pat Williams. Do you have a minute?

(Response)

John, I'm calling to ask a favor. As you may know, I've recently joined [Name of firm] and am beginning to talk to people who I might be able to assist in financial planning.

To help me do that, I'm developing a written summary of very brief comments from some of my past clients, talking about their experience working with me. I'm calling to see if you might be able to help me out with a short comment that I could use along with those from some other people I've worked with in the past.

(Response)

John, that's great, I really appreciate your help on this. If I could take just one more minute, suppose someone you knew asked you about your experience working with me, how would you answer that question?

(Response)

You know, what you just said would be perfect. Could I use that comment right there?

them directly and determining in person what their experience with me has been, you can feel free to do so."

That's the single most effective method of closing a meeting I know. From the Client's 99, it proclaims: "This is an adviser who feels very, very comfortable about the job he's doing for his clients and empathizes with the anxiety I'm feeling in making a decision." The adviser's conversion rate of initial meetings since he began the technique has risen significantly, yet the vast majority of times prospects simply take the list, thank him, and don't bother to call the clients offering the testimonials.

Some do, I should caution, so if you try this method, the clients giving testimonials have to know about that possibility and you have to be prepared to be accountable. But generally, simply offering the list and making it easy for the prospect to call sends a powerful message about your confidence in your work and the confidence that your clients place in you.

Clearly you can't give clients' names and phone numbers without their permission; that breaches confidentiality. But if you ask, the majority of satisfied clients will agree. "John, from time to time, when I'm dealing with prospective clients, they ask for the names of some clients they could check with," you could say. "I wonder if you could do me a big favor and when I'm asked, allow me to include your name and telephone number among the list of people they could call."

Testimonials and the other elements of a pre-meeting package are not difficult to assemble. They require some thought and effort, but if you follow the steps carefully, you'll find they pay off in developing trust and leaping over the two-minute hurdle.

Snapshots

✔ *The first element in a pre-meeting package is some background on your firm, such as when it was established, the number of clients, the assets it oversees, the range of products and investments, and any awards or other external tributes to its institutional strength.*

✔ *The second element is a one-page biography, listing how long you've been in the business, previous relevant experience, and any pattern in the clients you deal with or special needs that you fill. As well, mention associations, positions of responsibility, certification, and trust-building credentials such as teaching, writing, radio, or television exposure.*

✔ *If your trust-building credentials are slender, consider investing in them. You could teach a course at a community college or assume a position of trust with an association.*

✔ *If your trust-building credentials are still under construction, another less direct means to achieve the same purpose in the pre-meeting package is to devote some space to discussing your philosophy.*

✔ *A financial article you have contributed to a credible publication should ideally be another element of the pre-meeting package. As well, include a feature you have clipped from one of the better publications on our trust hierarchy.*

✔ *The final element of the pre-meeting package is testimonials. Prospects find it reassuring to read real comments from real people relating their experience with an adviser.*

✔ *Testimonials should include full names and some details such as professional status or community of residence, as well as the length of time the person has been your client.*

- ✔ *Testimonials do not exult that "this adviser doubled my money." The focus, instead, is on the service component: "My adviser is in contact, answers my questions, listens to my needs, helps me to understand my financial position."*
- ✔ *If you ask properly, 90 percent of satisfied clients are more than willing to provide testimonials. The key is who you ask and how.*
- ✔ *The four criteria for soliciting testimonials are: the client has to be fairly well satisfied; you must feel comfortable asking; the client should have an outgoing personality; and the client should bring some credibility and credentials.*
- ✔ *After asking for a testimonial don't fall into the trap of agreeing to have it sent to you later. Encourage the client to talk about how he sees your strengths, listen carefully, summarize a few essential points, and get him to agree to that statement.*
- ✔ *If you don't feel comfortable calling the client cold to ask for a testimonial, it's perfectly acceptable to send a letter first. You may include some sample testimonials from other clients.*
- ✔ *If you're a newcomer to the business, seek testimonials from people you have dealt with in the past.*
- ✔ *If somebody gives you a testimonial, don't forget to recognize and thank that person for helping you out.*
- ✔ *Once you've arranged for testimonials, you don't have to limit their use to the pre-meeting package. Testimonials can be a highly effective closing to the initial meeting with prospects.*

CHAPTER 11

Gaining Trust Through Profile

TRADITIONALLY MANY FINANCIAL ADVISERS HAVE BEEN INVOLVED IN COMMUNITY organizations such as the Rotary Club and Chamber of Commerce, or even political campaigns. They may have been attracted by the hope of broadening their base of prospective clients, but more often they've been motivated by a genuine community consciousness and a desire to help out.

But another aspect of such voluntary work, our research shows, is that it engenders borrowed trust. The adviser gains credibility with prospective clients, even if those prospects have no direct connection with the organization.

The specific group chosen can vary widely: a residents' association, PTA, school board, charity, hospital, or local business association. But the organization's nature does matter to a certain extent. It has to be credible to others, non-controversial, and not likely to offend clients. You don't want to be widely known as president of the local mud-wrestling association, be seen as raising money for someone accused

Figure 11.1

Developing Community Profile

1. Community involvement
2. Speaking to groups
3. Media
    a) Writing columns/articles
    b) Radio
    c) Getting quoted

of being a criminal, or take a high-profile position on an issue that has emotionally divided the community into warring factions.

In recommending involvement, I'm not talking about simply joining or even about attending meetings (Figure 11.1). While that can be of some potential benefit through the people you meet, it doesn't enhance your credibility much with outside prospects. For your community involvement to build trust, you must play a responsible leadership role. You have to serve on a committee, secure an appointment to the board, or be selected as a member of the executive.

In seeking profile through community work, think before you commit—and then be committed to what you choose.

One of the pitfalls some advisers stumble into is joining a host of organizations but not becoming sufficiently involved in any to make their mark and thereby raise their visibility. It's smarter to select one or two organizations, focus exclusively on them, and contribute in a manner that will be noticed. You're better off with that deeper commitment to one or two organizations than with a superficial involvement with eight or nine, showing up at meetings but taking it no further.

This shouldn't be done on impulse. It's part of your business strategy—an investment of time in brightening your appeal to clients which you want to plan carefully. A useful method is to list three or four organizations that appeal to you and then evaluate them, perhaps on a one to five point scale (Figure 11.2).

First, what's the credibility of the organization? The more exclusive, visible, and high profile the group, the more it will enlarge your credibility. The second criterion is the extent to which you are already involved in this area. It's much easier to gain a profile in an organization when you already have a foot in the door.

Third, you should be genuinely interested in the cause and generally like the other people involved. You can't fake commitment. People who join just to gain the trappings of office typically have difficulty following through on the commitments they make in that position. It becomes apparent quite quickly that they weren't motivated by a desire to contribute but by the lure of adding an extra line to their resume. In the end, that backfires, because word spreads.

The fourth criterion is whether a reasonable opportunity exists to reach a position of profile. Some board positions are so sought after that it's very difficult to gain any prominence. If so, direct your efforts elsewhere.

Figure 11.2

Community Organizations

Organization	______	______	______
1. Already involved (1–5 points)	______	______	______
2. Genuinely interested/ like the people associated (1–5)	______	______	______
3. Opportunity to associate with high-end prospects (1–5)	______	______	______
4. Not filled with other financial advisers (1–5)	______	______	______
5. Opportunity for access to positions with profile (1–5)	______	______	______
6. Impact on credibility (1–5)	______	______	______
POINTS (up to 30)			

Generating Prospects

Two other factors are worth considering because they bear on the likelihood of meeting prospective clients within the group to add to your business. While generating prospects is not your primary motivation, it's still worth fitting into the equation.

The first question is: To what extent will the organization afford you an opportunity to associate with high-end prospects? The second is: To what extent is the group relatively lacking in financial advisers? If you join an association where every third or fourth member is a financial adviser, your prospecting opportunities will be significantly constrained in comparison with a club with few competitors.

The age of the group's members might also be a consideration, since as we've noted earlier, the best prospects tend to be older. People in their fifties, sixties, and early seventies, while sometimes more conservative in their ways and less open to change, tend to have accumulated more significant assets. A problem in focusing your prospecting on younger people in their twenties or thirties is that while they may well be meaningful prospects in the future, at this stage of life they're still accumulating assets and struggling with the costs of family formation. They're buying houses and furniture, paying for day care and diapers, and haven't hit their peak earning period yet. They tend to be less fruitful as current sources of business than individuals in their late forties, fifties and early sixties. That probably should be reflected in the organization you're choosing as an outlet for your energy.

With those criteria, you should be able to find one or two local organizations that you can help and that can help you, building credibility with prospects and adding to your trust quotient.

Snapshots

- ✔ *Taking a leadership position within a community organization is a form of borrowed trust, helping an adviser to gain credibility.*
- ✔ *The organization should be credible to others, not controversial, and not likely to offend your clients.*
- ✔ *It's not enough simply to join an organization and attend meetings. You have to serve on a committee, get appointed to the board, or be selected as an executive member. For that reason, it's best to focus your energy on one or two groups rather than spread your efforts over eight or ten organizations and fail to fulfill your obligation.*
- ✔ *The four main criteria to consider are: the organization's credibility, the extent of your current involvement, your affinity for the people and the cause, and the opportunity to reach a position of profile within the group.*
- ✔ *Also worth considering are the opportunity the organization affords to meet high-end prospects and the extent to which other financial advisers are involved. A final factor is the age of members: you want them to be at an age where they have sufficient savings to be worthwhile prospects.*

CHAPTER 12

Earning Trust Through Patience

IN 1992 I RECEIVED A VIVID DEMONSTRATION OF THE POWER OF THE FINAL trust-building strategy available to advisers: earning trust through clearly demonstrated, sustained patience. After a workshop in which I had touted the advantages of borrowing trust by sending prospects articles from high-trust publications, I received a call from an adviser telling me he had tried the idea and it had bombed. He'd copied an article from the *Wall Street Journal,* mailed it with a covering note to 100 prospects in a relatively high-income area, and then followed up by telephoning each one. End result: one appointment, a meager 1 percent success rate.

He agreed to try again, but with a modified strategy. I asked him to find 100 names from another high-income area, with none of the individuals living closer than five houses from another prospect. The adviser sent a straightforward, non-threatening letter of introduction, with the same *Wall Street Journal* article.

The letter said: "It has never been more essential for people to stay abreast of changes in the financial marketplace. Over the next while, I'll be sending important articles on investment developments to a select group of people who might find this information of particular value. The attached article from the *Wall Street Journal,* dealing with the impact of global diversification on investment return, touches on some especially interesting developments. I hope that you'll find these and future articles of interest. Please feel free to call if you have any questions or if I can be of assistance."

He waited four weeks, avoiding any follow-up. He then sent an article from *Forbes,* with a handwritten note, "Thought you might find this of interest." After another four weeks, he sent a third article, from *Fortune.* This time he attached a business card, with a note on it: "For

Your Information." After waiting ten more days, he followed up by calling the recipients of the campaign.

After the first letter, nothing happened, other than a few recipients calling to request they be taken off the mailing list. A popular school of thought argues that once individuals are etched onto your prospect mailing list, they remain until they buy or die: Those are the only two ways of escaping. In today's environment, however, most advisers find that policy an exercise in frustration, with an associated waste of time, money, and energy. My view is that if someone is genuinely not interested, it's preferable to know sooner rather than later. Given that philosophy, you actually want to make it easy for those uninterested to let you know.

With the prospecting funnel now transformed into a pipeline, patience is essential.

After the second letter, the adviser received one call. A recipient expressed some interest and requested additional information. Shortly after the third letter, the adviser took three more calls. Finally, after waiting ten days and calling those prospects not yet in contact, he arranged another ten appointments. So this time he won fourteen appointments compared to only one appointment previously.

The Difference Is Patience

Much about the two efforts was the same: the identical adviser using material from a credible publication, following up with a phone call. But in the second trial the adviser was communicating a sense of discipline, patience, professionalism, persistence, and a commitment to education that was unusual relative to other advisers or salespeople who had approached these people previously.

Think about it from the Client's 99. After the first article, what did those prospects expect? Almost certainly, a phone call. They aren't naive. They know they're being courted. When the call didn't arrive, they no doubt concluded the adviser forgot. Salespeople, after all, are notorious for making promises and not following through.

The second letter would, of course, revive the same expectation that a phone call was just around the corner. But it didn't come. Now they were uncertain. After the third letter, they were quite confused, having to reformulate impressions of the adviser. Interestingly, a number of people told the adviser when he finally phoned, "I've been expecting your call." It's not a common experience for financial advisers when they're cold-calling prospects to have them say they've been waiting for the call.

That demonstrates, on a small scale, the critical importance of patience in earning trust. Clients are routinely scared off by advisers moving them along faster than they're inclined to go. That's not unexpected, given the different time frames prospects and advisers bring to the equation.

When the average adviser meets a prospect, how long does it take the adviser before he is ready to take on the client's business? About a nanosecond. He's ready. He's ready now, he was ready yesterday, he was ready last week—he's ready. How long does it take the prospect to be comfortable? Much longer: days, weeks, months and, in some cases, even years.

For the adviser to be effective, whose time frame does he have to operate from: his or the client's? The answer, clearly, is the client's. A challenge for an adviser, then, is to communicate to prospective clients "I'm interested in your business—it will be valued and well-received" without communicating "I'm desperate for your business and will put unwelcome pressure on you for it."

The Funnel Becomes a Pipeline

That emphasis on patience reflects a fundamental change in the business development process over the past decade, not just in the investment industry but in a broader range of enterprise. In the past, the business development process resembled a funnel. It had a fairly narrow mouth at the bottom and some holes on the side; it was a little rusty and the seam wasn't as tight as it might be. As a salesperson, you dumped a bunch of prospects into the top of the funnel, and some would slide through to the bottom. Most leaked out the sides or slopped over the top, but that didn't matter: you'd end up with some prospects flowing out the bottom of the funnel. It wasn't hugely efficient but it was fairly quick. You knew early on whether the prospect was going to become a client.

Today the prospecting process is like a pipeline instead of a funnel (Figure 12.1). Pipelines aren't vertical, they're horizontal, and natural gravity doesn't pull people through them. The prospecting pipeline is not even flat—it's actually tilted upward at about a 5 degree angle, working against you to slow progress down further.

As a financial adviser you have to identify prospects it makes sense to draw into the pipeline. But that's only the beginning. The next, more formidable challenge is to initiate a series of activities that will nudge those prospects through the pipeline. That doesn't mean that if you quickly build up sufficient trust with a prospect who is determined to buy immediately, you decline, protesting that they first have to experi-

Figure 12.1

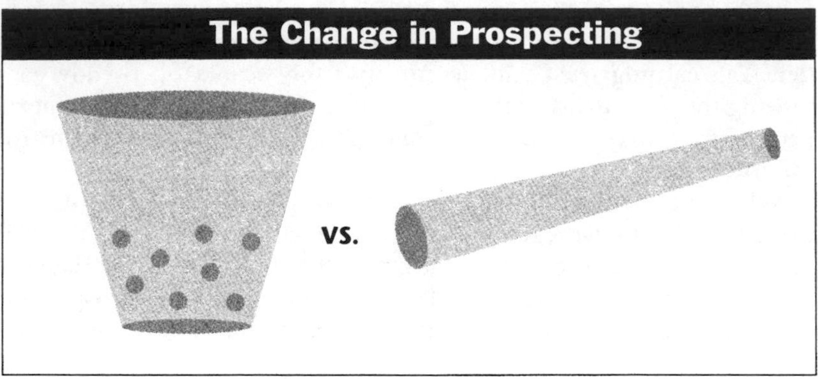

ence all the splendors you've deftly constructed into your pipeline. Obviously you accommodate people when they're ready. But you have to clearly understand a two-stage process exists in business development: it opens with identifying the prospect and putting them into the pipeline's mouth, while the second step is moving them through.

Let me distinguish between the two concepts we're dealing with here: sales and business development prospecting. A sale is an event. It occurs in a fixed period of time—with a beginning, middle, and end—which tends to be relatively short. Business development, on the other hand, is a process rather than an event. It too has a beginning, middle, and end, but the time span is much longer.

The reason it generally takes so long to convert a prospect into a client is that three ingredients must be in place for the sale to occur (Figure 12.2). First, the prospect has to feel a perceived need or detect a perceived benefit in doing business. Secondly, the prospect has to feel confident in your knowledge as a financial adviser. Finally, the prospect has to feel confident about your integrity; he or she has to

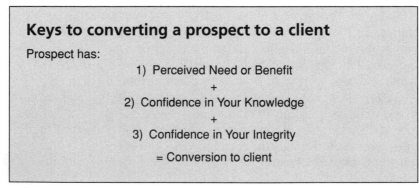

Figure 12.2

Keys to converting a prospect to a client

Prospect has:

1) Perceived Need or Benefit

\+

2) Confidence in Your Knowledge

\+

3) Confidence in Your Integrity

= Conversion to client

trust you. All three are required to turn the prospect into a client. Two out of three aren't sufficient.

The speed with which those three chips fall into place varies with the prospect. Typically, the quickest one to achieve is confidence in your knowledge. If you're an experienced financial adviser, prospects generally accept that you have a reasonable degree of knowledge, information, and insight into the investment process. Of course, that's less automatic these days as clients are more knowledgeable themselves. But usually the adviser's wisdom is not a big issue.

The challenges for the adviser more often are demonstrating benefit in doing business with her and building confidence in her integrity. In some cases the adviser wins confidence in her integrity, yet the prospect is happy where he is and in the short term no business is generated. In such instances the adviser must be patient and prepared to wait until the situation changes and the prospect is open to an alternative. More typically, however, the client feels some sense of unease about the prospective adviser. He's not terribly unhappy with her but also not entirely happy. He may trust her knowledge but not be quite sure about her integrity. Those anxieties can take months or even years to patiently overcome in the prospecting pipeline.

Patience and the Pipeline

It's important, in moving people into and along the pipeline, to adopt the view that just because somebody is not ready to do business now, that doesn't mean he or she won't be a worthwhile prospect in future. Some advisers become irritated when guests they invite to seminars are reluctant afterward to meet. "Those guys are deadbeats," the adviser will say. "They came and sat in my chairs, drank my coffee, and they're not prepared to meet. Write 'em off! They're losers!" Or he will set up at a trade show, gaining names from a draw at the booth, and when he later attempts to arrange a meeting, is rebuffed. "Wasted my time! Write 'em off! Toss the name away!" Advisers may even face such reluctance with referrals. The adviser will talk to the prospect for two hours, hold a second meeting, and the prospect is still not prepared to sign on. "Some people you can never please!" the adviser will gripe. "I'll move on to someone who appreciates the service I provide."

An alternate view is to accept that for some of the people who attended the seminar, visited the booth, or were referred from other clients, it doesn't make sense and likely won't make sense to conduct business: the chemistry doesn't exist, or they don't have the financial means. But for a significant number of those prospects, a reasonable level of chemistry has formed and a business relationship is likely to be productive. The adviser just has to work at it longer.

The challenge is developing effective follow-up to convert those prospects into clients. This requires sustained, low-key contact through intermittent mailings, occasional invitations to seminars, and periodic calls (not so frequent that prospects feel harassed), checking if they find the material of value, have questions, or are interested in a meeting. Something an increasing number of advisers are finding effective in this regard are regular lunch-and-learn programs for a handful of people in corporate boardrooms. The chance to sit around a boardroom table with three or four well-qualified prospects is more than worthwhile; it's a fairly low-cost method to come to know your prospects and for them to know you better.

The prospecting has to be organized efficiently, so that it doesn't become a drag on your time. It has to occur frequently enough so that the prospect remembers you and your interest but not so frequently as to annoy the prospect.

A Quarterly Model

A model we introduced effectively with one adviser is to identify prospects through seminars and put them into the pipeline, where they receive quarterly newsletters with information on markets and investing, and articles by credible sources. After every second issue—twice a year, therefore—the adviser hires a local student for very low-key follow-up. "Hi, my name is Abby Smith, I work with John Adviser at XYZ investment firm. John has been sending you some information. He has asked me to call to find out if you have any questions on any of the information you received and to see if you would be interested in scheduling a meeting to talk about some of the issues that are covered in the newsletter." During the course of a year—four newsletters and two calls—almost 10 percent of those prospects agreed to a meeting, and many of those converted into clients.

The key is the timing, of course. Imagine if those four mailings and two follow-up calls had taken place within a month instead of a year. On Monday, the prospects receive a newsletter. Next Monday, another newsletter, with a phone call on Tuesday. The third Monday, another newsletter arrives, and the fourth Monday they receive a fourth newsletter, followed quickly by a second call to check if they're interested. What do you think the results would be? Clearly, much less than in the more leisurely prospecting scenario.

That's an important lesson. The same number of newsletters and the same number of phone calls occurred in each scenario. The level of contact is identical. The difference is the pace—and the patience. In the first case you demonstrate discipline and a low-key approach: "I'm interested in your business, but not desperate for it." In the second case (even if, say, it was spread over a few months instead of one) you're sending a less-reassuring message about your anxiety level.

Now that we've moved from the funnel to the pipeline, we'll have to be more careful in monitoring the progress of our prospects. Figure 12.3 is a simple model that allows you to track the success of your prospect pipeline on an annual basis. It helps you to focus on the number of prospects currently on hand and the number you need to add in the coming year to remain at that level. (Figure 12.4 applies the same principles on a six-month window).

Let's say you've located 200 prospects through seminars, trade shows, and community groups. You expect a 10 percent conversion rate, so 20 of those prospects will become clients by the end of the year. You also anticipate deleting 30 percent from the pipeline as you determine that they are unlikely to become clients in the foreseeable future.

That leaves you with 60 percent of the prospects, or 120, continuing into the next year. If you want to begin Year Two with 200 prospects, it also indicates that you have to locate eighty more prospects in Year One. In forecasting the second year, remember you have two streams of prospects and, given their length of time in the pipeline, they will have different conversion and dropout rates. You might count, perhaps, on converting 10 percent of the newcomers but 15 percent of the longer-term group. Similarly, the deletion rate will differ. But the model provides a framework to plan your prospecting so that it's always an active, vital force in your business.

Figure 12.3

Prospect Pipeline Goals

	Year 1	Year 2	Year 3
Balance in pipeline going in	______	______	______
Added to pipeline	______	______	______
Converted to clients (5%–10%)	(______)	(______)	(______)
Deleted from pipeline (30%–50%)	(______)	(______)	(______)
Net Additions/Deletions	______	______	______
Balance in pipeline going out	______	______	______

Figure 12.4

Building Your Pipeline

	April–May	June–July	Aug–Sep
Balance in pipeline going in	______	______	______
Added to pipeline	______	______	______
Converted to clients	(______)	(______)	(______)
Deleted from pipeline	(______)	(______)	(______)
Net Additions/Deletions	______	______	______
Balance in pipeline going out	______	______	______

Inevitably, like other advisers, you're wondering about the optimum number of prospects to maintain in the pipeline. Unfortunately, no exact answer exists. You want as many as you can follow up and monitor reasonably on a consistent basis.

Some advisers limit their pipeline to twenty prospects and focus on those very intensely. Others have 2,000 and operate on a more mass-marketing approach. It depends on your style, the stage of your practice, and the kind and number of clients you prefer, as well as what other avenues for client development are open. If you have a significant client base, you should be developing a significant number of clients through referrals and other methods, so having a large prospecting pipeline may seem less important. If you don't have a large client base and are relatively new to the business, you'll probably be considering a larger prospecting pipeline.

Managing a Prospect Pipeline

It takes three elements to manage a prospecting pipeline effectively. The first is a significant amount of discipline and organization. If you're not well organized, you're unlikely to pull off a prospect pipeline. You also need to be computerized. File cards won't do the trick.

Secondly, you must dedicate money to the process as well as, obviously, your time and effort. For quarterly newsletters, it will probably cost about $5 per prospect for photocopying, mailing, labels and the like. For 200 prospects, that's a commitment of $1,000 (Figure 12.5).

You may prefer to handle the follow-up calls yourself, but many advisers find that as their practice develops it makes sense to hire someone to shoulder that burden. As a rule of thumb, we've found that a

Figure 12.5

The Economics of a Prospect Pipeline: 1999		
Prospects:	200	
Quarterly newsletter @ 1.25		$1,000
Assistant for twice year follow-up (400 calls @ 8/hour = 50 hours @ $10/hr + $25/appointment)		$1,000
TOTAL COST		$2,000
Cost/prospect:		$10

well-motivated college student or senior citizen, hired as a temporary cold caller, can make about eight contacts an hour. If you're aiming at 200 prospects twice a year, that entails fifty hours. For this work, you generally get what you pay for: a reasonable level we recommend is $8 to $10 an hour and, as an incentive, a bonus of $20 to $25 for every appointment generated. For fifty hours, that's another $500, and if out of the 200 prospects twenty appointments are arranged, you're facing another $400 to $500 incentive payment. So that's $1,000 for follow-up calls and $1,000 for the newsletters—a $2,000 investment, or roughly $10 per prospect to maintain the pipeline for a year.

Thirdly, if you're trying to earn trust through patience in your pipeline, you obviously need patience. This process can't be accelerated by mailing or calling more frequently. In fact, if you followed up after every mailing, instead of being more productive you would likely be less so. If every time prospects receive a mailing they also receive a phone call, the message communicated is that the newsletter is an excuse to call. Instead, through the process you are trying to demonstrate discipline, patience, professionalism, a commitment to education, and a desire, eventually, to work with the prospect as a client.

With care, you can make a prospecting pipeline work for you. It isn't as easy as in the old days, when the funnel and gravity dropped clients into our laps. But with discipline, organization, and patience, you can convert a steady stream of prospects into clients.

Snapshots

✔ *Clients are routinely scared off by the sense that the prospective adviser is in a hurry to grab their business and therefore trying to pull them along too fast. That's not unexpected, given the different time frames that prospects and advisers bring to the process. Advisers are ready at once to make a deal. Clients take much longer.*

- ✔ *In the past the business development process resembled a funnel. Today it's a pipeline.*
- ✔ *As a financial adviser you have to identify prospects worth drawing into that pipeline. The next, more formidable challenge is to initiate a series of activities that will tug the prospects through the pipeline.*
- ✔ *Unlike sales, business development is a process rather than an event. Like sales, it has a beginning, middle, and end—but business development takes much longer.*
- ✔ *To convert a prospect into a client, three factors must be in place. The prospect has to feel a perceived need or see a perceived benefit in doing business. The prospect has to feel confident in your knowledge as a financial adviser. Finally, the prospect has to trust you.*
- ✔ *In drawing people into and along the pipeline, it's important to adopt the psychology that just because people aren't ready to conduct business now doesn't mean they won't be worthwhile prospects in the future.*
- ✔ *Converting prospects requires sustained, low-key contact through intermittent mailings and occasional invitations to seminars. You have to initiate periodic calls (but not so frequent that it feels like harassment) to check if the prospect finds the material of value, has questions, or is interested in a meeting.*
- ✔ *A useful prospecting model is to send out quarterly newsletters, following up after every second newsletter with a phone call. You can hire students or senior citizens for follow-up calls, rewarding them beyond an hourly rate with a bonus for every meeting generated. The annual cost amounts to roughly $10 a head.*
- ✔ *It's important to monitor progress in your pipeline, calculating how many new prospects a year to add in order to compensate for those you convert into clients and those you delete as prospects.*
- ✔ *To manage a prospecting pipeline effectively takes discipline, organization, and computerization, money, time, and effort, and, finally, patience.*

CHAPTER 13

Organizing Prospect Development Activity

ONE OF THE FIRST ISSUES THAT EMERGES AFTER YOU BEGIN YOUR PROSPECTing pipeline is how to organize the flurry of activity. You're meeting people at different times, they're proceeding through the pipeline at an uneven pace, and you have to schedule them and yourself so that you maintain the momentum behind the delicate relationship.

Some advisers use Post-it notes: Wander into their office and you'll see walls plastered with yellow stick-on reminders. Others rely on file cards. Some fall back on memory. But increasingly, advisers realize they must automate. It's clear that advisers who aren't computerized will not be able to manage the longer-term process of client development. Fifteen years ago, back in the days of the funnel, a computer wasn't needed to manage prospects, because you knew in fairly short order who was going to become a client and who wasn't. Given the longer cycle time of the pipeline and the increased complexity of prospecting, automation is essential.

The easy part of automation is buying the computer. The hard part is figuring out how to use it and how to adapt it best to your needs. Three contact management systems are popular with advisers: ACT!, Maximizer, and Janna. They're fairly low cost and highly effective, after the initial learning curve.

An adviser without one of these packages will soon resemble an adviser without a car. You would not be very effective if you had to travel to clients' homes by bus. And you won't be effective without a proper information management system.

In figuring out what information to attach to the prospect's file, start by summarizing everything known already (Figure 13.1). How did you meet him? What's his current situation? Where does he work? What are his current needs? Are there any hot buttons you need to be alert to? What's the current arrangement between the two of you? Are there any barriers to doing business: What stands between the prospect and you?

What has been the prospecting activity so far? Has he attended seminars, received letters and newsletters? How many meetings or phone calls so far, and how did he react?

Next, you need to sketch out how you plan to move the relationship forward. Are you going to invite him to a workshop, send another newsletter, or call to suggest a meeting? What's the plan to tug the prospect down the pipeline?

The modern adviser needs up-to-date tools—and that includes a contact management system.

Maintaining the Data

After all that information is initially entered, it's easy to maintain. After every contact, you routinely note what transpired. Before initiating future contact, you can check the state of the relationship and not only refresh your memory about the last time you spoke with the prospect but also learn about his conversation with the student you hired to follow up on the recent mailing or whether he attended the seminar last fall.

Figure 13.1

Prospect Development Activity

Prospect Name:____________________ Completed as of:______

What Do I Know:______________________________________

How Met:____

Current Situation:_____________________________________

Needs:____

Current Arrangements:__________________________________

Key Barrier to Doing Business:____________________________

Past Contact: 1:______________________________________

2:______________________________________

3:______________________________________

Next Steps:____

Successful advisers sit down on a regular basis, perhaps quarterly or semi-annually, and review the progress of all their prospects. This allows them to develop priorities, deciding which clients should be accelerated and which might benefit from a more relaxed pace.

You have a car. But if you don't have a computer and contact management system, you are still in the horse-and-buggy era. The modern adviser needs modern equipment for the prospecting process.

Snapshots

✔ *One of the first issues that emerges after you begin your prospecting pipeline is how to organize the ensuing activity.*

✔ *In today's world of prospecting, you need a computer and a contact management program such as ACT!, Maximizer, or Janna.*

✔ *Begin using the system by entering all the information known about the prospect. Then keep it up to date.*

✔ *Each client file should include your plan for the future.*

✔ *On a quarterly or semi-annual basis, review your prospects and develop priorities.*

CHAPTER 14

Patience and Mega-Prospects

THE CRITICAL ROLE OF PATIENCE IN DEALING WITH MEGA-PROSPECTS WAS highlighted for me by a recent conversation with a very successful investment adviser, who had been in the chairman's club at his firm for many years. He decided to retire but stage-managed it brilliantly, bringing his daughter into the business three years before the retirement date so that she could take over. She was highly qualified, a chartered financial analyst for an insurance company, and began to pick up much of the client contact and to research the investment recommendations he was issuing.

When the actual time for retirement came, his clients were well prepared to transfer to his daughter. When he met with them, generally the decision was well received. So he was stunned when one of his best clients, a $2-million account, told him, "George, I want to thank you for the years of good service. I've really enjoyed the relationship. But I have to tell you I won't be leaving my account with your daughter. I'll be moving it to one of your competitors."

"Harry, obviously I haven't done an adequate job of communicating just how capable and well qualified my daughter is," the adviser protested. "The fact she's my daughter has nothing to do with it. She's a CFA and I can tell you with absolute assurance the level of service you'll receive from her will be every bit as high as it has been from me and maybe even higher."

"George, this has nothing to do with your daughter. Let me explain. About six years ago I was on the board of a local charity and, as it happened, one of the other board members was a broker who works for one of your competitors. I got to know him a bit, and one day received a call that his firm had developed some innovative strategies for people like me. He was wondering if we could get together for a sandwich or meet in his office to discuss those initiatives and how the ideas made sense for me.

"I thanked him for his interest but told him I was happy with my present adviser and it wouldn't be a worthwhile use of his time. His response, however, was interesting. He said: 'I'm pleased to hear that—for two reasons. I'm pleased first of all because you're well served; that's great. But I'm also pleased that given you're well served you are not out there looking for alternatives. I certainly wouldn't want the clients I'm doing a good job for to be scouting for a replacement. So I'm impressed you have that dedication and loyalty to your broker. But why don't we have lunch anyway?'

The bigger the prospect the more patience they require.

"So we had lunch, it was cordial, and it didn't go any further. About six months later he called again and said, 'Just calling to say hello and see how things are going. We've just published our quarterly investment review. I'd like to send you a copy because I think there might be some interesting ideas—particularly on page 3—for you to look at.'

"About six months later he invited me to breakfast. Again it was very pleasant. We chatted about a whole bunch of different things—frankly, not that much about investing but about the charity we were involved in, politics, and some other common interests. He has continued to contact me about every six months. Once a year or so we get together for a game of golf, or lunch, or attend a talk together.

"About a year and a half ago we were having a drink and he told me, 'I know you're happy with the broker you have. He's doing a good job for you and that's excellent. But should the circumstances change— should you run into a problem, or should your broker leave the business—I'd really like to have the opportunity to discuss working together. Do you think that might be possible?'

"I told him yes, that would be quite likely. And frankly, George, now that you are retiring, I want to give him an opportunity to show what he can do."

The Mega-Prospect List

Clearly that retiring broker's daughter had little chance of holding on to that account. The other financial adviser, through patience, discipline, and persistence, had positioned himself as the logical successor rather than her. Obviously, you can't afford to be that patient and disciplined with every prospect. Your week would be chewed up and you wouldn't last long in the business. But every adviser should have a top ten list of mega-prospects who are worth extraordinary wooing.

Those prospects should be very big—so big that if they became clients their account would immediately land them in the top five, or at least top ten, of your existing clients. A basis for a relationship should exist, some reason to believe the prospect would be disposed to work with you. You might read the latest newspaper article about Bill Gates and tell yourself, "Bill Gates is a mega-prospect if I've ever seen one." And yes, Bill Gates is a mega-prospect for someone. But unless you have a common interest that brings you together occasionally, or you went to school together, or you introduced him to computers, he's unlikely to be a prospect for you.

Those mega-prospects can come from a variety of sources. They could be childhood or college friends, a past employer, or someone you met through a common client. Serving on a prestigious board might expose you to prospects with significant assets. So might leisure activities.

I was reminded of the virtue of putting yourself in a position to interact with high-end clients by a broker who switched firms two years ago and as a result received a significant bonus. The broker and his wife were devotees of Italian cooking and he is an amateur gourmet chef, so they decided to celebrate by taking a cooking tour in Italy. Two courses were available: the first cost $2,000 for the couple and was highly appealing but the second, at $5,000, was more hands-on and offered a more elevated experience. They decided to indulge themselves with the enhanced course.

As it happens, only six couples took that Italian tour. Over the course of the trip the broker and his wife got to know the other couples fairly well. Two years later, three of the other five couples are clients of that financial adviser. And it's not because he spent the whole week talking business and handing out his business card. Quite the opposite: he was very low key, hardly talking about the fact he was in the business at all. But he had positioned himself—inadvertently, actually—through that cooking tour to develop a relationship with people who were mega-prospects. They enjoyed the relationship and were disposed to do business with him.

Thirty-Five Years and Counting

No hard-and-fast rules exist about how long you should cultivate a mega-prospect before giving up. I was listening to a tape recently featuring a very successful producer with high-end clients. He talked about cultivating prospects by taking them to charitable events, golfing, sailing on his boat, and to his cottage—he pushed very hard to build relationships with prospects. Someone asked: "How long are you prepared to persist in cultivating a prospect before you give up?"

The answer was, "I don't know." That puzzled the questioner: "What do you mean you don't know?" The adviser then explained, "The problem is I have only been in the business thirty-five years and I'm still talking today to some of the people I was talking to thirty-five years ago who have not yet become clients."

I'm not suggesting you should court a prospect for thirty-five years. But if someone meets all the criteria—truly a mega-prospect, has a predisposition to do business with you, and the vibes are right—you'll know in the course of dealing with him or her whether you're on track. If so, no reason prevents you from cultivating that relationship indefinitely, investing in a phone call every six months or so, and a meal, golf, or a tennis game or a movie together once a year.

Think back to that broker who won that $2-million account away from the other adviser's daughter. How much time had he invested? You could say six years. That's a long time to be patient. The other way to look at it, however, is that he invested twelve to fifteen hours. Each year he spent fifteen minutes on the phone and then a few hours having lunch, or golfing, or taking in a speaker. Not bad: twelve to fifteen hours to win a $2-million account!

A case could be made that if you have ten mega-prospects, you should be prepared to invest thirty hours a year on them in total. That works out to about forty-five minutes a week. It means you are going to be spending a breakfast, lunch, or a golf game once a month with one of them and making the occasional call. That's time well spent.

Thinking Big

I would also urge you not to censor yourself in contemplating targets. Too often advisers say, "Oh, that prospect would be too big. He's too wealthy, too important, and would never be interested in the kinds of services that I offer."

I was reminded of the pitfalls of self-censorship a few years back when I decided to contribute an article to a page in the *Globe and Mail* devoted to business change. The topic was attracting various contributors, and I figured it would be valuable to say that I was published on the Change Page. I invested four or five hours putting together what I considered was quite a good article and told my assistant to find out the name of the page's editor and send it along.

"Should I send it to anyone else?" she asked.

I thought for a moment and then said, "Tell you what: Why don't you send it to the *Wall Street Journal*? Call the *Journal*, find out the appropriate editor, and let's give them a try."

It was a bit of a lark and I didn't think about it again. A few weeks later I called the Change Page editor, and he couldn't have been less interested. He hadn't read the article, he wasn't going to read the article, the space was committed until 2010—thanks, but no thanks. I hung up the phone, disappointed but philosophical. Nothing ventured, nothing gained. I'd invested at most five hours, which wasn't much of a loss. I promptly forgot about it.

A week later the phone rings and on the other end is someone who introduces himself as the op-ed editor of the *Wall Street Journal*. He wants to run my article the following Wednesday. Now if someone had originally suggested investing five hours in an article for the *Wall Street Journal*, I would have thought that absurd and never would have agreed, because I would have figured the likelihood of the piece running was zero. The *Journal* is America's pre-eminent business publication. It's too big for me. They don't know who I am. They won't run anything I've written. The *Globe's* Change Page, yes; the *Wall Street Journal*'s op ed page, never.

Of course, I was censoring myself. It was through a fluke—my assistant's question, and my answer on a whim—that we tried. So it's a warning to all of us on the dangers of self-censorship.

Mega-prospects are a critical element of your prospecting process. They take care, time, discipline—and patience. But they are worth nourishing, because the return is so bountiful when realized.

Snapshots

✔ *Every adviser should have a top ten list of mega-prospects who are worth extraordinary wooing—perhaps even as long as thirty-five years.*

✔ *If you have ten mega-prospects, you should be prepared annually to invest thirty hours on them, in total. That's maybe one lunch or movie together a month and the occasional phone call.*

✔ *Don't censor yourself in terms of whom you target as a mega-prospect, figuring some people are too affluent or important to be your clients.*

CHAPTER 15

Client Referrals: What to Avoid

It's considered axiomatic in the investment business that the best source of new clients are referrals from current clients. Successful advisers confirm that adage, saying the vast majority of new clients are referred by existing ones. That belief has also been well documented by research. Our recent study, for example, of clients who changed advisers indicated that about half selected the new person based at least partly on a referral from family, friends, colleagues, and the like.

Many of the large investment dealers have surveyed their clients to find out if they would be amenable to providing their adviser with an introduction to people they know. Eighty percent of clients venture they would be willing. Yet when head offices canvass their advisers to determine what percentage actually ask their clients on a regular basis for such referrals, they discover that fewer than 20 percent—one in five—do.

That illustrates an interesting paradox in our business. Advisers want new clients. They know instinctively, anecdotally, and from research that referrals are the best source of those new clients. They are advised by head office research that clients are willing to provide those referrals. Why the blockage, then? Why don't more advisers solicit referrals on a regular basis?

A main reason, our research has found, is fear of rejection (Figure 15.1). Advisers worry that clients will rebuff them and the experience will be awkward and unpleasant. Related is the legitimate reluctance of advisers to put pressure on clients and cause discomfort. Clients might view the request as an imposition, feeling that recommending friends would violate friendships or even confidentiality.

Some advisers feel they might appear unprofessional by soliciting referrals. Others even question whether they have earned the referral.

"Gee, I'm not sure I even deserve this client, let alone his friends and neighbors," such advisers fret. "If I ask him about his friends and neighbors he might start questioning whether he should work with me."

Finally, some advisers claim they forget to ask for referrals in client meetings. But memory is a curious trait. I love desserts and at restaurants seldom forget to order one. I'm not as fond of vegetables and it's remarkable how often ordering vegetables will slip my mind. We all genuinely forget things—but often we forget because we want to.

There are wrong ways, and more wrong ways, and still more wrong ways to ask for referrals.

From the client's perspective, deterrents certainly exist to providing those all-important referrals (Figure 15.2). In some cases clients simply don't want to be responsible if something goes awry after they match up the friend and adviser. In other cases they're worried about confidentiality. But the prime concern is imposing on their friends and acquaintances. Clients don't want those friends and acquaintances feeling they took advantage of the friendship.

Indeed, that tantalizing 80 percent tally of client willingness to offer referrals is inflated, because the question was abstract. When phrased more concretely—"Do you have some acquaintances I can contact whose names I can take down right this minute?"—that 80 percent deflates dramatically. In our experience, 10 percent to 15 percent is more realistic as a positive-response rate.

That, of course, is one reason advisers don't solicit referrals more frequently. They know the real score: they will endure a significant number of rejections and may feel unprofessional as a result. If asking makes the client feel uncomfortable, the adviser pays a price. The rela-

Figure 15.1

Obstacles to Asking for Referrals

1. Fear of rejection
2. Don't want to put pressure on client
3. Might appear unprofessional
4. Feel I'm imposing
5. Have I earned a referral?
6. "Forget"

Figure 15.2

Obstacles to Clients Providing Referrals

1. Don't want to impose on friends/acquaintances
2. Responsibility if things go wrong
3. Confidentiality

tionship suffers. For many advisers it boils down to a simple equation: The price paid for seeking a client referral is greater than the reward.

The Wrong Way to Ask for a Referral

But there are right ways and wrong ways to ask for referrals. In this chapter we'll look at the principles behind the referral-generating methods that fail to work (Figure 15.3).

Let's start with pressure-based approaches. The classic method that is taught in sales training classes—indeed, that has been taught for decades—is the "who-do-you-know?" appeal. After a review with a client that has gone favorably, knowing the person is extremely happy with the relationship, you begin: "Mr Client, tell me, are you happy with the job that I've done for you?" The client is taken aback, having just spent an hour indicating how pleased he is. "Yes, of course I'm happy," he responds. You continue: "Well, that's terrific. I'm really pleased to hear it. Now tell me, who among your friends, neighbors or relatives would potentially benefit from the same kind of advice and service you receive? I can take their names right now."

This approach works in some instances—although only about 10 to 15 percent of the time. The clients feel an obligation, after expressing satisfaction, to respond favorably to the pressure. Still, most clients deflect the adviser's bid: "Well, I don't know anyone right now. If I come across somebody, however, I'll be sure to give you a call."

Worse, consider the thought process of those who actually tender a

Figure 15.3

Approaches Which Generally Aren't Effective for Most Advisers

1. Pressure-based ("Who do you know?")
2. Manipulative ("How are you doing?")
3. Based on guilt ("I get paid in two ways.")
4. Gimmicky ("Who do you want to retain as friends?")

name or two. Are they contemplating, as the adviser might hope, "Who do I know well who has the most money?" Unfortunately, no. Generally, what they're thinking is: "Whose name can I toss out so that if the person gets upset with me I won't mind that much?"

That leads to the KO referral. Unfortunately, KO doesn't stand for knock-out. It stands for kiss-off. Your clients scramble to come up with a name that allows them to kiss you off. "I know, I'll give the name of the jerk who offered me as a referral just a couple of weeks ago," a client suddenly remembers, jubilantly. "That'll teach him!" It's part of the Christmas-cake phenomenon of referrals, where the same names float around and around and around.

Sometimes, of course, the adviser obtains worthy referrals from the "who-do-you-know?" tactic. But too often the quality is suspect. You're not being directed to prospects with lots of money. You're securing relatively pain-free submissions from the client's perspective. So pressure-based methods generally don't work.

Avoiding Gimmicks

Gimmick-based methods also don't work. An adviser recently called me quite enthused about a referral method his firm had heard of that was supposedly sure-fire. Advisers were told that when a client asked them at the start of a conversation, "How are you doing?" their response should not be the conventional "Fine, thanks" but instead "Fantastic—absolutely great!" The client would inevitably be overwhelmed by that unexpected response—after all, everybody generally says "Fine" to that opening conversational gambit—and would be unable to proceed politely without inquiring about the cause of the euphoric mood. That allows the adviser to press for checkmate: "Let me tell you what happened—I'm so excited! I just got off the phone with one of my other clients, who told me she had been chatting to a friend of hers and suggested that person call me for an appointment. I can't tell you just how wonderful I feel when a client considers our relationship precious enough to recommend me to somebody else they know. It makes my day!"

I can understand how that approach might work. It certainly plants a seed in the client's mind. But a problem comes immediately to mind: If you try the tactic, consider what happens the next time the client asks you how you're doing and you reply, "Fantastic—absolutely great!" Your credibility and trust levels shoot down the drain.

Even without that danger, the fact remains the technique isn't terribly honest. It doesn't abide by the standards of integrity we should consistently meet. Move away from honesty, integrity, and truthfulness and you're on a slippery slope. Once you take a little step off, you start sliding down faster than you would prefer. The ploy might work for some advisers, but generally gimmicks don't work over the long haul for most people.

A third method that some advisers try I don't recommend because it's laced with guilt. At the start of a client relationship you say, "Mr. Client/Ms. Client, I get compensated for the work I do and the time I spend on your affairs in two ways. One of them, of course, is that I am reimbursed based on the investments you place with me. But that's only a small part of my compensation. The real compensation I get is when satisfied clients introduce me to other people they know. Tell me, if in a year from now you're happy with my work, do you think you'd be willing to introduce me to some of the people you know?"

Asked that way, most clients will respond, "Sure." What else can they say? Clients are no braver than the rest of us, and a year sounds a long way off. Eventually, however, those twelve months pass and you pick up the phone to sew them up. How will they respond? Will it be: "I'm so glad you called, because I remember that second method of compensation you discussed with me and I've been thinking of people I could introduce you to. Here's a list of ten wealthy friends."

As you can imagine, that doesn't routinely happen. Instead, you're back almost at square one with your "who-do-you-know?" appeal: "Mr. Client/Ms. Client, you may recall that a year ago we talked about how I get paid in two ways. The second and most important form of compensation was through my satisfied clients introducing me to friends. Based on our conversations, I know you've been very pleased with the work I've done. Now that we've had an opportunity to work together, who among the people you know might benefit from the kind of service and advice I offer?" It's a pressure tactic, with some guilt laid over it.

Give Me Your Enemy—Please

One of the more amusing referral approaches was relayed to me recently by an adviser who reached an affluent business owner in his community on a cold call only to be hit with a very hostile bombardment: "You guys are parasites! I have no interest in talking to you, let alone dealing with you. Go away and leave me alone." But the adviser rebounded, "Mr. Business Owner, I can understand how you feel and I respect that. But tell me, just before I let you go: Even though you are not interested, who among the people you know might be interested? Who among the people you know might it make sense for me to approach?"

It was a quick-witted and brave response, but the prospect wasn't impressed. "You haven't been listening!" he roared. "I just told you my opinion of you guys. As far as I'm concerned, you're the lowest form of life on this planet. I'm not interested in dealing with you, so why would I sic you on my friends?"

But the adviser bounced right back: "All right, I can understand that. If you don't want to introduce me to your friends, who among the people you *don't* like should I call?"

There was a slight pause and the business owner said, "Tell you what: Call Joe Smith. He's a competitor of mine. He's a jerk, you're a jerk; you guys deserve each other."

The adviser called Joe Smith, using the rather bizarre but still effective introduction to get passed on immediately to the new prospect by his secretary. "Mr. Smith, my name is Joe Adviser. I was talking to Mr. Business Owner, who suggested you might be interested in some of the financial services that I offer," he began. "I'm calling to see if you would be interested in setting a time to meet me." Joe Smith thought a moment and said, "I'm a little surprised—but sure, I guess if Mr. Business Owner thought it worth getting together, why not?"

As it turned out, the adviser gained a new client. So these inspired, offbeat approaches can sometimes work. But the difficulty is that when they succeed they encourage other advisers to try such low-percentage methods.

In that vein I recently came across an unusual technique aimed at new clients. After the initial session, the adviser is supposed to announce confidently, "Mr. Client/Ms. Client, you've made an excellent decision. As a result of our working together, you're going to become extremely wealthy. Five to ten years from now you'll be living in that big house you want to live in and driving that big car you want to drive. There'll only be one problem. The friends, neighbors, and relations you have now—who in five to ten years will still be living in the same house and driving the same car—are going to despise you. People hate others they know who do well. And they're going to ask, 'Joe/Mary, why didn't you tell me about that terrific adviser you began working with?' So tell me, who among all the people you know will you still want to be friends with five to ten years from now?"

Again, this is an approach that might work in some instances. But I suspect more often it turns clients off and inclines them to question whether they've made the right decision in picking that adviser, rather than motivates them to shovel out referrals. Besides, you don't need gimmicks and pressure tactics to obtain client referrals. Those stratagems are part of the ancient legacy of our business that we can set aside for more current strategies. Marketing methods are available that are easy to implement and far more effective in producing results, as we'll see in the next chapter when we look at the proper way to seek referrals.

Snapshots

- ✔ *A main reason advisers don't seek client referrals—even though they are the best source of new business—is fear of rejection. Advisers worry that it will be an awkward, unpleasant experience and that they will appear unprofessional.*
- ✔ *For clients the main stumbling block to providing referrals is that they don't want to impose on their friends and acquaintances. Related is the fear of feeling responsible if the relationship between their friend and adviser were to go awry.*
- ✔ *Avoid pressure-based approaches to referrals: "Who-do-you-know?"*
- ✔ *Avoid gimmicks: "I'm feeling fantastic today!"*
- ✔ *Avoid guilt: "The real compensation I get is when satisfied clients introduce me to other people they know, so will you do that a year from now?"*

CHAPTER 16

Maximizing Client Referrals

IN THE LAST CHAPTER WE LOOKED AT FLAWED APPEALS FOR CLIENT REFERRALS. Pressure-based, gimmicky, or guilt-edged tactics tend to sputter or backfire.

Four common principles underlie the referral-generation methods that are successful (Figure 16.1). The first principle is to create client apostles. This book opened with an anecdote about Dodee Frost Crockett and the client apostle she developed by helping her client get a second opinion on his cancer. You want clients who are so rhapsodic that they are spontaneously spreading the word about the kind of financial adviser they're lucky enough to have found.

How satisfied do clients have to be before they serve as client apostles? The answer is: ecstatic. Nothing less will do. So start with that goal. You want ecstatic clients.

Next, you need to make it easy for your clients to introduce people they know. It has to be low risk. A variety of methods can provide that opening. Some advisers use seminars and workshops, encouraging clients to bring along friends. In some instances advisers will put a charge on the workshop—say $10 or $20—but waive it if the client is accompanied by a friend or relative.

Newsletters offer another vehicle. Advisers who publish a newsletter can insert a note saying, "If you know anyone who might find this newsletter of value, we'd be happy to add them to the mailing list." Another opportunity to connect comes when reviewing a client's financial progress. The adviser asks if the research information is of value and after a positive response asks if anybody else the client knows might be interested in receiving a copy of the information.

In all three cases the approach is relatively low threat. And each provides some value for the prospect, another important principle to

Figure 16.1

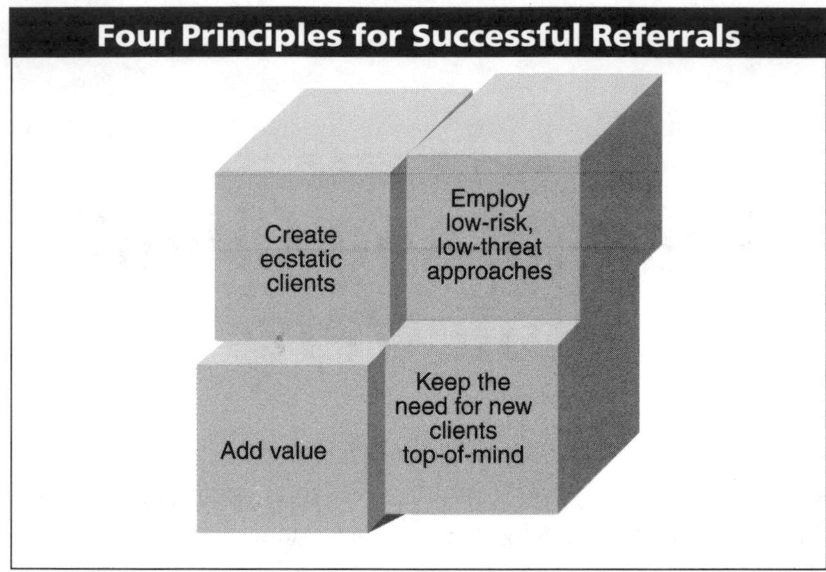
Four Principles for Successful Referrals
Create ecstatic clients
Employ low-risk, low-threat approaches
Add value
Keep the need for new clients top-of-mind

follow. Our firm has developed a letter, tied to seminars, that has been more effective in generating referrals than almost anything we have done (Figures 16.2, 16.3). Its expressed aim is to solicit feedback from clients in determining the seminars that would be most attractive. That's a valuable enough basis for writing, since you invest time and money in seminars and they should be broadly popular with your client base. In the process, though, you canvass recipients for the names of friends, family, or co-workers who might also appreciate an invitation to the seminars.

Advisers using this letter have managed to persuade between 25 and 30 percent of their clients to complete the questionnaire, with as many as of one name submitted per returned questionnaire of additional people to be invited to the workshops. Not every client, obviously, gives a name, but many offer more than one. So the adviser receives one potential prospect per response, with a quarter of the client base participating. (Figure 16.4 shows how this worked for one adviser.)

The Reasons for Success

That's a remarkable response level. It has been attained for several reasons. We've structured the approach to offer a reward for responding. Clients benefit from the seminars, and they can ensure they better fulfill their needs by giving input. The questionnaires are brief and not intimidating, no more than a page, and presented in a manner that allows a quick, easy response. In addition—and this is key—the adviser

Figure 16.2

Date

Any Client
1234 Any Street
Any City, Any State 56789

Dear Any,

I'm writing to ask for your help.

I am currently planning seminars for later this year on a variety of important investment topics. I would be most grateful if you would take two minutes to review the list of possible topics on the attached questionnaire and indicate the ones which you'd find of most interest; a stamped envelope is included for you to return this.

You'll be receiving an invitation to these seminars later this year. In the interim, please take a moment to indicate the names of any family, friends or co-workers who might also appreciate getting an invitation to these seminars.

Thank you in advance for your help on this.

Best regards,

Any Adviser

P.S. As a special thank you for taking the time to complete this questionnaire, one of the responses will be selected to receive dinner for two at (NAME OF RESTAURANT). Whether or not you are interested in attending these seminars, your business is very important to me; please contact me or my assistant (NAME OF ASSISTANT) at any time if you have questions regarding your account.

includes a return envelope with an actual stamp on it. Not a postage-paid envelope that gets redeemed only if returned or an envelope with a meter mark on it: the envelope must have an actual postage stamp. That taps into an interesting psychological process. Most clients won't want that stamp to go to waste. Some may steam off the stamp, but far more will take the time to fill out the questionnaire rather than let that stamp be squandered.

Finally, to encourage a response the adviser offers a modest incentive. The letter's postscript advises that to thank clients for completing the questionnaire, a draw will be held and one of the respondents will win a dinner for two at a local restaurant. The name of the restaurant

Figure 16.3

Which Seminars Would You Be Interested In?

1. Please indicate the seminar topics which you would like to see offered:

   - ❑ Conservative fixed income strategies.
   - ❑ Estate planning strategies: Keeping your estate in your family and away from the IRS (with lawyers from NAME OF FIRM)
   - ❑ Evaluating mutual funds: How to select the right fund
   - ❑ Investment opportunities in global markets
   - ❑ Investment strategies for business owners
   - ❑ Offshore havens and trusts
   - ❑ Peace of mind through asset allocation and a balanced portfolio: What it means, how it works
   - ❑ Planning for retirement: Developing a pre-retirement financial plan
   - ❑ Strategies to maximize your returns
   - ❑ Tax saving strategies (with an accountant from NAME OF FIRM)

2. Are there any other topics which you would like to see covered which are not included above, such as:

   ____

   ____

   ____

....

Dear Any Adviser, These people should receive an invitation to your upcoming seminars.

Name: ____________________	Name: ____________________
Address: ____________________	Address: ____________________
Phone #: ____________________	Phone #: ____________________

Please return in the attached postage paid envelope to:

Any Adviser
Any Firm
Any Address
Any City, Any State 56789

Figure 16.4

An Adviser's Results

- Questionnaires mailed to: 400 clients
- Questionnaires returned: 100
- Additional names for seminar invitations: 79
- Accounts opened: 6
- $s raised: $500,000

should be mentioned. Avoid McDonald's and invest a little more profoundly in this inducement, selecting one of the better restaurants in your community, one that would tempt clients.

Those four factors—something in it for your client, a relatively low commitment of time to complete the questionnaire, a stamped envelope, and the possibility of winning a dinner for two at a top-flight dining spot—produce a response rate of 25 to 30 percent. If you mail to 300 clients, you can expect as many as 75 to 100 responses and, let's say, 60 to 80 prospective introductions emerging from that effort. Are those referrals? Not in the true sense of the word. But they're certainly warm introductions. You can add those prospects to the seminar invitation list and in a significant number of cases ignite the prospecting process.

Adding Value

Let me give another example of generating referrals through providing value. At one of my workshops I was chatting with an adviser who works with a lot of business owners in his community. He had recently hosted a retirement-planning seminar with disappointing results. That's not unusual, as business owners are tough to attract to seminars.

We discussed what options were available to sharpen his relationship with those business owners and perhaps extend his reach to others. We looked at the concerns of business owners—what was their 99?—and realized a main problem is that they can be somewhat isolated and lonely. Even if they're running modest-sized operations, they tend to be solitary at the top, without a lot of colleagues to share their concerns.

The adviser returned to his office and tried a new tack, calling six of his business-owner clients and inviting them to a breakfast session in his boardroom two weeks down the road. It was scheduled from 7:30 A.M. to 10:00 A.M., with no specific purpose other than to generate a round-table discussion on common problems. It had nothing to do with the investment process—stocks, bonds, and mutual funds, which are his 99—and instead focused on their 99. Everybody showed up, they had coffee and donuts, and at 11:30 A.M. he had to boot them out of his boardroom.

It was, obviously, a very positive morning, and they all agreed to meet in two months' time. In addition, each promised to invite one other business owner to join them for the next session. Realizing he had hit on something, the adviser expanded. He immediately called another six business clients, tendered the same invitation, and after that proved successful, kept adding groups.

Currently, he runs five such groups, each meeting six times a year in his boardroom. He spends thirty mornings a year feeding his business clients and their friends coffee and donuts to talk about *their* problems. Why bother? First, by dint of sitting there and listening, he absorbs information about his Clients' 99—about their circumstances. Second, by organizing and sponsoring the popular sessions, he has strengthened his bond to those clients and other business owners like them. A number of clients have offered referrals. Those hadn't bubbled up before, so it suggests the sessions are stirring up such thoughtfulness. As well, some of the newcomers attracted to the sessions have become clients. In his view, it's time well spent.

But that was only the first step. After a year, he ambitiously decided to plan a seminar for business owners, remembering warily that the first effort had been an abysmal failure. This time he approached it differently. Instead of choosing an evening, he opted for a morning time slot. Rather than focusing on retirement planning, he canvassed his business-owner clients for suggestions on topics. As a result, the workshop featured an accountant who specialized in entrepreneurial practice talking about tax tips; a lawyer who specialized in business owners reviewing succession planning; a banker looking at how to develop deeper relationships with your banker; and a consultant advising how to motivate staff. The adviser played the role of host, introducing speakers and handling transitions; he was in the spotlight, but the major attention was not on him or his 99.

To his astonishment, over 200 people attended the workshop—less than half of whom were clients. The others were suggested by his clients when he appealed for names after the agenda had been formulated. One of his best clients had always resisted giving him introductions with the excuse "I can't think of anybody right now, but if I do later I'll let you know." This time, the adviser pointed out that the session incorporated many of that client's ideas and then asked if there were any acquaintances who should get an invitation. "Definitely," the client said. "I'll send you a list." It arrived the next day with sixty names.

Had the client met those sixty people since the last time the adviser pressed for names? Obviously not. The response was different because this time the adviser was providing clear value to the invitees. The client in question felt very comfortable passing along his friends' names, because they would benefit. And that's critical in the prospecting process.

Another opportunity for gaining referrals through adding value occurs when reviewing a client's financial progress. The adviser can take a moment to ask the client if the research information she has been receiving is of value. If the answer is yes, and presumably it will be, then the adviser can take the opportunity to ask the client who else she knows who might be interested in receiving a copy of that material.

In the future, one of the core philosophies for referrals will be: How do I provide value to the prospective client whose name I'm requesting, because only through that trade will my existing client really be comfortable forwarding names.

Remind the Client

The fourth strategy for obtaining referrals is to remain top of mind. Getting referrals, after all, is our 99, not the Client's 99. Our clients are busy, with many competing demands for their time, energy, and attention. Indeed, ask yourself a question: Despite your knowledge of the importance of referrals, when was the last time you volunteered one to your real estate agent, accountant, doctor, lawyer, banker, or, in fact, any service provider? Chances are it has been a while, even if you are very satisfied with their performance. Getting referrals from you is a top-of-the-mind issue for them but not for you.

It's the identical situation with our clients. We have to remind them periodically that we are still open for business—that we are, in fact, seeking new clients. That is particularly true of successful advisers; their clients figure they are doing so well and are so busy that they simply wouldn't be interested in the friend with a $100,000 account hunting for a new adviser.

Frankly, advisers foster that misguided impression. When clients ask how we're doing, we always respond very positively. "Fabulous." "Business is booming." "Busy, busy, busy." The last thing we want to say is, "Things are okay, but I could certainly use more clients." We don't say that—nor should we. But we must overcome the impression we convey to many clients that we are too successful for their friends and relatives.

Many different procedures are available for reminding your clients in a low-key, non-pressured fashion that you are open for new business. My firm has developed two simple letters for advisers that have proved highly successful. The first simply thanks the client for a recent purchase and then mentions you would always appreciate serving their acquaintances. It asks them if possible to pass on the enclosed business card to prospects or to send back the form at the bottom of the page with any names (Figure 16.5).

Figure 16.5

Date

Any Client
1234 Any Street
Any City, Any State 56789

Dear Any,

Thank you for your recent purchase. Your business is very important to me, so please contact me or my assistant, NAME OF ASSISTANT, if you have any questions regarding this transaction.

If you are pleased with the manner in which I have served you, and you believe that I might be able to help your family, friends or associates in a similar fashion, I would be very grateful if you could take a moment to indicate their names below or pass on the attached business card.

Thank you again for the opportunity to work with you.

Yours sincerely,

Any Adviser

....

Dear Any Adviser,

I think these people might benefit from your advice.

Name:____________________ Name:____________________

Address: ____________________ Address: ____________________

Phone #:____________________ Phone #:____________________

You can mention that we work together. ☐ Yes ☐ No

Fax to: Your FAX Number, or mail to: Your Name, Your Firm
Address
Address

THANK YOU VERY MUCH FOR YOUR ASSISTANCE

The second letter is more subtle (Figure 16.6). It accompanies an article of interest to the client and in a P.S. casually raises the referral issue: "Recently, several clients have asked me if I was available to work with a friend or relative. Referrals from satisfied clients are in fact the major method by which my practice has grown. Should you know of someone who might benefit from my help, please pass on the attached card. I would be pleased to meet with them to discuss their circumstances, without cost or obligation."

How frequently should you ask for a referral? One school of thought recommends asking every time you connect with your clients. Talk to them in the morning, you ask for a referral; talk to them in the afternoon, you ask again: "Oh, by the way, have you met

Figure 16.6

Date

Any Client
1234 Any Street
Any City, Any State 56789

Dear Any,

Almost all of us wish that we'd become aware of the value of money and started saving at an earlier age. These days, many parents and grandparents are particularly concerned about helping our children to develop good spending habits.

I was struck by the common sense advice in the attached article. If you happened to miss it, I thought you might find it of interest.

Best regards,

Any Adviser

P.S. Recently, several clients have asked me if I was available to work with a friend or relative.

Referrals from satisfied clients are in fact the major method by which my practice has grown. Should you know of someone who might benefit from my help, please pass on the attached card. I would be pleased to meet with them to discuss their circumstances, without cost or obligation.

anyone since we last spoke that perhaps I should contact?" A more reasonable rule of thumb would be to query once a year, although the time period will vary with the adviser. In this case, less is better. Any more and you risk being considered a pest.

Even if you are somewhat more aggressive than my guideline, it's vital that the client not be asked for referrals at every point of contact. Let's suppose a client receives an interesting article from you in the mail, with the attached business card noting your availability for referrals. She decides to hang on to the card in case somebody comes to mind, gratified by your thoughtful gesture in sending the article. Three months later another article arrives, again with the business card and the same P.S. requesting referrals.

From her 99, what's your motivation for sending the article? Is it because you care? Because you genuinely thought of her when you read the article? Or, does she figure you read a book on marketing and latched onto a sneaky new way of pressing for referrals?

My own view is that we should try to be in contact with our clients with an article of genuine interest perhaps once a quarter. Three of those communications should have no accompanying request for referrals, while the fourth probably should. By maintaining that ratio—one referral request for every four contacts—we ensure our clients are clear that our motivation in sending the articles is their personal education rather than extracting referrals in disguise.

Control Your Enthusiasm

Again it's a matter of patience and acknowledging the Client's 99. On that score, an adviser called me once complaining that he didn't receive any response when he tried the method. I was puzzled, because it has been successful with all the other advisers I've talked to. So I asked him to tell me exactly what he had done. "I followed your instructions precisely. I took the letter and copied it word for word. I used the article you showed us—great article—and attached some business cards," he said.

"Hold on a second," I broke in. "How many business cards did you attach?" He thought for a moment: "I don't know, maybe fifteen or twenty."

If you apply this method, try to control your enthusiasm. Some advisers insist that given the investment in postage and photocopying, it's only sensible to include two or three business cards. You probably won't land yourself in trouble if you attach two business cards. But the proper number is one. Let's not get greedy here. If the client wants to offer two referrals—or ten referrals—he'll find a way even if he only has one business card.

Other letters we've developed apply similarly to newsletters (Figure

16.7) and seminars you organize (Figure 16.8). The seminars letter is worthy of note: It invites the client and spouse to the session but notes that four spaces have been reserved for them, the extra two for friends who might find the evening of interest. It then adds: "Should your guests wish to meet with me to discuss their financial circumstances at some future point, I would be pleased to do so; there will, however, be no direct follow-up with anyone attending as your guest."

Some advisers, as you might expect, choke when they read that comment. Why plant the seed in the client's mind that we might be lusting after their guest's account? The reason is that it's already firmly rooted. When our company has researched letters sent without that tag line, the number-one reason cited for not inviting friends is, "I'm concerned that I'm going to be embarrassed because my friends will be followed up aggressively by the adviser and I'll feel badly as a result."

In their 99, that's the big barrier to inviting friends. So by your dealing openly with it and assuring them their fears are groundless, it's more likely your clients will feel comfortable inviting their friends and, in particular, their most affluent friends to the session, assuming it's of interest.

Let me stress that follow-up can take different forms, some quite subtle. If somebody attends your workshop through such an invitation

Figure 16.7

Dear Any Client:

This confirms that I will be meeting with you at my office next Thursday, April 6, to review the progress of your portfolio.

I look forward to seeing you at that time.

Regards,

Any Adviser

P.S. As you know, I am hoping to expand the number of clients like yourself with whom I work.

One of the best ways for someone to get a sense of my approach is through my newsletter. Prior to our meeting, I'd be grateful if you could think about two or three friends who might be looking for financial advice in the next while and would find my newsletter of value—I'd be happy to add them to my mailing list.

Figure 16.8

Dear Any Client:

I am writing to invite you and your wife/husband to attend a special thank-you dinner for some of my most valued clients.

The dinner will be held on DATE at the LOCATION; speaking after dinner will be NAME, Estate Planning Partner in the accounting firm of NAME OF FIRM. He [or she] will be speaking on Estate Planning and Tax Reduction Strategies for High Tax Bracket Individuals.

I have reserved four spaces for you—two of course for yourselves, the others for friends who might find the evening of interest. Should your guests wish to meet with me to discuss their financial circumstances at some future point, I would be pleased to do so; there will, however, be no direct follow-up with anyone attending as your guest.

Details of the evening are as follows:

Date:
Drinks:
Dinner:
Location:

I very much hope that you will be able to join me for what I know will be an entertaining, informative evening and look forward to seeing you on DATE.

Best regards,

Any Adviser

and six or nine months down the road she receives an invitation to another seminar, nobody is going to be too upset. It's a low-key approach, the choice is hers, and you're offering value. But other than that, when we say no direct follow-up, we really have to mean it. The adviser can't argue, "I didn't contact them for three days after the workshop. I gave them a chance." No direct follow-up has to mean no direct follow-up.

The Reassurance of Quasi-Referrals

Another opportunity to take advantage of your existing client relationships comes through quasi-referrals. Let's say the client is a business owner. You tell him: "I'm hoping in the period ahead to add more clients like yourself to my practice, and in coming months I'm going to be talking to other business owners. I was wondering if it would be all right to mention I work with you."

Most clients will quickly assent. It's an inoffensive request. Now when you contact a business owner, you can say, "I work with many business owners like yourself. In fact, among my clients is Mr. Smith of XYZ Printing. He said it was okay if I mentioned we work together, and I was calling to see if you would be willing to sit down and see whether some of the solutions that have been effective for other business owners might make sense for you."

It's not really a referral. But it does provide the prospects you're cold-calling with a greater degree of confidence and trust than they would ordinarily feel. You've borrowed an implicit testimonial from the original client—borrowed credibility.

Even if the prospects don't know the individuals who are the source of the quasi-referral, they are still reassured by the fact that you're working with somebody like them. Let's say you're canvassing a neighborhood: "I work with many people in Oak Ridges. Among my clients who have given me permission to mention them are Joe and Mary Smith on Belmont and Phil and Susan Brown on Pine. I was calling to see, since I'm often in the neighborhood, whether I could drop in and spend twenty to thirty minutes talking about your situation."

The credibility and comfort for the prospect rises dramatically with that quasi-referral, even if the two families mentioned aren't known by name or sight. You've differentiated yourself from other advisers by pointing out that you already have clients in place who resemble them.

You have to be careful with the tool. You don't want to abuse your client relationship. You certainly don't want to have clients feel pressured or squeezed dry, their name being bandied about all over the city. But used selectively, it can be an effective method of accelerating the trust-building process.

Saying Thanks

It is worth stressing that clients are under no obligation to provide referrals, nor should there be any expectation that a client will furnish one. Many financial advisers honestly believe that they are owed referrals for good performance. The truth of the matter is that increasingly clients take the view that the reward an adviser receives for doing a good job is that the client continues to work with him or her. My view is that a referral should be viewed as a bonus for a job extraordinarily well done and should not be treated as something you're entitled to.

It's also important to recognize that no matter how well you perform as an adviser, some clients will never provide referrals. Something in their makeup leads them to resist imposing on their friends or relatives, no matter how pleased they are themselves with your abilities. The best prospects for future referrals, therefore, are generally those clients who have tendered referrals in the past. They have demonstrated their happiness with your work and willingness to help in this fashion. So an important element of seeking referrals is to identify those clients who have handed out referrals in the past and to ensure they are properly acknowledged.

Advisers, therefore, need a more structured and more systematic approach than they have historically had for acknowledging referrals and showing appropriate appreciation (Figure 16.9). Even today, most financial advisers will simply thank the client when they receive the referral and leave it at that. While that might work satisfactorily in some cases, if that's your sole response to a referral, you are leaving on the table a significant opportunity to leverage that referral into others in the future. Instead, you should go out of your way to express appreciation—without leaving the client feeling bribed.

Within twenty-four hours of receiving the referral—forty-eight hours at most—you should send a handwritten note to the existing

Figure 16.9

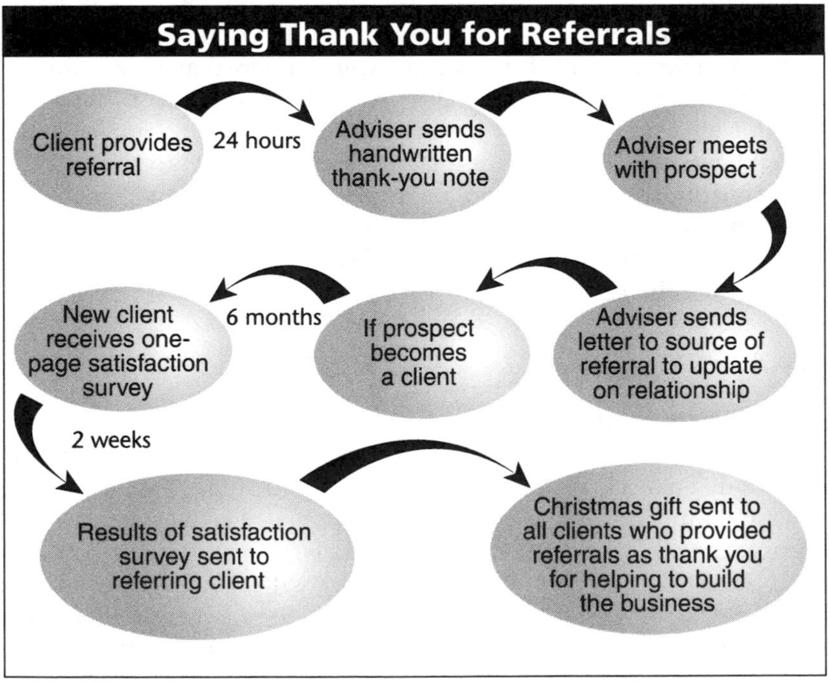

client thanking her for the referral. Nothing fancy, just a few sentences: "Thank you, Sally, for your confidence in introducing Jim Friend. Your support is much appreciated." That's all it takes.

Next, you should ensure your referral sources remain in the information loop. Many advisers fail to keep them informed of what transpires. Instead, when you think you know what the outcome is going to be, you might alert the original source by telephone. After the prospect becomes a client, a second note is the best touch: "Sally, you may recall that you introduced me to Jim Friend a few weeks back. I just wanted to let you know we have been working together. Thank you again for your confidence." Even if the news is bad—the referral has decided not to become a client or has not yet chosen an adviser—you may want to send a note bringing the client up to date and again thanking her for her confidence.

At this point advisers wonder whether they should recognize the introduction in a more tangible form. Cementing the appreciation with a gift in that way is wise, as long as the client does not feel bribed or sense commercialism. So avoid, say, a gift certificate with a dollar value attached, since that seems to put a price tag on the referral. But if the client is a John Grisham fan, you might want to send a copy of his latest book, or if she enjoys the ballet, two tickets to an upcoming performance would be appropriate, with a covering note: "Just wanted to thank you for the introduction."

One adviser sends a charitable donation to his favorite charity in recognition of the referral. In the note thanking the client, he adds: "P.S. As a special thank you I wanted you to know that I have made a contribution to the local hospital for sick children in your name." You could take that a step further by sending the donation to the client's favorite charity. From the client's viewpoint a $50 donation would be a reasonable, non-commercial recognition, and from your perspective that sum is quite trivial compared to the value of a referral. (For more ideas, see Figures 16.10, 16.11, 16.12.)

One financial adviser I know goes even further. After six months, he sends new clients a satisfaction survey with a few simple questions

Figure 16.10

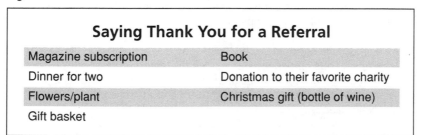

Saying Thank You for a Referral

Magazine subscription	Book
Dinner for two	Donation to their favorite charity
Flowers/plant	Christmas gift (bottle of wine)
Gift basket	

Figure 16.11

Magazine Subscriptions

Golf	Interior Design
Gardening	Cooking
Tennis	Travel

on one page. Almost always at that early stage of the relationship the new client is happy that his questions are being answered and a comfortable financial strategy is being put in place. When the adviser reviews that survey, he indicates to the new client his joy that everything is working out and adds, "I wonder if I could ask a favor of you. I'd like to send a copy of this along to your friend Sally Client, who originally introduced us." Almost always the new client agrees. And that opens up another opportunity to show your gratitude to the original client and reinforce in her mind that she made the right move. Now she can see in concrete form that her friend is being well served. She can feel confident when considering future referrals that they too will be well treated.

In December each year, one financial adviser invests in good bottles of wine and has each delivered—or delivers it himself—to all clients who provided a substantial referral over the course of the previous year, with a note: "Just wanted to thank you again for the opportunity to work together over the past year and for your confidence in introducing me to your friend, Jim Client." Invariably, January is his best month in terms of referrals. That gift reminds those clients that he appreciates referrals, and probably creates a slight obligation to think a

Figure 6.12

Welcome and Thank You!

A special welcome to all of the new clients who have joined us since our last newsletter. Thank you in particular to those clients who have mentioned our name to people they know.

As a small sign of our gratitude, four times a year, we randomly select a client who has introduced our service to a friend for special acknowledgment. Receiving dinner for four this month at the XYZ restaurant are Mr. and Ms. Existing Client and their friends, Mr. and Ms. New Client.

little more seriously about others they know who might also benefit from his services as a financial adviser.

Another financial adviser recognizes referrals when he holds his annual client appreciation event. Every client is invited to hear a guest speaker, but those who provided a referral in the previous year are invited beforehand to a special private dinner. He makes it clear to them in a brief toast at the dinner that "while I value all my clients I wanted to pay a special thank you to each and every one of you who over the course of the last year have made the effort to introduce me to friends."

Some readers may feel that's a lot of effort to acknowledge referrals. And it is. But it's not as much effort as is required to bring new clients on board through methods other than referrals. Since one referral will often lead to another, this diligence makes a lot of sense. At the same time, it's important to be careful about not creating a pattern or creating expectations on the part of clients who provide multiple referrals. So you may not want to recognize each and every referral with a separate gift. It's remarkable how quickly something that is treated as a bonus the first time becomes expected the second time. That's the virtue of an annual gift or commemoration of referrals: It presents an opportunity to be a little different each time. The key, remember, is that the client feel thanked but not bribed.

Finally, having spent so much time last chapter discussing referral pitches we should shun, let me conclude with two excellent sentences to close a positive client meeting. They're simple and straightforward: "Mr. Client/Ms. Client, in the period ahead I'm very much hoping to add to my practice more clients like yourself. Should you know of someone or come across someone you think might benefit from the same kind of advice you've received, I'd be grateful if you'd pass my name along." No pressure, no gimmicks—but it puts the message across that you're open for business. If you develop ecstatic clients and from time to time in a low-key fashion remind them that you value referrals, more often than not you'll find yourself with an increasing string of referrals from existing clients.

Snapshots

- ✔ *The first principle for obtaining successful referrals is to create client apostles. You want clients who are so enamoured about the service you provide that they are enthusiastically spreading the word about the financial adviser they're lucky enough to have found.*
- ✔ *The second principle is to employ low-threat, low-risk methods to make it easy for your ecstatic clients to introduce people they know.*

- ✔ *A letter developed by our firm, tied to seminars, has been more effective in generating referrals than almost anything we have done. It asks for client feedback in determining the seminars; canvasses them for the names of friends who might appreciate an invitation; and offers a draw for a dinner for two at a popular restaurant as an incentive to generate responses. Remember, though: the questionnaire must be brief and easy to fill out, and you must use a real stamp on the enclosed self-addressed envelope.*
- ✔ *The third principle for obtaining referrals is to add value, as did the adviser who built up his business-owner clientele by adopting their 99 and holding sessions on their non-investment concerns.*
- ✔ *The fourth principle for obtaining referrals is to remain top of mind. You must periodically remind clients that you are still open for new business.*
- ✔ *A rule of thumb is to raise the referral issue once a year with a client.*
- ✔ *The following reassurance works well in letters inviting clients to bring friends to an event you're sponsoring: "Should your guests wish to meet with me to discuss their financial circumstances at some future point, I would be pleased to do so; there will, however, be no direct follow-up with anyone attending as your guest."*
- ✔ *Don't forget to thank your clients for a referral. Keep them informed of what happens after the referral is given and consider an annual recognition of referrals by your clients.*
- ✔ *Here are two handy sentences to close a client meeting: "Mr. Client/Ms. Client, in the period ahead I'm very much hoping to add to my practice more clients like yourself. Should you know of someone or come across someone you think might benefit from the same kind of advice you've received, I'd be grateful if you'd pass my name along."*

CHAPTER 17

Doing Business with People You Know

TRY THIS EXERCISE: TAKE A SHEET OF PAPER AND WRITE DOWN THE NAMES OF everyone you know—friends, relatives, neighbors, co-workers, past employers, shopkeepers, and the like. Most people find it fairly easy to reach, relatively quickly, 100, 150, or even 200 names. Now, mark an asterisk behind everyone on the list whom, from what you know about their financial means and personality, you wouldn't mind having the opportunity to serve as an adviser. Finally, cross out all the people in that subset whom you currently work with. Use Figure 17.1 to help you.

Most advisers who try that drill wind up with a list of between fifty and 100 people they would gladly work with but who aren't presently clients. In fact, not only are they not clients but the adviser has never approached them about the possibility of becoming clients.

That lapse arises for many reasons. In some cases advisers are reluctant to approach those potential targets for fear of jeopardizing friendships or breaching confidentiality. But the main reason is simply that we don't want to intrude—we don't want to be viewed as attempting to commercialize a personal relationship.

But that misjudges the situation. Imagine this scenario: You decide that you need to find a lawyer to update your will. You have two alternatives. You can call a lawyer who you know—maybe through the church, or the PTA, or the golf club, maybe an old classmate. The second option is to search the Yellow Pages.

The vast majority of people will call someone they know. The reason is simple, yet for our purposes profound: Given the choice, people prefer to conduct business with people they know. It's true of financial advisers, as the lawyer scenario demonstrates. It's true of our friends. It's true of our acquaintances.

The key, therefore, is to capitalize on that truism without ignoring

Figure 17.1

Categories to Consider		
Know personally: (relatives, close friends)	______	______
Past co-workers/employers:	______	______
Know casually: (Church, PTA, hockey, neighbors)	______	______
Classmates from school:	______	______
Via community activity: (coaching, scout leader, boards)	______	______

the reservations that traditionally block us from soliciting such business. We need methods to approach those friends that are comfortable for both parties. If we can manage that, we'll convert some of them into clients without impairing the relationship we already enjoy with those who aren't interested.

"By the Way, I'm a Financial Adviser"

Four simple principles form the basis for such cautious, comfortable approaches to friends and acquaintances (Figure 17.2). It begins by letting them know what we do. However, in doing that, I'm not for a moment suggesting you immediately place a bulk order for business cards to pass out to everyone you meet and already know. Not only is that not professional but it wouldn't be effective. It wouldn't be comfortable.

But suppose you're talking to someone at a party or a ball game who you know casually. And suppose you ask them the nature of their work. They are highly unlikely to be offended by that question. People love to talk about what they do. They'll answer your question and, more often than not, duplicate by asking what you do. At that point, you should not respond with: "Glad you asked. I'm actually a financial adviser with the XYZ firm and I happen to have with me a prospectus for an exciting new issue that if we act quickly could be made available to you right here and now." Instead, you want to say, simply, "I'm a financial adviser with the XYZ firm." Leave it at that. If the person wants to know more, he or she will ask. If not, you've accomplished your purpose, which is just to plant the seed so that the individual knows what you do, in case some day soon it comes to a choice between the Yellow Pages and an acquaintance.

Although that's a fairly basic concept, it's remarkable how many people in our business and similar businesses fail to follow it. I was talking once with a senior partner at a large accounting firm. He told me about the time a large corporate law firm in their city relocated into their building and his group decided to host a welcoming reception in their boardroom for the firm's partners. The accountant walked into the reception and to his shock across the room spotted a friend he had played tennis with every week for several years. He went over and said, "Doug, I'm really embarrassed. I didn't know you were a lawyer. I thought you were a doctor." His friend replied, "Listen Jeremy, there's nothing to be embarrassed about. I thought you were a dentist."

So make sure your acquaintances know you're not a dentist or a doctor. And you don't have to wait for them to ask directly. Other opportunities to mention it generally arise. Let's suppose somebody tells you she is a pharmacist and owns a local pharmacy. That's an opportunity to connect her comment to your interests. "Gee, I'm an investment adviser with XYZ firm and one of the recommendations from our research department is Johnson & Johnson, particularly because of this new drug they're launching. Tell me, have you any information from the sales people handling that new drug? And what's your opinion of it?" Will the pharmacist feel offended by those questions? No, she'll feel flattered because you've solicited her opinion. But in the process you casually have let her know, in an extremely low-key fashion, how you earn your living.

Communicate Interest

After accomplishing that first goal, the next step is to communicate interest. Let people know—again in a low-key fashion—that if they wish to conduct business with you, you would be pleased to comply. Suppose you meet someone who is a lawyer at a social gathering or a meeting of a board you've joined. A few days later you get a note in the mail

Figure 17.2

Principles of Doing Business with People You Know

1. Let people know what you do
2. Communicate interest
3. Make it easy for people to take the first step
4. Maintain balance

from him: "Enjoyed chatting with you the other day. I came across this article that I thought might be of interest." The piece, from a legal publication, discusses a new ruling on the liability of financial advisers.

Would you be affronted to receive that article? Obviously not. You would be flattered. He listened to you and expressed an interest. What happened to your likelihood of picking him if you need a lawyer? Clearly it increased. He communicated an interest in you and at the same time hinted, "If you're interested in doing business with me, I would be pleased to do business with you."

In that vein, suppose you meet somebody at a social gathering or a board meeting, and a few days later he receives a note from you: "Enjoyed chatting. Thought you might find the attached article of interest." Included is an article from a high-trust publication such as the *Wall Street Journal* or *Forbes* on an investment issue. Obviously the more the item is related to his individual circumstances the better, but it doesn't have to be too specific. Will the individual be upset? I don't think so. You've quietly reminded him of your occupation and indicated interest in doing business, should he be interested. You've made it easy for him to take the first step in developing a relationship.

Figure 17.3

Date

Ms. Any Acquaintance
1234 Any Street
Any City, Any State 56789

Dear Any,

As you may be aware, I recently joined NAME OF FIRM as an investment adviser.

On the evening of DATE, a seminar on strategies to minimize taxes is being held in conjunction with NAME, C.A. tax partner with the accounting firm of NAME OF FIRM and NAME, estate lawyer, with the law firm NAME OF FIRM. It occurred to me that you might find the seminar of interest; an invitation is attached should you wish to attend. I would be delighted to have you as my guest.

If you would like to attend, please give my assistant, NAME OF ASSISTANT, a call.

Best regards,

Any Adviser

Fast-forward six months. You open your mail one day and it includes an invitation to a seminar that your lawyer friend and some other partners in his firm are sponsoring on estate planning. "If you're free on Thursday evening, we'd be pleased to have you along," a handwritten note adds. Would you feel imposed upon? Of course not. You're being given an opportunity to attend a session of value: you might learn something and even meet some prospective clients. But even if you're not interested in attending, you won't feel offended, since the choice to go or not has been left to you.

So flip that scenario around: Suppose you send an invitation for one of your seminars to some of the people you casually know. Are they going to be offended? Chances are that they won't—assuming the topic is of genuine value and interest (Figure 17.3).

The key, however, is to maintain balance. Keep the frequency of such contact fairly low, maybe once a year. These people are in a different category from your prospect pipeline, where the contact is about once a quarter. You don't want them feeling you intruded on the personal relationship. The last thing you want is that when you walk into a room, everyone immediately scurries for cover because you're viewed as only interested in people for their cash-register possibilities. But if you remember people prefer to do business with people they like, and in a low-key fashion let them know the nature of your work and communicate interest, you can build your business through the people you know.

Snapshots

✔ *Given the choice, people prefer to do business with people they know.*

✔ *The first step in approaching friends and acquaintances for their business is simply to let them know what you do.*

✔ *The second step is to communicate an interest.*

✔ *The third step is to make it easy for them to move to the next stage and develop a business relationship with you.*

✔ *If you keep your initiatives low key, nobody will be offended, and some of the people you know will gladly choose to do business with you.*

CHAPTER 18

Creating the Motivation to Meet

WHEN WE FIRST EXAMINED THE FIVE-STEP PROCESS TO BE SUCCESSFUL—making initial contact, building trust, creating the motivation to meet, closing the sale, and turning a transaction into a client—I noted that each was important, but the critical stages were the first two: developing the initial contact and building trust. After you've taken those two steps, developing the motivation to meet is a natural outgrowth. If you have been operating from the Client's 99, demonstrating that you can provide value, you have already been creating the motivation to meet.

Historically, a sales-training tenet has been that when courting a client who already has an arrangement in place, you must create dissatisfaction with the existing relationship in order to propel the customer to switch. But with so many investors poised or prepared to switch—some of our research has shown that 15 to 20 percent change their financial-advice arrangement in a given year—it's not necessary to create dissatisfaction. A significant number of investors are dissatisfied already. You simply must be positioned as one of the alternatives they consider.

Our firm's research has delineated a few approaches that create value and provide a motivation for prospects to meet. The first opening flows from the quite unrealistic expectations many people hold about their likely retirement age. In one survey we asked individuals in their forties when they hoped to retire:

- 33 percent said at age fifty-five or under;
- 32 percent indicated age fifty-six to sixty;
- 28 percent opted for age sixty-one to sixty-five;
- 6 percent said over sixty-five; and
- 1 percent replied they were never going to retire because they wouldn't be able to afford it.

Most of those expectations are not even close to realistic. All studies on preparedness for retirement—the extent to which consumers have set their financial house in order—inform us it's impossible that so many people will be able to retire before the traditional mid-sixties gatepost. Interestingly, consumers are actually well aware of that even as they serve up those unrealistic predictions.

Determining retirement needs is so complicated that most investors require an adviser to help with the calculation.

Anxiety About Retirement

In another research study we asked consumers how concerned they are about outliving their retirement savings. Sixty percent indicated they were either somewhat or very concerned. That was particularly true of respondents in the thirty-five to fifty-five age bracket, but strong even for individuals in their sixties. When we analyzed the responses by net worth, as expected, it correlated—the lower the asset level, the more concerned individuals were. But as much as 53 percent of those with a net worth between $100,000 and $250,000 were worried about outliving their retirement savings.

In part that concern arises as most people have no idea what finances their retirement requires. When you ask how closely they've calculated the sum they need, only one-seventh of respondents have spent a fair amount of time or feel they have a good sense of what's required. About 40 percent figure they have a pretty good sense, and the remaining 40 percent haven't the vaguest notion. Again, while the results correlate with income and net worth—the higher the income and net worth, the better knowledge people feel they have—less than one in four respondents with a net worth exceeding $100,000 believed they had a good view of their retirement needs.

That's not unexpected. After all, calculating retirement needs is not a simple task. Most people would face difficulty computing it on their own. On the expenditure side, you must begin with some rudimentary cash flow estimates of future needs, based on today's dollar, and factor in both inflation and tax rates. On the income side, you must calculate possible sources of revenue, adjust that for inflation, factor in pensions, and develop some reasonable assumptions about the likely return yielded by your current savings. Most consumers can't complete such a complicated analysis on their own.

So it should be no surprise that most people don't know what will be needed to live post-retirement. And advisers can capitalize on that uncertainty when seeking an initial meeting. Marketing Solutions research finds a positive response to the following offer from advisers: "One of the services I provide, if you're interested, is to spend some time talking about what you expect your retirement needs will be and calculating whether you're on track to meeting those goals. We'll look at when you intend to retire and the standard of living you plan to have at that time."

Providing Value

If you've already developed trust with the prospect, this is a very successful technique for eliciting a meeting. You're providing value. You're not beckoning, "Come to a meeting and I'll tell you about some hot new stocks." Instead, you're saying, "I'm going to provide you with information of real substance."

The anxiety many investors harbor about their asset mix offers another opening to gain a first meeting through providing value. Consumers view the markets as increasingly volatile and, given that economic climate, are uncertain whether their current investments are the most appropriate. When we probed that anxiety with the question "How satisfied are you that your savings are in the right investments for the period ahead?" we received some interesting results. Thirteen percent of respondents were absolutely confident. Another 53 percent declared they were quite satisfied. The balance, about one third of those surveyed, admitted to being only somewhat satisfied, moderately comfortable, or not satisfied at all. The unease displayed by that third offers an opening to an adviser promising to provide additional information and assistance.

Such anxiety, by the way, is not restricted to low-end investors. One out of five respondents with over $250,000 in investments indicated they were not at all satisfied or only somewhat satisfied that they had adopted the proper asset mix.

So the second technique for creating the motivation to meet—after you've established familiarity and trust—is to tell a prospect, "One of the things we do for the people we work with is to offer a second opinion on how their investments are structured, given the current economic climate and what's predicted for the period ahead. If you're interested, we'd be happy to sit down with you to review your objectives and how your investments are currently allocated. We may determine the current arrangement is absolutely appropriate, but at the minimum you will have obtained a second opinion on that investment profile."

These two methods will help you provide the motivation to meet by taking advantage of the anxiety and dissatisfaction already in the marketplace.

Snapshots

- ✔ *If you have been operating from the Client's 99, demonstrating that you can provide value, you have been building the motivation to meet.*
- ✔ *In today's environment it's not difficult to create the dissatisfaction that might lead a prospect to switch financial advisers. A significant number of investors are dissatisfied already and are intending to move or prepared to move.*
- ✔ *Most people don't know what they will need to live post-retirement. Advisers can capitalize on that unease when seeking an initial meeting by offering to help prospects calculate whether they are on track to meeting their retirement goals.*
- ✔ *Another effective technique is to offer a second opinion on the prospect's current asset mix.*
- ✔ *In both cases, you're offering information of substance rather than touting hot new stocks.*

CHAPTER 19

Closing the Sale

THE FINAL STEP IN CONVERTING A PROSPECT TO A CLIENT IS CLOSING THE sale. You've established contact, built trust, and motivated the prospect to meet by providing clear value. Now the rubber hits the road.

More nonsense has been written on closing methods than on the rest of the selling process put together. "Close early, close often" is a maxim, for example, that resounds through the halls of many sales organizations. And as many sure-fire, no-fail techniques abound as sales trainers. The classic method is an alternative close, which plunges the prospect into choosing between two options the salesperson conjures up without raising the delicate issue of whether the person even wants to buy. "Would you be interested in this widget in red or blue?" "Would you like 5,000 or 10,000?" "Would you like to meet on Monday or Tuesday?"

If that doesn't work, you can sample from such delights as balance-of-time closes or weight-of-pain closes. Momentum closes have always amused me. The principle is quite simple: If you can lure the prospective client into saying "yes" four or five times in a row, in theory he or she will have formed a habit and you can sneak in the critical question of purchasing your product.

"Did you have a good weekend," the adviser begins.

"Yes."

"Did you have a chance to get out for a game of golf?"

"Yes."

"Did you have a good game?"

"Yes."

"Did you enjoy the weather?"

"Yes."

"Would you like to buy a million dollars of IBM stock?"

While my retelling makes those notions seem absurd, in fact reputable schools of thought promote closing along all those lines. I suggest it makes more sense to step back and consider the sales process in context. Throughout that process, advisers must fixate on the Clients' 99. Prospects and clients are constantly weighing the benefits of doing business with us against the risks. So in closing, as in everything else, our challenge is to enhance the benefits and reduce the risks.

Ask questions. Ask more questions. And then ask some more questions.

A Rookie's Dilemma

Imagine a new salesperson who has been in the business for only a week arrives at work one morning excited because his grandmother has opened the door for him to meet with her next-door neighbors. The neighbors recently came into some money which they want to invest, but they happen to be leaving imminently for a long European trip. They intend to decide before departing and, not having an adviser, are a rookie's dream.

The salesperson calls them and receives a courteous welcome. "We'd be pleased to talk with you today, because we're leaving tomorrow," the man says. "But you should know we are pressed for time, so we can only give you half an hour. You should also know we are intending to meet with two other financial advisers. As long as you're comfortable with those arrangements, we'd be happy to sit down with you."

They schedule a meeting for later that morning. In preparation the salesperson digs out the sales manuals from his training sessions, which detailed the five-step process that in various forms is universally taught in sales training (Figure 19.1). The first step is building rapport: making the client feel comfortable and developing empathy. The second stage is investigating and asking questions. The third phase, after hearing the answers, is providing solutions. Next comes identifying and responding to objections, while the final element is getting commitment and closing the sale.

In various forms those five steps permeate the thinking of all salespeople in this business. But the rookie has only half an hour. So he asks you: Which step should I spend the most time on?

A Short History of Selling

While you're considering that, let's put the selling process in perspective. Until the mid 1950s, if you entered sales you received no training.

Figure 19.1

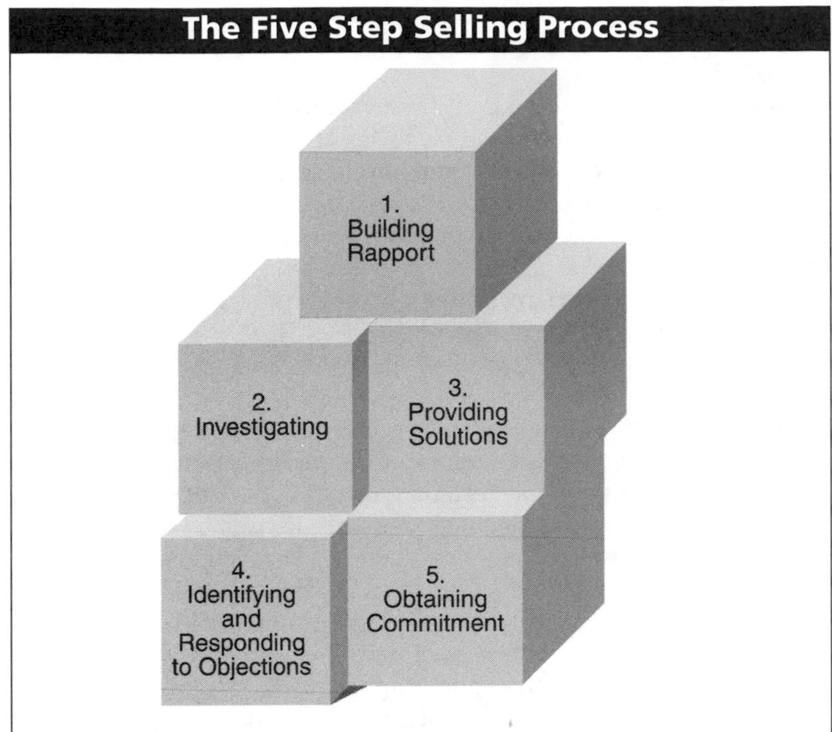

Selling, it was believed, couldn't be taught. Selling was an innate art. You were either born an effective salesperson or you weren't. If you were lucky, you might receive some training by being sent out for a day or two with one of the experienced salespersons, learning by osmosis.

In the late 1950s and early 1960s Xerox developed its professional selling skills program, PSS, which revolutionized the field because for the first time a structured approach to selling was encouraged. PSS transformed what had been considered a pure art into part science. Selling obviously still has a subjective component. It's not carried out by formula. It's not mechanistic. But for the first time, thanks to Xerox, a structured selling process started to evolve.

The five-step process derives from the PSS approach. An entire generation of salespeople found their effectiveness improving dramatically because for the first time they had formalized direction. Researchers studied which parts of the model were the most important. As with our rookie salesperson, where should you spend the most time to spawn a healthy sales experience? Some people argued rapport-building, because rapport is the essence of selling, the key to converting a prospect into a client. Others talked about the importance of framing recommendations, while still others championed objection-handling. Finally, as might be expected, a group held firm to the notion that closing was all that mattered: The most successful salespeople were the most avid and gifted closers.

Research reveals that none of those vaunted steps drives sales effectiveness. The only factor that seems to correlate consistently with a successful sales experience is the step that tends to get overlooked: the amount of time spent asking questions, getting the client to talk, and listening. And that's the answer to the rookie salesperson's query—he must devote the most time to getting the clients talking, through asking questions, and he must listen intently to what they are trying to tell him.

Building Rapport

Let's investigate the process more deeply. Clearly, building rapport is important. You must establish a minimum degree of comfort so the client feels you're on the same wavelength. Otherwise, the ball game is over.

Many sales training programs have outlined somewhat manipulative techniques for establishing that rapport. For example, salespeople were taught that when you sit down in the prospect's home or office, you should scan the surroundings for something that hints at her interests, personality, or hobby, and then devise a way to establish a common bond, because that forges rapport.

Perhaps you note from the diploma on the wall that you both attended the same university; you could comment on that connection. Or you notice a photograph of her grandchildren, and so you compliment her on those beautiful youngsters. Maybe a golf trophy holds pride of place on the mantel, so you talk about golfing. In the process, you're building ties.

The hazard in this approach is demonstrated by an anecdote, perhaps apocryphal in nature, about a new salesperson who on his first day calls on a buyer. Since he has been well trained, he glances about the office for something to establish rapport. No personal touches are evident, other than one very obvious item: a large stuffed moose head directly behind the buyer.

Naturally, he says to the buyer, "Gee, that's a good-looking moose head."

The buyer looks back at it and remarks, "You think so? I think it's kind of ugly myself. Hate the thing."

The salesperson recovers, "Yeah, now that I look at it more closely, I can see what you mean. But it's interesting. Where did you shoot it?"

"I didn't shoot it."

Again the salesperson is confused but he soldiers on: "Oh. But you are a hunter?"

"Never hunted in my life," is the unexpected response.

None of the role-playing in the sales-training classes prepared the novice salesperson for this bizarre sequence of events. He departs from the script and queries, "If you don't mind me asking: You're not a hunter, you didn't shoot it, you don't particularly like it—then why do you hang the moose head in your office?"

The buyer snorts, "The reason it's there is so salespeople can come in and ask me dumb questions about it, we can get that over with, and then move on to business. Now what would you really like to talk about?"

While most people are more polite about it, often that same concern is dominating prospects' thoughts when we're chit-chatting about the weather or the kids: What do you really want to talk about? It doesn't mean that when you're meeting clients you have known for years, or you know outside the client relationship, or with whom you share common interests that you shouldn't engage in those familiar warm-ups, catching up on their lives. But contrary to the general perception, as a rule when you're meeting with prospects you don't know well, you should use the preliminary stage as a launch pad to set the agenda for the meeting itself.

"What we agreed," you begin, "is that we're here today to talk about so-and-so, this-and-that, and some-more-of-that. We're going to take, based on our conversation, roughly forty-five minutes. Are you comfortable with that?" That businesslike approach conforms to the two-minute rule: You're not meandering but showing purpose and efficiency. And it prepares you to move quickly into the key part of the closing process: the questioning.

Getting the Client to Open Up

The key to that process is to pose questions that encourage the prospective client to open up. That requires non-threatening queries that are open-ended and that inspire the client to elaborate. Ask questions like:

- "What experiences have you had with investing up to this point?"
- "What is it about investing in the past you found most enjoyable?"
- "What is it about investing you found least enjoyable?"

As the prospect talks, get in the habit of saying:

- "Tell me more about that."
- "Could you elaborate on that?"
- "Could you give me a little more detail on that?"

Once you've extracted information, the next step is to formulate appropriate recommendations. Some salespeople practice the grenade approach to selling. They act as if they're in a foxhole, armed with several boxes of grenades, while their client is stationed in a trench nearby. They pick up a grenade and lob it over. After it explodes they peek out to see if a white flag has risen. If no white flag appears, they reach down for another grenade—they have lots—and throw that over, checking again for the white flag. They keep throwing and throwing, until the buyer concedes: "All right, I'll buy."

The premise is that if you make the right recommendation—lob the right grenade—the client will buy. So the more recommendations you lob, the more likely you are to hit a nerve with the client. "Are you interested in these conservative government bonds? No? Well how about these hog bellies?"

While that attitude may occasionally work in your favor, more frequently it operates against you. Pressing an idea your client views as inappropriate doesn't increase her confidence that her adviser truly understands her needs and is weaving recommendations to her situation. Contrary to the grenade-lobbing premise, substantial research demonstrates the fewer recommendations you make, the more likely a successful outcome, providing those recommendations meet the Client's 99 as revealed by your questioning.

Dealing with Objections

Most salespeople desperately hope to avoid the next stage in the sales process: dealing with objections. Salespeople have traditionally viewed objections as the enemy. If we pulled out grenades for lobbing recommendations, we called in the heavy artillery for this battle, employing our tanks to crush any objections. Objections seemed to stand between us and the treasured land.

Interestingly, research has discovered that often the best financial advisers are remarkably poor in dealing with objections. They're stellar at building rapport, excellent at asking questions, fine at presenting solutions, but they're not particularly adept at handling objections. The reason, I've concluded, is that successful financial advisers don't have much experience dealing with objections.

The people who manage objections the best are the promoters calling out of boiler rooms, selling penny stocks. They spend all day fielding objections, so they become skilled at deflecting concerns. Successful financial advisers operate in a totally different manner. They don't provoke a lot of objections, so why should they be skilled at handling them?

Our research shows that if advisers invest time at the front end asking questions that enable them to frame recommendations which satisfy the client's needs, objections fade. Such prudence persuades clients that your recommendation is aligned to their needs, rather than being advanced because it's the investment of the week or carries a higher commission.

Of course, objections will arise. The instinctive reaction is to quash them and, accordingly, advisers have been taught various defensive approaches. One popular tactic is a diversion based on apparently shared feelings. Let's say the client worries the investment would be too risky. You respond: "Ms. Client, I understand how you feel. Most of my clients have felt the same way. On closer examination, however, they found that the investment wasn't too risky, and in fact the greatest risk you face is that you will have insufficient resources to live on when you retire. I understand how you feel—other clients have felt the same way, believe me—but they discovered it was nothing to worry about."

That's an effective method, in many cases, of vaulting past the objection. But you haven't answered it. It has been cast aside temporarily, because the client feels pressured, since those other, presumably smarter clients aren't concerned about the same investment. But you pay a price, since the objection remains as a submerged concern that could resurface.

I've watched salespeople in meetings suppress an objection with this handy diversion and then, when they press to close the sale, the client unexpectedly hesitates. "I need some time to think about it," the client will say. Or, "I'm not sure yet."

The salesperson walks away frustrated: "Those darn clients, they can never make up their minds! I wish I could deal with clients who weren't perpetually procrastinating." Some of those clients may indeed be procrastinators, congenitally unable to form a decision. But most of them are perfectly capable of smooth decision-making in all other aspects of their lives. Arguably, the stumbling block is that the adviser has foiled rather than faced their expression of their concerns.

I believe you should encourage rather than stifle objections. After presenting recommendations, you should say, "Mr. Client/Ms. Client, at this point often people I talk to will have some questions that haven't been answered or perhaps concerns on some of the things I've outlined. That's perfectly natural. What among the things that we've talked about so far are you not entirely clear about, have some questions about, or perhaps are concerned about?"

A client can easily voice his concern after that invitation. He might indicate he doesn't have any concerns, in which case you cheerfully move on. But if he does have an objection, you certainly want to hear it. By asking the question, you haven't created the concern. It was already there. But you've brought it to the table, where you can deal with it.

Begin by ensuring that you fully understand the problem. Ask some open-ended questions, in a non-threatening way. "That's a very common concern. I hear it often. Tell me why you feel that way" is a reassuring way to continue exploring the objection. Make it as safe as possible for the client to express his feelings.

After you have fully heard the objection, you must calculate whether it's valid. Perhaps you have recommended stocks, and he balks: "I owned stock once and I made a little money, but frankly I didn't sleep soundly for the whole period I owned it."

It's quite possible that prospect shouldn't own stock. "Mr. Prospect," you might respond, "many people share your feelings, and that's absolutely understandable. Why don't we look at some alternatives that perhaps you'll be more comfortable with."

On the other hand, it's possible that the client doesn't fully understand because you haven't communicated properly. In fact, the concern about risky investments—clients' fears that they will lose their money—is probably the number-one objection confronting advisers. But our response is generally misdirected at our 99 rather than the Client's 99. We rebut with charts and graphs that gratify us, because that's our 99, but don't have nearly the same client impact.

Marketing Solutions research found the best way to react to that concern is to place it in context. Offer an analogy:

"Mr. Prospect, I understand how you feel. Certainly none of us wants to think we might lose our money. So that's a concern many clients have; you're not alone. What you really have to decide is your priorities. We can find investments without that short-term volatility, but the cost is that in the process you might not get where you want to end up.

"It's like taking a plane trip. You board a plane heading from New York to Los Angeles. What percentage of the passengers are on that flight because they enjoy flying? Virtually nobody. They're on board because they need to get from Point A to Point B, and flying is the most efficient and effective method. For some, it's the only way of reaching that destination, because they don't have the time to drive, take a bus or train, hitchhike, or walk. It's the only alternative.

"Let's say an hour after takeoff the plane hits turbulence. Many passengers, particularly those who haven't flown before, become quite apprehensive. They're convinced it's the end—the plane is about to crash. If parachutes were readily available, they would evacuate. Experienced travellers, on the other hand, shrug their shoulders. They're not happy with the turbulence, but they recognize it's the price you sometimes have to pay for getting from Point A to Point B. They tighten their seatbelts, try to divert their attention to other matters, and wait it out.

"That's what investing really is. Investments that bump up and down from time to time are the price you pay to travel efficiently to your financial destination. But you have to make those decisions for yourself. Only you can decide if you're prepared to put up with some turbulence. There's no right or wrong answer. But you have to understand that if we select investments that don't have any turbulence, you will pay a price."

In our research, that effectively places investing in perspective. Since advisers should anticipate turbulence—as well as client concern over such turbulence—it's worth bringing the objection to the fore, so that it can be discussed well before it becomes an entrenched obstacle.

Less Is More

Closing is the final step. Many articles counsel that you have to cast your line, asking for the order five, six, or seven times before reeling it in. In other words, expect to hear "no" four, five, or six times before obtaining the glorious "yes."

In the early '90s, however, an organization called Huthwaite, Inc. conducted research, summarized in Dr. Neil Rackham's book, *Spin Selling*, that demolished that belief. They observed 575 calls by American Airlines representatives, monitoring how many times the seller asked for the order, and correlated that with the ultimate effectiveness of the call. They found the most effective number of times to ask for an order is once: 60 percent of the time a sale resulted from just one request. The next most effective frequency was twice, producing a 35 percent success rate. In third spot was zero times: That suggests you're better not asking for the order at all rather than to ask three or four times. (Figure 19.2).

Figure 19.2

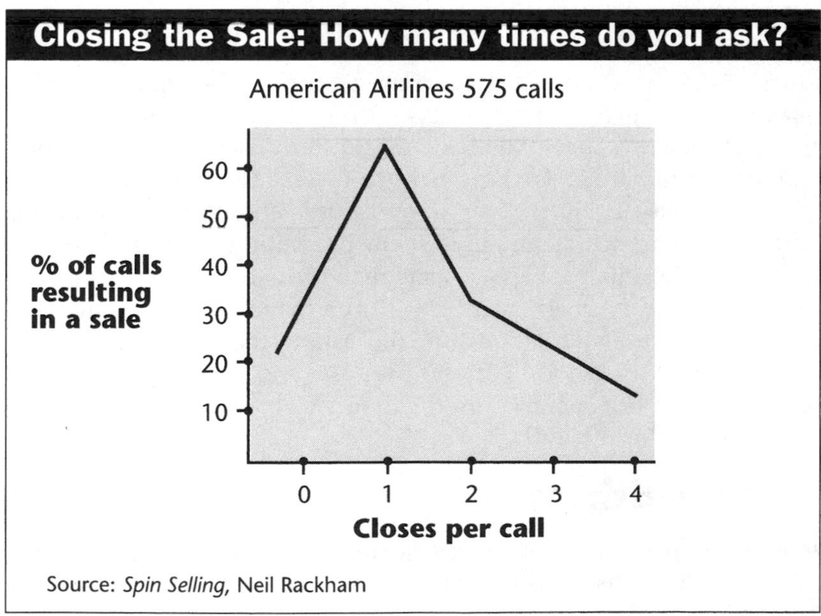

Figure 19.3

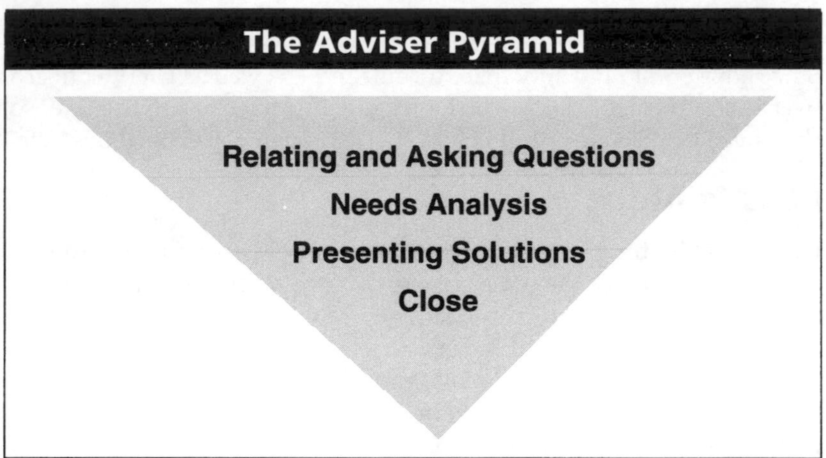

If you think about the client relationship, that's perfectly logical. If you prematurely ask the client for a decision on the sale and he or she declines, the relationship deteriorates. The client has experienced unwanted pressure. You've been rebuffed, forced to retreat a step. The relationship has suffered. Ideally you only want to close once. You want to ask the client for the order once and only once.

Traditional salespeople with a pressure-based orientation have often portrayed the selling process as a pyramid. While that metaphor is helpful, unfortunately their characterization of the process has been distinctly unhelpful, because they turn everything upside-down. They have viewed the pyramid's top part—relating, asking questions, and determining needs—as the least important elements. Instead, they've concentrated on the bottom: presenting solutions and getting the order. Advisers have to reverse that pyramid (Figure 19.3). The least amount of an adviser's time should be spent at the bottom, closing, with some time spent presenting solutions. But the most time, as our rookie salesperson with a half-hour to present learned, should be spent at the top of the pyramid, interacting with the client, forming a relationship, and asking the open-ended questions that will lead to a successful proposal and elicit any objections so the sale can be concluded on the first try. That will be the effective selling model for the future.

Snapshots

✔ *More nonsense has been written on closing methods—the final step in the selling process—than on the rest of the selling process put together.*

- ✔ *Instead of trying the latest sure-fire closing technique, it's wise to look at the sales process in context. The challenge in closing is to respond to the Client's 99, notably the client's balancing of the benefits of doing business versus the risk.*
- ✔ *Until the mid-1950s it was believed that selling couldn't be taught, since it was an inborn art. Xerox's professional selling skills program, PSS, revolutionized the field because it provided a structured approach to selling that evolved into the current five-step process.*
- ✔ *Research shows the only factor that correlates consistently with a successful sales experience is the step that traditionally tended to get overlooked: the amount of time spent asking questions, getting the client talking, and listening.*
- ✔ *Building rapport is important but generally overdone. Contrary to the general perception, when you're meeting with prospects you don't know well, you should as a rule use the preliminary stage to set the agenda for the meeting itself, then move on to questioning.*
- ✔ *The key to the questioning process is to ask questions that encourage the prospective client to open up. This calls for non-threatening questions that are open-ended and inspire the client to elaborate.*
- ✔ *Once you've extracted information, the next step is to formulate appropriate recommendations. But avoid the indiscriminate, grenade-tossing approach. If you press an idea that your client doesn't view as appropriate, it doesn't increase confidence in you. Substantial research demonstrates that the fewer recommendations you make, the more likely you are to have a successful outcome, providing those recommendations meet the Client's 99 as revealed by your questioning.*
- ✔ *Historically, salespeople viewed objections as the enemy. But it makes better sense to encourage objections than to stifle them.*
- ✔ *Sometimes the objections are perfectly valid and should be heeded. The most common objection is risk. That is best dealt with by the airplane turbulence analogy, which allows clients to clarify their own willingness to take risks.*
- ✔ *With closing, less is more. Try to ask for the sale only once.*
- ✔ *When interacting with a prospect, the most time should be spent trying to understand their needs by asking questions.*

CHAPTER 20

Prospecting Through Trade Shows

A PROSPECTING VEHICLE MOST ADVISERS TRY, PARTICULARLY WHEN NEW AT the business, is to arrange a booth at a local trade show. They hand out material; collect the names of prospective clients, generally through a draw; and after the event pursue the people they met. But the majority of advisers who test that technique abandon it in frustration after the first or second attempt. They don't find it a productive use of their time.

A major impediment, rarely considered, is that most trade shows create the wrong environment for financial advisers. If you set up at an automobile show or a home show—two of the biggest draws in many communities—people are there to tempt themselves with the latest innovations in cars or homes, not to discuss saving for the future. They will probably be oblivious to you amid the many dazzling attractions that lured them to the event. They might even feel imposed upon by your approach.

Another obstacle is the clutter. Drawing attention is often an enormous challenge. As well, when you're positioned standing or sitting behind a booth at a trade show, passersby immediately view you as a salesperson out to pitch something. That's not the most positive context to initiate an advisery relationship.

Still, booths can be a highly effective prospecting vehicle—providing we employ them properly. We have to view the show as an efficient channel to talk to a large number of prospects, some of whom might qualify for our prospect pipeline and a few of whom might be interested in doing business soon. We have to rearrange our approach to overcome the barriers at trade shows and maximize our attainable goals.

The first step is to critically evaluate the venue itself. It's smart to focus your energy on trade shows and meetings that have a financial or business orientation. Pure consumer shows don't generate the right ambiance to initiate a financial discussion.

Location, Location, Location

Once you've selected an appropriate venue, take care arranging your location within the show. Booth location is critical, yet too many advisers leave that to chance. They arrive the morning of the show to discover where they're stationed—whether they have been lucky or unlucky. In most cases it doesn't take much more money to secure the most advantageous location, and sometimes you won't even have to pay extra if at an early stage you remark, "I would like, before committing, to have an indication of where my booth will be."

With care and thought, and operating from the Client 99, trade shows can be effective prospecting vehicles.

Often advisers press for a busy location, perhaps by the entrance. But that's generally the least-conducive place for holding a decent conversation with prospective clients. Instead, you want a location with a reasonable amount of traffic—you don't want to be stuck off in a corner—but not so much traffic that you can't focus individually on people wandering by. Ideally, you also want to be placed at the end of a row, since it's easier to chat privately there than between two booths. It's worth paying a modest premium to reserve such a spot, as it will considerably enhance your effectiveness.

Once you have obtained the right venue and right location, the next focal point is arranging the look of your booth. It has to project a professional image. A card table, a leftover poster from 1989, and some brochures don't cut it. If you intend to invest your time on a trade show, you have to invest energy and money on a professional backdrop that broadcasts the proper message rather than undercuts your efforts. Often head office will have such materials available or in some cases you can borrow them from fund companies. They ensure a perfectly professional image for your booth.

The Value of Eye Contact

Once you have the right venue, right location and right look, the next step is to yank yourself out from behind the table. The most common mistake of advisers at trade shows is to place a table at the front of the booth and sit or stand behind it, waiting for prospects to approach them. The table is a barrier. Get rid of it. If you absolutely need a table for printed material, shove it to the back of the booth. With the booth's front area open, plunk yourself there and make eye contact with prospective clients.

In the past, when I ran election campaigns in downtown Toronto, we arranged for volunteers to pass out literature in the morning at subway stops as people were streaming to work, the premise being that they would have some time to read our campaign offerings on the subway. Many times volunteers would return and say, "That was terrible! It was so humiliating. People ignored me, brushed by me, refused the material. I'll never do it again."

We'd return together to the subway station. As people approached I'd look them in the eye, smile, and say, "Good morning." Almost always, people in return would respond, "Good morning." Then I'd extend the literature toward them and say, "Can I offer you one of these?" Again, almost always, they'd say, "Sure."

I have no idea how long they spent actually looking at the material. It's a numbers game—some glance at or read the material, others throw it in the garbage when they pass the corner. But very seldom were people rude. Very seldom did they brush by. Why? Because of the eye contact, the smile and the brief connection made as they smiled in return.

The same principle applies for prospecting at a trade show. As people wander by, since you can't chat with everyone, evaluate from appearances the likelihood that an individual might be a suitable prospect. Create eye contact with those who appear promising and wish them a "Good morning" or "Good afternoon." When they respond, as most will, with a duplicate greeting, you've opened an avenue for discussion.

Non-Threatening Openings

Now you need a non-threatening way to continue the connection. You want to give the person a solid reason to talk further, which is the only way to establish a relationship. One effective technique we've tried is asking, "Have you had a chance to take an investor literacy test?" In most cases, they respond, "No, I haven't." You continue, "Well, would you like to? It'll only take three or four minutes, and you'll find out how much you know."

Obviously not everyone will be interested. But a significant number will say, "Sure, that sounds kind of interesting." You're providing value, giving them a chance to check their knowledge.

When they've completed the test (Figure 20.1), you need a relatively low-threat follow-up. That's not: "I have an opening available on my schedule tomorrow morning at 9:15." Instead, try something like, "You know, we have a seminar on retirement planning coming up and I'd like to send you an invitation. Could I do that?"

Figure 20.1

Investor Literacy Test

This test is based on telephone interviews conducted by Marketing Solutions among principal or joint financial decision-makers in 1,000 Canadian households with savings and investments of $10,000 or more. The telephone interviews were conducted in 1996. The results for all respondents as well as the correct answers follow.

1. To the best of your knowledge, if you have invested in a mutual fund containing bonds or mortgages and interest rates went up, what would happen to the value of your fund? Would the value of your mutual fund likely increase in value, stay the same or decrease in value?

- ❑ Increase in value
- ❑ Decrease in value
- ❑ Stay the same
- ❑ Don't know

2. To the best of your knowledge, what is the maximum percentage of RRSP investments that can be put into investments outside of Canada?

- ❑ 20%
- ❑ Under 20%
- ❑ Over 20%
- ❑ Don't know

3. Let's say you had a choice of receiving $1,000 in bank interest, $1,000 in rental income, $1,000 in dividends from a Canadian stock or $1,000 as a bonus from an employer. Which of these should give you the most dollars after deducting the taxes owed?

- ❑ Dividends
- ❑ Net rental income
- ❑ Bank interest
- ❑ All the same after taxes
- ❑ Bonus
- ❑ Don't know

4. Let's say you've been investing in shares typical of those sold on the Toronto Stock Exchange for the last 20 years. To the best of your knowledge, in how many of those 20 years did the stock market go up?

- ❑ 12 out of 20
- ❑ 15 out of 20
- ❑ 10 out of 20
- ❑ 7 out of 20
- ❑ 4 out of 20

5. Let's say that you had a $100,000 five-year GIC with a chartered bank. If the bank that you held the GIC with went out of business, what is the maximum amount of your funds that would be protected by the Canadian government through the CDIC?

- ❑ $60,000
- ❑ $100,000
- ❑ $75,000
- ❑ $25,000
- ❑ $40,000
- ❑ Don't know

6. Please tell me which of the following investments, over the long term, that is since 1950, provided Canadians with the best returns, before any taxes which were due? To the best of your knowledge is it:

- ❑ Canadian Savings Bonds
- ❑ U.S. stocks
- ❑ Long-term corporate bonds
- ❑ Canadian stocks
- ❑ 5 year GICs
- ❑ Don't know

7. And which of those same investments over the long term, since 1950, provided Canadians with the worst returns before any taxes that were due?

- ❑ Canadian Savings Bonds
- ❑ U.S. stocks
- ❑ Long-term corporate bonds
- ❑ Canadian stocks
- ❑ 5 year GICs
- ❑ Don't know

8. To the best of your knowledge, which of the following best describes a "capital gain"? Would it be:

- ❑ The profit you make when you sell stocks or bonds
- ❑ The annual increase in your net worth
- ❑ The interest you received on an investment
- ❑ The increase in value of your RRSP investments
- ❑ Financial gifts from another family member
- ❑ Don't know

Investor Literacy Results

Overall results for the 1,000 Canadians
Correct Answers: 2.7 out of 8
Incorrect Answers: 3.0 out of 8
Did Not Know: 2.3 out of 8

1. To the best of your knowledge, if you have invested in a mutual fund containing bonds or mortgages and interest rates went up, what would happen to the value of your fund? Would the value of your mutual fund likely increase in value, stay the same or decrease in value?

❑ Increase in value	% Answering Correctly: 36%
☑ Decrease in value	% Answering Incorrectly: 52%
❑ Stay the same	% Answering Do Not Know: 12%
❑ Don't know	

2. To the best of your knowledge, what is the maximum percentage of RRSP investments that can be put into investments outside of Canada?

☑ 20%	% Answering Correctly: 22%
❑ Under 20%	% Answering Incorrectly: 27%
❑ Over 20%	% Answering Do Not Know: 51%
❑ Don't know	

3. Let's say you had a choice of receiving $1,000 in bank interest, $1,000 in rental income, $1,000 in dividends from a Canadian stock or $1,000 as a bonus from an employer. Which of these should give you the most dollars after deducting the taxes owed?

☑ Dividends	% Answering Correctly: 36%
❑ Net rental income	% Answering Incorrectly: 32%
❑ Bank interest	% Answering Do Not Know: 32%
❑ All the same after taxes	
❑ Bonus	
❑ Don't know	

4. Let's say you've been investing in shares typical of those sold on the Toronto Stock Exchange for the last 20 years. To the best of your knowledge, in how many of those 20 years did the stock market go up?

❑ 12 out of 20	% Answering Correctly: 18%
☑ 15 out of 20	% Answering Incorrectly: 49%
❑ 10 out of 20	% Answering Do Not Know: 33%
❑ 7 out of 20	
❑ 4 out of 20	
❑ Don't know	

5. Let's say that you had a $100,000 five-year GIC with a chartered bank. If the bank that you held the GIC with went out of business, what is the maximum amount of your funds that would be protected by the Canadian government through the CDIC?

- [x] $60,000
- [ ] $100,000
- [ ] $75,000
- [ ] $25,000
- [ ] $40,000
- [ ] Don't know

% Answering Correctly: 56%
% Answering Incorrectly: 29%
% Answering Do Not Know: 15%

6. Please tell me which of the following investments, over the long term, that is since 1950, provided Canadians with the best returns, before any taxes which were due? To the best of your knowledge is it:

- [ ] Canadian Savings Bonds
- [x] U.S. stocks
- [ ] Long-term corporate bonds
- [ ] Canadian stocks
- [ ] 5 year GICs
- [ ] Don't know

% Answering Correctly: 22%
% Answering Incorrectly: 60%
% Answering Do Not Know: 18%

7. And which of those same investments over the long term, since 1950, provided Canadians with the worst returns before any taxes that were due?

- [ ] Canadian Savings Bonds
- [ ] U.S. stocks
- [ ] Long-term corporate bonds
- [ ] Canadian stocks
- [x] 5 year GICs
- [ ] Don't know

% Answering Correctly: 17%
% Answering Incorrectly: 61%
% Answering Do Not Know: 22%

8. To the best of your knowledge, which of the following best describes a "capital gain"? Would it be:

- [x] The profit you make when you sell stocks or bonds
- [ ] The annual increase in your net worth
- [ ] The interest you received on an investment
- [ ] The increase in value of your RRSP investments
- [ ] Financial gifts from another family member
- [ ] Don't know

% Answering Correctly: 52%
% Answering Incorrectly: 38%
% Answering Do Not Know: 10%

In most cases, again, people will cheerfully agree. And that avails you the opportunity to capture their name, address, and phone number for your prospecting pipeline. Another alternative is to build in a draw for anybody who completes the investor literacy test. That provides an added incentive to take the test and requires them to leave their name and particulars. Some advisers even offer a handout that allows test-takers to compare their performance with others who tried it. People love tests, love to know how they score, and love to know whether they're smarter than the next person.

If you follow the process I've just outlined, in no more than six to eight minutes you will have identified through a visual scan some possible prospects, established initial contact with some, chatted briefly with one, provided some value, started to build some trust, and edged him or her into the prospect pipeline. That's obviously more effective than heading off to the trade show without careful thought and passing out material indiscriminately, hoping for some fireworks.

The downside to this approach is that you can't talk to everyone. You'll only hit 5 to 10 percent of the people attending the show. But the return you get from targeting whom you talk with—even if only in a rough way—and then dealing with them in some depth to start building a relationship is much greater than if you simply sit behind a booth, not differentiating yourself from everybody else flogging their wares at that particular trade show.

Snapshots

✔ *The majority of advisers who try trade shows as a way to find prospects abandon the approach in frustration after the first or second effort. But booths can be very effective prospecting vehicles—providing you use them properly.*

✔ *You have to view the show as an efficient channel to talk to a large number of prospects, some of whom might qualify for your prospect pipeline and a few of whom might be interested in doing business soon.*

✔ *Focus your energy on trade shows and meetings that have a financial or business orientation rather than car, home, or boat shows.*

✔ *Locate your booth in a reasonably busy area but one that affords you enough quiet and privacy to talk comfortably with guests. It's worth paying a modest premium for an end-of-row position.*

✔ *Your booth must project a professional image. Often head office will have the right props available. In some cases you can also borrow them from fund companies.*

- ✔ *Don't let the traditional table out front in such booths serve as a barrier between the public and you. With the booth's front area open, locate yourself in that spot, pick out likely prospects, make eye contact, and wish them a "Good morning" or "Good afternoon."*
- ✔ *One effective technique is then to offer them a chance to take an investor literacy test. Afterward, you can advise them of an upcoming seminar and capture their names for your prospecting pipeline. Or you could give them an opportunity for a draw, again capturing names and particulars.*
- ✔ *In no more than six to eight minutes, you've visually identified some possible prospects, established contact with some, chatted briefly with one, provided some value, started to build some trust, and edged him or her into the prospect pipeline.*

CHAPTER 21

Running Effective Seminars

SEMINARS EMERGED AS ONE OF THE HOT PROSPECTING TOOLS OF THE '90S. Whether advisers run sessions at which they are the featured expert or bring in guest lecturers, the ability to leverage their time through mingling with a lot of prospects and clients at one time is obviously attractive.

Three components are required for an effective seminar program. You have to get prospects into a room. You have to deliver an effective, motivating message while they're present. And you have to convert those attendees into clients, over time.

To run an effective seminar program, all three elements are mandatory. You can lure prospects to the event and deliver a stimulating message, but if you can't convert them into clients, the seminar wasn't effective. Or you can deliver a rousing message but if you didn't draw a large number of prospects, again you won't receive much of a return for your time and effort. So all the factors are important.

Some advisers are intimidated by public speaking and find that element the hardest of the three. But you can always delegate the speaking to someone else—an analyst from your firm, a representative of a mutual fund company, a local accountant—while still maintaining the host role in front of prospects for yourself. What you can't delegate—and therefore the toughest element—is getting the prospects into the room.

Before attracting them to the session, however, it helps to know the seminar's exact objective. This can differ widely from adviser to adviser. Some seminars, for example, are designed to generate short-term sales. I've attended seminars where at the outset the adviser locks the doors and announces, "Putting on this seminar costs $6,000, so nobody's leaving until we pay the $6,000 back." It's known as the time-share approach to hosting seminars.

Another tactic, somewhat more subtle, is to place a strong emphasis from the seminar's start on booking a meeting. "If you don't book a meeting before you leave today you'll miss the opportunity of a lifetime, you'll die destitute, you'll be eating dog food in your retirement. . . ." Not my favorite, but it does work for some advisers.

Other seminars are product focused, which is fine, if that's your objective and you clearly outlined it in the invitation. On the other hand, the bait-and-switch technique doesn't work: inviting prospects to a talk on tax-saving strategy only to hit them with a two-hour sales pitch on limited partnerships. It erodes your trust, enrages your guests, and empties your prospect pipeline.

Advisers must ensure that the quality and value of seminars will be high and the sales pressure low.

The seminar approach that our firm considers most fruitful is to focus on education and cultivating relationships. The seminar glides people into the pipeline and slides them along if they're already inside.

You should view a seminar as part of a long-term series rather than an isolated event. Many advisers experiment with a seminar, find it harder work than anticipated, and abandon the strategy. But any program has a learning curve. If you aren't prepared to dedicate the time, effort, and discipline to moving along that learning curve, you probably shouldn't be attempting that form of prospecting anyway. Whether it's advertising, direct mail, or seminars, you must commit fully to the activity as an ongoing part of your prospecting arsenal.

The number of prospects you intend to target obviously affects the workshop's structure and location. Some advisers aim at small groups, running the sessions in their office or a convenient boardroom. Others focus on large-scale events and rent outside space. It depends on your priorities and budget. Another consideration is whether you or a guest will be the main speaker. In many respects, the best alternative is to combine, since an outside speaker can imbue confidence in your prospective clients.

The final issue is budget. Too often advisers fail to consider all the costs involved in a seminar—rental, refreshments, audio-visual expense, promotion, speaker honoraria, mailing and staff costs. Halfway through the preparations, they frantically discover it's costing far more than anticipated, so they cut corners. Afterward, they're surprised it hasn't been more successful. You need to tailor the event to a realistic budget, established at the beginning of the prospecting process.

Why Is the Seminar Being Held?

Since the springboard to a successful seminar is persuading people to attend, the key question we must tackle is: What's the barrier to their coming? As with all of human affairs, the answers are diverse. Some people are too busy. Others have attended a previous seminar with a similar subject matter. For some, the topic simply lacks any appeal. But the number-one reason prospects don't attend is that they're nervous they might have a bad experience. They worry that it will be a waste of time, they'll be pressured, or the quality of the workshop won't be particularly high—in essence, their confidence in the likely quality and value of the experience isn't sufficiently high.

In arranging the seminar, therefore, advisers must address that apprehension. It should be done on three fronts: the offer or the reason for coming, how you spread the word, and the follow-up.

Let's start with the offer, since the workshop topic will be one of your first decisions. It's almost always better to make the topic broad in nature, and educationally oriented, as opposed to product focused. Prospects tend to be wary if they're invited to a seminar on "The Five Best Stocks to Buy Today." Some people will certainly turn out, but you will draw fewer than to a workshop titled "How to Select the Stocks That Are Right for You."

People want education and information from seminars, and the more strongly you communicate that those will be the event's essence, the more likely they'll be to show up. In our research, by the way, the number one hot-button for seminars has been—and likely will continue to be for the foreseeable future—tax-savings strategies.

After settling on a topic, you need to pick a speaker. If you're a good speaker, that's one possibility. But remembering the hesitation that prospects instinctively feel about attending workshops, it's worth considering how much added credibility and trust the seminar will inspire if you feature an outside speaker. This is obviously a touchy issue since the adviser pays the shot. On more than one occasion I've been told, "It's tough to lure people to a seminar, and I've only got them for an hour to ninety minutes. I want all the light to shine on me. I don't want to share the visibility." But our research shows consistently that with a credible outside speaker—most commonly an accountant or a lawyer—attendance increases. People are more confident they will have a good experience and obtain valuable information.

Other factors support that direction as well. Your credibility, if you are on a panel with an accountant and lawyer, for example, heightens as you link yourself to their credibility. You face significantly less work because you only have to prepare comments for part of the seminar. And your likelihood of gaining referrals from the other professionals on the panel shoots up because of the exposure you generously granted them.

The key is to share responsibility, not abdicate it. You still want to remain in the spotlight. You probably want to speak for at least half the program. After all, at the end of the session you don't want your prospects exclaiming, "Wasn't that accountant fascinating! I think I'll give him a call about helping me with my taxes." That's not the objective. You want to borrow the other professionals' credibility to leverage turnout but not restrict your own role to the point where your own credibility isn't boosted by the session.

Location Is Key

Advisers often overlook the importance of seminar location. They decide on cost, booking the public library or the Holiday Inn to keep the outlay low. But they may pay a big price in attendance and credibility for that saving. Prospects judge the seminar's merits in part on location. In our experience, the best seminar locations are somewhat exclusive and carry a certain cachet. Private clubs and country clubs often work best because they add a subtle message about the adviser's status. They also give people who have not seen the inside of the club an extra incentive to attend.

Refreshments are the final element of the offer you extend to invited guests. To run a successful seminar you certainly don't need to incur exorbitant costs for fancy hors d'oeuvres or a big meal, but it makes sense to offer light refreshments, be it wine and cheese or coffee and pastries. Pick the best you can afford, given the size of the event and what people would expect at that time of day. It definitely affects the mood of the guests and again transmits a statement about you.

Mike Robertson, a Houston broker who spoke at one of our Top Performers conferences, prospects at the very high end, targeting individuals with more than half-a-million dollars to invest. He hosts luncheon seminars in various cities across the United States, booking a private room in the best restaurants. He'll then mail his select list of prospects a personally addressed invitation, in the process offering a statement about the caliber of his clients and the kind of people likely to be joining the invitee for the seminar.

After you have the offer—topic, speaker(s), location, and refreshments—you have to get the word out. That is actually a two-edged consideration: Who do you want to invite and how do you intend to reach them?

You could buy a large newspaper ad and invite everyone interested. While that has the virtue of broad distribution, newspaper advertising often gets submerged in the clutter, and you lose control over who appears. Those attending would be self-selecting and the people eager to come may not be your ideal prospects. A similar approach, but more targeted, would be direct mail. It takes more effort, but you could buy a mailing list or select an area that is likely to generate the type of prospects you're eyeing.

Seminars, as we've discussed before, are an excellent, low-threat avenue for inviting friends and acquaintances in the hopes of moving them closer to working with you as an adviser. They are helpful for sliding prospects along the pipeline. Current clients will find value in the seminar and might, as we've discussed, recommend friends for your invitation list. Past clients also shouldn't be overlooked. Many firms have a list of former clients who switched, perhaps along with their adviser, and maybe the subsequent experience has not been totally satisfactory; a seminar invitation might be the first step to returning them under your tent.

Finally, don't forget to ask your guest speaker if any of his or her clients should be invited. It's a way of leveraging the speaker's participation, extending the guest list, and broadening your exposure to what are undoubtedly appropriate prospects for your business.

Advertising the Seminar

Once you've decided who to invite, you have to convey the message to them. Generally, mass-marketing vehicles such as ads, posters, and even direct mail won't hit your main targets. Mailed invitations are usually the most effective vehicle. The key, though, is their appearance. Again, the invitation makes a statement, and it must heighten your appeal and the seminar's appeal. These days engraved invitations, similar to those for weddings, work best.

Mike Robertson, after booking exclusive restaurants, sends the invitation with a wedding-style reply card. It reads: "Mr. Robertson, I will be joining you for lunch on May 18th. For my entrée I would prefer (check one) filet mignon or shrimp scampi." Why bother with that card? As Mike says, "I don't care if people eat the filet mignon, the shrimp, or the breadbasket. What I want, however, is to send a very clear message to those prospects about the kind of event it's going to be, who it's targeted to, and who else is likely to be there." The invitation, with reply card, subtly presents that message.

Mike also has a fascinating follow-up for invited guests who fail to show up at the seminar, despite having confirmed their attendance and receiving a reminder call the morning of the event. He phones them the next day and says, "Mr. Prospect/Ms. Prospect, it's Mike Robertson here. I'm calling to apologize. You know there were so many people at the seminar yesterday—it was so successful—that I unfortunately didn't have a chance to come around and say hello. But

I'm calling to chat and find out how you enjoyed it. What did you think of the program?" About half the time people are so embarrassed they agree to meet with him even though they didn't attend.

It's important to remember, as Mike's experience shows, that not everyone who promises to attend actually does. Some people forget. For others, more pressing business intervenes. In still other cases, since the workshop is not considered a very high commitment by the invited guests, it doesn't take much to divert them to spend their time elsewhere. They glance at the TV listings, notice a new episode of *Friends*, and decide to stay home instead. If it had been a repeat they would have attended, but a new show takes precedence.

Some develop cold feet. As the event approaches, they decide not to expose themselves to the possibility of an uncomfortable experience. Finally, perhaps underlying all those other reasons, some guests don't perceive the seminar as offering any great value for them.

That is familiar territory. Many advisers find it worth applying the same technique here that they employ to add value and reduce the risk in initial meetings: a confirmation letter with an information package. The cover letter outlines the seminar line-up. It's supplemented by material fleshing out the topic and speaker, along with one or two articles from credible outside sources. It increases the prospects' confidence that the experience will be positive and also elevates the sense of obligation to attend, reducing the chance that *Friends* will divert them.

Delivering an Effective Message

After all that preparation, the seminar date arrives. You've drawn 50, 100, or 150 prospects to the affair. The challenge now is to deliver an effective message, remembering again that the focus should be on education as opposed to hard sell. Multiple speakers are generally more effective, not only because of their added credibility but also because they allow for more breaks and offer contrasting styles, making it easier for the audience to pay attention.

A related issue is the session's length. Within reason, shorter is probably better than long. Given our 99, we can listen to ourselves pontificate for a long time. It's not quite the same from our Prospect's 99. As a rule of thumb, if you're the sole speaker, an hour is the absolute maximum that an audience will pay attention. A speaker has to be superb to hold someone's attention longer. With a couple of speakers, perhaps you can edge the session up to an hour and a quarter or an hour and a half.

Those practical time restrictions are why lunch-and-learn seminars in a boardroom make eminent sense. They lend themselves to a relatively short presentation: prospects are in by noon, finish their sandwich by 12:15, the talk begins, and they're out the door by 1:00 or

1:15. Those sessions often are easier to attend, as part of the work day, rather than evening seminars which require prospects to rush home, eat a quick dinner, and go out again despite the appeal of that new episode of *Friends* they noticed.

Visuals and handouts are absolutely critical at seminars. Without such material, it's much harder for the audience to pay attention and retain the information. Generally, the seating at seminars is not conducive to paying attention: rows and rows of chairs, with nothing to write or rest your hands on. It's far more productive if you can arrange for your prospects to be seated at round tables. They can jot down notes, enjoy coffee or tea, and generally feel more relaxed and comfortable. It will cost more, because a bigger room is required, but the enhanced experience suggests it's worth considering.

A pitfall of most seminars is that they're one-way: the speaker talks and the audience listens. Mostly that's unavoidable, but it helps if you foster audience involvement, periodically stopping, writing down key ideas, and encouraging your guests to take notes.

Sparking Audience Involvement

One exercise that stirs up intellectual juices is, coincidentally, the 99 Game. Everybody is handed a sheet of paper, with the numbers 1 to 99 scrambled about the page (Figure 21.1). You begin, "I know it has been a long day and many people are here in body, but sometimes it takes the mind a little longer to catch up. We all know the virtues of a quick break of physical exercise. We're going to try a very short bout of mental calisthenics. The page before you has 99 numbers on it. When I say 'start,' circle the number one, then the number two, then three, and see how far you can get in thirty seconds."

After the time's up, you ask, "How many found all 99?" People laugh, because nobody came even close. "All right, let's get serious," you continue. "How many found 20? How about 15? How about 10?"

Generally you'll find some who managed to get between 10 and 20. After congratulating them, you say, "Obviously this group needs help. It has been a long day, so let me give you a hand." Ask them to draw a line down the middle of the page vertically and then another horizontally, creating four quadrants. Then point out, if nobody picks it up immediately, that the numbers increase in a counter-clockwise position from quadrant to quadrant. Number 1 is in the upper right-hand quadrant, 2 in the upper left-hand quadrant, 3 is in the quadrant below that, and so on.

With that explanation, advise them, "I want you to now continue from where you left off, but this time I'm only going to give you fifteen seconds." After they try again, ask how many found it easier this time.

Figure 21.1

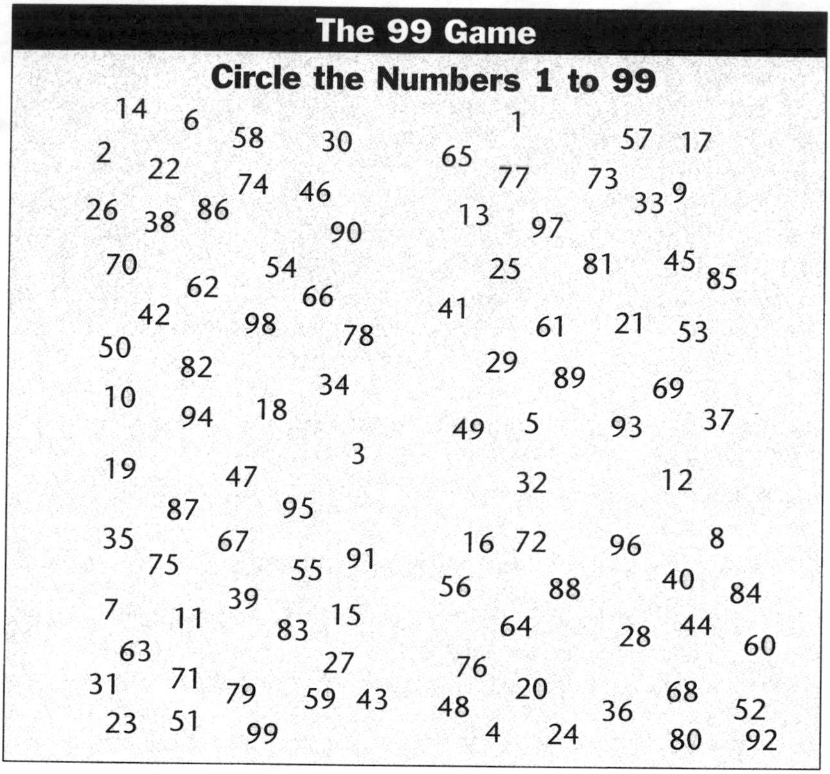

The 99 Game

Circle the Numbers 1 to 99

14 6 1
2 58 30 65 57 17
22 74 46 77 73 33 9
26 38 86 90 13 97
70 54 25 81 45 85
62 66 41
42 98 78 61 21 53
50 82 29 89
10 34 69
94 18 49 5 93 37
3
19 47 32 12
87 95
35 67 16 72 96 8
75 55 91 56 88 40 84
7 11 39 83 15 64 28 44 60
63 27 76
31 71 79 59 43 48 20 68 36 52
23 51 99 4 24 80 92

Everybody will. Then ask how many circled as many numbers the second time as the first, even though they had half the time. The bulk of the audience will raise their hands.

"Why was it easier?" you ask. Someone will answer, "Because I knew where I was going." That's your cue: "Exactly. You knew where you were going. You had a plan. And just as you need a plan to be able to circle the numbers from 1 to 99, you need a financial plan if you are to achieve your retirement plan in the most direct manner possible."

Starting seminars with the 99 Game has two advantages. It makes a forceful point about the importance of financial planning. It also sparks involvement.

You can also end the seminar with another audience participation technique that presses home the importance of financial planning. That second game should be foreshadowed at the opening of your presentation. "Over the course of the evening, we're going to be talking about a broad range of ideas that hold the potential for helping you to increase your income and to retire in greater comfort," you begin. "Sometimes people come to sessions like this hoping they'll find ideas that will allow them to become wealthy with no effort on their part. Unfortunately, I have to tell you right now I don't know very many ideas or approaches that will let you do that. But there is one, as a matter of fact, that I've come across quite recently—and I'll share it with you before the evening is out. It has the potential of significantly increasing your income with absolutely no effort on your part. Let me repeat: no effort whatsoever. So what I'd like is a volunteer who will remind me before the evening is over to let you in on this secret."

After obtaining the volunteer, you resume, "Great. That will be one idea, but unfortunately just one. Everything else we talk about tonight will require some effort, some application, and some discipline on your part." The program continues and at the end of the evening you remark, "I think I've covered everything I wanted to cover tonight. I thank you again for coming. I don't think there's anything left untouched, right?" The volunteer, or somebody else, will of course take that less-than-gentle hint to remind you of your promise to help them get rich without any effort.

"Thanks for reminding me. I did make that commitment and we try to honor all of our promises," you note. "What I'd like you all to do is stand up for a moment—it has been a long session—and stretch your arms. Perfect. Now I'd like you to reach under the table in front of you. Underneath, you'll each find a ticket that has been attached with tape. That ticket is for Saturday's lottery, in which the first prize is $5 million.

"It may be that someone in this room can ignore everything we've just talked about and retire with no effort by winning that $5 million. But if you don't have the winning ticket, good luck in putting the ideas we've discussed into practice."

That's one of the best methods I know for ending the seminar with a bang—on a positive, upbeat note. It's also something people will be talking about as they leave and will remember long past Saturday night's lottery draw.

Handling Questions

Seminars normally close with a question period. I'm jaundiced, however, about the effectiveness of that tradition. After a tightly scripted, well-presented seminar, the adviser throws the event open to chance. Sometimes—maybe one out of ten times—a few cogent and coherent questions will immediately emerge, and everyone will be enriched.

But 90 percent of the time you get no questions, with an embarrassing silence that forces the audience to feel guilty, or a few weak or even extraneous questions. You could also elicit unwelcome impromptu speeches by questioners hoping to match your one-hour presentation, which could drive everyone to wish they were back home watching *Friends*. The risk of opening the session to questions is greater than the reward, because you've lost control. You don't know what will come next. You may be forced to cut people off, or humor them and bore others. All that transpires just when you should be winding up on a positive note.

Figure 21.2

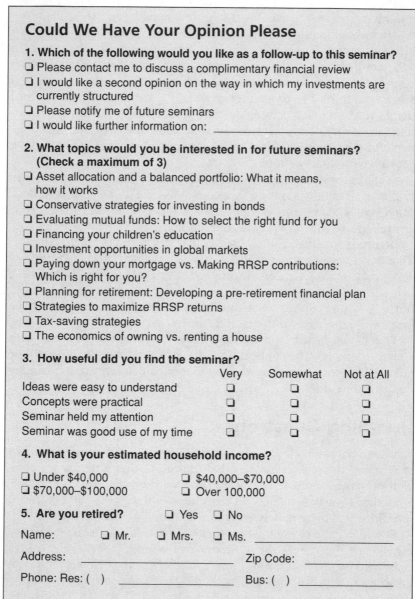

Could We Have Your Opinion Please

1. Which of the following would you like as a follow-up to this seminar?

❑ Please contact me to discuss a complimentary financial review
❑ I would like a second opinion on the way in which my investments are currently structured
❑ Please notify me of future seminars
❑ I would like further information on: ______________________

2. What topics would you be interested in for future seminars? (Check a maximum of 3)

❑ Asset allocation and a balanced portfolio: What it means, how it works
❑ Conservative strategies for investing in bonds
❑ Evaluating mutual funds: How to select the right fund for you
❑ Financing your children's education
❑ Investment opportunities in global markets
❑ Paying down your mortgage vs. Making RRSP contributions: Which is right for you?
❑ Planning for retirement: Developing a pre-retirement financial plan
❑ Strategies to maximize RRSP returns
❑ Tax-saving strategies
❑ The economics of owning vs. renting a house

3. How useful did you find the seminar?

	Very	Somewhat	Not at All
Ideas were easy to understand	❑	❑	❑
Concepts were practical	❑	❑	❑
Seminar held my attention	❑	❑	❑
Seminar was good use of my time	❑	❑	❑

4. What is your estimated household income?

❑ Under $40,000 ❑ $40,000–$70,000
❑ $70,000–$100,000 ❑ Over 100,000

5. Are you retired? ❑ Yes ❑ No

Name: ❑ Mr. ❑ Mrs. ❑ Ms. ______________________

Address: ______________________ Zip Code: ______________

Phone: Res: ( ) ______________ Bus: ( ) ______________

If you insist on a question period, ask prospects to write them on cards. A member of your staff can circulate to pick up the questions, which you can screen. Alternatively, don't hold a formal question period. End with the usual thanks and remind your audience that you and the other speakers will be available to answer any questions. That way nobody is held hostage to somebody else's questions, and the evening doesn't spiral out of control just as everyone's getting tired and edgy.

After the event you want to convert attenders into clients. The best method is the tried-and-true feedback form. We've developed a one-page form requesting feedback on the session, suggestions for future seminars, and, above all, information on the best way for individual follow-up (Figure 21.2). People will complete them, particularly if as a reward you offer a draw with some modest prize.

Naturally, you don't just follow up with those individuals who indicate on the form that they wish to be contacted. At the same time you don't want to be intrusive. You don't want people to feel misled about the obligation they entered into by attending the seminar.

If some people don't indicate a desire for follow-up, you can phone to chat about the seminar, going over some of the items on the feedback form in greater depth. That might end with the inoffensive question, "May I send you some further information?" If they're not interested—or if you choose not to make those phone calls because you fear the effort will be misinterpreted—you put those people in the prospecting pipeline and begin the development process.

A good investment after the seminar is to send everyone a personalized thank-you note for attending, perhaps with a trust-building article attached. After all, the seminar was a trust-heightening effort. It's worth a little extra cost and effort—as with the prior information package, the refreshments, the larger room with tables, and those lottery tickets—to make it a memorable, pleasurable experience that will knit stronger ties for the future.

Snapshots

- ✔ *Seminars are one of the hot prospecting tools of the '90s.*
- ✔ *An effective seminar program requires three elements. You have to get prospects into a room. You have to deliver an effective, motivating message while they're present. And you have to convert those attenders into clients, over time. What you can't delegate—and therefore the toughest element—is bringing the prospects into the room.*
- ✔ *The most effective seminar approach is to focus on education and cultivating relationships. In that vein, it's best to view the seminar as part of a long-term sequence rather than an isolated event.*

- ✔ *The number of prospects you intend to target affects the structure of the seminar and where it's held.*
- ✔ *Set a realistic budget for the seminar.*
- ✔ *It's generally best to make the seminar topic broader in nature and educationally oriented, as opposed to product focused. The top topic for seminars is tax-savings strategies.*
- ✔ *Attendance goes up when the adviser shares the speaking limelight with an accountant, lawyer, or other professionals who add their expertise and credibility to the evening.*
- ✔ *The best seminar locations are somewhat exclusive and carry a certain cachet.*
- ✔ *Light refreshments help to enhance the evening.*
- ✔ *Engraved invitations are the most effective vehicle for getting word out about the seminar. You may want to follow up with a reminder and an information package.*
- ✔ *Don't bore your audience. Remember: Multiple speakers are easier to listen to. Shorter presentations are better than long. If you're the sole speaker, an hour is the absolute maximum that an audience will pay attention. If you arrange a couple of speakers, perhaps you can nudge the session up to an hour and a quarter or an hour and a half.*
- ✔ *Visuals and handouts are critical. And consider seating everyone around round tables.*
- ✔ *Encourage involvement, through techniques like the 99 Game and the lottery-ticket closer.*
- ✔ *Avoid a formal question period since you lose control.*
- ✔ *A feedback form will help you leverage the evening for follow-up.*

CHAPTER 22

Developing Professional Referrals

WHEN WE LOOKED AT THE PROSPECTING TRUST SPECTRUM, REFERRALS from professionals topped the list. That's no surprise to anyone who has been in the business for any period of time. Nothing beats the immediate credibility of being introduced to a client by his or her accountant or lawyer. If you're good enough for the professional, you're almost always considered good enough by the client.

Despite that, the vast majority of advisers who have tried to cultivate referral relationships with accountants and lawyers have failed. To reverse that miserable record, let's analyze the process for developing solid referral relations with fellow professionals to highlight the obstacles that have prompted the failures.

Five steps are essential for sound referral relationships:

1. understanding the Accountant's and Lawyer's 99;
2. identifying and targeting the right accountants and lawyers;
3. comprehending the need to reassure professional referral sources about the quality and experience you'll provide any clients they recommend;
4. finding ways of adding value to referral sources; and
5. maintaining sustained, low-key contact with those referral sources.

Often that first step trips us up: We fail to devote proper attention to our Referral Sources' 99. Their priority is to help existing clients fare better by finding solutions to their problems. At the same time, those professionals want to ensure existing relations with their clients aren't jeopardized. Sometimes a conflict arises between those two instincts. Even if accountants and lawyers suspect a client might be better off with some professional financial advice, they could imperil the relationship with that client through the referral.

In seeking a referral relationship, we have to remember that for most accountants and lawyers the downside risk in granting a referral overwhelms the potential upside gain (Figure 22.1). They fear losing clients because of a poor experience with the referred financial adviser more than they are beguiled by the possibility of having happier clients through the referral.

At the same time, not very far behind that fear in the Accountant's 99 and the Lawyer's 99 is the thirst to attract new clients. The current decade thrusts accountants and lawyers, like the rest of us, into a new world. They've discovered—at both large and small firms—the need to market more actively and extensively.

A reciprocal mindset and some Starbucks coffee can fuel professional referrals.

Another concern they nurse amid the information explosion is keeping up to date, notably on peripheral matters for which they are expected to hold some expertise but often don't have adequate information. That's particularly true for accountants, notably with small and mid-sized firms, where they don't have the central resources to provide the know-how that a large firm can muster. Clients expect their accountants to be informed about investment issues. But many accountants don't have that proficiency and can't meet their clients' needs for financial and investment information.

Their own personal financial fears are another key element of their 99. Like everyone else, accountants and lawyers worry whether their own financial affairs are in proper shape for the future.

Figure 22.1

Concerns of Accountants and Lawyers

1. Existing clients
   a) helping clients do better
   b) not jeopardizing existing relationships
2. Attracting new clients
3. Keeping informed on what's happening
4. Personal affairs

Who Do You Approach?

After educating ourselves on their 99, we need to figure out who specifically to approach (Figure 22.2). The accountants and lawyers you choose should clearly be top quality: You must be comfortable that they run a sound practice, pay attention to detail, and are trustworthy. You also want to pick those with a business base that meshes well with your marketing needs. While that correlation may seem automatic, in fact not all accountants and lawyers—even with the best will in the world—have the opportunity to refer clients to you.

The lawyers and accountants you target should also have a reciprocal mindset. I've encountered many advisers who have invested a fair amount of time in fostering relationships with accountants or lawyers, feeding them clients, and yet no prospects flow their way in return. When they sheepishly (or angrily) raise the issue, they learn that the accountant or lawyer doesn't believe that providing referrals is professional. That's particularly true with large firms, but such traditional restraint holds even in some smaller firms.

Finally, the chemistry has to be right. A referral relationship is a partnership, and without the requisite chemistry the partnership won't be sustained in the long term.

Some advisers ignore these considerations, to their detriment. Rather than concerning themselves with the other professionals' 99, they figure that simply by advising of their availability they'll turn the referral tap on. So the adviser looks up "accountants" in the phone book, calls the first one listed, and informs him or her, "It's John Adviser over at XYZ company. I'm calling to let you know I'm available to help out any of your clients, so if you happen to run into somebody with money, send them over." After that, he moves on to the next accountant on the list, and so on. Then he sits back waiting for the phone to ring. When it doesn't, he says, "Another dumb idea. Clearly professional referrals don't work—back to cold calling." I exaggerate,

Figure 22.2

Attributes of the Right Referral Partners

1. Top-quality partner
2. Business base
3. Reciprocal mindset
4. Chemistry

of course, but only slightly, given the flimsy marketing schemes some advisers have used to develop relationships with fellow professionals.

The other common trap is to target the wrong accountants and lawyers. Our instinct, understandably, is that bigger is better. So the financial adviser woos partners in the large, prestigious law firms and national accounting groups. While in some cases that has led to fruitful relationships, in more cases it's a bust. Generally your best opportunities are with the small to mid-sized firms rather than the elite.

Smaller firms are inclined to be more marketing oriented. They tend to be less conservative. Big firms, particularly in major metropolitan centers, tend to cater to large corporate clients. You could develop a wonderful relationship with a senior accountant at a top firm, but if that accountant's sole responsibility is to manage the audit of your community's largest bank, the chances that he or she will be interacting with many prospective referrals are slim.

Smaller Is Better

It's best to concentrate on small and mid-sized firms, ideally with accountants and lawyers in their thirties and forties. If they're much younger, they probably haven't yet developed a business base that will generate relatively immediate referrals. If they're much older, they're possibly set in their ways. We've found that accountants and lawyers in their fifties and sixties tend to be more reluctant to dispense referrals. Despite those general prescriptions, your own age has to be factored in. The right chemistry is more likely to bubble forth with professionals of your own generation.

It's worth pointing out, in this vein, that another common mistake is that some advisers scramble to deal with every professional they can scrounge up in their target group. The risk is that by targeting everybody you end up targeting nobody. Instead, you should start by establishing a sound referral relationship with two or three people in each profession. If you still have surplus energy, you can add an extra person or two to the various categories.

If you are targeting only a few professionals in each category, you want to ensure they're the best bets. One way to begin is with existing relationships. You may already have a referral relationship with an accountant or lawyer that's operating at a low level but can be intensified. You might also turn to friends, relatives, or neighbors in those professions.

An alternative that many advisers have found fertile is to learn who fulfills their best clients' accounting and legal needs. You might edge into it by asking one of those clients: "Gerry, I wonder if you could help me. From time to time some of my other clients ask me to refer an accountant or lawyer they might use. Tell me, what kind of experience have you had with your own accountant and lawyer?" If he's positive about that relationship, you push further: "That's interesting. Do you think your accountant would mind if I were to call her with a view to getting together and knowing her better, so I might refer some of those clients her way?" Of course, the client will assent.

"That's great! With your permission, I'll give her a call," you conclude. "If you don't mind, I'll tell her we work together."

When you call, you say, "Ms. Accountant, it's John Adviser here, with XYZ firm. I was talking to a common client we have, Gerry Investor, and he was relating how positive working with you has been. You certainly seem to have a fan in Gerry. Let me tell you why I'm calling: From time to time I'll run into clients who aren't happy with their accounting relationship or don't have an accountant. I'm looking for an accountant I might refer them to. I was calling to inquire if you would be willing to sit down at some point and talk about the approach you take, so that if I come across clients who would be a logical fit I'd be able to refer them."

What will be the accountant's response? You can count on it being significantly better than the response she just gave to that financial adviser who phoned to tell her he was open for business and if she had any clients with money to shoot them right over. But the major advantage to this approach, rather than going automatically to people you may be close to such as your high-school chum or sister-in-law's third cousin, is that the odds are higher that the professional has other clients like the high-quality joint client you initially consulted.

This approach requires more time, but it's worth the trouble to target the right level of accountants and lawyers. Some advisers are even more systematic, sending a letter to a select group of clients—say the top 10 percent—asking for input on the professionals they work with so the adviser can develop a pool of professionals to assist clients, somewhat in the way Dodee Frost Crockett of Merrill Lynch in Dallas helps her clients (Figure 22.3). The strategy scans a wide array of professions: accountants, lawyers, architects, insurance brokers, real estate agents, and perhaps even bankers.

Providing Reassurance

After locating the right professionals, we have to provide reassurance that their clients will benefit and have a superior experience working with us. Accountants and lawyers have an innate conservatism and, from their 99, will be wary of passing along clients to us. That's understandable, given we would be similarly cautious.

Suppose you received a major referral from an accountant whose practice, to your mind, wasn't top flight. She had a reputation for cutting corners, perhaps, or not completing filings on time. If a client

Figure 22.3

Date

Any Client
1234 Any Street
Any City, Any State 56789

Dear Any,

I'm writing to ask a favor.

Recently, a number of clients have asked me for suggestions as to a professional to whom they can go for advice.

As a result, I'm developing a short list of professionals in different categories whose name I'll pass along to my clients who have need of their services.

If you work with someone who you've been particularly impressed with and whose name you'd be willing to let me pass along, I'd be very appreciative if you'd indicate their name below and mail or fax this page back to me.
Many thanks for your help on this.

Best regards,

Any Adviser

....

Dear Any Adviser,

I've had a good experience with the individual(s) below and would be pleased to have his/her name passed on to other clients.

	Name	Firm	Telephone
Accountant:	___________	___________	___________
Architect:	___________	___________	___________
Insurance Broker:	___________	___________	___________
Lawyer:	___________	___________	___________
Real Estate Agent:	___________	___________	___________
Other:	___________	___________	___________

were to ask you to recommend an accountant, would you mention that one, despite the debt you owe her for the recent referral? Obviously not. You don't want to take a chance of jeopardizing your relationship with your own client, should the subsequent relationship with the accountant falter.

So we have to build trust with the accountants and lawyers we eye for referrals, just as we build trust with prospects and clients (Figure 22.4). A starting point is emphasizing common clients. It's useful to highlight our personal credentials through a pre-meeting package. It's also critical to demonstrate our style and patience—our adherence to the Banker's Rule. They want somebody safe, conservative. It's another opportunity to tap into our arsenal of trust-building articles from the *Wall Street Journal, Fortune,* and *Forbes.*

In providing this reassurance, we knock down the obstacle of their suspicion and need for reassurance. But that simply eliminates a negative. We haven't furnished a positive reason to provide referrals. To develop a vigorous referral relationship we must add some value to their practice so they can perceive the benefit of providing referrals.

Adding Value

While this may seem an imposing hurdle, actually five areas are available for financial advisers to add value (Figure 22.5). The first is to position yourself as an information resource, soothing the professional's anxiety about keeping up to date on financial affairs.

Some financial advisers concentrate on developing a reputation as the best and the most accessible source of investment information for the professionals they've targeted. They'll regularly send articles, sometimes on a bi-weekly basis. They'll mail a newsletter, be it their firm's or one they've developed personally. They'll periodically host presentations in their boardroom for small groups of professionals, briefing them on the latest in the marketplace.

I know an adviser who carries this one step further. He tells ac-

Figure 22.4

Building Trust with Potential Partners

1. "We have a client in common."
2. "We have a mutual acquaintance."
3. "I'm developing a group of business people to work together to help each other attract new clients."

Figure 22.5

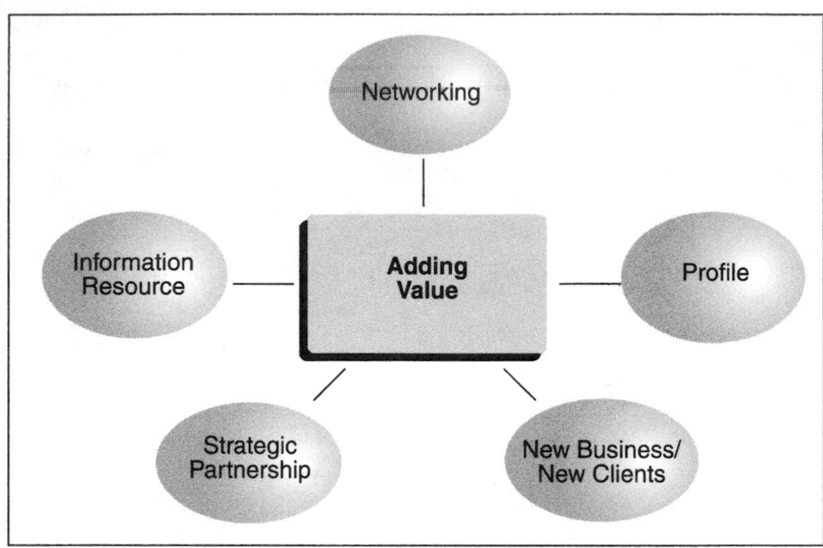

countants and lawyers to call him if they ever run into a question from a client that they can't answer on an investment or financial issue. If he doesn't have an answer, he'll research it and phone them back without delay. Note that his message isn't "Send your clients over to me," but "Send your problem over to me, and I'll find the information to help you shine." The adviser is conveniently filling a gap that accountants and lawyers face and fear.

Another alternative for adding value is to meet a second concern of accountants and lawyers: extending their network of professionals. They need to expand their source of referring professionals, just as we do. Some advisers have spearheaded an ongoing networking group, parlaying that effort into a robust referral relationship.

Networking breakfasts are quite simple to arrange. The group gathers routinely—say, once a month—in someone's boardroom from 7:30 to 9 A.M. Members are drawn from different specialties within the central professions. Taking part might be a tax accountant, a general accountant, an estate lawyer, a family lawyer, a corporate lawyer, a commercial real estate agent, a residential real estate agent, a life insurance broker, a property and casualty insurance broker, an architect. A funeral director might be a member. A management consultant is one of the most active members of a group I'm familiar with.

A low-key approach is to contact potential members and just advise them you're assembling a group of professionals to meet on a regular basis to exchange information. The purpose, in these times of swift-moving change, is to keep everyone more knowledgeable and current about other fields, in order to better advise clients when questions arise. A more direct approach is to indicate you want them to join a referral network that will allow a variety of high-quality professionals to expand their relationships so they'll have other professionals to refer clients to and receive referrals from.

Advisers generally have positive results from these breakfast groups. The response from the other professionals is usually enthusiastic, since they confront similar problems expanding their client base. The downside is that it takes considerable effort to organize the group initially and the payoff doesn't tend to be immediate.

One adviser arranged for nine professionals to meet at his office. The pattern is for the breakfast meeting to revolve around a talk by one or two of the participants about emerging issues in their area of expertise that will be of interest to the other professionals. The adviser volunteered to make the first presentation—on global markets, bond prices, and interest rates—and it was well received. He returned to his office, closed the door and waited for the phone to ring. Nothing happened. The next meeting was in someone else's boardroom, with another speaker. Again he invested time to attend, in return picking up some new information and enjoying some cordial conversations with the others. He returned to his office, waited for the phone to ring with the real dividends from that day's investment, but again nothing happened.

It took three meetings before he obtained his first referral. It took another two meetings to secure a second. But after the first six months the pace picked up: after each meeting, he'd receive a few referrals within a week or two of the gathering. So the process took time to ignite, but once operating on all cylinders it was quite powerful. That experience, if you think about it, is simply human nature. Just as with client referrals, people prefer to refer friends and acquaintances to people they know. After we've built a relationship through sustained, ongoing contact, we'll be top-of-mind when accountants and lawyers encounter a client who needs sophisticated financial advice.

Helping to Build Profile

Advisers can also add value to other professionals by helping them build profile. With accountants and lawyers facing the same marketing challenges we do, financial advisers can lend a friendly hand by showcasing them before our clients. You invite an accountant to speak for twenty to thirty minutes on tax-code changes at a seminar, or ask a lawyer to explain estate planning. Generally, they'll be enthusiastic, as they need the profile. Or you could approach that accountant and lawyer to write a short article of 300 words for your newsletter, to be published with their photograph and full credit.

Again, they are generally delighted because it provides visibility. You're adding value to the relationship you are nurturing.

Some advisers, particularly in smaller communities, are apprehensive about such invitations because they have several accountants and lawyers as clients and don't want to upset anybody. But this need not be a problem. Advisers have avoided giving offence by designing a broad program of seminars and newsletters that illuminates the talents of all these other professionals.

One adviser, for example, went in turn to three accountants he was targeting, with a pitch along these lines: "Over the next twelve months I intend to hold three seminars for my prospects and clients in this community. The first seminar, early in the year, will be on tax planning, the spring seminar will be on dealing with your banker, and the fall seminar will be on creditor-proofing. I wonder if you'd be interested in speaking at the creditor-proofing seminar, which will be of particular interest to business owners."

The accountant, interested in profile, was, of course, pleased. More to the point, when she received an invitation to the initial seminar on tax planning, she wasn't upset to notice a rival on the platform. She knew the adviser's plan and that she would share the spotlight in turn.

You can apply the same strategy to newsletters. If you're planning a full year's program, you could approach a lawyer in your community: "One of my new initiatives this year is to invite outside experts to participate in the newsletter I publish for clients and prospects. I have a slot available in the spring issue for a piece on estate planning. I'm wondering if you could prepare a column for that edition."

One particularly ingenious adviser approached three local accountants to participate in a tax-planning panel. While some co-ordination and diplomacy was involved, he killed three birds with one stone, building better links to all three accountants through one session. Moreover, he drew a significantly larger turnout for the session from prospects because the perceived value of attending a session with three accountants is probably higher than a session with only one. Even better, he persuaded the accountants to share the workshop's cost. That is the ultimate demonstration of the potential of giving profile to accountants and lawyers in your community as part of your marketing program.

Providing Referrals for Them

The fourth method of adding value to accountants and lawyers is to provide them with referrals. The other indirect boosts will be appreciated, but nothing matches direct referrals. The old axiom remains true: The best way to get a referral is to give a referral.

While not every client of yours will be looking for the services of an accountant or lawyer, a surprising number will. It should be standard procedure on becoming someone's financial adviser to learn whether that client has written a will, has a lawyer and is satisfied, and engages an accountant to prepare taxes and is satisfied. Sometimes you'll discover clients are perfectly happy with their existing professionals. Often, however, you'll find they are unhappy or have a need for an accountant or lawyer they've yet to fill.

That provides an opportunity to tell your clients or prospects, because sometimes the matter is raised with prospects, that you can be of service. "One of the things I do, for clients who need it, is to put them in touch with appropriate accountants, appropriate lawyers, or other professionals," you advise. "If you're interested, I'd be happy to give you the names of three accountants some of my clients are happy with. It might be worthwhile talking with them."

When the client leaves, you have the opportunity to pick up the phone and tell those three accountants or lawyers that you have just passed on their name to Joe Client, who may contact them. Placing those calls increases the likelihood you'll receive referrals from those professionals in return.

Some advisers quickly point to a glaring inconsistency in that approach: "Hold on now. You're telling us that we should give a client the names of three accountants or three lawyers to call. But when those professionals are providing a referral to a financial adviser, I only want one name on the list—mine."

That's true. It's an irreconcilable contradiction. When you're providing referrals to clients, it's smarter and safer to offer more than one name. It gives you an opportunity to make some extra calls, advising two or three accountants or lawyers that you've provided a referral, rather than being limited to only one. More importantly, if you refer a client to an accountant or lawyer and the relationship doesn't work out—there's no chemistry, or a serious problem arises—who is on the hook? The answer is you. But if you provide several names and things don't work out, you still may be perceived to bear some responsibility but ultimately the choice has been the client's.

Some advisers seek out opportunities to provide referrals by sending a letter informing clients that if they ever need an accountant, lawyer, or other professional the adviser has developed a referral list based on input from fellow clients (Figure 22.6). That creates the opportunity for more referrals, even if it's not an immediate necessity. Clients keep the offer in the back of their mind and take advantage down the line. It also reminds clients of your interest in helping them with all aspects of their business affairs.

Figure 22.6

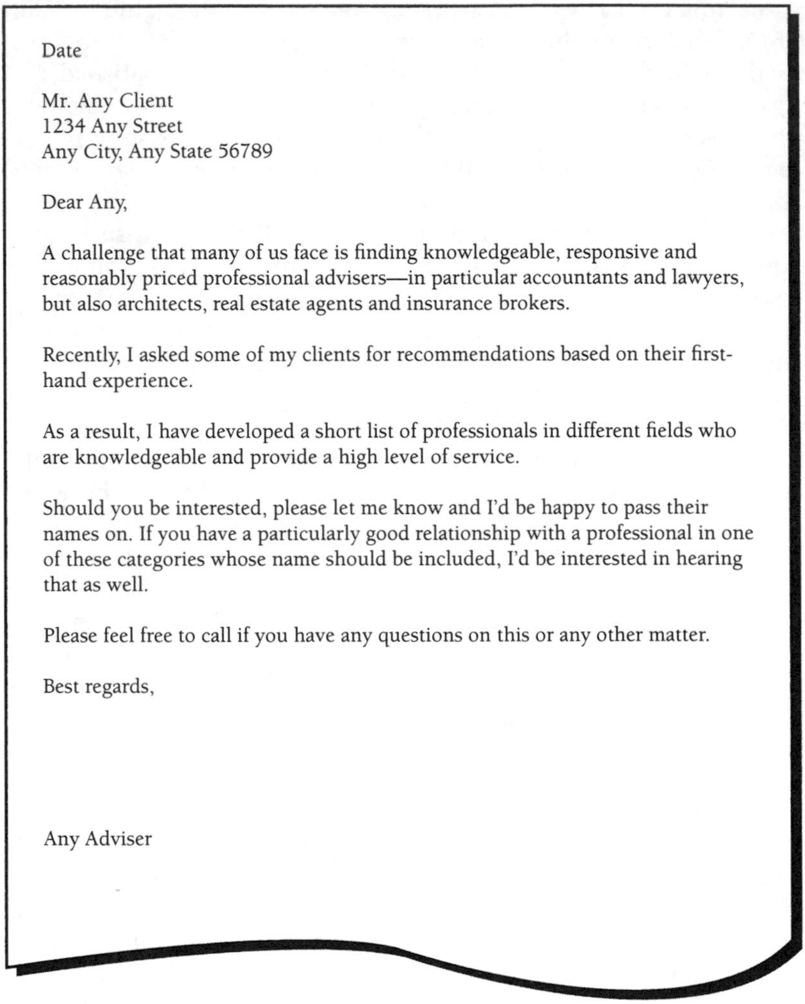

Date

Mr. Any Client
1234 Any Street
Any City, Any State 56789

Dear Any,

A challenge that many of us face is finding knowledgeable, responsive and reasonably priced professional advisers—in particular accountants and lawyers, but also architects, real estate agents and insurance brokers.

Recently, I asked some of my clients for recommendations based on their first-hand experience.

As a result, I have developed a short list of professionals in different fields who are knowledgeable and provide a high level of service.

Should you be interested, please let me know and I'd be happy to pass their names on. If you have a particularly good relationship with a professional in one of these categories whose name should be included, I'd be interested in hearing that as well.

Please feel free to call if you have any questions on this or any other matter.

Best regards,

Any Adviser

Strategic Partnerships

The final approach to adding value is a strategic partnership. That's a somewhat overused and sometimes overblown phrase sprouting up in the business press these days to describe two or three different companies with common purposes working together. I know one adviser who began by agreeing to put out a joint newsletter along with a prominent accountant, a lawyer, and a life insurance agent in his community. Each took a page in the four-page newsletter, which appeared quarterly, providing education rather than pushing products. They rotated positions so that each was featured on the front page once a year.

Client lists, however, weren't shared; they all mailed directly to their own clients.

After the first issue, the adviser received a call or two, but certainly no spectacular response, given the added exposure to three other professionals' full client list. After the second newsletter, the response was better. But as with our liftoff scenario, it took four newsletters before the real explosion. Again, that shows it takes time to build trust with new prospects.

After a year the four professionals expanded the relationship into seminars. Each sponsored a seminar for his own client base, which he moderated and chaired, but the other three professionals attended as participants. Again, they didn't share client bases or lists and no direct opportunity was offered to follow up. But a significant number of inquiries resulted. If you analyze the situation, each professional was taking his personal credibility with his client base and, over time, patiently imparting it to his partners.

Those procedures for developing referrals from professionals—from understanding the Accountant's/Lawyer's 99 to adding value—must be cemented by developing a proactive communications policy toward those fellow professionals. Every couple of months, you should be in touch with them. It might be nothing more than a phone call. It might be sharing a breakfast, lunch, or simply a cup of coffee. But you must maintain sustained contact. Assuming six key professionals on your list, each of whom you want to contact every second month for an average of half an hour—sometimes a phone call, sometimes a lunch—works out to a three-hour commitment in that two-month period. Over a year, it's twelve hours—perhaps the most productive twelve hours of the year in terms of business generation.

Finally, in considering the self-interest of lawyers and accountants as you forge links, don't forget the personal dimension. At the end of the day we all prefer to deal with people we like. And one thing we appreciate is for them to express a real interest in us—to show some understanding, sympathy, and empathy for our circumstances. One reminder of that interest which has proven phenomenally effective is to send your accountant-friends a package with a half-pound of Starbucks coffee about two weeks before taxes are due. The covering letter recognizes that the weeks ahead will be unusually hectic, something advisers can sympathize with, given their own pressures during registered retirement savings plan season. "While I can't offer any advice on getting those returns completed," the notes says, "I hope the enclosed coffee helps you and your staff get through some of those late evenings" (Figure 22.7).

That's not a big thing; actually, it's a little thing. But for financial advisers who have sent the coffee, it has had a powerful impact. It re-

Figure 22.7

Date

Ms. Any Accountant
1234 Any Street
Any City, Any State 56789

Dear Any,

For people in the investment business, the period leading up to February 28—the last day for RRSP contributions—is the most hectic of the year.

Over the next couple of weeks, I suspect that your life will be equally hectic, with lots of long hours working on last-minute tax returns. While I can't offer any advice on getting those returns done, I hope that the attached Starbucks coffee helps you get through some of those late evenings.

Best regards,

Any Adviser

minds the accountants you were thinking of them. It differentiates you, next time they're in a position to make a referral.

Snapshots

- ✔ *Nothing beats the immediate credibility when you're introduced to a client by an accountant or lawyer.*
- ✔ *The five essential steps for developing professional referral relationships are: understanding the Accountant's 99 and the Lawyer's 99; identifying and targeting the right accountants and lawyers; reassuring referral sources about the quality of the experience you'll provide clients they recommend; finding ways of adding value to referral sources; and maintaining sustained, low-key contact with those referral sources.*
- ✔ *In seeking a referral relationship, remember that for most accountants and lawyers the downside risk in a referral overwhelms the potential upside gain. They fear losing a client because of a poor experience with the referred financial adviser more than they are attracted by the possibility of having a happier client through the referral.*

- ✔ *At the same time, not very far behind in the Accountant's and Lawyer's 99 is their need to market more aggressively to attract new clients. They are also concerned about keeping up to date on peripheral matters where they are expected to have some expertise but often don't have adequate information and support. They also worry whether their own financial affairs are in shape for the future.*
- ✔ *The accountants and lawyers you target should be top quality. They should also have a reciprocal mindset, and the chemistry must be right.*
- ✔ *Small and mid-sized firms are generally preferred targets, ideally with accountants and lawyers in their thirties and forties.*
- ✔ *You could find those accountants and lawyers through friends, relatives, or neighbors. But a better alternative is to ask your best clients who handles their accounting and legal needs.*
- ✔ *Some advisers send a letter to a select group of clients—say, the top 10 percent—asking for input on the professionals they work with so the adviser can develop a pool of professionals to assist clients.*
- ✔ *After finding accountants and lawyers to target, you have to build trust. A starting point is emphasizing common clients. It's useful to highlight personal credentials through a pre-meeting package. It's also critical to demonstrate your adherence to the Banker's Rule. They want somebody safe, conservative. It's another opportunity to use your stockpile of trust-building articles from the* Wall Street Journal, Fortune, *and* Forbes.
- ✔ *You should also provide positive reasons for working with you by adding value to those professionals' business.*
- ✔ *One method of adding value is to position yourself as an information resource for those professionals, soothing their anxiety about keeping up to date on financial affairs.*
- ✔ *A second method is to help them extend their network, inviting them to join a group of professionals who meet to share information and ideas over breakfast.*
- ✔ *A third method is to help build their profile, showcasing them before your clients at seminars and in newsletters.*
- ✔ *A fourth method is to provide them with referrals (and to call them immediately to let them know you've done so). But remember: It's smarter and safer to give your clients two or three possible names rather than one when providing a referral.*

- ✔ *The final method to add value is a strategic partnership. You might consider sharing newsletters or seminars with a select, compatible team of other professionals.*
- ✔ *It's important to maintain regular contact with the accountants and lawyers you're working with. You should be in touch every couple of months.*
- ✔ *A little Starbucks coffee can go a long way.*

CHAPTER 23

How to Differentiate Yourself

WE TALKED EARLIER IN THE BOOK ABOUT THE NEW REALITY WHICH FINANCIAL advisers confront, that getting a referral is only the beginning, not the end of the client acquisition process. In particular, when you are talking to high-end prospects you will invariably be in competition with other financial advisers.

The challenge you face is to differentiate yourself from that competition. How do you ensure that the prospect feels more comfortable working with you than with all those other available advisers? How do you convey a superior level of professionalism and trust that will differentiate you from your competitors?

The opportunities for differentiation arise at four stages: before a meeting, during a meeting, at the meeting wrap-up, and after. In many regards, the most important stage is before the meeting, and that's why I've previously stressed the two-minute rule and the critical importance of your initial impact on the prospect. I discussed the value of setting the scene with a pre-meeting package—one excellent vehicle to differentiate yourself from competitors. I also mentioned the financial adviser who called to let prospects know that a private parking spot would be awaiting them on their arrival. A third way to differentiate yourself at this point is through the professionalism expressed by your reception area. Ensuring that you have today's *Wall Street Journal* rather than last year's *Time* magazine is another chance to differentiate yourself.

One financial adviser has implemented a clever routine for first meetings. He alerts his receptionist that he is expecting a prospect and, if possible, obtains a physical description of that prospect from the referral source. When the prospect walks through the door, the receptionist says, "Oh, you must be Richard Prospect. Mr. Adviser has told me to let him know the moment you arrive."

The prospect has never set eyes on the adviser, but already he has received a powerful signal about the importance and seriousness that adviser attaches to working with him. This probably contrasts starkly with equivalent sessions at competing advisers' offices, where the receptionist took several exasperating minutes before paying him any attention, scanned a list of scheduled appointments to check if he was to be allowed through the sacred portals, and then told him that he'd have to wait five minutes because the adviser was busy.

Talk is cheap; tangible specifics will differentiate you from the competition.

Differentiating Yourself in the Meeting

The meeting itself offers the second stage for differentiation. Ensure a positive start by telling the receptionist, in front of the prospect, to hold all your calls: "No interruptions." There are two reasons for that order. First, you really don't want any interruptions: After all, this is a crucial meeting. Secondly, you want to signal to the prospect that she is going to be taken seriously.

As I've stressed, your office should look professional—a place where clients feel comfortable having their money administered. You want to minimize clutter. Make sure your degrees are visible. Eliminate any possible triggers of doubt about how objective you are: If you've received trinkets or trash from fund companies, get them out of sight. (They should never have been in your office in the first place.) The Banker's Rule must apply to your office as well as the reception area.

More and more financial advisers are recognizing the importance of the appropriate courtesies and stylistic flourishes at this point: Offering coffee or a soft drink is appreciated, and having it served in chinaware or glass is better than in styrofoam.

On the more substantive side, start by outlining the meeting's purpose. This preamble should recognize that prospective clients often feel apprehensive. We know they worry that this may be an uncomfortable interaction in which they will feel pressured.

So address those concerns head on by assuring the client that this meeting won't involve any sale. That's not sacrificing anything, since the research shows it's probably going to take two or three meetings to turn the prospect into a client.

Begin with: "Ms. Prospect, I'd like to achieve two things today. First, I'd like to get to know you, your circumstances, what your needs are, and where you are hoping to wind up financially in the future. Secondly, I'd like to give you the opportunity to get to know me. If it is okay with you, I'd rather not get into any specific discussion of investments today. If after today you would like to meet further to talk about that, I would certainly like to—but is it all right with you if today we just use the meeting to get to know each other?"

That preamble has a remarkably positive effect in defusing the prospect's tension and making her less defensive. Now she no longer has to worry about being fooled, and you have the opportunity to engage in a productive dialogue about her financial issues.

You may want next to take the opportunity briefly to review the pre-meeting package. Don't dwell on it, but hit the high points. If the prospect hasn't had a chance to read it fully—or even if she has—make sure she understands that she can call you at any time with questions and concerns.

Indeed, that invitation should extend beyond the package. One financial adviser points to a bookshelf with a plethora of personal finance texts. He tells prospects that one of the elements of value he provides to clients is that he loans them at no cost books from his collection on investment planning, mutual funds, and taxation.

As you slip in these examples of special service, try to make them as concrete as possible. Lots of financial advisers will say that they are committed to service. Words are cheap. Tangible specifics will differentiate you (Figure 23.1).

Figure 23.1

Strategies to Differentiate Yourself

Before a meeting	During a meeting	Meeting wrap-up	After a meeting
1. Pre-meeting package	**1.** Office look (Banker's Rule)	**1.** Client survey results	**1.** Follow-up note
2. Parking spot	**2.** Preamble (Purpose of the meeting)	**2.** Client testimonials	**2.** Article
3. Reception appearance (professional)	**3.** Brief review of pre-meeting package		
	4. No interruptions		
	5. Personal finance lending library		

Ending Properly

If the beginning of the meeting is the most important component in any interaction, the next in importance is the end. It sets the stage for whether the relationship will stop or continue. It sounds the final notes the prospect will walk away remembering. You need to think carefully, therefore, about how to wrap up the session. You need a conclusion that will ensure prospective clients go away thinking you are better than any other adviser they have met.

I've already mentioned the idea of ending with client testimonials the prospect can follow up, if desired. You can also offer client phone numbers—again showing the prospect how willing you are to be checked out.

One financial adviser shows prospects a survey of client satisfaction which he hired a local accounting firm to conduct with his existing client base. That's not a big gamble: If you poll most clients they'll be positive, or else they would no longer be your clients. (The real issue, of course, is not whether they are satisfied but how satisfied they are.)

At the meeting's conclusion, this adviser tells prospects: "I have a deep commitment to client service. We pride ourselves on the things we do to make sure our clients receive the best level of service and advice that we can possibly provide. About a year ago I commissioned a survey of my clients. Here's a copy of the report that I received, along with a copy of the original letter to clients and the survey." Think about the impact that concrete demonstration has on prospects, compared to the adviser who simply says, "We're committed to client satisfaction." This approach is tangible and specific—a powerful mix.

A final way to differentiate yourself is in your activities after the meeting. Assuming that you have secured a follow-up meeting, you don't want prospects to feel taken for granted. The investment of a minute and a half and a postage stamp helps in this regard. Send a follow-up note letting them know how much you enjoyed meeting them and how you look forward to the next get-together. You may also want to include an article pertaining to something you talked about in the meeting, taken from a top business publication, reinforcing that you are the kind of adviser they will feel comfortable working with.

That's a lot of work. A few years ago it wouldn't have been necessary. It used to be that if you received a referral—well, you got a client. But given how competitive the environment is today and how discerning clients have become, the only way to capitalize on that referral opportunity is to recognize that you are in competition and begin to differentiate yourself from the crowd. With that in mind, in the next chapter we'll look at an important strategy for differentiation—target marketing.

Snapshots

- ✔ *The challenge you face today is to differentiate yourself from the competition.*
- ✔ *The opportunities for differentiation arise at four stages: before a meeting, during a meeting, at the wrap-up, and after the meeting.*
- ✔ *The most important stage is before the meeting. Remember the value of a pre-meeting package and the example of the financial adviser who called to let prospects know a private parking spot would be awaiting them. Ensure your reception area is professional, and prepare your receptionist to greet prospects in a way that indicates their importance to you.*
- ✔ *Ensure a positive start to the meeting by asking the receptionist to hold all your calls.*
- ✔ *Keep your office appearance professional—and replace those styrofoam cups.*
- ✔ *Begin the meeting by addressing the Prospect's 99, telling her you want to get to know each other this session and if it's all right with her, don't want to get into any specific discussion of investments yet.*
- ✔ *As you slip examples of special service into your discussion, make them as concrete as possible.*
- ✔ *Your conclusion should ensure that prospects walk away thinking you are better than any other adviser they've encountered. Testimonials are useful. So is a survey of client satisfaction.*
- ✔ *A final way to differentiate yourself is in your activities after the meeting. Don't forget a follow-up note, possibly along with a financial article of interest.*

CHAPTER 24

The Move to Target Marketing

IMAGINE YOUR BROTHER REMINDS YOU THAT YOUR NIECE CELEBRATES HER tenth birthday this weekend and you decide to pick up a gift Saturday morning. For most people, the initial instinct—sometimes the only instinct—is to head to Toys Я Us. It assures wide selection: You'll find something that will delight the child. Pricing will be competitive, although it's not pricing that attracts customers to Toys Я Us, because you could find the same toys elsewhere at significantly lower cost. But you trust Toys Я Us to stock what you need, since that's its focus.

And it's not just Toys Я Us. From sporting goods to hardware to office goods, specialty retailers in the last fifteen years have thrived, chopping away at the base of the broad mass-merchandising department stores from one side while the discounters chop away from the other side. Unless retailers can compete on price with the Wal-Marts of this world, they better have a strong, distinct niche. The businesses in the middle have been clobbered.

A Bad Time for Generalists

That's not just true of retailing. Generalists haven't fared well in most categories over the last decade and a half. Take physicians. The general practitioners who two decades ago saw children in the morning, a patient with a hernia in the afternoon, and delivered a baby in the evening have seen their practices erode. Patients have gravitated toward specialists such as pediatricians and obstetricians. The same trend has been occurring in other professions, such as accounting and law: a squeeze on the generalist, to the specialist's advantage.

The reason is simple. Generalists do well, as long as they're just competing with other generalists. But the moment a specialist appears on the scene, with greater expertise and a more potent focus on a narrow marketplace, generalists have trouble competing for that specific target group.

Let me give you another example, based on our research. Imagine an affluent client calls one day so delighted with your work that he wants to give you a gift and won't take no for an answer. The present is a cruise anywhere in the world for you and your spouse. Unwilling to hurt his feelings, you accept.

In future, the winners are likely to be the first advisers who move to target marketing.

Preparing to book the cruise, you turn to the Yellow Pages and find two options under Travel Agencies. The first is Round-the-World-Travel, established in 1930. Its advertisement proclaims: "We've been where you want to go." The second possibility is The Cruise Shop, specializing in cruises of all types. Which would you chose?

When we've asked consumers, 80 percent select The Cruise Shop, despite competition from a long-entrenched travel agency that has presumably been satisfying customers for many decades. If you're looking for a cruise, you choose the source that you expect to have the best information, selection and advice—the best value. If you were considering a bus trip across Europe, you wouldn't phone The Cruise Shop. You would tap Round-the-World Travel for that, unless another specialist alternative was available.

This dynamic shift from generalist to specialist permeates the economy. But financial advisers, for the most part, have resisted the trend. The principal reason is that most financial advisers haven't had the discipline to focus their marketing activity. Therefore, as a generalist financial adviser you've been luckier so far than those department stores, general practitioners, and Round-the-World Travel. You've been competing, as a rule, against other generalists. And generalists do fine, as long as they are competing against other generalists.

In the period ahead, however, given specialization's advantage, it's inevitable that the pattern of other areas of the economy will hit ours as well. And normally the big winners are the first to shift. They lead the pack rather than chasing the others.

Prospecting for Physiotherapists

Let me give you an example of someone who dipped her toes in early. In 1993 after a workshop a financial adviser approached me to discuss her practice. She had been with her firm for a few years and was getting by, doing well enough to hang onto her position but not much better than that. More importantly, she was having no fun and was questioning whether this profession was right for her. She woke up every Monday morning with knots in her stomach at the prospect of another week on the phone, cold calling.

In discussing her options, I asked what she did before becoming a financial adviser. "Really nothing related to this," she said. "I was a physiotherapist and ended up running a physiotherapist clinic, which I sold. That's when I came into this business." Given that background, in the next few minutes we sketched out a simple plan of attack that would position her to target physiotherapists in her community. It consisted of attending local physiotherapist association meetings, finding out whether an opportunity existed to write for the association's newsletter, and seeking out a speaking opportunity at an association meeting. Nothing unusual, but all targeted at this one, tangible group.

I didn't give that conversation much thought until about a year later when she called to report some good news and bad news. She had attended the next meeting of local physiotherapists, and the person next to her, engaging in chit-chat, happened to ask where she worked. She explained that she had previously been a physiotherapist but was now actually a financial adviser. She had come to the meeting, she said, because she wanted to stay in touch with events in the physiotherapy community. As luck would have it, the person sitting beside her declared, "Actually, I happen to have a financial question that maybe you could help me with." The adviser left the meeting with a client.

Over the course of the next year she continued to attend meetings. She initiated a regular column on financial matters for the physiotherapy newsletter, since it came out monthly and the editor had trouble filling space. She spoke at the September meeting on cash flow management and retirement plans for physiotherapists.

The good news, then, was that over twelve months she had built her profile in that narrow community and as a result picked up forty clients from within it. She had established a database with the names of more than eighty other people from that community whom she was cultivating after they had indicated some degree of interest. The bad news, however, was that she was running out of physiotherapists. What could she do?

We chatted again and hit upon the idea of expanding the approach to two other target groups: nurses and chiropractors. They were allied fields, in which she could apply the same strategy. In the period that followed she again successfully marketed herself to those groups, and her clientele grew.

Her experience points to some of target marketing's advantages (Figure 24.1). You can build trust more easily through the visibility you gen-

Figure 24.1

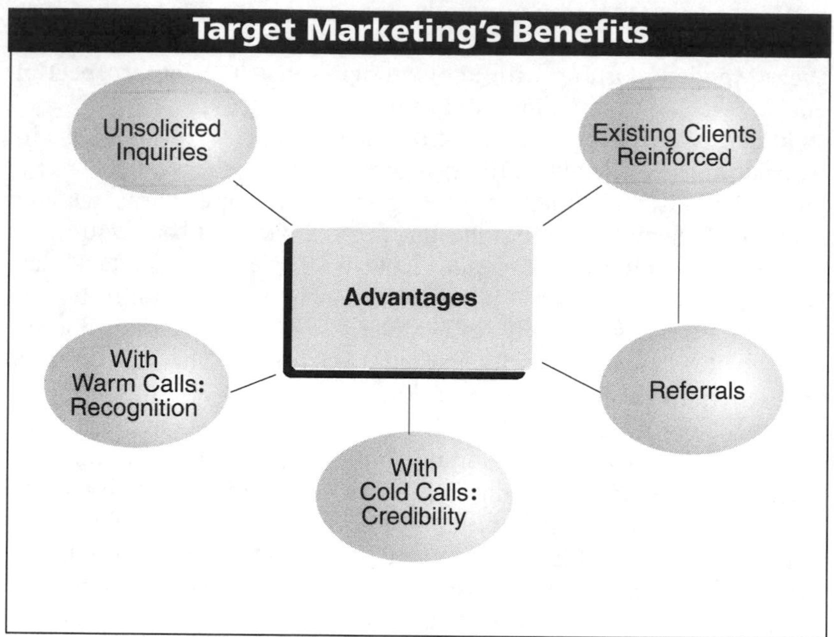

erate within the designated group. You can probably differentiate yourself from other financial advisers, not just by visibility but also because you can add value: You become more knowledgeable than any other adviser about the group's specialized needs and can better serve members. The potential to generate positive word-of-mouth leading to referrals surges, since you are the expert within the community and easy to refer. It's also a very efficient way to market. You're dealing with a common group with common needs and strong links between the members.

But the strategy has disadvantages as well. By definition you are limiting the prospects you target. You're making a fundamental decision to zero in on one, two, or perhaps three communities—the rifle rather than shotgun approach. For the moment, at least, you're setting aside all the other alternative groups. It's also possible you may select the wrong group.

Even if the target seems a natural fit and in the short term is productive, the group itself might face difficulties over the long run. Financial advisers who targeted real estate developers in 1990 might not have been serene about that decision with the real estate slump in 1995. Or, the group might be too small for your needs.

Another difficulty is that just as the potential for positive word-of-mouth can grow exponentially in target marketing, so can negative word-of-mouth. An unhappy client within a broad practice is not a fatal blow. The client moves on, and you focus on all those who remain. But it isn't so easy in target marketing. By definition, people within the targeted group probably talk to one another a lot. It's much harder to escape negative word-of-mouth inspired by a crabby client.

Being the Expert Resource

Many indications suggest target marketing is an option that more and more financial advisers will be forced to explore. As clients become more knowledgeable, they will want to deal with the expert resources for their area. They want the people positioned in their minds as the best qualified for their particular needs.

A parallel would be to imagine yourself stumbling across a body on the street late one night. A knife sticks through the rib cage and you pull it out, only to have a police officer arrive on the scene at precisely that moment. You find yourself down at the local police station, allowed one call. Who do you phone?

Some people in that situation might phone the lawyer in the Yellow Pages with the largest ad. Others might call someone they know, seeking a recommendation. But most people would step back and consider: Who is the best person available to rescue me from this mix-up? Is Eddie Greenspan available? On important issues, people gravitate to the resource they consider most expert for their particular circumstances.

When you reach Eddie Greenspan, you're also unlikely to ask him to fax a proposal on how he intends to handle the matter, with an outline of his fees. You're more likely to plead, "Mr. Greenspan, I have a serious problem. Can you fly here immediately. It doesn't matter what you charge; cost is not an issue." On important matters, you want the best.

But let's try another scenario. On this same dark night on the same dark street, as you head home, instead of a body lying in wait for you, it's a police car, and the officer pulls you over for speeding. But you weren't breaking the speed limit: you're being harassed by the local police force. Furious, you decide to fight back. Would you hire Eddie Greenspan? Not likely. Instead, you would probably thumb the Yellow Pages, call a few lawyers, and check their fees. On trivial matters, you tend to accept what's convenient.

That's true of us, and it's also true of our clients. And since financial advice is important rather than trivial, we have to position ourselves in the minds of a significant client base as being the best, or among the best, for their needs. That's difficult to accomplish in an entire community, unless it's a very small one. The only way to manage it in an larger community is somehow to segment the market and focus on a subset of the broader group. We don't need to position ourselves as the best for everybody. We only need to be perceived as the best by a clear, definable segment of that whole market.

That's what target marketing is all about. Sometimes people get confused and figure that if they target market, they can't accept clients outside their target group. So if someone is target marketing veterinarians and receives a referral from a veterinarian to his brother-in-law who is a doctor, the adviser is supposedly compelled to say, "I'm sorry, I can't deal with him because I only deal with veterinarians."

In fact you can take on any clients and referrals you receive. Target marketing simply involves focusing your marketing energies on one particular group so that you can better meet its needs. You direct your time, energy, and resources toward that group. But you don't reject other clients you already have or other prospects that wander your way.

Interestingly, advisers who target market find less price resistance. Just as Eddie Greenspan doesn't get people quibbling over his fees, once you've identified yourself as the best adviser in a narrow area you reap a financial reward. You'll find it less likely that prospects will try to negotiate downward on price, and more likely they'll be willing to pay a premium to work with you.

The physiotherapist-turned-adviser who decided to return to her roots identified a number of benefits from concentrating her marketing efforts. She found that every time she wrote a column for the association newsletter her existing clients' comfort level in working with her seemed to rise. The flow of referrals within the physiotherapy community also increased. It's easier to refer a colleague to the person perceived as the best community resource. When she attended meetings she sometimes had five or six clients introducing her to other physiotherapists in the room.

Meanwhile, she continued to cold call, but within the target market. When she called, often people would remark that they had heard her speak or they read her columns. Sometimes they were actually flattered that this expert—the best resource in their community—was contacting them. Indeed, it's probably wrong to call that a cold call. It was a warm call. And even when they didn't recognize her name and hadn't heard her speak or read the columns, she still could begin with more credibility: "I specialize in meeting the needs of physiotherapists."

Another advantage was that she started to receive unsolicited inquiries. Every financial adviser's dream is to pick up the phone and discover it's a prospect calling you. The position she attained encouraged that to happen.

The final advantage was that she was happier. Monday mornings were now enjoyable. She looked forward to getting to work and starting the week. She liked her work better because it was more fruitful, the negative elements had disappeared, and her new career had united with her old passion for physiotherapy and allied fields. Target marketing, for her, was a marvelous breakthrough.

Snapshots

- ✔ *Generalists have lost ground in the past decade and a half. When a specialist has appeared on the scene with greater expertise and more powerful appeals to a narrow marketplace, generalists have had trouble competing for that target group.*
- ✔ *Most financial advisers have resisted the trend to specialization, in large measure because few have had the discipline to focus their marketing activity.*
- ✔ *The penalty for that refusal to target has so far not been great, since generalists do fine as long as they are competing against other generalists.*
- ✔ *Targeting allows you to build trust more easily through the visibility you generate within the designated group. You can add value to that group by becoming more knowledgeable than any other adviser about the group's needs, and as a result serve members better.*
- ✔ *The potential to generate positive word-of-mouth and referrals escalates with targeting, since you become the expert within the community, and it's easy to refer friends to you. It's also a very efficient way to market.*
- ✔ *The main disadvantage is that you are limiting the prospects you target, by using the rifle rather than shotgun approach.*
- ✔ *A danger of target marketing is that you could pick the wrong group. It could be too small or headed for difficulty as an industry or profession.*
- ✔ *Just as the potential for positive word-of-mouth can grow exponentially in target marketing, so can negative word-of-mouth.*
- ✔ *On important matters people want the best. On trivial matters they tend to accept what's convenient. Since financial advice is important rather than trivial, you have to position yourself in the minds of a significant client base as the among the best for their needs.*
- ✔ *Being perceived as the best is hard to accomplish in a large community. Instead, segment the market, focusing on a subset of the entire group.*

- ✔ *Target marketing doesn't mean sacrificing clients or prospects outside your designated group. It simply involves focusing your marketing energies on a particular group so that you can better meet its needs.*
- ✔ *A physiotherapist-turned-adviser who decided to return to her roots found writing a column for an association newsletter raised her existing clients' comfort level. The flow of referrals also increased.*
- ✔ *Given the advantages of specialization, the pattern will inevitably take hold in our industry. Normally the big winners are the first to shift, leading the pack rather than chasing others.*

CHAPTER 25

Selecting a Target Market

TARGET MARKETING REQUIRES PATIENCE. THE INSTINCTIVE REACTION OF many advisers after hearing about target marketing is to lunge into the first possible market that comes to mind and try to sell immediately. They assume that the natural attachments within the group will automatically handle the delicate issues of building trust and profile.

For effective target marketing, however, you should proceed carefully, with intelligence and patience. First, you should identify several possible target groups. Then you must research those groups, learning about members' needs and any competition for their business, to verify whether they are feasible targets.

After selecting the best target, you have to build a profile, employing the various trust-building suggestions we've mentioned earlier in the book. Arrange writing and speaking opportunities, attend meetings, and participate in events such as golf tournaments and fund-raisers. Only after laying that foundation can you effectively sell to the group.

In evaluating a target market, the first criterion is that members have sufficient resources to invest. The group may be alluring for other reasons, but if members aren't in a position to invest—or there aren't enough members—it's unlikely to be a rewarding group. You might admire the work of young artists in your community and feel you would enjoy associating with them, but they aren't a group likely to generate much business at this stage in their lives.

You also have to be sure the group will have enough resources tomorrow to support a target-marketing specialist. Do any obvious threats exist that could jeopardize their economic future? Wholesalers of tobacco products might be an excellent target market today, but down the road they may not remain as attractive.

Second, you should steer clear of groups that are over-prospected or already have a dominant adviser in place. Some professions that tend to be among the initial target markets considered, such as physicians, are also classically over-prospected. The existence of a dominant adviser does not preclude entering that market but turns it into a much tougher struggle. The noise level is heightened, and the obstacles to developing credibility are more pronounced. It's harder to access the trust-building vehicles such as the speaking and writing opportunities because the topics aren't fresh and competition abounds. You want a target group that's not over-prospected; ideally, nobody should be currently targeting this group.

Specialists can steal clients from generalists—even generalists masquerading as specialists.

Third, the target market needs to be accessible through existing organizational and communication links. Members must meet and communicate with one another, through meetings and publications, so that you can build visibility and profile as the group's expert resource. Have they established a trade association? Do industry publications exist? Do they hold conventions and meetings? How often, and where? If the group hasn't banded together in an association, members don't meet, and no steady communication vehicles have been established, it will be extremely difficult to be successful.

In researching the group's communication processes, you need to discover who are the leaders—the individuals who exert influence and who you would initially try to bring onside so they might open doors to others. If it's an industry association, does it have an executive director? If it's an ethnic group, has somebody served as president for the last fifteen years, or does everybody look up to a distinguished elder?

Fourth, the group must share the affinity that doctors display toward one another. Being able to tell a physician-prospect "I specialize in meeting the needs of doctors," or "I work with ten other physicians in the community" produces an instantaneous, visceral connection. Credibility is being silently transferred, as the physician-prospect considers, "I have some needs in common with those people, so if you work with them, I'll listen more seriously to you."

Contrast that position with calling a prospect and saying, "I specialize in meeting the financial needs of graduates from the local university." Those graduates share something in common, but they don't generally feel a strong affinity to one another unless they attended at the same time. In target marketing, you should seek groups that feel unique and display affinity.

Fifth, the group should be a natural fit: You should enjoy dealing with its members. If you have a visceral reaction against lawyers, for example, they're probably not your best prospecting target, even if they conform to the other criteria. The chemistry must be present.

Finally, it's best that you have a starting point for making inroads with the group. That base may be, as with our physiotherapist-adviser, a common background. Perhaps you're an accountant, so you might target accountants. Perhaps you're an engineer, in which case that group is a logical target. If prior to becoming a financial adviser you worked as a sales representative for a pharmaceutical company, you might target pharmacists, or physicians. Or you might have common interests with the target group, such as a love of sailing (Figure 25.1).

One way to identify target groups is to study your client base and look for repeaters. That indicates a likely chemistry and a base from which to mount your offensive.

Some Target Markets to Consider

With those criteria in mind, let's scout some possibilities (Figure 25.2). Professions are obvious target markets: chiropractors, dentists, doctors, veterinarians, accountants. . . . The list goes on and on.

Many advisers focus successfully on an ethnic group. Typically, if you're part of an ethnic group—particularly one that hasn't traditionally been a source of many financial advisers—you have an excellent opportunity to differentiate yourself from advisers who aren't members of that segment of society.

Small businesses can be thriving target markets. Some financial advisers concentrate on auto dealers or print-shop owners. Others will select a group as narrow as McDonald's franchise-holders.

Figure 25.1

Requirements for an Effective Target Group

1. Resources to invest
2. Not over-prospected/no dominant adviser already in place
3. Accessible via existing groups/common communication methods (members communicate)
4. Natural for you (you like dealing with them)
5. You can add value
6. Base from which to start in place
    - common background
    - common interests
    - existing client(s)
    - repeaters in client base

Figure 25.2

Possible Target Group Categories

1. Professions (chiropractors, dentists, veterinarians)
2. Ethnic groups (Italian, Chinese, Indian, Korean)
3. Small business (auto dealers, printshop owners, McDonald's franchisees)
4. Occupations (controllers, salespeople, CEOs)
5. Affluent hobbies (tennis clubs, country clubs, sailing, flying)
6. Residential communities (community association, residents' association)
7. Personal activities (bridge club, little league, church groups)

A fourth alternative is to pick an occupational group. Professional salespeople could form a target group, or corporate controllers and financial vice-presidents.

Some advisers target affluent hobbies. They set out to be the adviser of choice at a local country club—the first person who the members of that golf club, whatever their occupation or ethnicity, will think about when considering an adviser. The adviser sponsors golf tournaments or club awards, plays a prominent role on the club's key committees, and seeks out opportunities to speak at meetings. Not only golf fits the bill: You could spotlight tennis, sailing, or even something as narrow as flying.

Residential communities are not an obvious target, but some financial advisers have picked a narrow residential area and become the adviser of choice for people in the residents' association or other community groups. Some advisers focus on personal activities such as bridge clubs, baseball leagues for the young or old, or church groups.

Your targeting approach could also be product-driven. You can focus on new issues, a specific industrial sector such as technology, or high-yield bonds. The investments in that situation determine the people you then target.

Broad vs. Narrow

Once you develop a critical mass of five or six clients within any of these possible target groups, it's much easier to develop other clients within the community, since you've now become a safer choice to deal with. You're the expert (and friendly face) for that group.

In evaluating those groups, however, keep in mind the other issues mentioned earlier. Members of the group must have the resources to invest, or it's not a feasible target. They must feel affinity with each other. Communications and other links must be accessible. Those are all absolutes; without them you're wasting your time. It's also preferable if members of the group are not over-prospected and you have a base to serve as a launch pad.

One of the critical philosophical challenges advisers confront in target marketing is how broad or narrow the target should be. An adviser might say, "I can understand the value of target marketing, of positioning myself as an expert for a specific group. But I want to target market in such a way that I'm not leaving anyone out. So I'm going to position myself as the expert resource for people with money."

Unfortunately that marketing approach resembles an advertisement I saw recently for a noted restaurant. Midway through the copy it declared, "We specialize in French, Italian, and North American food." That's a business which realized the value of specializing to compete, but then decided to claim it specialized in everything. The intended message is: "No matter what your needs are, we specialize in it." But to specialize in everything is to specialize in nothing—to be a generalist. And a generalist, even pretending to be a specialist, will lose out to a true specialist. If you want French cuisine, you would probably pass on this restaurant in favor of one truly specializing in that style.

While this is an extreme case, that instinct is not uncommon. Even if you're somewhat more disciplined, you might decide, say, to specialize in business owners. They have the resources and an affinity. Generally they have connective tissue: associations with newsletters and meetings.

The risk, however, is that the group is still somewhat broad and another ambitious adviser can dive in underneath you, slicing off an attractive chunk of your targeted market. He decides, "I'm going to target restaurant owners. I'll go to the local meetings of the restaurant association, write for its publication, and try to speak at an association meeting. I'll also host two seminars this year for the group on enhancing productivity and new marketing ideas."

If you're typically talking to a restaurant owner in the morning, a general contractor in the afternoon, and the owner of a print shop in the evening, you'll find in time that it will be difficult to compete against the financial adviser who is targeting just restaurant owners. You have become the generalist. He is the specialist—and more attractive to that group, because he's wrapped up in their 99.

But even he is not secure. Another smart financial adviser can stroll along and sense a market opportunity. She figures, "There's an intriguing sub-group of the restaurant-owner universe that has affinity, resources, and communications ties. That's McDonald's franchise-holders. I already have two clients that own McDonald's franchises. I'll start attending their meetings, develop a special newsletter targeted to their needs, and organize a special trip to the annual meeting of McDonald's. I'll also see if sufficient interest can be found for a tour of restaurant operations throughout the country. The franchise holders would pay the cost of the trip, but I would arrange it and be front and center."

The adviser who targeted restaurants in general will still keep most of them and be able to expand, because he is the pre-eminent authority in that broad category. But he will have difficulty attracting and holding McDonald's franchise owners, because the competing adviser has become their specialist. Whenever a financial adviser picks out a sub-group that has more affinity to the sub-group than to the larger group, that adviser has a chance to control that niche.

The broader your choice of target group, the more prospects you can hit. More business owners are available than restaurant owners, and there are more restaurant owners than McDonald's franchise owners. That's the advantage of a broad group. But the narrower you target, within reason, the better the profile you'll be able to build within the group, meeting members' needs, and the more insulated you will find yourself from a competitor sliding in underneath you.

As a financial adviser you are arguably better off as the pre-eminent resource in three or four sub-groups rather than the pre-eminent resource in one large group. Of course, the size of your city affects the strategy. In a larger community you have more flexibility because of the larger population to draw upon. Lots of McDonald's franchises are present, not just one. In smaller communities, the group must inevitably be broader to sustain the marketing initiative. As well, in the smaller community you're more protected from someone lopping off a subgroup, because it's likely too slender to be viable.

Strategically, a number of factors come into play as you shift to target marketing. The process is not automatic. The group or groups you should pick may not be obvious. It entails balancing the various factors and making a strategic choice.

Snapshots

✔ *The first step in target marketing is to identify several possible target groups. Then you should research those groups, finding out more about members' needs and the competition, to ensure the groups are feasible targets.*

✔ *The first criteria for a target market is that members have sufficient resources to invest.*

- ✔ *Second, the group should not be over-prospected or already have a dominant adviser in place.*
- ✔ *Third, the target market must be accessible through existing organizational links and communications vehicles.*
- ✔ *Fourth, the group must feel affinity.*
- ✔ *Fifth, the group should be a natural fit for you.*
- ✔ *Finally, it's best that you have a starting point for making inroads with the group.*
- ✔ *Some possible target markets are based on professions, ethnic groups, small businesses, occupations, affluent hobbies, residential communities, personal activities, or investment products.*
- ✔ *One of the critical philosophical challenges advisers confront in target marketing is how broad or narrow the target market should be.*
- ✔ *The broader the target group you choose, the more prospects you can hit. But the narrower the target, within reason, the better you'll be able to build a presence within the group, meeting members' needs, and the more insulated you will be from a competitor sliding in beneath you.*
- ✔ *As a financial adviser you are probably better off being the pre-eminent resource in three or four sub-groups rather than the pre-eminent source in one large group.*
- ✔ *The size of the community you work in affects your strategy. A larger community allows you more flexibility because of the greater population to draw upon. Even narrowly targeted groups can contain many potential clients. In smaller communities the group you target must inevitably be broader to sustain the marketing initiative.*

CHAPTER 26

Beginning Target Marketing

LET'S PRESUME YOU'VE DECIDED TO TARGET MARKET. YOU HAVE IDENTIFIED three to five possible target groups and with the help of Figure 26.1 evaluated your fit against each using our suggested point system. One group clearly emerges with the highest score. Now you have to research that pacesetter carefully, to learn its 99. What are the main problems confronting group members? What are their current hot buttons?

Recently I needed to learn more about dentists for a workshop. I called my own dentist and asked if I could schedule ten minutes at a convenient time to talk on the telephone about the issues and concerns of dentists. When dentists got together, what did they worry about? He was quite happy to oblige, and we had a pleasant ten-minute chat—it doesn't take any longer to cover the territory. Eight key points surfaced, ranging from the effect of fluoride, to financial pressures and the need to operate a dental practice like a business, to the fear of AIDS (Figure 26.2).

Getting Information

In investigating your target group, you would follow the same procedure. The first source of information is generally a member of the group whom you already know. It's important to respect his or her time and keep the conversation brief, certainly under fifteen minutes.

You explain, "The reason for this talk is that I want to get a better understanding of the group's needs because I'm considering focusing some part of my practice on it. I'm not going to try to sell you anything. This is simply information gathering." At the end you thank him and push for additional contacts: "Listen, this has been wonderful. I really appreciate it. I'm wondering whether I can ask a further favor: Do you know two or three other people I might be able to have a brief conversation with about dentistry?"

Figure 26.1

Evaluating Target Groups

	Name of Group	Name of Group	Name of Group
1. Resources (1–5 points)	______	______	______
2. No dominant adviser/ not over-prospected (1–5)	______	______	______
3. Accessible via existing communication methods (1–5)	______	______	______
4. Fit (1–5)	______	______	______
5. Base from which to start (1–5)	______	______	______
Total (out of 25)	______	______	______

The second source would be trade publications. Find back issues and read them carefully. They will not only alert you to the issues facing the group but also indicate whether an opening exists for you to write a column on financial matters for that particular publication. The back issues might also reveal whether somebody has beat you to the punch and is already prospecting within the group.

A third source is the industry association. Often it's possible to sit down or at least talk on the telephone with the executive director, a staffer, or an executive member. You want to know the group's unique needs. "I'm thinking about putting together a series of workshops that would focus on specific concerns of dentists," you might say, "and I want to better understand what are the circumstances and needs of dentists today."

Finally, don't overlook other suppliers to the group who might have a wealth of information to offer. If you're targeting dentists, consider talking to accountants, lawyers, or bankers who have a lot of dentists as clients. You could contact the dentistry dean at the university or distributors of dental equipment. All those people interact regularly with dentists and can offer insight on their 99 and how to make inroads into the target group (Figure 26.3).

Building Profile

After those two steps—identifying and researching the target group—you have to begin building profile within it (Figure 26.4). Recently I

Figure 26.2

TARGET GROUP: Dentists

CONTACT: Dr. Allen Kent

TELEPHONE: 555-4826

KEY POINTS:

1. Effect of fluoride in toothpaste & better education in schools and homes—kids have fewer cavities.
2. More and more insurance plans covering treatment—attracts patients who wouldn't have come previously, but caps amount can charge (based on out-of-date fee schedules).
3. Overall under increasing financial pressures (especially newer dentists, for whom cost of establishing a practice is high with banks more cautious about loaning large sums to purchase equipment to get started).
4. Need to manage dental practice like a business—need staff of dental hygienists/assistants and delegate routine work to make a good living.
5. Increasing trend to treat adults with corrective procedures/orthodontics.
6. Finding and maintaining qualified staff a bigger and bigger issue.
7. AIDS
8. Stress level among dentists one of the highest among any profession—high levels of burnout.

SOURCES OF ADDITIONAL INFORMATION

1.	Dr. Barbara Olnychuk	555-1234
2.	Dr. Peter Bernas	555-5678
3.	Dr. Tom Elliott	555-9123

worked with a financial adviser who, as it happened, had targeted dentists. He already had several dentists as clients, so that provided a base on which to develop profile. Over the course of a couple of meetings we developed a five-point marketing plan to position the adviser as the pre-eminent financial resource for dentists in his community:

1. He decided to attend some of the local dental association's monthly meetings as well as the annual meeting. Attending every month seemed over-ambitious, so we settled for every second meeting.
2. He had already approached and had some luck with a quarterly publication for dentists called *Dental Practice Management*: The editors were interested in the possibility of his writing a regular 750-word column.

Figure 26.3

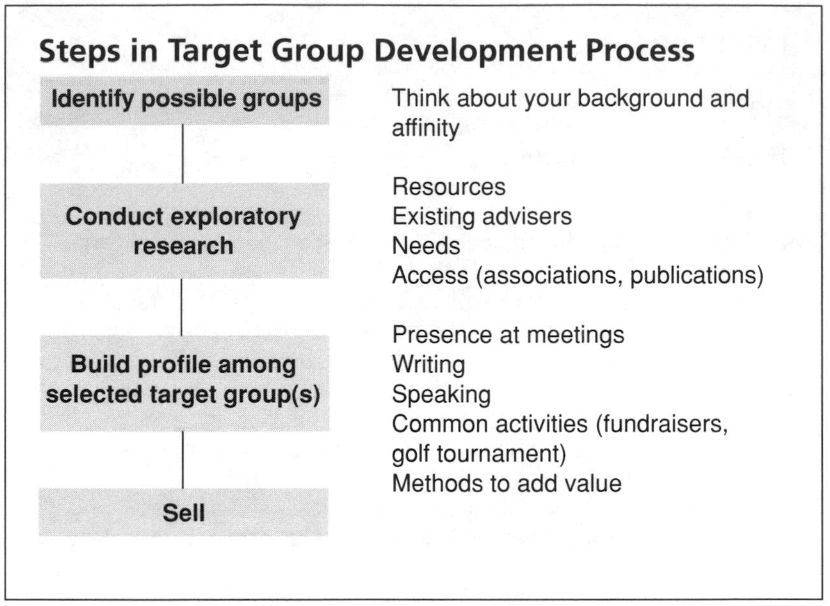

Figure 26.4

Target Group: ______________________

Opportunities for Building Profile:

Associations	1. ________
	2. ________
	3. ________
Writing Opportunities	1. ________
	2. ________
	3. ________
Existing Suppliers	1. ________
	2. ________
	3. ________
Speaking Opportunities	1. ________
	2. ________
	3. ________

3. He figured he would hold a spring seminar on tax strategies for dentists, featuring a local accountant with a significant number of dentists as clients, and a fall seminar on estate planning with a local lawyer as guest speaker who also specialized in dentists. He would, of course, act as host and remain in the limelight at the events.
4. In the course of his research on dentists he had come across a number of compelling articles relating to practice management, staffing, financial affairs, and marketing. He decided to send a mailing every second month to all dentists in the community with a collection of such articles, totaling no more than four pages.
5. He also intended to approach the local dental association to pursue an opportunity to speak at one of its functions.

Calculating the Time Commitment

Most financial advisers would agree that his approach was sound and would establish his credibility and visibility. It would carry him a long way down the road to being the expert on financial advice for that particular target group. But many advisers might question the effort involved, which seems quite overwhelming. How do you maintain an existing client base and stream of revenue while investing in a new target market?

Let's review his activities, then, to calculate exactly how much time you would actually be committing if you undertook a similar initiative. Start with the association's six meetings. You would obviously want to arrive early and leave late, since much of the benefit derives from mingling with dentists before and after the formal meeting. That might amount to three hours per meeting, or a total of eighteen hours annually.

The quarterly articles would require research and, even if material was available from convenient sources like head office, adequate time to shape them to your own particular personality and slant. The column has to be high quality, because if it's not, it isn't worth doing. Let's assume each article would take twelve hours to prepare (although your time commitment, remember, could be cut down dramatically by hiring a journalism student to conduct an interview and write the article). If the twelve-hour estimate seems understated, consider that for a 750-word article that amounts to roughly sixty words an hour, or about a word a minute. In total, the four articles would demand forty-eight hours of preparation.

The two seminars involve considerable effort, but much of it—the preparation of invitation lists, typing of labels, liaising with caterers—can be delegated to your staff. Still, you have to handle the planning and co-ordination, meet with the outside speaker, prepare your own talk, oversee the publicity, and check the site. It's reasonable to estimate you will spend forty hours per seminar, or eighty hours over the year. That's not a huge amount of time, given that you should attract a large crowd, leveraging the event off the popularity of the guest speakers and their own client base.

The articles you need to distill for the target group involve a lot of reading, but much of that is simply part of an adviser's normal burden of keeping informed. Let's assume it takes three hours extra to prune through and select the package of articles. The rest of the work—photocopying and mailing—is a staff function. So that costs you eighteen hours of time over the year.

The half-hour speech to the association meeting is the final item of the marketing strategy. It requires extensive time to research, write, practice, and practice again. For some advisers, the total time required would be infinity: they could start today and never finish. If you're not comfortable speaking, this avenue is probably not worth pursuing. The rule of thumb on presentations is that you should generally spend an hour in preparation for every minute of the presentation itself. So if it's a thirty-minute talk, expect to spend about thirty hours beforehand.

Together, all the marketing initiatives for the target group amount to 194 hours over the course of the year. That's a cautious estimate, because we wanted to do a high-quality job. But even that conservative appraisal works out to less than four hours a week.

The question you have to ask, as you consider target marketing, is: Would that be the best investment of time compared to other possible investments of three to four hours a week? Some advisers might shrug off target marketing, figuring they would be smarter to spend that period each week prospecting through other methods. But for many advisers, this could be the best possible use of the time, because it would launch them into a position of prominence in a specific, attractive community. Bear in mind, as well, that after you build your reputation within the targeted group, less time will be required to maintain your position than was demanded to build it. It's the Liftoff Dynamic.

You won't be able to drop all the activities, of course. You have to protect your flank. If you tell the quarterly publication's editor you want to cut back to writing a column only twice a year, some other financial adviser might be invited to fill the gap. But maintaining your position will require less time, because you can be more selective in the activities you follow.

Slow and Sustained

The time you invest in profile-building has to be spread out over a long period for a couple of reasons. First, that makes it manageable while you continue the rest of your practice. But it also has to be extended because, as I've indicated before, trust-building works best when it is a sustained, ongoing process. Faced with an outlay of 194 hours, you could take four weeks off your regular work and devote fifty hours each week to building visibility and profile in the newly targeted market. But your efforts would flop. The issue isn't just finding a block of time. It's finding that time over a sustained period.

All too commonly, advisers fall into the trap of short, episodic bursts of activity before losing focus and drifting on to other pursuits. If you appear at three association meetings, bursting with energy and exuberance, and then seem to disappear, you will hurt rather than help yourself. To position yourself within the target group and maintain that position, you need a high degree of discipline and focus.

In these trust-building activities, you'll find the toughest is gaining the opportunity to speak at an association meeting. Probably not many meetings are held, and if it's an attractive group often other speakers are already lined up for those precious slots. More importantly, until you have built up trust, the program committee will be quite apprehensive. They may be concerned that as soon as they hand you the microphone you'll start flogging product, and they'll be embarrassed because they effectively endorsed you.

Getting an article published is generally easier, and that's usually the first point of penetration. Industry publications seem perennially short of features, and editors are usually eager to fill space. Tell the editor, "I deal with many dentists, and talking to them recently I've heard a lot express concerns about retirement. I've written a column on the topic that I'd like to send along to see if it's a good fit for your publication."

Notice you don't say, "I'm interested in writing a column and if you're interested I'll write it." From the Editor's 99, that's asking for a bigger commitment than simply reading what's been written, and she is less likely to give you the go-ahead. It's much easier for the editor to agree to have a look if you've indicated the potential interest and already have the article completed.

If she asks you to send it along, you may have to scramble to write the piece, but the door is ajar. If the column meets her standards and you receive positive feedback, suggest a second piece. After that, you can propose a regular column. But you're better to edge along one step at a time, rather than beginning by shooting for a monthly column. From the Editor's 99, that's a bigger risk and commitment than she is likely to make. But if you're patient with this, as with all your target marketing activities, credibility will build and it will pay off in the longer term.

Snapshots

✔ *After using the scorecard in Figure 26.1 to evaluate various possible target markets and select the best fit, it's time to research the group.*

- ✔ *Does the group have the resources today and will it have the resources tomorrow to support a target marketing specialist?*
- ✔ *Are any other advisers canvassing members of the group directly or as part of a larger group?*
- ✔ *How do group members communicate?*
- ✔ *Do they have a strong affinity?*
- ✔ *Who are the key influences in the group?*
- ✔ *Finally, what's their 99? What are the current hot buttons?*
- ✔ *Begin soliciting information through someone you know who belongs to the group. It's important to respect his or her time and keep the conversation brief.*
- ✔ *Find back issues of the trade publication or its equivalent, and read them to learn the issues facing the group and also to determine whether an opening is available to write a column on financial matters.*
- ✔ *Talk with key officials in the industry association to learn what's happening.*
- ✔ *Don't neglect to talk to suppliers to the group.*
- ✔ *After researching, begin to build profile. Your plan ideally might involve regularly attending association meetings, writing for a trade publication, hosting seminars, sending out mailings with interesting articles, and speaking at events.*
- ✔ *Those efforts will probably require an average of three to four hours per week. For many advisers, that could be the best possible use of that amount of time, because it would launch them into a position of prominence in a specific, attractive community.*
- ✔ *Remember that after you build your reputation within the targeted group, less time will be required to maintain your position than was needed to build it.*
- ✔ *The hardest marketing activity in a target group is gaining a speaking opportunity at an association meeting. Writing for the association publication is easier, but remember to proceed slowly with the editor, winning trust.*

CHAPTER 27

Building a Target Market

ONCE YOU'VE STARTED TO ATTAIN PROFILE AND DEVELOP TRUST WITH YOUR target market, you want to capitalize by approaching members and discussing their investment needs. The challenge is, as always, to look interested without seeming over-eager or desperate and applying unwanted pressure on the prospect (Figure 27.1).

Marketing Solutions has devised two letters to send a prospect you've met at an industry function, in our example a dentist at an association meeting. The two letters are similar in most respects, noting that you were happy to meet him and are enclosing an article that might be of interest. The difference is in the nature of the article attached. One comes from the *Wall Street Journal,* on the growing financial pressures confronting dentists. The second article was actually written by the financial adviser himself, for a forthcoming issue of *Dental Practice Management* (Figures 27.2, 27.3).

While you can advance a compelling case for both packages, our research found that the *Wall Street Journal* article delivers a better first impression than the *Dental Practice Management* column. The *Wall Street Journal,* as we've noted before, generates a lot of credibility but in this case, more significantly, it serves as a much lower-key follow-up to the initial encounter. The *Dental Practice Management* piece, written by the adviser, inevitably sets the dentist's defenses on edge: What's this adviser trying to sell me? And the last thing you want is to be perceived as somebody who attends dental meetings as a thin excuse to sell. Arguably, the best solution is to send the *Wall Street Journal* article initially and then two months later follow up with the *Dental Practice Management* column.

It's critical that you guard against looking as if you are trying to make incursions into the group simply to pitch products. That's why, for exam-

Figure 27.1

ple, I recommend that if you're targeting a narrow group—again, say, dentists—you decline any invitation to set up a booth at the annual convention. When the dentists walk through the doors of that convention or trade show, what are they thinking about all the people behind booths? The answer: those individuals are out to sell something. Seldom will their bankers, lawyers, or accountants be lined up behind those booths. You want to be a partner with the dentists, on the same level as them, not positioned as somebody inferior trying to grab for their wallet. The Banker's Rule applies here as well as to general prospecting: You want to appear as professional as the most professional advice they receive.

Similarly, it would be a mistake to send a letter like the sample in Figure 27.4, talking about interest rate predictions and the urgency of locking in investments at the current high rates. At first glance this might not seem much different from the other sample letters, since it attaches an article which should be of interest. But whose 99 are you operating from when you send a letter about locking in at high interest rates? It's really your 99 rather than the Client's 99. More importantly, the letter positions you as somebody out to sell something. And you have to be careful when focusing on a target group—particularly a professional group—not to cast yourself in that image.

Contrast that with the letter in Figure 27.5 inviting dentists to a seminar on planning options to ensure retirement or a scaled-down

Figure 27.2

Date

Dr. Allen Kent
1234 Any Street
Any City, Any State 56789

Dear Dr. Kent,

I enjoyed meeting you at the ADA meeting on Tuesday evening.

Further to our conversation on the growing financial pressures facing dentists, I thought you might find the attached article from the *Wall Street Journal* of interest. It talks about how some of the issues we discussed are affecting dentists south of the border and what some are doing as a result.

I look forward to seeing you at upcoming meetings of the ADA.

Best regards,

Any Adviser

practice by age 55. It's at a country club, jointly presented with an accountant from a prominent firm. Notice that while you are charging $50 for the seminar (implicitly conveying that it must be valuable if other dentists are willing to pay the price), the entire admission fee is being donated to the local dental association scholarship fund. You're asking for a signal of serious business commitment by requiring participants to spend money to attend, but the flavor is much loftier and more low key, suggesting value rather than arm-twisting. The response to this approach has been very positive, because it builds credibility and positions you as an adviser rather than a salesperson. And that must be the key element of all your communication with the group.

Figure 27.3

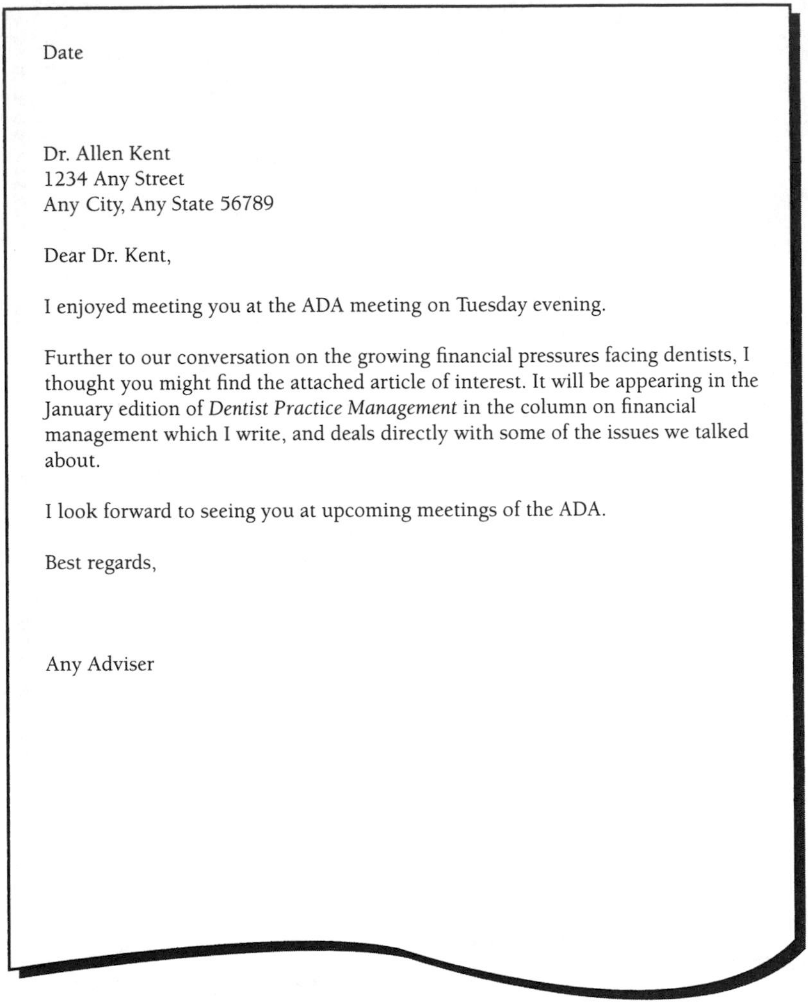

Date

Dr. Allen Kent
1234 Any Street
Any City, Any State 56789

Dear Dr. Kent,

I enjoyed meeting you at the ADA meeting on Tuesday evening.

Further to our conversation on the growing financial pressures facing dentists, I thought you might find the attached article of interest. It will be appearing in the January edition of *Dentist Practice Management* in the column on financial management which I write, and deals directly with some of the issues we talked about.

I look forward to seeing you at upcoming meetings of the ADA.

Best regards,

Any Adviser

Finding New Ways to Do Business

When planning your marketing strategy for the target group, you have to follow the normal trust-building steps we've developed for general prospecting and the general mix of clients. But it's also an opportunity in some measure to alter the way you work to better meet this specific group. You can differentiate yourself not just by building credibility within the group but also by offering some services that are tailored to that particular cluster.

For example, suppose you are a financial adviser in the snow belt of Canada and the northern United States. You decide to target semi-

Figure 27.4

Date

Dr. Allen Kent
1234 Any Street
Any City, Any State 56789

Dear Dr. Kent,

These days, one of the key issues in making sound investment decisions is predicting the direction of interest rates.

I thought you might find the attached predication of interest rate trends by the Conference Board, which came out just last week, interesting reading. A peaking of interest rates is predicted in the period ahead—if that's correct, now's the time to lock in the current high interest rates.

Please feel free to call if you have any questions or if I can be of assistance.

Best regards,

Any Adviser

retired or retired people who winter in a warmer climate, heading down to Florida, California, or Arizona. What are their unique needs? First, and critical to your operation, is that they have a special problem with access to their advisers, since they're away for part of the year. Secondly, they have security concerns, as their houses are unattended for an extended period of time. Thirdly, they face difficulties staying in touch with events in their communities while away.

Let's say you decide to hold a workshop for these snowbirds (Figure 27.6). The first change to your normal practice would be in selecting the date and time: The best period for them tends to be Saturday morning. They don't have the pressures of work and family that com-

Figure 27.5

Date

Dr. Allen Kent
1234 Any Street
Any City, Any State 56789

Dear Dr. Kent,

In a recent survey conducted for the *American Journal of Dentistry,* over half of dentists indicated that they hoped to retire or scale down their practice by age 55.

The only issue that they saw as potentially standing in their way: Being able to pull back without sacrificing their standard of living.

Last spring, a number of your colleagues attended a seminar on precisely this topic. Held at the Markham Golf and Country Club from 6 P.M. to 9 P.M., it outlined some of the financial planning issues and options facing successful dentists planning for their retirement. Assisting me in presenting this seminar was Joanne Rogers of Doane Raymond, a C.A. who works extensively with dental practices.

The seminar was so well received that Joanne and I are offering a follow-up session on the evening of May 20 for those dentists who were unable to attend the first one. The entire $50 admission fee will be donated to the American Dental Association Scholarship Fund; all the details are outlined in the attached invitation. (Some of the comments from your colleagues who have attended the last seminar are included as well.)

Since discussion is a key part of the seminar, space is of necessity limited and reservations will be taken in the order they are received. I hope to see you on May 20—please feel free to call should you have any questions before then.

Best regards,

Any Adviser

pel your other clientele to prefer weekday sessions in the evening or at lunch. Evening would work for these snowbirds, but a seminar over brunch draws particularly well.

For speakers, instead of the accountants and lawyers you normally spotlight in seminars, you might want to turn to a representative from the local police and somebody from an insurance agency to talk about residential protection during an extended absence. If your snowbird clients winter in Florida, you might acknowledge their 99 by telling them, “To help you, I’ve established a 1-800 number for my office so you can call anytime with questions and concerns. Beyond that, I intend to

Figure 27.6

Enjoying Your Place in the Sun This Winter

Featuring:

Minimizing Out-of-Plan Health Insurance Costs	Mary Smith AARP
Tax Implications of Wintering Elsewhere	Joe Jones Ernst & Young
Legal Consequences of Second Home Ownership	Peter Johnson Johnson & Elliott law firm
Leaving Your Home with Peace of Mind	Sgt. William Brady Miami Police Department

Date: Saturday, February 19, 2000
Place: Great Hall, Carleton University
Time: 8:30 A.M. Coffee/Registration
9:00 A.M. Presentation
Noon Adjournment

Sponsored by the Local Newspaper and Your Firm
For more information call______________________

make a significant sacrifice, and leave my frigid, snowbound locale two or three times this winter to travel to Florida and meet with my clients one-on-one to answer any questions that develop while they're away. As well, if we're working together, once a week I will send you a package of photocopies from the local newspaper with items of interest."

You have rearranged elements of your practice to meet the Client's 99. You have increased the chance of gaining referrals, by enhanced service to this target community. The newsletter, in particular, when it has been tried by advisers, tends to be a prime source of conversation among other snowbirds who aren't working with the specific adviser and want to keep abreast of news from home.

Finally, you are building competitive insulation. A generalist adviser who approaches any of your clients is highly unlikely to steal them. The only way that generalist adviser can match you is by also changing work methods.

On this recurring theme of specialized vs. generalist, it's important to stress that the seminar you host for snowbirds on home security is unlikely to be compelling for other prospects or clients, even those who are retired but not planning to be away for extended periods. Unless they're thinking of adopting such a lifestyle in the future, they're unlikely to attend.

Should you care? Absolutely not. If enough snowbirds are available for a successful seminar—clients and new prospects you can tap through the local senior-citizens council, travel agents, and other professionals—it doesn't matter that you couldn't lure the hundreds of thousands of people in your community who aren't snowbirds. The essence of target marketing is producing a strong appeal to a narrow group rather than relying on a low, indifferent appeal to a broad group. If the group you target is sufficiently large and has appropriate resources, you can be better off with the focused appeal.

A Chance for Innovation

Target marketing allows more flexibility in developing approaches to meet your Clients' 99. Let's say you're targeting restaurant owners. Instead of falling back for seminars on issues closer to your 99, like retirement planning, you can be more innovative by responding to their 99. The opportunities, actually, proliferate. You could bring in a consultant to highlight successful marketing techniques for restaurants. You could invite a consultant on personnel issues to comment on effective motivation and staffing techniques. A banker specializing in financing restaurants could discuss the principles of dealing with financial institutions. You could host a seminar on anti-fraud and anti-theft defenses to minimize slippage at restaurants. All those topics probably have greater appeal for those clients and prospects than the familiar chestnut of retirement planning, which generalist advisers are offering.

Similarly, you could sprinkle articles on those types of topics throughout your newsletter for the target market. Stories could offer marketing tips, new trends in restaurants, and motivation techniques, as well as investment-related information. It's added value that they will heartily appreciate and that will bond them more closely to you. The newsletter may be of no interest to someone running an auto dealership, but you shouldn't care in the slightest. A strong appeal to a narrow group can serve you well.

Similarly, suppose you decide to target professional salespeople: real estate agents, wholesalers, commercial leasing agents, computer salespeople, commission salespeople in the textile industry, and other high-earners in this category. What's their 99? Given the pressures they face, they would probably be interested in seminars on stress management or time management. They have an unquenchable thirst for ideas on selling, so you could invite in a consultant to talk about new methods for developing relationships with prospective clients. You could establish a networking group in which the various salespeople could exchange leads and tips. The newsletter could develop similar themes, honing in on your target market's 99, adding value that insulates you from generalist competitors.

New Communities for New Advisers

I held a workshop recently for rookie brokers in Toronto, a highly competitive metropolitan market in which it is difficult to differentiate yourself. One of the brokers asked a tough question: If I was coming into the business now, what would I do? In response, I sketched out another variant of target marketing for large, metropolitan centers.

I suggested taking out a map and drawing a circle perhaps sixty miles outside the city. Then you should search for two to five communities just beyond that circle, which have populations of about 6,000 to 10,000 people. You would then visit those communities, seeking for your future prospecting two small towns that don't have dominant advisers and are a fairly short drive apart.

You should then commit yourself to spending a day every two weeks building profile and credibility in those target communities. A morning in one community, an afternoon in the other—not a huge commitment. You should establish a part-time office, because it's difficult to build credibility when you tell a prospect, "Step into my office; let me open the back door of my car." To obtain that space, you could approach a local insurance or real estate agent, although for higher credibility your best bet would be a lawyer or accountant. That might also help you to initiate a deeper relationship with them.

An early step is to check whether the local newspaper has a regular column on financial affairs. With no dominant adviser, chances are strong that the opportunity exists to pioneer such a column. Since it's a smaller community, you may have to commit to spending $1,000 or $1,500 in advertising over the year to write that feature, but it would be money well spent. Similarly, you should approach the radio station about a weekly or biweekly financial commentary or a more extensive show every month or two in which you would take calls and arrange for outside experts to call in.

Next in building profile, you should introduce yourself to influential people in the community: lawyers, accountants, doctors, mayor, councillors, ministers, the Chamber of Commerce president, and civic administrators. You should join the Kiwanis and Rotary clubs and make a point of attending meetings. Find out the key charities and help out with the Christmas food drive or the United Way. If the community has a hospital board, you might offer to serve on the fund-raising committee (you won't face a lot of competition, let me assure you). Come out for golf tournaments, bonspiels, and other social activities. Through that, you start to become a fixture in the community.

Get a list of business owners who are fairly accessible and call them, advising about your new office and asking if you could stop by to meet them. Offer to speak to the business executives' group, seniors meetings, and individual companies on issues like retirement planning or tax savings. Even if you didn't have to offer an advertising quid pro quo for that column, it might make sense to spend some money on ads and to sponsor a hole at the local golf tournament. It won't amount to much, because the cost of such ventures in small communities isn't high.

After about a year, you might be more ambitious and attempt a broader seminar, since you've established some awareness and credibility. You might bring in an outside speaker, perhaps jointly hosting the event with a local accountant. At that juncture you might also want to sponsor a client appreciation event, something which has worked very well for advisers in smaller communities. Ideal would be a barbecue at a local park on a Saturday morning, with everyone you've met so far invited. In a smaller community, that has the potential to be the social event of the week, if not the month.

If you follow those initiatives—if you're persistent and visible in the community every second week—would you have established yourself as the credible source of advice in the community? Absolutely. The more crucial question, however, is: Would you have received a better return on that investment of one day every second week—10 percent of your time—in this project than through following conventional prospecting methods such as going to trade shows and making cold calls? In some cases, probably no. But in most cases, I believe the answer would be yes.

That return won't be felt immediately, whereas the adviser out cold-calling does garner some immediate short-term results. But after twelve to eighteen months, the adviser who has chiseled out 10 percent of his or her time to build trust against a defined target group will wind up ahead of the game.

Snapshots

✔ *The initial challenge in approaching target market prospects is to look interested without seeming desperate and applying unwanted pressure.*

✔ *Of two packages Marketing Solutions has devised for low-key follow-up after an initial meeting with prospects, the better one included an article from the* Wall Street Journal *on growing financial pressures confronting the target group. You should wait until the recipients' defenses are reduced to send the article you wrote for the industry publication.*

- ✔ *Guard against looking like somebody making incursions into the group simply to pitch products. If you're targeting a narrow group, avoid setting up a booth at the annual convention.*
- ✔ *Our research found it was a mistake to send a letter urging members of the target group to lock in at current interest rates. More effective with professionals was a letter touting a seminar on planning options to ensure retirement or a scaled-down practice by age fifty-five. The event was successfully held at a country club, jointly sponsored with an accountant from a prominent firm, at a cost of $50 to be donated to a charity associated with the group.*
- ✔ *Target marketing allows you to reshape your work activities to better connect with the specific group. You can differentiate yourself by offering services tailored to that particular group, as with the adviser marketing to snowbirds.*
- ✔ *Those new initiatives for the target market build competitive insulation against generalist advisers.*
- ✔ *While targeted seminars and newsletters won't interest people outside the specific group, if you appeal strongly to a narrow group that meets the criteria, you can fare better than through a weaker appeal to a broad group.*
- ✔ *If you live in a large, metropolitan area, you might consider targeting some smaller communities on the outskirts without a dominant adviser.*

Section III
Keeping Clients

CHAPTER 28

Providing Value to Your Clients

THE 1990S, FOR GOOD REASON, HAVE BEEN CALLED THE VALUE DECADE. And that trend will persist. In category after category, clients migrate to those businesses that provide clear, concrete, substantive value. Financial advice is no different. In Keeping Clients, we must focus on adding value so that our top clients become ecstatic apostles, telling everybody about our virtues. We do that through the Value Cycle, a client-centered process made up of six vital elements.

For most clients, the Value Cycle commences with a financial plan (Figure 28.1). It's the foundation for the relationship with the client and the value that you provide. The plan should not be sixty pages of charts, graphs, statistics, and densely spaced type. Neither should it be flimsy—for example, two pages, with one of those a cover page.

As I noted in Chapter 1, for most clients there will be a gap between future financial needs and likely financial capacity. The financial plan puts those issues on the table and presents an agreed-upon solution. The financial plan is a vital part of retirement preparation and, more importantly, at the core of the value proposition that you provide. A financial plan gives clients the sense that they are in control. They can now sleep soundly at night.

Improving Our Advice

The second component of the Value Cycle is the advice that you provide. Historically, the quality of advice from many financial advisers was somewhat hit-and-miss. As clients become more discerning, advisers are having to increase the caliber of the advice that we give. Advisers will have to develop a better understanding of things like optimizing risk and return, and balancing portfolios. The standard of advice simply has to improve.

The third component of value that advisers provide is the products used to execute our advice. Traditionally, it has not been uncommon for clients to be sold product that might not be the absolute best for their needs. Those products, however, might have carried the best commissions or been the only ones the financial adviser could sell. As clients become more knowledgeable, an unquenchable demand will emerge for an open system in which clients will search out the financial advisers who can sell them the best possible products to meet their needs. As clients read the many columns in newspapers touting various financial products and the many books evaluating those alternatives, they won't accept second best.

Are you creating value for clients? Does your value proposition exceed the competition's?

The fourth element of value that advisers present is reporting. For many clients, it's worth stressing, reporting is a constant source of frustration. Quite simply, they don't understand the statements that they receive. The statement might have too little information or too much information—and it's not presented in a form that meets their needs.

This is not rocket science. Clients, typically, want to know how they have done in the last year and how they have done since they started

Figure 28.1

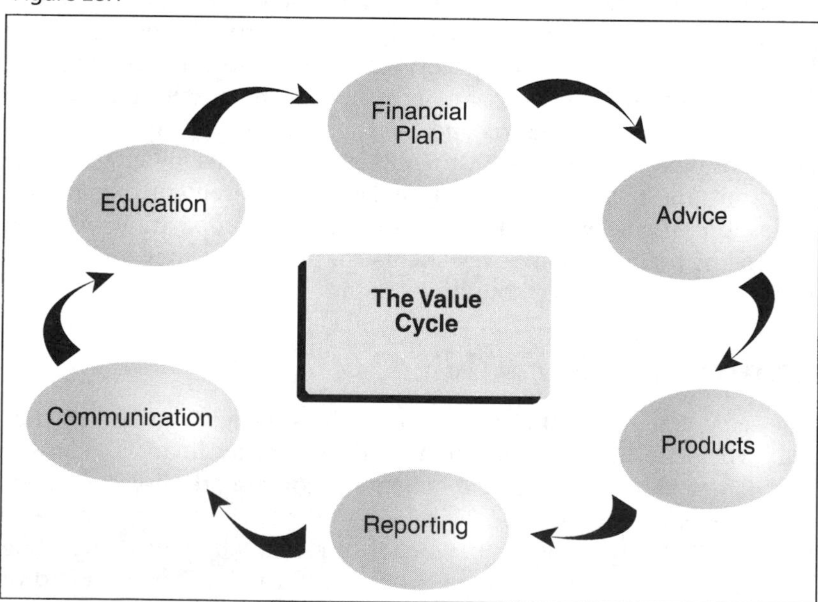

investing. They want that information in both absolute dollar terms and percentage returns. And too often, that information is missing.

One of the challenges for financial advisers is that you are generally constrained in how information is reported to your clients. You are not in control of what head office mails. But that doesn't prevent you as a financial adviser from adding value—supplementing the information that head office provides. More and more, as I indicated in Chapter 1, financial advisers are discovering the power of being able to say to a client, "In addition to the statements you get from my firm, I have found that often clients benefit from receiving some additional statements that are in a different format. Here are three alternatives I use for my clients. Which one would be most appropriate and useful to you?"

A Shot Across the Bow

The fifth element of the Value Cycle is communication. We know from experience that the quality and, in particular, the quantity of communication to clients is paramount in assuring them that they are receiving value from their adviser. And we also know that quantity is more important than quality. A ten-minute phone call every quarter is more important than a one-hour meeting once a year. Depending on the nature of the client, both may be required. But frequent contact for most clients is the jewel that often keeps them from walking away. Frequent contact convinces them they are receiving value from the relationship.

As our client base grows, maintaining that regular contact can become a major challenge. I recently was talking with a financial adviser who had just lost a very substantial client with more than $1-million in assets. The client had walked, suddenly—or at least, suddenly from the financial adviser's viewpoint. When the adviser finally had a chance to see him afterward, the client essentially said, "Look, I never heard from you. I didn't think you were all that interested in my account and I decided to move it somewhere where it would be valued."

The client was gone. But it wasn't too late to ensure that didn't happen with other clients. Fortunately, that financial adviser treated the incident as a shot across the bow. We talked about how to transcend his difficulty of not seeming to have enough hours in the day to accomplish everything he wanted.

We focused on freeing up some time for this urgent priority of ongoing communications with his best clients. He agreed that he could set aside Tuesday and Thursday afternoons, from 1:30 to 5 P.M. He then sent a letter to those clients:

"Dear John/Joan: Staying in regular contact with my clients ranks among my top priorities. Recently, I reviewed a list of my very best clients and realized that we haven't talked recently. It occurred to me that a brief conversation might be helpful, as a way both to get caught up on recent market developments and to answer any questions you might have." The letter then advises that to avoid an extensive game of telephone tag, the adviser's assistant will call to arrange a convenient time for a telephone appointment.

In some cases clients simply indicated that they were happy and saw no need to talk. Everything was okay—which was fine. The adviser had benefited from extending the offer. Other clients were interested in chatting but found Tuesday or Thursday afternoons inconvenient, so that led to some telephone appointments in the mornings or evenings and on weekends. That's inevitable, since clients naturally expect that their adviser will adhere to their schedule.

In the bulk of the cases, clients were delighted to talk to the adviser and agreed to a telephone appointment on a Tuesday or Thursday afternoon. With his assistant's help, the adviser managed about five appointments on each of those days, generally for fifteen to twenty minutes per client, although some ran longer. At that rate, he was able to manage ten clients a week, or forty a month. In that quarter, he spoke to 120 of his clients with an investment of two afternoons a week.

That completed, he had a choice. He could begin the cycle anew with that group, or he could drill down deeper into his client base, hitting another 120 clients. That's an example of how with a little discipline and systematic effort you can add a significant amount of value to your client relationship in a key area: communication.

The sixth stage in the Value Cycle is your commitment to education. Clients increasingly express the desire to understand their investments better. And they look to their financial adviser to educate them. Often clients are frustrated by how difficult it is to get their advisers to help them understand investments.

It's critical that advisers commit themselves to this task, through such vehicles as seminars and financial newsletters. One financial adviser I know puts on relatively small, brief seminars for his clients—they are busy people and can't make a heavy time commitment—but he also tapes the events and circulates copies to clients. Whether those tapes ever get listened to or not, he has signaled his commitment to this element of the value proposition.

It is helpful to review your own activities to see how they relate to the Value Cycle. Are you creating value for clients? Are you touching a variety of bases? Does your value proposition match or exceed your competitors? The surest way to see your client base disintegrate before your eyes is to fall short of the value that your clients expect to receive from a financial adviser.

Snapshots

- ✔ *In Keeping Clients, we must focus on adding value so that our top clients become ecstatic apostles, telling everybody about our virtues.*
- ✔ *The Value Cycle generally begins with a financial plan.*
- ✔ *The financial plan answers three linked questions that clarify the gap between what a client will need at retirement and what he or she can be expected to have on hand. It then lays out a foundation for overcoming that gap, which often revolves around increasing savings or accepting more volatility in investments.*
- ✔ *The second component of the Value Cycle is the advice that you provide. As clients become more discerning, advisers will have to ramp up the caliber of the advice that we give.*
- ✔ *The third component of value that advisers provide is the products used to execute our advice. As clients become more knowledgeable, they won't accept second best.*
- ✔ *The fourth element of value that advisers present is reporting. Clients, typically, want to know how they've done in the last year and since they began investing, in both absolute dollar terms and percentage returns. If head office isn't providing proper reports, you may have to handle that challenge yourself.*
- ✔ *The fifth element of the Value Cycle is communication. Don't wait for a shot across the bow. Arrange for a system of regular contact with clients—particularly your top clients.*
- ✔ *The sixth stage in the Value Cycle is your commitment to education. Clients expect their advisers to help them understand investing.*

CHAPTER 29

Listening

LISTENING IS A CRITICAL SKILL IN KEEPING CLIENTS. YOU CAN BE THE WORLD'S most skillful questioner, but if you don't listen to your clients' answers, you are unlikely to keep them happy or make a sale. Questioning and listening are complementary skills, both essential to advisers because research shows they correlate more frequently with successful outcomes than other attributes. You can be mediocre in closing techniques, dreadful in objection handling, and a not terribly compelling presenter of recommendations but still attain success. However, if you haven't developed acute questioning and listening skills, your long-term future in this business will be limited as you deal with more knowledgeable, more discerning clients and prospects.

To gauge your listening ability, try the quiz in Figure 29.1. Answer the questions honestly, since you're only cheating yourself if you fudge. Add up your totals in each of the three categories: "always," "most of the time," and "sometimes." Multiply the number of instances you answered "always" by 5 and the number of occasions you answered "most of the time" by 3. You don't receive any points for answering "sometimes"—with this quiz or with clients. The top possible score is 60, 5 points awarded for each of twelve "always" responses.

Few advisers merit a score of 40 or higher. Occasionally in workshops one person will reach that level. Some attain 30 to 40, a fair number score 20 to 30, and a few end up between 10 to 20. (We don't ask how many people score below 10, because they haven't heard a thing we said all day.)

Effective listening starts with the 50-50 rule. When talking with prospects or clients, your rule of thumb should be: 50 words for you, 50 words for them. In fact, research suggests that's actually a little high for the adviser's share. A better goal is that the prospect should

Figure 29.1

How Well Do You Listen?

		Always	Most of the time	Some-times
1.	Do you ask lots of open ended questions so that clients actively participate in discussions?	❑	❑	❑
2.	As clients are talking, do you give them your full attention rather than thinking about your rebuttal or next remark?	❑	❑	❑
3.	Do you allow prospects to express their complete thoughts without interrupting?	❑	❑	❑
4.	Do you ask clients to elaborate on their comments?	❑	❑	❑
5.	Do you avoid getting impatient or frustrated when clients don't make a decision as quickly as you'd like them to?	❑	❑	❑
6.	Do you summarize and verify areas of agreement or disagreement at key points in the conversation?	❑	❑	❑
7.	Do you write down key ideas (and your own thoughts) while prospects are talking?	❑	❑	❑
8.	Do you ignore distractions while listening?	❑	❑	❑
9.	Do you concentrate fully even though the conversation is boring or the client is going on and on?	❑	❑	❑
10.	Do you listen as intently to clients you don't particularly care for as to those you like?	❑	❑	❑
11.	Do you try to understand your client's unspoken, underlying motivation and look for hidden meaning?	❑	❑	❑
12.	After clients finish a thought, do you leave a moment of silence to give them a chance to continue?	❑	❑	❑
Total		____	____	____
X		____	____	____
=		____	____	____

speak 60 to 80 percent of the time. The more the prospect talks, the more likely the adviser will gain a positive outcome.

Ludwig Mies van der Rohe, a noted German architect, coined the expression "less is more." That's as true of selling as architecture. However, that insight runs counter to the instincts of most financial advisers. We spend many hours diligently researching, raising our level of knowledge, and familiarizing ourselves with a plethora of statistics. Often we assume we can impress clients by showing how well-informed we are. We proudly spew out everything we know, sure that it will overwhelm clients into signing on the dotted line.

The truth is exactly the opposite. In an experiment recounted in *Psychology Today,* researchers sent teams of two university graduates with identical backgrounds and resumes to job interviews with the same employer. The first graduate crammed into that interview as much information as possible about personal achievements and why he or she was the ideal candidate for the job. The second student spent some time outlining achievements but devoted about 60 percent of the interview to asking intelligent and well-researched questions about the company, the industry, and the job itself. In almost every case the second student won the job.

Learning to Listen

That philosophy, however, is one of the hardest things for advisers to accept and, even when they do accept it, to practice. If you want an eye-opening experience, try sticking a pocket dictating machine or recorder in your briefcase before your next sales encounter. Leave it on during the session, and replay it later. Don't focus on what you or the prospect said (although that might prove instructive as well). Instead, monitor the respective amounts of time each of you spent talking. For most advisers it's a depressing disclosure.

Advisers who operate by telephone a great deal can try another route to compare the amounts of time they and their clients talk. One adviser took advantage of a chess clock, which is essentially two clocks linked together. When you stop one, the other starts ticking. It's a graphic way to record how much each person talks as the conversation unfolds, providing immediate feedback to change behavior. After a few weeks the adviser didn't need the chess clock anymore, because he had developed new habits to replace the old pattern.

Hidden tape recorders and desktop chess clocks may seem awkward if not foolish, and such close monitoring of time almost obsessive. But in many cases those methods can open your eyes to how flagrantly you are violating the 50-50 rule. Given that listening correlates with success, and you can't be listening to clients when you're talking at them, they can point to vital behavioral changes many advisers must make.

The 50-50 Rule in Practice

Several years ago I delivered a two-part workshop, the two sections divided by a span of a week. When I asked the advisers if they had put any of the ideas in place during that intervening week, one adviser told the following story:

"I had a meeting the day after the workshop with a very, very upscale prospect I had been cultivating for a number of years. I'd met with him twice before, presenting what I felt were solid ideas. The meetings went okay, but he wasn't prepared to act. So this time I decided to try the 50-50 strategy you suggested.

"The meeting was scheduled for forty-five minutes. At the outset I said I wanted to share some ideas with him, but first I wondered if I could ask some pertinent questions. He agreed, and I asked about his previous investment experience, his views on the market, and his concerns about investing. Time passed quickly, and when I looked at my watch, to my horror I saw there were only ten minutes remaining and I had yet to launch into my investment ideas.

"I told him it had been a pleasure chatting and I had learned a lot, but I had promised to keep the meeting to forty-five minutes. Since I wanted to honor that commitment, I wondered if we could talk about those investment opportunities some other time. But the prospect said, 'No, go ahead. I've got some more time.' Half an hour later, I walked out with a new account."

Perhaps that successful result was in the cards anyway. Perhaps the prospect had finally decided this was the time to open an account. But it was an interesting coincidence that on the first occasion when the adviser's priority was to ask questions—to listen rather than talk—the prospect's comfort level in dealing with that particular adviser rose high enough to sign on.

Your first priority when meeting with a prospect or client, particularly when your trust is still in the formative stages, is not to talk but to listen. Practice the 50-50 rule, asking questions, getting the prospect to open up, and paying careful attention to the answers.

For many salespeople that will involve a change of habits—and few things are harder to change than habits. One salesperson I know put a sign on his desk that said "50-50." Another has a large note taped to his telephone with the acronym "SUD," reminding him to "Shut Up, Dummy!" when talking to clients.

In the words of Confucius, every long journey begins with a single step. If changing gears all of a sudden seems intimidating, you could incorporate a listening hour into your daily routine. Designate the time between 10 and 11 in the morning, for example, to concentrating as hard as you can on talking less and listening more. Salespeople who have tried that incremental step have been astonished by the results, finding they could gradually extend the practice to the whole day.

As you contemplate those changes, it's also worth reminding you of the two-minute rule. If that's the critical period of the relationship with a client, and listening is vital to success, it's important that you immediately indicate to the prospect that you are someone who listens. But in trying to impress the client in that brief period of time, an adviser's instinct might be to do all the showing and telling—100-0, not 50-50. Instead, as soon into the two minutes as you possibly can, you should be asking the questions that will get clients talking about themselves, their needs, and their interests.

The Pause That Refreshes

Even when you've implemented the 50-50 rule you'll sometimes find it difficult to prod prospects to open up. Fortunately there are a few techniques you can use to help such reticent prospects become more forthcoming. One of the simplest is called "Pause-one-two-three." Whenever you've asked a question and a prospect has completed the answer, you mentally count: Pause one, Pause two, Pause three.

The gap in conversation creates a powerful silence, a vacuum that the prospect will be inclined to fill. If she hasn't completely finished her thought or something relevant has flickered to mind while she has been speaking, she will resume without you having to scramble to figure out the next question. It's remarkable how often after that deliberate pause you will hear a really salient piece of information. Of course, before you reach Pause 19 or Pause 20, it's advisable to speak, so the prospect knows you're not comatose. But a short, three-beat pause can refresh the conversation wonderfully.

The Value of Note-Taking

Another listening tip is to take notes so that your mind stays focused. One of the greatest barriers to listening is our own desire to talk. Often when prospective clients are speaking, they will mention something that triggers a thought in us. It might have been an incorrect statement, a new idea that flashed through our mind, or a concern that must be directly dealt with. The adviser's tendency—and we all do it—is to stop listening, fixate on that thought, and begin formulating a response. We're no longer focusing on the prospect's continuing discourse but on our own ultimate intervention.

The solution is to get into the habit of writing down what a prospect or client is saying. That helps you to erase it temporarily from your mind—instead of being transfixed by a specific comment—and to continue listening. When your turn to speak arrives, you refer back to your notes to refresh your memory, without having lost most of the other parts of the conversation. You can even leave a specific space—say, the top of the page—for marking down points you immediately know you will want to refer back to. It's worth stressing that in taking notes you don't have to imitate a court stenographer, assiduously copying down every word. Usually just a word or phrase will suffice.

Research with university students confirms that the best way to increase listening effectiveness during lectures is to take notes. Even if they never look at those notes again, the mere act of marking down key points dramatically increases retention and the quality of listening. So taking notes will definitely improve your listening.

Your notes will also help you keep tabs on clients for future reference. Following a meeting you can put the notes in a file—preferably after taking a few moments to embellish them—so that the next time you're preparing to talk to that client you can consult them to refresh your memory on previous issues and concerns. Those notes, to some extent, become your record of the Client's 99.

Finally, by taking notes you communicate to prospective clients that you are truly listening to them. If you ask the prospect, "Do you mind if I take notes while we talk?" she will invariably agree. But what you are tacitly communicating when you ask permission is: "What you have to say is important; I want to listen to what you say; and my focus is on hearing your needs." Those are three highly important trust-building attributes that should be regularly communicated to prospects and clients.

You also communicate that you are listening by the questioning style, discussed previously, of pressing for elaboration: "Could you tell me more about that?" or "Can you elaborate on that a bit more?" Obviously if you are seeking more information, you're intent on what has already been said.

Summarizing and verifying what has just been discussed also shows that you have been listening. "Let me see if I hear you clearly on this: What I heard you say is X. Is that correct?" Again, you are clearly determined to listen carefully.

Empathizing comments also serve this purpose. "I understand how you feel." "I know what you mean." And, of course, your body language communicates interest in the client. Lean forward rather than slouching back in your chair. Maintain eye contact. Nod to indicate empathy. Don't keep looking at your watch. And, to state the obvious, look interested while the prospect is talking.

The Value of Recall

Some years ago a client retained my firm to produce a video in which we interviewed top-performing salespeople from a variety of fields. The technique of a very successful real-estate agent has stuck with me, because it relates to this critical area of listening.

She begins every meeting by reviewing what the client said at the previous encounter. "At our last meeting," she might note, "you indicated that you were looking for a home in the range of $250,000 to $300,000, in an area that was child-oriented and no more than a half-hour commute from downtown. Have I missed anything, or has anything changed since we last spoke?" Almost always the client confirms her comments, and she moves into her proposals: "Great! Based on that, here are some houses that I'm going to show you."

She has found that approach plays a significant role in her success. First, she is communicating that she has been listening. Secondly, she is making sure that nothing has changed since the last encounter. We've all had the experience of being halfway through a meeting only to find out the ground rules have altered. She avoids such embarrassing and wasteful situations at the outset.

Thirdly, she is reminding clients of their objectives. Sometimes, clients forget. They don't stay focused, particularly in a long meeting. The review at the start of the meeting highlights the main goals that the client and adviser are working toward together.

Fourthly, she is clearly communicating that her recommendations are squarely in the Client's 99. She's not making those recommendations because they're convenient for her—because she'll be paid more, for example. She's presenting them because they flow naturally from the client's own objectives, which she has carefully listened to.

Finally, the real-estate agent has found the technique forces her to be a more disciplined listener. Knowing she will begin the next meeting by summarizing the previous session's key points forces her to stay intently focused on the client's words.

The Danger of Preconceptions

Of course, if you're listening, it's important that you hear accurately. The biggest stumbling block we face in that regard is preconceptions. As an example, before going any further read the phrase in Figure 29.2 on the next page.

In workshops, most people—perhaps as you did—read the words as "Paris in the Spring." In fact, they're wrong. It reads: "Paris in the the Spring." But we skip over the extra word, because we're seeing what we expect to see.

Figure 29.2

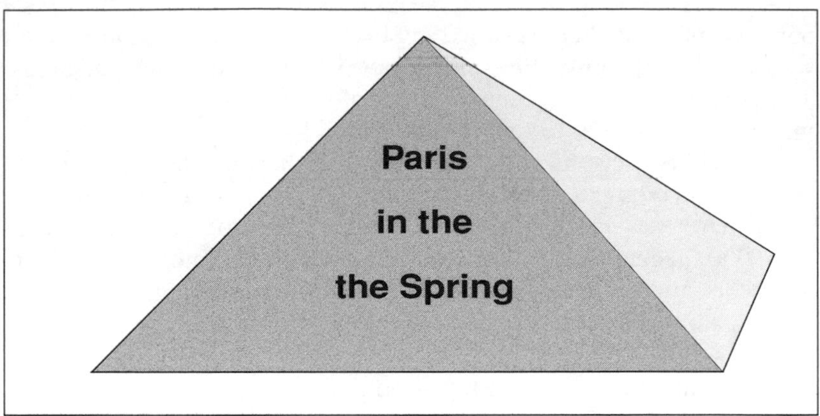

I observe this commonly in another context. In restaurants I like to order a club soda with lemon, which is much less customarily ordered than a club soda with lime. Because of that, I enunciate lemon clearly, I emphasize lemon—and nine times out of ten, I receive a club soda with a slice of lime. It happens in all manner and quality of restaurants. I doubt the waiters or waitresses are deliberately trying to irritate me, or attempting to reduce their tip. What happens is that as soon as I say "club soda with," they stop listening because they've heard it so many times they assume they know already what I'm going to say.

Imagine you're meeting with a prospect who has been recently referred to you. He's sixty-five, just retired from a company, with a $250,000 retirement package to invest. What are his investment needs?

Most likely, you've figured he wants safety, capital preservation, and income. But the truth is you haven't the foggiest notion what his objectives are, because you haven't even met him. You may have a fairly accurate perception based on the many other people with similar backgrounds you have advised. But this may be the exception, the ninety-ninth person out of 100. Maybe he already has $5 million or $10 million in real property, generating a healthy income, and this latest quarter of a million is play money. And even if you were accurate in your initial assessment, if you don't take time to hear him tell you his objectives but plunge right into your sage recommendations, you are subtly communicating that he is a bit irrelevant to you.

Clients want to feel listened to, not sold to. You'll find working on your listening skills rewarding, because it bonds you more closely to your clients. Listening, and the questioning skills that complement listening, will drive success with prospects and clients in the competitive years ahead.

Snapshots

- ✔ *You can be the world's most successful questioner, but if you don't listen to your clients' answers, you aren't likely to keep them happy or make a sale.*
- ✔ *Effective listening starts with the 50-50 rule. In fact, research suggests that's a little high for the adviser's share and a better goal is ensuring that the prospect speaks 60 to 80 percent of the time.*
- ✔ *Less is more, as is shown by a study of university graduates applying for a job. Almost always the applicants who asked questions rather than extolling their own virtues won the job.*
- ✔ *Check what proportion of an average meeting or phone conversation you currently spend talking. To find out, try taping yourself, or borrow a chess clock.*
- ✔ *Even when you've adopted the 50-50 rule, you'll sometimes find it difficult to get prospects to open up. Try the "Pause-one-two-three." technique. You'll find a little vacuum goes a long way.*
- ✔ *Take notes to keep your mind focused on the conversation.*
- ✔ *After the meeting put the notes in a file so next time you're preparing to talk to the client those notes are available to refresh your memory on previous issues and concerns.*
- ✔ *If you ask the prospect, "Do you mind if I take notes while we talk?" what you are tacitly communicating is: "What you have to say is important; I want to listen to what you say; and my focus is on hearing your needs."*
- ✔ *You also communicate that you are listening by offering questions that encourage elaboration: "Could you tell me more about that?" or "Can you elaborate on that a bit more?"*
- ✔ *Summarizing and verifying what has just been said also indicates that you have been listening intently: "Let me see if I hear you clearly on this. What I heard you say is X. Is that correct?"*
- ✔ *Empathizing comments help as well: "I understand how you feel." "I know what you mean."*
- ✔ *Body language communicates interest. Lean forward in your chair rather than slouching. Maintain eye contact. Nod to indicate empathy. Don't check your watch, and look interested while the prospect is talking.*
- ✔ *Consider applying the technique of the real-estate agent who routinely summarizes the previous meeting with a client in order to ensure that*

nothing has changed and her recommendations are geared to the Client's 99.

- ✔ *In listening it's important that you hear accurately. The biggest stumbling block we face in that regard is preconceptions.*
- ✔ *Don't assume you know what your clients want because you've served others like them. Clients want to feel listened to, not sold to.*

CHAPTER 30

Achieving Client Ecstasy

MY FIRM WAS RECENTLY APPROACHED BY AN INVESTMENT DEALER TO improve an underachieving office. Twelve brokers worked out of that branch, and we extracted a commitment that for three months each would put in an extra hour a day on our special program. Some decided to come in earlier or stay later. Others chose to work through the lunch hour, and still others contributed that extra time on the weekend. Whatever the choice, they were each pledging sixty hours, which handed us a large chunk of time to shape the program.

We divided the brokers into two groups of six, chosen to be roughly equal in experience and sales. With one group we concentrated on prospecting new clients. We held seminars, ran a small advertising campaign, cold-called, and networked in the community. At the end of the three months, they significantly increased their production. They were happy, and head office was happy. It was win-win all around.

With the second group we focused on existing clients. We ran update workshops for clients, developed a newsletter, and heightened contact levels. The participants initiated more check-in calls to clients and held meeting reviews that normally wouldn't have been scheduled. For every dollar increase in production the first group achieved through prospecting new clients, this second group improved by $11 through better service to existing clients. We called it the Rule of Eleven. Massaging existing clients was eleven times as effective as prospecting.

Some mitigating factors should be considered in judging the experiment. As prior to this time the advisers had not been spending as much time with existing clients as necessary, they were picking easily available, low fruit. Obviously advisers will hit a point of diminishing returns with existing clients, when the incremental benefit of expending more efforts will diminish over time. As well, we have to remember that new-client development is a long-term process. That first group of advisers would eventually realize benefits from those prospects that simply hadn't materialized in the initial three-month period.

But despite those caveats, the experiment clearly demonstrated the value of happy clients. The advisers found existing clients had more assets to be invested—but those were only forthcoming after deeper relationships were constructed. The clients were more willing to pass on friends to their adviser as a result of the warmer relationships. The workshops the advisers presented also provided an easy route for tacit referrals.

Client ecstasy is the fortification—the walls, moat, and barbed wire—to protect your franchise.

Earlier, looking at the evolving consumer, we discussed the need to achieve a higher level of satisfaction in order to deal properly with today's more discerning and demanding client. Client satisfaction isn't satisfactory any longer—it's too low a standard, as obsolete as the pole-vaulting records of several decades ago. Today we have to vault higher. We have to aspire to thrilled clients, delighted clients, ecstatic clients.

The Advantages of Client Ecstasy

Although that more challenging goal could be deemed an added cost by the adviser, requiring spending more money and more time on people you've already corralled, in fact, as the experiment shows, seeking client ecstasy should be viewed as unleashing an array of benefits.

Ecstatic clients become apostles, generating referrals for the adviser, as our experiment showed. You receive more business now and in the future from such clients, without worrying whether they are shielding assets from you or considering abandoning you for another adviser. Meetings are more efficient: Ecstatic clients are more likely to take your advice and less likely to subject you and your proposals to the third degree. Negotiations over price are less common, and if they occur, aren't as hard-edged, because ecstatic clients are more willing to pay a premium for your advice rather than using a discounter.

The final advantage, and by no means the least, is that you will feel better dealing with ecstatic clients. We all derive two kinds of income from work: We accumulate the financial income that puts gas in the car and pays the mortgage, but we also receive psychic income, which can be just as important. We want to enjoy the day at work and feel appreciated by the people we work with. I've found that when successful advisers wake up on Monday morning and look forward to the week ahead, they are motivated less by financial income than by psychic income. Having ecstatic clients generates that psychic income.

Defending Our Fortress

Clearly, achieving client ecstasy puts us on the offensive. But we shouldn't underplay the defensive aspects. Competition is highly intensified today, and clients may be at risk.

Long-term advisers often tell me how glad they are to have entered the business years ago and to have established a loyal client base in comparatively placid times, rather than having to build from scratch today. True, but as I always point out, others in the past have expressed the same comfortable sentiments, only to see their own franchise wither away later.

Twenty-five years ago, for example, you would hear identical comments from owners of family restaurants. "I'm really glad we built up our clientele and our reputation when we did," the owner would say. "We have a solid image in the community for providing good food at good prices. I would hate like heck to be starting today and having to compete against McDonald's."

Ten years ago retailers in clothing, books, shoes, and sporting goods were taking the same confident line: "Am I ever glad we opened this store when we did. We've had a chance to develop a base of loyal clients who appreciate the selection, price, and service level. People know us and we know them. I'd hate to be starting from scratch today, competing against Wal-Mart."

Over the next decade those client bases evaporated. Many family restaurants and retailers—even outlets providing substantial value—are now gone, and others are seriously hurting as their client bases have thinned. And our business is not immune.

Today if you're a successful adviser with a strong base, you probably recognize that you shouldn't take your clients for granted, but you believe you can rely on them. Out in the distance you see some dust. You might figure the wind is strong and blowing the sand out of the desert. But another possibility exists: It may not be sand blown up by wind but dust kicked up by the horses from modern-day Attila the Huns, heading your way.

That dust is an early-warning signal. Those Huns coming after our customers aren't going to be arriving today, or perhaps even tomorrow. But they are on their way.

The sensible strategy is to defend your base. Build a big wall. Then dig a deep moat and stock it with piranhas. Then build another wall outside that moat, with barbed wire on the top. Because at the end of the day, the biggest asset you have as an adviser is your customer base. That's your franchise; you can't jeopardize it.

That dust may just be sand blown up by the wind on the horizon. But you can't take a chance that it's not the competition heading this way to steal your customers. You must protect yourself by investing the time, effort, and energy to build client relationships to the highest possible level, because client ecstasy is the fortification—the walls, moat, and barbed wire—to protect your franchise.

Snapshots

- ✔ *Working over a three-month period with an underperforming office, Marketing Solutions found that massaging existing clients was eleven times as effective as prospecting. While that ratio would change over time as slow-blooming prospects flourished, the experiment clearly showed the value of happy clients.*
- ✔ *Today's advisers have to aspire to client ecstasy.*
- ✔ *Seeking client ecstasy shouldn't be viewed as a cost factor but as showering a rainbow of benefits.*
- ✔ *Ecstatic clients generate referrals and offer more business personally. Meetings become more efficient, negotiations over price are less common and if they occur, are less hard-edged.*
- ✔ *You will feel better dealing with ecstatic clients: Your psychic income will soar.*
- ✔ *Seeking ecstatic clients is also a defensive maneuver. Competition is highly intensified today and clients will be at risk. Client ecstasy is the strongest fortification for protecting your franchise.*

CHAPTER 31

Achieving Minimum Standards

BEFORE DISCUSSING WHAT CREATES ECSTATIC CUSTOMERS, LET'S STEP BACK A moment and consider the minimum standards clients expect simply to remain satisfied. For that, let's consider why dissatisfied clients leave us.

As we've learned, Marketing Solutions research shows the number-one cause of client defection is not performance but lack of contact. So the first step to achieving a minimum standard of satisfaction is ensuring we have a sufficient level of client contact. Beyond that, we have to:

- provide an acceptable level of service and responsiveness;
- maintain a minimum threshold of performance in our investment returns; and
- ensure we are creating realistic expectations in the minds of our clients and managing those expectations effectively.

Let's explore each in turn. Contact level, we've learned, is critical. And in contact, frequency is more important than duration—or to put it another way, quantity outweighs quality. A five-minute phone call once a quarter is more effective as a sign of contact than a two-hour meeting once a year. Depending on the client, both types of contact may be mandatory, but it's important to recognize that regular contact is one of the most critical requirements for maintaining a satisfied client.

Some advisers figure they can satisfy the contact requirements with monthly or quarterly statements and newsletters. While clients don't object to statements or newsletters, they don't necessarily view them as contact. Contact has to be voice-to-voice over the telephone, or face-to-face in a meeting or seminar. In the ideal world, the contact comes from you. But if that can't be arranged, hearing from one of your associates is certainly superior to no contact: "I'm calling on the suggestion of John (or Jane) Adviser."

After ensuring a minimum level of regular, sustained contact, you have to establish acceptable service standards. When clients gripe about service, generally they pinpoint three or four elements. They are upset, first of all, by lack of access: They feel unable to reach their adviser. They also complain about telephone calls not being returned, questions not being answered, or administrative errors being made and not quickly corrected. So if you want satisfied customers, you have to develop a minimum baseline level of service and ensure that it is continually met.

The crucial questions are whether you helped to set a client's expectations or even know what those are.

Clients also demand acceptable returns. While most clients understand that periods occur when their investments underperform the target, sustained periods of underperformance produce a problem. Indeed, a benefit of developing ecstatic clients is that it buys you patience—sometimes a lot of patience. But no knowledgeable client's patience is infinite, and you have to deliver acceptable threshold levels of returns. If you attain higher than the threshold, that's wonderful. But you must at least meet the threshold.

Meeting Expectations

So you must achieve minimum standards on three fronts: contact, service, and performance. But that process can be disastrously short-circuited if you define minimum standards differently from the client. And most advisers, unfortunately, aren't proficient enough at establishing minimum standards when they bring new clients on board.

Let's take contact levels, for example. You've just completed a meeting with a demanding client. Perhaps the client has been rough on you in the past or has left a previous adviser. During the conversation, contact levels aren't mentioned and you breathe a sigh of relief. You're off the hook, you figure, because the client has no expectations about the frequency with which she will hear from you.

Actually, that's absolutely wrong. Clients always have expectations. The crucial question is whether you contributed to setting those expectations or even know what they are. So it's vital at the onset of the relationship to tackle head-on these key areas—contact, service, and performance—and ensure the expectations are sensible and agreed upon by both parties.

On contact, you should say, "Ms. Client, I have a policy that each of my clients hears from me a minimum of once a quarter. Depending on circumstances it might be more often—and obviously if you call me, we'll be talking more as well. But you can be assured that even if you don't call me, you're going to hear from me once a quarter. The vast majority of my clients find that works out very well. Are you comfortable with that?"

The occasional new client may indicate that's insufficient, necessitating some stickhandling on your part. But now you know that you have a difference of perception. The great majority of clients, however, will declare the level of contact reasonable. With that assent, you have set clear, achievable expectations.

Notice you don't ask the client, "How frequently do you want to hear from me?" The risk in that open-ended question is she will reply, "I don't know. How about once a week?" That would throw on the table an expectation that's completely unachievable and unrealistic. At that point it would be difficult to retreat to your preferred standard of once a quarter. So while on many client matters you probe with open-ended questions, on expectations you need to be more directive, steering the client toward achievable, mutually acceptable levels.

Similarly, you need to establish clear expectations around administrative screw-ups: "If a mistake ever occurs, I want to hear from you. The person in our office who handles administrative matters is Phil. You can call him directly and he'll take all the particulars down. Typically it takes us less than a week to resolve such administrative issues, and you'll certainly be kept abreast of what's happening in the meantime."

It's also important to remember that as your business grows over the years, your longer-term clients will need to be brought up to date on any new patterns of handling their problems and any new people working with you. Their expectation that they will always deal with you, for example, might have to be amended.

Communicating Your Service Standards

On this issue of setting expectations, I recently ran into a curious situation. I was talking to a client who had fired one broker and moved onto another, and naturally I asked why.

"Well, you know, the guy that I was dealing with seemed like a nice guy and he worked pretty hard," the client said, "but frankly, he wasn't knowledgeable enough."

When I asked what led to that conclusion, he responded, "What would happen is I would be talking to the adviser and I'd ask him questions. Frequently he would say, 'I'm not absolutely positive on the answer to that, so why don't I do some research and get back to you later this afternoon?' He would typically get back to me in two or three hours, but I just felt I'd be more comfortable with somebody who was more knowledgeable than that."

Presumably that client is now dealing with an adviser who, no matter what the question, will fire back an immediate answer. The first adviser was doing the right thing, yet got fired for his pains. Why? Because he didn't set realistic expectations. He should have been saying, "Joe, I can provide you an answer right now, but rather than giving you something that maybe isn't 100 percent, I'd like to check a few things and get back to you in a couple of hours' time."

Beyond setting expectations, you have to communicate your service standards to clients. I recall one adviser who, after a workshop, set new standards that included a promise that every phone call would be returned the same day. When I later inquired about the outcome, she shrugged. "It was a little disruptive initially, and sometimes staff members had to stay late to phone back, but now it's working out reasonably well. You know, though, I'm not getting a sense that I'm receiving much of a payoff in terms of clients appreciating that we're going to that extra effort. I don't mind, but I expected a more positive reaction," she admitted.

"How have you communicated to the clients that you're doing all this?" I asked.

"What do you mean?" she said. As it turned out, she hadn't drawn to her clients' attention that it wasn't just by a happy circumstance that calls were quickly returned but rather part of a deliberate, ongoing policy by this adviser to meet her clients' needs.

These days, telling a client you pride yourself on superior service is too general and provocative a statement. You're not unique in talking about commitment to service, and many of the organizations that bray the loudest on this score provide the worst service. So you have to be specific, setting out achievable targets your clients are aware of and appreciate.

Toward that goal, Figure 31.1 presents a statement of philosophy that spells out clearly for clients and prospects what to expect. It covers the financial plan, co-ordination, investment philosophy, tax planning, accessibility, monitoring, and communication. When we've tested that statement of philosophy on clients, the response has been very positive.

The reason is that it's tangible and measurable. You're setting yourself apart from those other people making empty promises and claims about service standards, by offering to deliver specific services the client wants. In particular, we find a marked positive response to the pledge to return all business calls on the same business day and to the fact that the adviser maintains a collection of books on personal finance which are available to clients.

So to achieve a minimum level of client satisfaction, remember to focus on three key areas: contact, service, and performance. We have

Figure 31.1

Statement of Philosophy

1. My relationship with my clients starts with the development of a comprehensive financial plan to achieve their long-term financial goals. As part of this plan, we cover the investment, insurance, tax and estate planning aspects of each client's situation.

2. I strive to serve as my clients' chief financial adviser. As part of this role, I coordinate the activities of existing professional advisers such as tax accountants and estate lawyers. If required, I also tap into my own network of professional advisers.

3. My investment philosophy is essentially conservative in nature. Operating within each client's risk profile, an investment portfolio is structured which will achieve long-term growth without undue risk—as a result, both my clients and I sleep soundly at night.

4. Tax planning and minimization is a key component of the financial plan for most clients. As part of the overall plan, strategies such as income splitting, prudent use of leverage, and family trusts are evaluated.

5. Each client's account is monitored on an ongoing basis to take advantage of opportunities created by changing circumstances. In addition, each plan is reviewed annually and appropriate adjustments made.

6. I make myself as accessible to clients as possible. All telephone calls are returned the same business day, either personally or by my assistant.

7. I believe that my best client is one who is fully informed. As a result, I have a strong commitment to client communication through regular newsletters, seminars, and guest speakers. In addition, I maintain a library of some of the very best books on personal finance, available for loan to all my clients.

to make sure the expectations held by our clients—particularly our new clients—are well aligned and realistic. Once we develop those expectations, rather than keeping them a secret we must communicate them to our clients in clear, concrete terms.

Snapshots

- ✔ *The prime reason for client defection is lack of contact. The first step to achieve a minimum standard of satisfaction is to ensure that you have a sufficient level of client contact.*
- ✔ *Clients also demand a minimum threshold of financial return on their investments.*
- ✔ *You have to provide an acceptable level of service and responsiveness.*
- ✔ *You have to create realistic expectations in the minds of your clients and manage those expectations effectively.*
- ✔ *Frequency of contact is more important than duration. A five-minute phone call once a quarter is more effective than a two-hour meeting once a year.*
- ✔ *Clients don't view statements and newsletters as contact. Contact must be voice-to-voice, or face-to-face in a meeting or seminar. The contact should come from you, although an associate can substitute.*
- ✔ *When clients gripe about service, generally they are upset by lack of access to the adviser. They also complain about calls not being returned, questions not being answered, and administrative errors being made and not quickly corrected.*
- ✔ *Failing to discuss expectations with a client doesn't mean expectations aren't there. It just means you haven't helped to set them and maybe aren't even aware what they are.*
- ✔ *In setting expectations with a client, open-ended questions can backfire. Be more directive, steering the client toward achievable, mutually acceptable levels.*
- ✔ *Beyond setting expectations, you have to communicate your service standards to clients, perhaps through something like a Statement of Philosophy.*

CHAPTER 32

Positioning Yourself As an Adviser

In conversations with investors, it's clear that today's consumer distinguishes between someone who is a salesperson and someone who is an adviser. It's also clear which they prefer.

Figure 32.1 lists twenty dimensions on which our research shows clients differentiate between those two approaches. Take a moment to run through the list, and check which of the two alternatives best fits you. Again, for this exercise to be effective in helping you to improve your style, it's important to be honest, filling out the questionnaire before reading further and discovering the answers.

Finished? Now add up the number of checkmarks in the right-hand column beside the first ten categories, 1 to 10. Next, add the checkmarks in the left-hand column for the final ten categories, 11 to 20. Count that score out of 20.

In every case, consumers told us that those answers for which you marked points are the characteristics that correspond to someone who operates as an adviser rather than a salesperson. No doubt most of them fit your style. But in planning for the future, why not start by picking one dimension on this table where you could improve and thereby strengthen your position as an adviser. Make that a priority for a few months. After that seems under control, try another characteristic. It's important, because in the future being perceived as an adviser won't just be desirable. It will be essential.

Snapshots

- ✔ *Today's clients distinguish between a salesperson and an adviser, preferring the adviser.*
- ✔ *You can position yourself better as an adviser by strengthening those dimensions where your style more resembles a salesperson than an adviser.*

Figure 32.1

How Would Your Clients Rate You?

1. **Backup**	❑ Operates on his/her own	❑ Is backed up by a team
2. **Confirmation**	❑ Seldom confirms details of meeting in writing	❑ Often confirms details of meeting in writing
3. **Contact Level**	❑ Only contacts clients when has something to sell	❑ Periodically contacts clients to bring them up to date
4. **Credentials**	❑ No professional designation	❑ Has professional designation or degree
5. **Dress**	❑ Dress is very stylish, flashy	❑ Dress is conservative
6. **Follow-up**	❑ Often fails to meet commitments or follow through	❑ Usually meets commitments and follows through
7. **Manner**	❑ Talks quickly, high-pressure manner	❑ Talks slowly, low-key manner
8. **Notes**	❑ Takes few notes	❑ Takes lots of notes
9. **Office**	❑ Office is cluttered, messy	❑ Office is clean, neat
10. **Organization**	❑ Is poorly organized, operates "out of control"	❑ Is well-organized, operates in control
11. **Pace**	❑ Always calm; has time to talk	❑ Is often in a hurry, rushed
12. **Preparation**	❑ Is well prepared for meetings	❑ Is poorly prepared for meetings
13. **Pressure**	❑ Almost never feel pressure to buy when dealing with him/her	❑ Quite often feel pressure to buy when dealing with him/her
14. **Priority**	❑ Get the sense that always places the client first	❑ Get the sense that often places own interests first
15. **Professional Upgrading**	❑ Invests a lot of time in professional upgrading	❑ Invests little time in professional upgrading
16. **Questions**	❑ Asks a lot of questions	❑ Asks few questions
17. **Research**	❑ Takes time to reflect and do research before offering solutions	❑ Offers quick, immediate solutions to problems
18. **Response to Questions**	❑ Is thoughtful, thinks responses through	❑ Is spontaneous, provides immediate reactions to questions
19. **Response Time**	❑ Quick to respond to calls	❑ Slow to respond to calls
20. **Talking**	❑ Likes to achieve a balance between talking, listening	❑ Likes to spend most of the time talking

CHAPTER 33

Feedback

WE'VE ALL HAD THE DISMAL EXPERIENCE OF DINING OUT IN A SMALL GROUP and suffering through a dreadful meal. The service is indifferent, the atmosphere insipid, and the price way out of proportion with the value. Throughout the meal everyone is heatedly complaining that they will never return to the restaurant again. But when the maitre d' or owner comes over and solicitously inquires, "How was dinner?" we curiously fail to tell him the truth. Instead we politely mumble, "Fine."

If you review that dynamic, somebody who quite possibly has sunk a life savings into this operation has invited input, and we've lied. We're not forthcoming because we have an easy out: We never have to come back to that restaurant—and we won't. Supplementing that, of course, is the natural aversion most of us have to confrontation.

Carry that interaction back to your own business and your quest for client ecstasy. One of the primary ways to ensure you're on track with your client base is soliciting feedback. The key, however, is in the asking. And too often, like that maitre d', we fail to unearth the truth.

A common trap we fall into is when during a client meeting we ask how satisfied he or she is, and the client, like those frustrated diners, says, "Fine, I'm quite satisfied." We walk away like that maitre d' reassured about the relationship. No alarm bells having sounded.

In both cases, although feedback has been sought, the clients don't believe the request is sincere. Ironically, that cynical feeling is more likely to strike when we're unhappy as customers, since we suspect feedback has been ignored in the past or the situation wouldn't have grown so desperate. We assume that restaurateur is simply fulfilling some drill recommended at maitre d' school and isn't really interested in our comments. We suspect that even if we said "The meal was terrible," he would cheerfully reply, "Glad to hear it," and move on to the next table.

Getting Honest Feedback

If the restaurateur was seriously seeking feedback, after our initial "Fine," he could press further: "I'm pleased to hear that, but tell me—what one thing could we have done tonight to make your experience more enjoyable?" Or, "I wonder whether I could ask a favor. I'd like to buy you a drink, if I could, and get you to tell me what would you do differently if this was your restaurant."

To get honest feedback, you have to communicate that you genuinely value that feedback.

Are we more likely to provide honest feedback if the question is asked in that way? Absolutely. That's particularly true when the restaurant isn't quite as hopeless as I described, but drifting in that middle range where improvements could turn it into an attractive dining spot for us and others in future.

By asking properly, the restaurateur helps himself in two ways. First, he receives honest feedback that he can act upon. As well, our chances of returning as customers escalate. We feel better about that restaurateur because he seems truly to care about our point of view. We're also curious to see whether he implemented the changes we discussed.

The same dynamic applies to our business. When you ask, "Are you pleased with the service you're getting?" you hope your clients will say yes. But you haven't really questioned about the relationship in a manner that makes it easy, comfortable, or inviting for them to respond. You also haven't extracted anything to improve your performance.

If you really want to learn your clients' views, you have to advance to the next stage, stating, "I'm pleased to hear that, but what one thing could we do that would make dealing with us more pleasurable for you?" Or: "If you were in my shoes, what would you do differently to improve the level of service you receive?" If you probe in that manner, it's surprising the gold you'll dig up. Clients will be much more willing to share their point of view. After all, unlike the restaurant diners, they have a longer-term stake in your business and want improvements.

Some advisers proceed beyond that one-to-one feedback, canvassing clients through formal questionnaires. The key, if you adapt our sample letters and questionnaire, is to keep the request short and to the point (Figures 33.1, 33.2, 33.3). The questionnaire should not appear intimidating and should be easy to complete.

Figure 33.1

How Good a Job Am I Doing?

	Dissatisfied	Needs Work	Adequate	Good	Excellent
1. Performance of your investments	1	2	3	4	5
2. Comfort with your level of risk	1	2	3	4	5
3. Confidence that you have a coherent investment strategy	1	2	3	4	5
4. Written communication/ statements					
a) Frequency	1	2	3	4	5
b) Quality	1	2	3	4	5
5. Frequency of telephone contact from me	1	2	3	4	5
6. Investment options and recommendations clearly explained	1	2	3	4	5
7. Ability to reach me when you call	1	2	3	4	5
8. Your questions are answered clearly	1	2	3	4	5
9. Your account is handled without problems or mistakes	1	2	3	4	5

What one thing could I do to improve the service you receive in the coming year?

____

____

____

____

Name: ____________________________________

Figure 33.2

Date

Any Client
1234 Any Street
Any City, Any State 56789

Dear Any,

One of my goals is to constantly look for ways in which to better serve my clients.

In advance of our meeting next week, I'm writing to ask you to give some thought as to how I could better meet your needs in the upcoming year.

As a starting point, I'd appreciate it if you could take a moment to complete the attached "report card" for the past year, to use as a reference point when we meet.

I look forward to seeing you on Wednesday.

Best regards,

Any Adviser

Communicating That You Care

It's important, through this process, to communicate to clients that you sincerely want to hear from them—that you're not just going through the motions. Back in the 1980s when customer service came into vogue, all kinds of service establishments—notably hotels and restaurants—began displaying or handing out customer satisfaction cards. At first customer participation was high, but it has dropped precipitously. One reason is that the cards are no longer unique. But a more important reason is that customers who have completed the cards haven't seen any meaningful changes, and so they wonder whether the organization is really serious.

When I was recently in a hotel in Pittsburgh I noticed, on top of the television, a card that claimed, "$100 for your opinions." Intrigued, I read on. "We'd be grateful if you would take a moment to complete the short satisfaction survey on your night table. Every month we draw one of the responses and send a check for $100 as a thank you."

Although I don't complete many of those cards anymore, I filled that one out. Why? Cynics might contend that I was in Pittsburgh and there wasn't much else to do. Others might say that the $100 motivated

Figure 33.3

Date

Any Client
1234 Any Street
Any City, Any State 56789

Dear Any,

I'm writing to ask a favor.

My number one priority for (INSERT YEAR) is to ensure I'm providing my clients with the highest possible level of service.

To help me do that, I'm writing to ask you to take three minutes to complete the attached assessment of how I'm doing right now and note ways in which I can serve you better; simply return it in the enclosed stamped envelope.

Thank you in advance for your assistance on this. I'll be circulating a summary of the results to you and my other clients later this year.

Please call if you have any questions in the meantime.

Best regards,

Any Adviser

P.S. As a small thank you in advance for taking the time to respond to this questionnaire, I've made a contribution to the United Way on behalf of you and my other clients.

me. While both of those factors may have contributed, ultimately what provoked me was the feeling that someone really wanted to know my opinions. The hotel wasn't simply going through the motions.

If you send your clients a feedback questionnaire, you want to be sure you communicate that same message to them. As with the questionnaire on seminar possibilities we discussed earlier, include a self-addressed envelope—with a real stamp on it. You might indicate in a P.S. that you're making a donation to a local charity in gratitude for your clients' assistance, or, as at that hotel, respondents will become eligible for a draw of some kind. The amount of the draw doesn't matter.

What's crucial is that you've gone the extra mile to recognize the effort you're asking clients to make in returning the questionnaire.

Handling the Response

Before sending the questionnaire, you should spend some time considering how you'll handle the response. If a client checks off a few areas of your performance that "need work" or even rates an item "dissatisfied," the expectation is that you'll be in touch to deal with that.

Let's imagine the client is irritated by what he feels is low contact level by his adviser. The questionnaire arrives, and he figures, "It's taken her awhile, but finally she has asked. That's great." His satisfaction level increases. But then he doesn't hear from the adviser. After a period, his satisfaction level drops again—but not just to the pre-questionnaire level. It plummets below that, because the client concludes, "The whole thing was a charade. My adviser wasn't really interested in feedback. She was faking it—and wasting my time!" One of the key principles of feedback, therefore, is if you're not prepared to deal with the answers, don't ask the questions. (One way to show you're serious is to report back to clients through a letter like that in Figure 33.4.)

Sometimes advisers get excited about feedback and send all their clients a questionnaire. If you have 300 clients and then are flooded with 100, 150, or even 200 responses, you'll have difficulty following them all up. It's more sensible to send questionnaires to 10 percent of your client base at a time—perhaps every month. If you skip December and a summer month, you can canvass your entire clientele over a year, but in a steady manner that gives you the opportunity to follow up on each of the responses when they flow in.

Feedback questionnaires can be a versatile tool. Some advisers send them out as a warm-up to a meeting. If a review is scheduled, the client is asked to prepare the assessment for discussion at the meeting.

But they're not so versatile that they can be combined with a referral solicitation. I've seen some client satisfaction questionnaires that are two or three pages long, testing the client's patience, but a few clients begin to fill them out nevertheless, pleased their adviser is seeking their opinion. Then on the last page they stumble onto a final question: "Who among the people that you know would you recommend that I contact about the possibility of working together?" At this point any goodwill generated through the questionnaire dissipates. "Aha!" the client says, "I knew it! I knew it was too good to be true. My adviser has an ulterior motive."

How you solicit feedback doesn't really matter. It's an individual decision, depending on your style and size of operation. But make sure, unlike that maitre d', that you ask in a way that encourages clients to

Figure 33.4

Date

Any Client
1234 Any Street
Any City, Any State 56789

Dear Any,

Recently, I circulated a survey to you and my other clients, requesting some feedback on how I can serve you better.

I am delighted to report that over 40% of my clients took the time to answer: 95% of responses indicated that they were satisfied, with particular strong ratings on communication and comfort with the level of risk.

That being said, there were indications of room for improvement with interest in more communication. In response, I am pleased to let you know that I will be sending you a quarterly newsletter, commencing in the very near future. In addition, you will be receiving an invitation to a seminar, in which I will be reviewing investment developments.

Many thanks for the continuing opportunity to work with you. Attached for your information is a summary of the responses to the survey.

Best regards,

Any Adviser

P.S. As a small token of my thanks, one of the responses was drawn at random for a dinner for two at NAME OF RESTAURANT. The lucky winners were NAME OF CLIENTS from NAME OF CITY/TOWN.

respond comfortably, and that when you receive the feedback you visibly act upon it.

 Snapshots

- ✔ *Soliciting feedback is one of the prime ways of ensuring you're on track. The key, however, is in the asking. Too often advisers don't learn the truth because they don't ask properly.*
- ✔ *When you ask a client, "Are you pleased with the service you're getting?" you hope the answer will be yes. Instead of patting yourself*

on the back, however, move to the next stage: "I'm pleased to hear that, but what one thing could we do that would make dealing with us more pleasurable for you?" Or: "If you were in my shoes, what would you do differently to improve the level of service you receive?"

✔ *If you canvass clients through a formal questionnaire, keep it short and to the point. The questionnaire should be unintimidating and easy to complete.*

✔ *It's important, through such a questionnaire, to communicate to clients that you really want to hear from them and aren't just going through the motions.*

✔ *Include with the questionnaire a self-addressed envelope—with a real stamp on it. You might wish to indicate in a P.S. that you're making a donation to a local charity in gratitude for your clients' assistance, or that respondents will become eligible for a draw.*

✔ *Before sending the questionnaire, spend some time considering how you'll handle the results. Clients who indicate dissatisfaction expect you to follow up by talking to them and making changes. If you're not prepared to do that, don't bother sending out the questionnaire.*

✔ *It's more sensible to send questionnaires to 10 percent of your client base at a time, perhaps every month. If you leave out December and a summer month, you can canvass your entire clientele over the course of a year.*

✔ *Feedback questionnaires can serve as a warm-up to a meeting. But don't mix them with a request for referrals, or your motives will be questioned.*

CHAPTER 34

Practicing the SOS Principle

INTERACTIONS WITH CLIENTS ESSENTIALLY HAVE TWO DIMENSIONS. CLIENTS look to you to deliver on the product-service dimension, forging financial plans, recommending investments with suitable returns, and running your office efficiently. But clients also develop a personal relationship with their adviser and want to enjoy the dealings. They expect to look forward to talking with you and being able to trust you. Every client evaluates an adviser on those two dimensions: product service and relationship.

These two factors can be combined into a four-quadrant model for evaluating business interactions, as in Figure 34.1. We can quickly eliminate Quadrant 1 from consideration. With no product-service ties or relationship, that person is a stranger to the adviser and no business connection will exist unless change occurs on one of those two dimensions. But the other three quadrants bear on our work.

Quadrant 4 portrays an all-too-common combination. The adviser has a strong, positive relationship with a client but not much resonance on the product-service dimension. The person likes the adviser, appreciates going out for drinks, but isn't very confident about that adviser's investment knowledge. At one time that was still sufficient for a client-adviser relationship. Then, advisers served their friends. But today, with more demanding clients, relationship ties won't carry advisers over the long haul unless they're also delivering at least at a minimum acceptable level on the product-service side.

Consider the reverse combination, depicted in Quadrant 2. The adviser delivers strongly on the product-service side but lacks much of a relationship with the client. It's a supplier situation, which isn't inherently bad. In fact, advisers will inevitably be viewed as suppliers of investment services by some clients, especially if those advisers have a

Figure 34.1

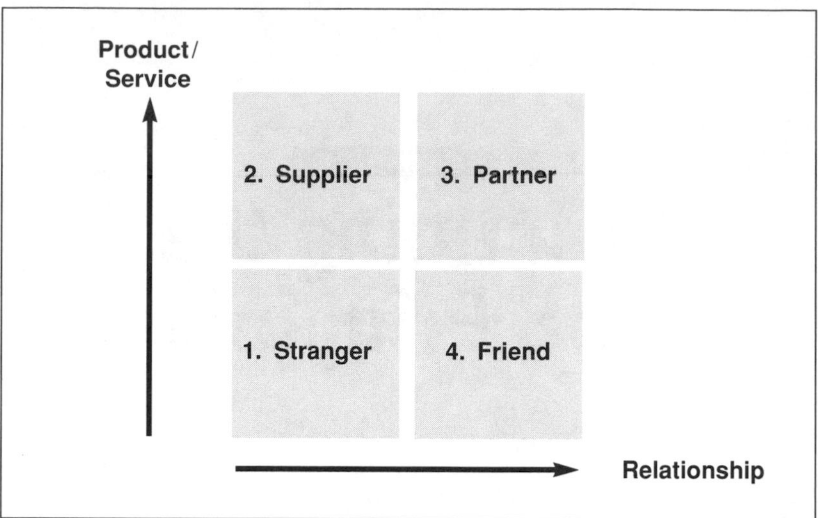

large client base. Historically, adopting a supplier mentality—providing the strong returns and service which that requires—has allowed some advisers to build large, successful practices.

Unfortunately, a myriad of other suppliers are available. And the risk exists that someone will deliver more effectively on the critical product-service scale. As well, if that dimension is the main basis for our affiliation to our client, we can be damaged by external events beyond our control, namely market downturns. If we encounter a period of choppy market performance, we're vulnerable with clients for whom we're simply suppliers.

Clearly, we want to position ourselves in Quadrant 3. We want to deliver well on both the product-service and relationship dimensions. We want to be a partner.

Protecting against Market Fluctuations

Advisers sometimes question the devotion I urge to building relationships: "Why don't we just focus on investment returns?" they protest. Certainly that's possible, if you believe you can generate double-digit returns, quarter after quarter, year after year. No need to worry about relationships under that scenario. Your clients will probably be ecstatic because you're performing so well on the product-service dimension that nothing else counts.

However, I constantly hear advisers expressing concern that they can't be 100 percent confident of their ability to deliver high returns in the short term. Those yields aren't controllable; the markets can sour.

But we can control, in the short and long term, the relationship to our clients. Relationships create the patience that ties our clients to us if for a period of time we slip below the acceptable level on the product-service dimension.

Over the years I've interviewed a broad range of clients, from those ecstatic with their adviser to those who have fired their adviser. Repeatedly I've met clients who had exceptionally high returns, yet still fired their brokers. I've found that most of those advisers lost the clients because the relationship was flimsy. The clients didn't feel comfortable working with their adviser, often because they felt pressured. I remember one client saying that each time his adviser called, a knot formed in his stomach because he feared it would be a stressful experience. Although his broker was delivering excellent performance results, the client decided life was too short to deal with somebody he didn't like.

On the other hand I've found many cases where investment returns were only average, yet the clients were ecstatic. They extolled their adviser's virtues because he or she made them feel special—made them feel the adviser cared about them.

The most powerful sentiment advisers can create in their clients is that feeling of caring—not just about the clients' money but about the clients themselves. Clients believe the adviser is someone they can trust to put their interests first. Now advisers do care about their clients, so the issue here isn't a failure of caring. In the memorable words of the prison captain from Paul Newman's 1967 movie *Cool Hand Luke*, "What we've got here is a failure to communicate."

Advisers must do a better job of communicating that they care. And the key to that is to follow the SOS Principle. In this case, SOS stands for Suspension Of Self-interest.

The Three SOS Traits

When you think about activities that communicate you care, three qualities stand out. The activities must not be self-serving. They must be personal. And they must be unexpected.

Imagine you arrive home to find a letter from your lawyer. Inside is a note—"Thought you would find this of interest"—with an article, "Five Reasons to Update Your Will Today." Is your reaction, "What a great guy! I'm so happy I'm dealing with this thoughtful lawyer!" I don't think so. Your response is much more likely to be: "He wants to sell me something."

Imagine instead that the enclosed article was "Five Things You Can Do Today to Save Taxes Tomorrow." You'd now have a different response (assuming that this wasn't a tax lawyer). Because now there would be nothing particular in the gesture for him.

That dichotomy is fundamental for our client activities. The key to having your clients feel they're dealing with somebody who cares is to have periodic communication in which nothing explicitly can be gained by you as an adviser through that communication.

If that happens, it guarantees a favorable reception during more commercial interactions. Ironically, that package from your lawyer might well have been sent because your lawyer was concerned for you that your will is outdated. He wasn't panting over the possibility of generating a measly $100 from rewriting your will. He might have just dealt with the messy ramifications faced by relatives after a client died without a proper will and was now engaging in some friendly preventive maintenance. But you assumed he couldn't possibly be motivated by your interests, because of the personal opportunity for profit. If he had operated more regularly from the SOS principle, your reaction would have been more charitable.

With that in mind, it's important to review all your communications with clients—particularly your best clients, with whom you definitely don't want to fall into a supplier mentality—and consider how many of those communications are free of self-interest. Ask yourself in how many instances the client would have figured, "Obviously they're sending me that (or calling me, or inviting me to this workshop) because they care. There's absolutely nothing in it for them in doing that."

For most advisers, very few communications fall into that category. But as we go forward, we need to carve out a small chunk of our week—I suggest 5 percent, about two to three hours—to focus on SOS activity. Those two or three hours in which we suspend self-interest can add leverage to the remaining hours in the week, in which we concentrate on the product-service dimension.

As well as being devoid of self-interest, the activities you carry out in those critical hours should be personal and unexpected. Let's return to our earlier scenario: Again you receive a package from your lawyer, this time a newsletter without a covering note. Would you feel valued or special? Of course not, because you know every client received the newsletter.

Now let's suppose the same newsletter arrives with a business card or a Post-it note pointing you to an article on page 3, perhaps relating to a recent investment he knows you made, or to the latest court decision on the treatment of expenses for self-employed salespeople. How do you feel this time? Obviously more intrigued, because this time the lawyer has singled you out for a personal communication, even in the midst of a mass mailing.

SOS activity should also be unexpected. Imagine it's early December and you open your mail to find a Christmas card from your lawyer. Will you say, "Wow! What a surprise! Does he ever care!" Not likely. You may appreciate the courtesy, but you won't be excited by it. In fact, if the card didn't arrive, not many clients would miss it. They wouldn't be walking around grumbling, "My lawyer doesn't care because he didn't send me a Christmas card."

But imagine in early January a card arrives from your lawyer announcing, "Happy New Year." Inside a note adds: "Thanks for the opportunity to work together last year. Best wishes for the coming year." It cost the same to send that card, but the response will be different—far more enthusiastic. The effort stood out because it was unusual and unanticipated. Through such unexpected gestures, we signal that we're not treating our clients automatically. We care about them and take time to cater to their needs as individuals.

Communicating That You Care

How you communicate caring depends on you, the nature of your operations, and your clients (Figure 34.2). Although the activities must have a personal touch, some can be organized in a mass way, because they can be executed so as to appear personal. Others will be highly individualized, geared to the specific interests of one client. If you walk into a bookstore and see a new guide for small-business owners, you might purchase a bundle of copies to send to the various business owners on your client list as an SOS signal. On the other hand, you

Figure 34.2

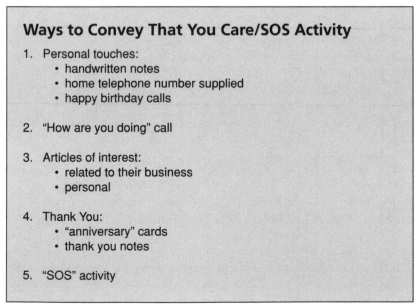

Ways to Convey That You Care/SOS Activity

1. Personal touches:
   - handwritten notes
   - home telephone number supplied
   - happy birthday calls
2. "How are you doing" call
3. Articles of interest:
   - related to their business
   - personal
4. Thank You:
   - "anniversary" cards
   - thank you notes
5. "SOS" activity

might buy only one copy of a book on the Galapagos Islands, for the client who will be vacationing there next month.

One adviser, when statements are sent by head office to his clients, mails a photocopy out himself, with a personal, handwritten note attached. "We're on track." "We're performing ahead of schedule." "This investment looks a little weak, but we've reviewed it recently. It still makes sense to proceed." That personal touch is tied to the crux of the relationship: the investments. It shows his clients their adviser is paying close attention to their needs between meetings. If doing this monthly seems daunting, try splitting your clientele, mailing to a quarter of them every month. This will also make the notes seem less routine.

Providing your home telephone number can serve as another opportunity to let clients know you care. Often I ask advisers at workshops whether they put their home telephone number on their business cards. Generally, about 25 percent provide it, while 75 percent don't. The reason is obvious: We're sufficiently harassed at the office and don't want to inflict more bother on ourselves at home. But advisers who give clients home phone numbers report they actually receive a minimal number of calls at home—maybe one a month. That one call might have come anyway, because the client could have tracked you down if you're in the phone book. More importantly, you generally want to receive that call, because it's urgent.

So providing home phone numbers is a high-return, low-cost SOS activity. By signaling your constant availability to clients, you gain some benefits without much downside. But even if you opt to provide your home number, you should carefully consider your method, because two different options exist with quite different SOS dividends.

One alternative is to say, "Ms. Client, here's my business card. It has my home phone number printed on it. My clients generally prefer to call me at the office during business hours, but if a pressing problem arises, feel free to call me at home." Clients receive that courtesy positively, and you collect some credit.

But an even better approach is: "Ms. Client, here's my business card. Let me write my home phone number on it for you. My clients generally prefer to call me at the office during business hours, but if a pressing problem ever occurs, feel free to call me at home." The message of personal concern has been intensified by that one twist. In the first case the gesture is not particularly personal, since the number is printed on the card and the client realizes everyone is receiving it. In the second instance the client feels special—you wrote the number down exclusively for her.

Saying Happy Birthday

Birthday calls are another method of letting clients know you care. But it must be calls, not cards, to adhere to our SOS guidelines. At a presentation for life insurance agents not long ago I had the temerity to suggest that when their clients received the agents' annual happy-birthday cards it did not spur them into wild cries of ecstasy. Clients weren't doing cartwheels around the room, stunned and delighted that the agents remembered them. Sending the card doesn't hurt, but it also doesn't particularly help agents, because it's humdrum and routine, conforming to the life-insurance agent stereotype.

It's easy to be a critic, of course. Somebody asked me, and it was a fair question, what I'd do instead. I suggested picking up the telephone at 9 A.M., calling the client, and saying simply, "Just wanted to be among the first to wish you a happy birthday." Nothing more, nothing less. Now you have to be judicious in using that approach. If one of your clients is the CEO of a major multinational enterprise, that may not be the most appropriate form of interaction. But for most clients, especially seniors, making that call is a personal touch that stands out and is appreciated.

Another effective technique is using "How-are-you-doing?" calls. Marketing Solutions research, as I've indicated, has found that many clients feel their advisers don't contact them enough. But beyond the quantity of contact, a secondary problem looms: the quality of contact. Our firm often interviews clients who complain, "I hear from my adviser reasonably regularly, but every time he calls it's to sell me something." If your clients only hear from you when you're selling, it's hard for them to believe your motivation for placing the call was their interests rather than yours. It's hard for them to believe you care about anything but their wallets.

An antidote is to engage periodically in "How-are-you-doing?" calls. Pick up the phone and tell the client, "I'm not calling for any particular reason. I just thought of you this morning and figured I'd call to say hello and see how things are going." After the initial shock (which clients recover from) and suspicion (which disappears quickly if you don't try to sell them anything), clients respond positively to the chance to just gab with their adviser, someone they would prefer to be more than just a supplier.

The Non-Investment Connection

A third method of communicating you care is to send articles of interest. Unlike those trust-building articles from the *Wall Street Journal* and various financial magazines, these can be drawn from a broader array of publications and on a wide range of subjects. While there's nothing wrong with sending articles on estate planning, investment, or globalization, they serve a different purpose of reinforcing your professionalism and showing a commitment to education. To deepen client relationships, you have to proceed further, sending articles where there's clearly nothing in it for you in the short term.

One adviser, for example, subscribes to half a dozen golf magazines. Every few months he finds a particularly stimulating one-page article—perhaps some putting tips, or a close-up of a new course his clients might be interested in playing, or a review of some new equipment. This adviser maintains a client information database, and so he sends a copy to the sixty clients his database lists as golfers. He includes a short cover note: "Came across this and thought you would be interested."

What does an article on putting have to do with stocks, bonds, and mutual funds? Absolutely nothing. What does it have to do with communicating that the adviser cares? The answer, of course, is: Absolutely everything.

This activity is also liberating, since it doesn't limit you to articles on investing. You can apply some target marketing concepts in this SOS work, even if you have a general clientele, slicing off special interests. Your clients, like you, probably find it a challenge to keep up with their reading. As you squeeze in your own reading time, you can help by keeping them in mind. I know advisers who make it a rule to find some article in every publication they read—be it a financial or general one—that they can send to one or more of their clients. The article might be on a company, a supplier, foreign competition, tennis elbow, an exciting recipe, or a new book. That gesture builds deeper relationships.

Saying Thank You

Another sort of SOS activity falls under the classification of thanks. Indeed, I find it remarkable how often advisers are abysmal at saying thank you. Given our strong communication skills, it's surprising we aren't more effective at letting clients know their business is appreciated. It's not that we're not appreciative; we are. But we don't communicate that sentiment.

Sending thank-you cards helps. One adviser, after attending a workshop I gave, set up a neat system. Every day at 3 P.M. his assistant comes into his office with three thank-you notes. She won't leave until he has completed notes of appreciation to three clients: "Thank you for taking the time to talk." "Thank you for taking the time to meet." "Thank you for your confidence." "Thank you for your patience." "Thank you for being a client." He's received more positive feedback from those simple cards than from taking clients to dinner, taking them golfing, or making other expensive gestures. When building relationships, often little things have the biggest impact.

Another adviser found a different way to say thank you. He bought some cards with Happy Anniversary on the outside but blank inside. When clients receive them they're puzzled, because it's not, as far as they know, an anniversary. They turn inside to find the adviser has written, "In reviewing your records, I noticed it has been twelve months since we began working together. Just wanted to say thank you." That works, he has found, in other time frames: two years, five years, or even six months. Of course, there are limits: I wouldn't suggest sending a card saying, "In reviewing my record, I noticed it has been three weeks since we began working together"—the client might figure that's the longest you've held on to a client! But the power of saying thank you shouldn't be underestimated.

One useful exercise is to list all your clients who are business owners. Then, beside each name, mark down who might be introduced to that owner as a source of business. Nothing will demonstrate good will as much as that expression of caring. Let's say the client is a printer and you call to say, "George, when I was seeing another client of mine yesterday, he was cursing his printer who had screwed up a shipment: it was late and wasn't right. I mentioned that you and I work together and that perhaps he should try you. I told him he might get a call from you. His name is Peter Client." That printer's reaction, obviously, will be extremely positive.

Beyond referrals, you could simply show some interest in helping such clients with their business. Suppose you have a meeting with a major client who owns a pharmacy. You mention, "Janet, just before we get started, as a matter of interest I took some time on Saturday morning to visit some of the other pharmacies in this community. I noticed they're doing some things differently from you, and I'm curious as to why that might be." The message you're sending is that you value her beyond the short-term benefits you'll derive from her investments. Again, it's the little things that build deep relationships, not the big things.

You could even give your clients some business yourself. If one of them owns a restaurant, you may want to propose having a special dinner for your client base some Monday night when restaurants are typically slow or even closed, perhaps involving a cooking demonstration. Some advisers take advantage of such a venue to hold wine-tasting sessions—one of them arranges for the wine columnist at the local paper to serve as guide. We've seen magicians or comedians booked for such events, or Olympic athletes.

Turning a Transaction into a Client

Even when dealing with client accounts, openings exist for SOS inroads. New clients offer excellent opportunities which advisers have traditionally missed. We put a lot of time and energy into courting prospects, but once they sign we view that as the culmination rather than the start of a process. In reality all we have gained is a transaction; we must extend that into developing an ecstatic client.

That new client is probably convinced that now that you've won her business, you won't be as keen on serving her needs. But let's say that ten days later you call. "Ms. Client, you should have received a confirmation of your first purchase by now. I'm just phoning to be sure you've received it and to take a few minutes to go through it with you, to be sure there's nothing that is ambiguous or needs explaining."

Let's say four weeks later the phone rings again, and once more her helpful adviser is on the line. "Ms. Client, you should have received your first statement by now. Again, I'm just calling to take a minute to go through it with you and be sure that nothing is unclear."

Together those two phone calls probably take five minutes. But in those five minutes, look what you've achieved through SOS: You've signaled to the client, unmistakably—since no payoff could directly accrue to you in placing the calls—that she's important and special, valued beyond the business she provides.

Again, we don't spend our life in these SOS endeavors. Just 5 percent of the work week—two to three hours. You can slip it in between other work, like those 9 A.M. birthday calls or those cards signed at 3 P.M. every day. Or you can choose slack periods of the week: a lot of advisers prefer 3 P.M. to 5 P.M. on Friday afternoons, for example, to engage in SOS work.

Not long ago I watched a video featuring a very successful investment adviser. The producers also interviewed his wife, who talked about something her husband does that drives her crazy, but which I thought was brilliant. When they watch *60 Minutes* on Sunday night, he brings a pad of paper into the living room, puts a blank videotape in the VCR and turns it on. As he watches each segment, he notes down any of his prospects or clients to which it might apply. If an episode, say, spotlights Luciano Pavarotti, he writes down the names of prospects or clients who are opera fans or who serve on the board of the Metropolitan Opera Company. He does that for each of the three segments.

When he returns to the office at 8:30 A.M. the next day, he immediately calls those prospects and clients. He'll say, "Hi, it's John Adviser here. I'm calling because I thought of you last night when I was watching *60 Minutes*. Did you happen to see it?" If the person watched the show, he says, "Wasn't that a great interview with Pavarotti? It was just terrific and I thought of you when I saw it. I just wanted to call and share that with you." If the individual missed the show, the adviser says, "They did a really great interview with Luciano Pavarotti. As it happens, I taped it. Why don't I send you over a copy?"

Again, that's not a time-consuming activity. It probably takes three to five minutes to talk to the client. But the payoff is that the adviser reminds the client that he or she is really special. Beyond that, the adviser finds an interesting after-effect that happens too often to be coincidental. A month to six weeks after each of those calls, more often than not a referral rolls in from the client, who has told somebody else about this wonderful adviser. You can't expect that to happen, but it's remarkable how often it does. If you make your clients feel special and valued through SOS activity, they'll tell friends about the excellent partnership they have with you.

Snapshots

- ✔ *Clients evaluate advisers on two dimensions. They look for you to deliver on the product-service dimension and to develop an enjoyable personal relationship.*
- ✔ *A strong, positive relationship but not much resonance on the product-service score was at one time sufficient for a client-adviser association. Today that won't carry you over the long haul unless you're also delivering on the product-service side at an acceptable level.*
- ✔ *If you deliver strongly on the product-service side but lack much of a relationship with the client, it's a supplier connection. Inevitably you'll be viewed as a supplier by some of your clients, especially if you have a large client base. But you can be damaged by external events such as market downturns.*
- ✔ *You want to position yourself to deliver well on both the product-service and relationship dimensions. You want to be a partner.*
- ✔ *Relationships create the patience that holds clients to advisers even when they slip below an acceptable level on the product-service dimension for a period of time.*
- ✔ *The most powerful sentiment you can create in your clients is the feeling that you care—not just about their money but about your clients themselves.*
- ✔ *The key to achieving that state is to follow the SOS Principle: Suspension Of Self-interest.*
- ✔ *Activities that communicate you care reflect three traits: They must not be self-serving, they must be personal, and they must be unexpected.*

- ✔ *For clients to feel they're dealing with somebody who cares, periodic communication must occur in which nothing can be gained by you as an adviser.*
- ✔ *It's important to review all your communications with clients—particularly your best clients, with whom you definitely don't want a supplier relationship—and estimate how many are free of self-interest.*
- ✔ *Advisers need to carve out a chunk of the week—about 5 percent, or two to three hours—to focus on SOS activity.*
- ✔ *Besides lacking self-interest, the activities you carry out in those hours should be personal and unanticipated.*
- ✔ *Although the activities must have a personal touch, some can be organized in a mass way but be executed so as to appear personal. Others will be highly individualized, flowing from the interests of a specific client.*
- ✔ *One adviser, when statements are sent by head office to his clients, mails out a copy himself, attaching a personal, handwritten note.*
- ✔ *Providing your home telephone number can serve as another opportunity to let clients know you care. Take advantage of the psychological advantages of personally writing the number on the cards you hand out.*
- ✔ *Other methods of letting clients know you care include Happy Birthday calls and "How-are-you-doing?" calls.*
- ✔ *You can communicate you care by sending articles of interest drawn from a broad array of publications such as golfing magazines.*
- ✔ *Advisers must learn to do a better job of saying thanks. You could try sending out thank-you cards, perhaps a few daily, as does the adviser whose assistant stands over him at 3 P.M. every day until he completes that task. Or you could send Happy Anniversary cards, to mark your anniversary with the client.*
- ✔ *When it comes to building relationships, it's often little things that have the biggest impact.*
- ✔ *With clients who own businesses, look for opportunities to send them new customers and to show a personal interest in their enterprise.*
- ✔ *When dealing with client accounts, openings exist for SOS inroads. In particular, ease new clients through the period after they sign on.*
- ✔ *Even watching television can provide opportunities to show you care.*

CHAPTER 35

Breaking Through the Clutter

BEFORE FOUNDING MARKETING SOLUTIONS, I WAS A PARTNER IN AN ADVERTISING and marketing consultancy. One of the overriding challenges in advertising is simply getting noticed. It's called "breaking through the clutter": finding a way for your own ad or commercial to be noticed amid the noise generated by all the others.

That same problem faces financial advisers trying to send a signal to clients about how keenly their business is valued. Again, competing noise makes it hard to be noticed. That's particularly true of large clients who are courted often, receiving lots of communication and positive messages. How do we stand apart?

The solution is not to spend more money but to search for ways to be different. In this chapter, I'll offer a host of ideas, but only to ignite your own creativity. The key is to search for methods to display personal attention, to surprise, and to stand out (Figure 35.1).

As an example, for years when I was a partner in that advertising consultancy, we would send our clients at Christmas a bottle of wine or chocolates, naturally of the highest quality. They were always grate-

Figure 35.1

Break Through the Clutter

- Seek uniqueness
- Key is to convey thought/personal attention
- Look for a way to make everything you do "surprising"

fully received and nobody ever returned them, but we didn't sense that we were kindling much excitement when we delivered that gift.

One year, in the fall, Tom Peters released a new book, *Thriving on Chaos.* We bought fifty copies, shipping one to each of the CEOs and marketing vice-presidents of our top twenty-five clients. The note inside read: "Hope this helps both of us to thrive through the chaos of the coming year." The response was fascinating. We received half a dozen notes thanking us and several phone calls with similarly enthusiastic sentiments. The bottles of wine and the chocolates—which, by the way, cost more than the book—had never drawn such ardent notice.

In giving gifts to top clients you must stand apart from the conventional.

Customizing Your Gift

The book, of course, was different, whereas wine and chocolates were traditional. The book was also somewhat personal, more customized to those particular customers' concerns than the wine or chocolates. They were trying to thrive in chaos. In fact, as the practice evolved further, we matched the books more intimately to the specific client's business. Our financial services clients received *The Rise of the House of Morgan,* while our high-tech clients got *Father and Son,* the story of the Watsons at IBM.

We found that the more we honed the book's subject matter to our clients' own business and interests, the more gratified they were and the more effective the gift was. We were sending a message that we'd given our offering some thought. It wasn't something we were stamping out for every client. It was special, indicating we considered them special.

That's a principle that advisers need to bear in mind in all their activity. It hit one adviser when his best client was about to get married. He called me for advice, wondering how he could let the client know how much he valued the relationship. With 500 people at the wedding, he wanted his gift to stand out—against tough competition. We talked it over and he ended up sending a quite modest gift—embarrassingly modest—but it broke through the clutter. When his client and new wife checked into the Club Med in Guadeloupe, the clerk at the reception desk handed them a card. They opened it to find a message from their adviser: "Congratulations and best wishes. I hope that you both enjoy the scuba lessons."

The adviser had taken the trouble to dig out where they were staying and arrange the lessons as his gift. The first day after the honeymoon, early in the morning, the adviser's phone rang. It was the client, effusively thanking him. Now how many of the other 500 guests at that wedding do you suppose received a personal phone call of thanks that morning? I doubt very many. It had nothing to do with the amount of money spent on the present: the adviser, when we originally chatted, was willing to spend far more than he paid for the scuba lessons. The gift worked because it was different. He had separated himself from everybody else doing the predictable. He had broken through the clutter.

Marking the Birth of a Child

Let me paint a picture for you. Your best client, after years of trying, has just succeeded in having her first child. It's a very special occasion and naturally, like most advisers, you are inclined to send flowers to the hospital. How big a bouquet do you need to order to break through the clutter—to indicate your joy and the special nature of the relationship? Actually, the bouquet would have to be so huge it fills the room. Everybody, after all, is sending flowers; while yours will be welcomed, they won't stand out without such a dramatic step.

Instead, you could devise something that sets you apart. If you want to deliver flowers, what about sending them the day the client returns home? But you could be much more imaginative than that.

You could send a certificate for a photography session to capture the new arrival's first portrait. You could arrange weekly maid service for that critical first month after the birth. You could pay for a catered meal to be sent to the house that first day back—or even for the entire first week. You could personally deliver a bottle of Dom Perignon for the new parents to celebrate on their return home. You could send the new mom a certificate for a day at a spa when she gets back on her feet. You could schedule a limousine to take the client and baby home from the hospital, with a card saying: "Congratulations. Hope this new arrival gets out into the world in fitting fashion."

None of those ideas may be appropriate for you. They might not fit with your personality or orientation. You can easily find others: The point is to be unique—to stand apart from the conventional.

Making Heroes

One company whose president served on the board of the local ballet traditionally sponsored a ballet performance for the firm's clients and their spouses. Guests were treated to dinner beforehand, and the evening was always warm and congenial. But after the initial year the company had the impression the event wasn't creating much excitement.

The first time you arrange a gift it tends to be exciting; the second time, it's less so; and the third time, well, it's ho-hum. You break through the clutter on the opening round, but very quickly clients absorb that event into their experience and it becomes part of the routine. The challenge is to keep inventing different approaches. The problem is that if you keep raising the ante, the stakes rise higher and higher.

The company above decided to be innovative. Instead of inviting clients and spouses, it invited clients and their children who were taking ballet lessons. This time it sponsored a matinee performance, with a reception afterwards which the performers from the ballet also attended, in costume. The cost was considerably less, as the expense of the preshow dinner had been eliminated. Yet the reaction was dramatically higher, because the company had made those parents heroes in the eyes of their kids. Let me tell you: that breaks through the clutter.

In Toronto many fund companies host advisers in their private boxes at Blue Jays ballgames—as happens with other companies, cities, and sports across North America. While that was exciting when the stadium first opened in 1989 and when the Blue Jays were a championship club, it has lost its appeal with repetition and a less-successful team. Companies have difficulty attracting the top advisers to their evenings, and as the quality of guests is ratcheted down, the level of excitement is ratcheted down as well.

One fund company recently decided to take a different tack, inviting advisers and their kids to an afternoon game. While the advisers had lots of opportunities to watch baseball games from a SkyDome box—indeed, that was the problem—it was a novel experience for the kids. Again, the company was making their clients look like heroes in front of their kids. Few things build loyalty like that.

A Silver-Plated Response

I was reminded of the power of breaking through the clutter when I talked to an adviser about the phenomenal reaction he received to a low-cost gift he was supplying clients with children or grandchildren. This was, I should stress, a very successful adviser, with a ski chalet and a condo in Palm Springs, both of which he used to entertain clients.

Whenever a client had a child or grandchild, his assistant would clip the birth announcement from the newspaper and take it to the print shop downstairs to be blown up and laminated. Then the adviser would place it in a silver-plated frame and send it to his client with a congratulatory note. The cost was less than $50, but the reaction was powerful—more powerful, in fact, than when he had lent some of those same clients his condo and saved them $2,000 on their vacation. The gesture was intensely personal, making the client feel special (even though, as with many of these clutter-crashing gifts, from the adviser's end it was actually a routine, able to be employed widely through his client list). The adviser noted that while clients were appreciative when borrowing the condo, he sometimes sensed they felt some cynicism as well: "We deserve this—after all, we helped to pay for it." He never got that sense with his silver-plated frame.

Client appreciation events offer another opportunity to break through the clutter. These affairs have become common recently and are quite productive, when the adviser makes the clients truly feel special. The challenge is to design an event that seems extraordinary. Too many advisers host a seminar some evening or Saturday morning, with wine and cheese and a guest speaker, and label it a client-appreciation event. While clients may appreciate the event, they don't see it as special. They don't talk about it enthusiastically the next day—or next week—to everybody they meet.

What works? Some advisers run golf tournaments, focusing in particular on top clients. Some host boat cruises or theater nights. One adviser struck gold with a Death By Chocolate evening. He's based in a cold climate in Alberta, and booked a local hotel one January evening for the extravaganza. When clients arrived, a jazz quintet was playing, couples were dancing, champagne was being served. On each table, as a starter, there was a small box of Belgian truffles, with a Death By Chocolate buffet to follow. The adviser arranged draws of prizes that were donated by key suppliers, so that every fifth or sixth client left a winner.

The event involved a significant amount of effort and considerable expense by the adviser. But the feedback and word-of-mouth afterward was phenomenal, far surpassing anything else he'd sponsored. While he could have scheduled two or three client workshops for the cost of that one client-appreciation event, the feedback convinced him seminars could not possibly have been as effective.

Another financial adviser has started a tradition: Each June he hosts a Family Fun Day on a Saturday for all his clients to bring their children and grandchildren. He arranges for clowns, jugglers, and face-painting and even pays the local fire department to bring its cherry-picker so kids can be lifted up and pull lollipops off trees. Naturally, there are hot dogs, chips, and ice cream. It's not very expensive but it has a marvelous impact on clients, since in taking an interest in their children and grandchildren, the adviser is expressing an interest in them beyond the next sale.

One financial adviser I know leveraged the Oscar awards into a successful client-appreciation event. *The English Patient* had just won the Academy Award for best film, and he was sure most of his clients had not yet seen it. He booked an evening at a local theater and invited all of his clients to a private showing. He provided popcorn and pop, and simply stood at the front of the theater at the beginning, telling those who attended: "Just wanted to take the opportunity to express my thanks to you for the opportunity to work together. Enjoy the film." It wasn't a high-cost event. Including popcorn, it cost him under $5 per client. But he received a phenomenal response. He intends to make it a regular event, each year identifying one Oscar-winning film that his clients have probably not seen or would enjoy viewing again.

Special Events for Special Clients

Follow that lead in planning your own events, and make sure yours are out of the ordinary. That's especially the case with your best clients. While we all like to be democratic, if somebody is going to feel particularly ecstatic, it's nice if that somebody is a top client. A trap I've noticed in customer appreciation efforts is advisers deciding that with a client base of, say, 500 people, nothing large scale can be attempted because of the cost; the event therefore has to be small scale. My view is that it's smarter to hold a really special event for 50, or 100, of those clients—something to knock their socks off—and then down the road sponsor something more modest for the rest. But you want to be remembered, particularly by your best clients.

Let me close with a clever idea by one adviser that allowed him to break through the clutter. He maintained a significant amount of business with the Templeton fund and was able to arrange a lunch with Sir John Templeton on a Toronto visit. He interviewed Sir John, just as a member of the media might, and sent his clients a copy of the tape along with a picture of the two of them together. Clients lapped it up. The tape positioned their adviser as someone unique—somebody who had access to investors of Sir John Templeton's stature. It was obviously of interest, and, most importantly, it broke through the clutter.

In the future, as the marketplace becomes more crowded and competition increases, we will have to look for ways to break through the clutter.

Snapshots

✔ *Advisers must find ways to break through the clutter and get noticed amid all the noise.*

✔ *The solution is not to spend more money but to find ways to be different.*

✔ *A book that is targeted to the recipient's interest can be a wonderful Christmas gift, instead of the traditional bottle of wine.*

✔ *Scuba lessons for a top client and his wife on their honeymoon helped one adviser to shine.*

✔ *After a top client gives birth, look for something beyond the traditional flowers: a certificate for a photography session, weekly maid service for the critical first month, a catered meal to be sent to the house that first day back from the hospital, or a limousine to take her and baby home from the hospital in style.*

- ✔ *Make your clients look like heroes in front of their children, as did the companies that arranged a special ballet matinee or a day in a SkyDome box for clients and kids.*
- ✔ *A silver-framed response to the birth of a client's child or grandchild will be long remembered.*
- ✔ *Follow the Death By Chocolate lead in planning your own customer appreciation event. Make sure your event is out of the ordinary. In some cases that might mean hosting something just for your top clients.*
- ✔ *Remember the adviser who got so much mileage out of a lunch with Sir John Templeton.*

CHAPTER 36

Making Clients Feel Special

THE CHALLENGE FOR THE ADVISER IN BUILDING RELATIONSHIPS, AS I INDICATed in Chapter 34, is to make the client feel special. One standard method is to link yourself to positive emotional experiences, as a friend naturally does. The adviser who sent the framed birth announcements was doing that—and it's part of the reason for the unexpectedly warm response he triggers.

One adviser, who had three clients with children graduating from university, noticed a paperback, *How to Get Your First Job,* while browsing in a bookstore. He bought three copies and dispatched it with a covering note, congratulating the clients on the special moment and suggesting the book might be of interest to their children.

He didn't think anything of it again until the clients all called to thank him profusely for his thoughtfulness. He didn't expect such a strong, positive reaction from an investment of $7.95, and indeed the response had no connection to the expense. His gesture was effective because he was communicating to his clients that he was paying attention to them—they were special, like friends.

That can be a very effective technique when clients face enjoyable moments, from anniversaries to promotions—even divorces, if it has been a difficult and unhappy marriage. Any positive emotional event for a client is an opportunity for an adviser to build a deeper relationship.

Some financial advisers worry that they might appear to be overreaching or presumptuous by involving themselves in such personal events. That is a legitimate concern. But your objective as a financial adviser should be to develop a relationship that's strong enough with all of your clients and certainly your best clients that everybody feels comfortable with these kinds of expressions. It has to be driven by the client, however. Some clients are somewhat standoffish, uninterested in these kinds of interaction, and that's fine. Part of your challenge is to know your clients well enough to recognize those who would appreciate such tokens of appreciation from you.

Again, let me stress this need not cost a lot of money. I know a financial adviser who began sending every client who was a golfer a sleeve of golf balls on his or her birthday with a note: "I just wanted to add my birthday wishes . . . and I am including a small gift. Hope you enjoy it." Obviously all those clients could afford golf balls. Most of them probably have more golf balls than they know what to do with. But the clients were invariably touched. It wasn't that they had been saved $6—it was the tapping into a positive moment that made the gift effort so worthwhile.

Advisers need to be more deliberate and organized about showing appreciation to clients.

The Message, Not the Medium, Counts

One of the most powerful ways to make clients feel special is to remember the seven key words when talking to them: "I thought of you the other day." Not "I thought of you the other day because we have a sales contest this quarter, and since I'm a just a little short, you sprang to mind," but "I thought of you the other day because I value you as a client and as a friend."

At Marketing Solutions we encourage advisers in annual planning to list their top twenty clients and put down beside each their interests and hobbies. Perhaps they love thrillers, collect stamps, avidly garden, or passionately follow sports. Next to that, write down something you could send to each client over the course of the year with a note attached: "I thought of you when I saw this." It could be a magazine, a book, a memento. It doesn't really matter. What you send isn't as important as the gesture of sending something—letting your clients know that you're thinking of them.

Let's imagine you're in a bookstore and come across a home-renovation magazine. You recall that one of your clients is renovating her home. So you plunk down four dollars to buy the magazine and send it over with the requisite covering note. Suppose your client already has the magazine? Is the four dollars wasted? Has it been thrown into the garbage, even if your copy of the magazine winds up there? Absolutely not. The benefit isn't in the magazine itself; it's in the signal you've given that the client and her renovation project are special to you—that you're thinking of her even when you're not generating revenue from the process.

One adviser recently related an interesting experience. A top client was a business owner who, after years of cajoling, had finally been convinced by his wife to take a holiday cruise. The adviser checked out what ship they were booked on and arranged to have a large fruit basket stationed in their room with a note: "Congratulations on your long-overdue and well-deserved holiday. I hope this is the first of many to come." It cost $50, a tiny sum when compared to the client's value over the years. When the client returned he called to thank the adviser for the gesture. End of story.

Well, not quite. A week later, the client's wife called. As it happens, the adviser has never met her, having dealt exclusively with her husband. "I just wanted to phone and tell you how much we appreciated your gift, how thoughtful it was," she said. "And I was wondering: I was talking to some friends at the club, and we were hoping you'd be willing to come and talk to us about investing. We don't know much and would like to learn more."

It turns out she was on the program committee for the ladies' luncheon series at the most exclusive country club in the area. Needless to say, the adviser managed to find time in his schedule to honor her request. While that opportunity wasn't—indeed, couldn't have been—on his mind when he sent that fruit basket, it's an example of the kind of return you will get, over time, from systematically going to the trouble of making your clients feel special.

The point is not to be manipulative but rather to let those clients whose relationships we value know how important they are to us. The expressions of appreciation are genuine—those clients *are* very important to us. The trouble is that we generally don't express our gratitude enough. We have to be more deliberate and organized about showing appreciation, and that begins by finding out and noting their interests.

Treating Clients as Friends

If you want your clients to feel like friends, it helps to treat them like friends. A top-tier client of one adviser complained to me recently, "You know, my adviser does a pretty good job, but one thing bugs me. It probably shouldn't, but it does. At least three times in the last two years he's asked me during our conversations what my wife does for a living. It irritates me that he has to keep asking."

It's a reasonable expectation for clients—particularly top clients—that their advisers will remember their spouse's occupation. Frankly, even if it's an unreasonable expectation, advisers can't change that. So if you want to make clients feel like friends, you have to know the same things about them you know about friends.

Some advisers have steel-trap memories and can easily remember minutiae about clients and their families. But most of us need help. As we discussed when we looked at organizing for prospecting, notes can be kept in standard files. The best option, however, is to maintain a client database. In that database you would list the kind of information shown in Figure 36.1.

You don't build that data bank by calling clients and interviewing them for thirty minutes. The information has to be gathered in the

Figure 36.1

Client Database Information

Client: ______________________________

Telephone: Residence: ______________________________

Business: ______________________________

E-mail: ______________________________

Fax: ______________________________

Other: ______________________________

Date of Birth: ______________________________

Where Prefers to be Called: __________ Best Time to Call: __________

Occupation: ______________ Industry: ______________

Key Competitors: ______________________________

Past Employers: ______________________________

Universities Attended/Degrees: ______________________________

Interests: ______________________________

Spouse: ______________________________

Spouse's Occupation/Company: ______________________________

Children (Year of Birth) ______________________________

____

____

Past Investment Experience: ______________________________

Other Comments: ______________________________

____

course of normal conversation. Luckily, it generally emerges, but advisers often don't retain it. So you have to note the information as it's offered, review it before meetings, and supplement it after each client conversation.

Let me add that it's possible to get carried away with this. You don't want to begin a conversation with your client, "Jonathan, how's it going? How's the golf game? I remember the last time we talked you birdied the 17th hole and were slicing a bit on the three wood. Have you fixed that slice?" That sort of approach quickly becomes transparent, and the last thing you want is clients feeling you're being less than honest in dealing with them.

Snapshots

✔ *Advisers should make their clients feel special, like friends.*

✔ *One effective method is to link yourself to positive emotional experiences, such as birthdays, anniversaries, and graduations.*

✔ *One of the best ways to make clients feel special is to remember the seven key words: "I thought of you the other day."*

✔ *List your top twenty clients, their interests and hobbies, and something you could send to each over the course of the year with a note attached: "I thought of you when I saw this."*

✔ *The point is not to be manipulative but—like the adviser who sent the fruit basket to the cruise ship—simply to let those clients whose relationships we value know how important they are to us.*

✔ *If you want your clients to feel like friends, an obvious method is to treat them as such. That involves remembering what they tell you about themselves and their family. The best way of keeping track of this information is to maintain a client database.*

CHAPTER 37

Blow-Away Service Experiences

EARLIER I DISCUSSED THE IMPORTANCE OF PROVIDING RESPONSIVE, RELIABLE service to our clients. You must cement that customer focus into your day-to-day routine. But in the course of running our practices, opportunities periodically arise to go above and beyond the minimum that clients expect and provide Blow-Away Service Experiences, or as I call them, BASEs. These BASEs are the grand-slam home runs of our client-satisfaction efforts.

The trick is to identify and capitalize on these moments. Ironically, some will occur after mini-disasters. And many will be relatively small-scale acts—small things that clients magnify, because the gestures are unexpected and unusually considerate.

One adviser found such an opening when a client called needing a check quickly. The client lived out of town, two hours away. The adviser directed his assistant to drive out to drop the check off. The client was surprised and overwhelmed by the adviser's dedication. While you don't want to disrupt your office regularly with such BASEs, similar opportunities arise from time to time for blow-away service, and you should seize them.

I recall once losing my wallet while in London, England. Although I was able to procure some interim cash, I was now without credit cards. I called American Express at 2 P.M. The representative asked me, "Mr. Richards, what time are you leaving?" I replied, "4:30."

"No problem—we'll have a replacement card out there for you," he promised. I was pleased, but not overwhelmed. That's the expected service from American Express, and I was, after all, paying an annual fee for it.

At 4:20 I looked at my watch. The courier hadn't yet arrived with the card, and naturally I was anxious. Just then the phone rang; the hotel receptionist told me someone had arrived from American Express. I rushed down to the lobby and was greeted by a man who introduced himself as Peter Markham. "We spoke earlier this afternoon, Mr. Richards. I've come to drop off your American Express card."

I thanked him but expressed my surprise, since I'd assumed the card would be sent by courier rather than being dropped off personally. "Well, normally we do it that way," he said, "but you know, sometimes couriers can be late. I was coming off shift anyway, and as you're practically on my way home, I thought I'd drop it off myself."

It's important to touch all the BASEs—particularly after your team dropped the ball.

Little Things Count

Was that a big thing or a little thing? A little thing, clearly. But that BASE made a dramatic impact on this client, because it underlined the importance American Express as an organization places on my comfort. It had risen above the expected in providing personal attention.

I was talking recently to a client who commented about visiting his adviser's office for a meeting and being offered coffee while the adviser completed a phone call. He had only been there once before, yet the receptionist said, "You take one cream and two sugars, don't you?"

The client was amazed. "That's right, but how did you know?"

"Well, you were here previously and had coffee," she replied. "I made a note then as to how you like it." Again, a little thing. But it was unexpected and the client felt special.

Another client's adviser—out in Vancouver, where they experience rain more than occasionally—came out of a meeting to find it had just started pouring. He didn't have an umbrella, but the adviser told him, "No problem. We keep some extras for exactly that purpose. Why don't I lend you one? You can drop it off when it's convenient or bring it back the next time you come in. Whatever works for you."

The client was blown away. That had never happened before in dealing with other professionals and businesses. I followed up with the adviser. "At the beginning of the year, we buy enough umbrellas to have 100 on hand," he said. "They're pretty cheap—just this side of disposable umbrellas, really—and cost us $8 apiece. We generally lose half of those in a year, so it costs us $400 annually. Frankly, the mileage we get out of being able to lend them to clients more than compensates for the cost."

Turning a Problem into a BASE

Even when you hit a problem, a possibility often exists to recover and turn it into a blow-away experience. I give a lot of workshops in Vancouver, and on one occasion, only nine of the ten boxes of binders arrived, leaving us without materials for ten participants. We photocopied and shared, but naturally I was upset and since it was a two-day session, I was anxious to ensure the binders arrived for the next day.

During the first break I called Federal Express. The customer-service agent said, "Mr. Richards, I can't tell you how sorry we are. We've just spent $2 million to avoid exactly this kind of problem, but it seems wherever people are involved, human error creeps in. Your tenth box made its way to Newfoundland, and unfortunately they're fogged in, so we can't fly it out to you.

"But let me tell you what we've done. I spoke to your assistant and we've already picked up a replacement set of binders from your Toronto office. They will be arriving in Vancouver imminently and we'll get them over to you right away. It goes without saying that there will be no cost for the entire shipment. But what else can we do? Would it be helpful if our general manager wrote a letter of apology to each of the participants who were inconvenienced?"

What happens to my predisposition toward Federal Express after that incident? It actually goes up. They sent part of my shipment to the wrong coast, yet I'm more likely to retain them in the future because they recovered so fantastically from the mistake. If they goof on the next shipment, then they have a probably insurmountable predicament. But consumers have tolerance for occasional error. The problem, then, isn't the mistake; it's how you deal with mistakes.

Recovering: The Three Steps

In recovering from mistakes, follow the three steps from the above example. First, acknowledge the error—"You're absolutely right, we screwed up"—and empathize with the client: "I know how you feel. It's frustrating for you and I can assure you it's frustrating for us." Second, fix the problem quickly and directly. Third, look for a way to go beyond that in service, to acknowledge your concern and turn it into a positive experience. Research shows that recovery from errors can be one of the most effective means of blowing away clients with the level of service you provide.

That doesn't mean you should deliberately make mistakes so that you can impress your clients with your flair for recovery. For most operations, lots of opportunities to recover from mistakes will present themselves over the course of time. The principle you must entrench in your staff's minds is that whenever an error occurs, they have to deal with it immediately, even if you're not available. They must acknowledge the problem and empathize with the client; and then they must go above and beyond the call of duty in redressing the situation.

Blow-away service experiences lead to ecstatic customers. Clients are always telling me, and others, about BASEs they encounter: The adviser's secretary who keeps tab on their coffee preferences or the thoughtful adviser who stocks a closet full of umbrellas for his clients. I tell people about my experience with American Express and Federal Express. That's how the little things—and big things—add up.

Snapshots

✔ *In the course of running our practice, opportunities periodically arise to go above and beyond the minimum that clients expect and provide a blow-away service experience, or BASE.*

✔ *The trick is to identify and capitalize on these moments.*

✔ *Many BASEs will be relatively small-scale acts that clients magnify, because they are unexpected and unusual—like the adviser's secretary who keeps tabs on the coffee preferences of clients, the adviser who provides umbrellas on rainy days, or the American Express representative who delivers personally instead of taking a chance on a courier.*

✔ *Some opportunities will occur after mini-disasters, like my experience with Federal Express.*

✔ *In recovering from mistakes, follow three steps: (1) acknowledge the error and empathize with the client; (2) fix the problem quickly and directly; (3) look for a way to go beyond that in service, to acknowledge your concern and turn it into a positive, blow-away experience.*

✔ *Remember: BASEs lead to ecstatic customers.*

CHAPTER 38

Doing Well by Doing Good

IN THE LIST OF ATTRIBUTES CLIENTS SEEK IN AN ADVISER, FINDING SOMEBODY with a social conscience who contributes back to society doesn't tend to be very high on most lists. That being said, an increasing desire is emerging on the part of many people to feel good in all respects about the companies and professionals they deal with. We see that in the success of organizations like the Body Shop and Ben and Jerry's, which are doing well by doing good.

Some advisers have tapped into that sentiment by sharing their success with the community and letting clients know about it. Classic examples are the advisers who sponsor golf tournaments for a good cause or donate to charity in lieu of Christmas gifts, quietly letting clients know.

You have to be highly comfortable with such initiatives, or they will inevitably appear forced or phony. But if it fits your instincts, consider allocating some money in your marketing plan to making a contribution back to the community. It doesn't have to be a huge amount of money, by the way. Often $500 will make an impact on some community need.

Without blowing your own horn, let your clients know what you've done. You might advise the media or mention it in an aside in a newsletter, talking less about your contribution and more about the group being helped. Advisers with such a bent have found their clients felt better dealing with a socially conscious adviser. As we move forward, with the spread between people at the top of society and bottom likely to grow, doing well by doing good is a technique that will be available to more and more advisers.

Snapshots

- ✔ *The success of organizations like the Body Shop and Ben and Jerry's demonstrates the increasing desire of many people to feel good in all respects about the companies and professionals they associate with.*
- ✔ *Some advisers have tapped into that sentiment by sharing their success with the community and letting clients know.*
- ✔ *If it matches your own instincts, consider allocating some money in your marketing plan to making a contribution back to the community.*
- ✔ *Without appearing to brag, let your clients know what you've done.*

Section IV
Implementing

CHAPTER 39

Leveraging Your Time

WE'VE TALKED EXTENSIVELY IN THIS BOOK ABOUT VARIOUS IDEAS AND activities that financial advisers can employ to improve their client relationships and their effectiveness in dealing with prospects. As you've been reading, no doubt you have been seized by a mixture of conflicting emotions: exhilaration at the prospect of trying some of those new ideas, but an equally powerful sinking feeling that they will be impossible to implement because, to a lesser or greater extent, they each require time. And like most advisers, you are probably now working as hard as you can—or want to.

The only alternative is to leverage your activities. You can leverage your activities through technology. You can leverage your activities by better use of staff. You can leverage your activities by a more disciplined approach to planning.

The challenge for every successful financial adviser—it accompanies success, actually—is to strip away non-essential activities that can be handled by somebody else in order to focus on the key items that only the adviser can carry out. A liberating step is to build into your business some systems that automatically take care of certain routine activities. I call this putting your practice on autopilot.

A good example was the adviser concerned with the predicament that can arise if the client doesn't receive adequate contact after initially coming on board. The client displayed enough trust to give the adviser her money, but that's only the beginning part of the trust spectrum. She could easily lose that basic level of trust if she doesn't hear from the adviser for twelve months after the courtship concludes. More to the point, we want our clients at the top level of the trust spectrum.

That financial adviser arranged for an assistant to call every new client a week after the initial order was placed and say, "Ms. Client, my name is Joe Staff. I'm calling at the suggestion of John Adviser. You should have received your first confirmation by now. I just wanted to be sure that you received it and answer any questions that you have, to ensure nothing is vague or uncertain."

Two months later the assistant calls again. Same formula: Are you receiving statements and have you any questions? The calls generally don't take long, but they reap large dividends, reassuring the client that the courtship has become a committed relationship.

Top advisers have a strong commitment to investing in staff, technology and knowledge.

What's important to note here is that the financial adviser has little involvement with these phone calls, even though they are heightening his ties to the client. He set up a system where every client automatically receives those two phone calls. He then delegated the work and only hears about it when some unusual problem erupts that demands his attention. Otherwise, the check-up calls run on autopilot while he concentrates on other affairs.

Autopilot Steps

Another adviser has established a similar routine for recognizing special occasions for his clients. If a client receives a promotion, or retires, a fruit basket is sent with a congratulatory note. The adviser's involvement is limited to pressing a key on his computer that he has specially programmed. When he's in a client file and wishes to note a particular occasion, he presses the key and the name is automatically added to the list. At the end of the week the computer spits out the list for his assistant, and fruit baskets are sent. Again, he has automated the process.

Another adviser was surprised by the enthusiastic reaction when he sent a book called *The Insider's Guide to Disney World* to a long-term client who had mentioned he was visiting the entertainment showcase with his family for the first time. The adviser has since bought a bunch of copies, keeps them in the office, and anytime a client mentions a visit to Disney World, he simply writes a short note and his staff takes care of the rest.

Staff can also be leveraged to help you communicate efficiently with your clients. I talked earlier about the virtue of telephone appointments. If it's handled properly, nothing is wrong with your assistant phoning a client to arrange a convenient time for the two of you to chat. That significantly cuts down the time and energy you have to expend on telephone appointments, which all too often require more effort to arrange than is ultimately involved in the session itself.

Seminars are another example of leveraging your time. In a single evening you can connect to twenty-five, seventy-five, or 200 prospects and clients. It's not as intimate as one-on-one meetings, but it's certainly better than no interaction at all. And you are sending a positive signal even to those who can't attend but still appreciate your commitment to client education.

Investing in Your Business

One of the essential prerequisites for automating your process is a commitment to investing in your business. At Marketing Solutions we have found many different patterns to success among top financial advisers. No two financial advisers are the same, but we have observed one common trait—without exception they have a strong orientation toward investing in their business. They invest in staff. They invest in technology. They invest their own time to become more knowledgeable.

It's important as we head into the uncertain future that financial advisers be willing to invest in their practices. Money spent must be viewed not as an expense but as an investment. Staffing is particularly crucial in this regard. Talking to financial advisers about mistakes made in their practice or what they wish they had done differently, Marketing Solutions has found they invariably cite waiting too long to hire their first staff member, and then waiting too long to hire subsequent staff.

Financial advisers tend to be too conservative. Failing to hire staff as soon as you can afford to is a trap, because it prevents you from gaining the productivity that person will unleash, which invariably more than compensates for the extra salary. But let me highlight a second trap that can also occur: failing to pay the going rate when hiring. Often financial advisers will wonder how little money they can get away with in hiring. That's the wrong question. The real question is: How much can I afford to pay? Up to a point, a direct correlation occurs between productivity and the compensation package. Paying an extra $5,000 to hire a person who is superior rather than average or below average will often be the best expenditure of $5,000 you can make.

As a financial adviser, you want a strong backup team. You want superior people who can take initiative and accept delegation. You want as much of your practice on autopilot as possible, so that you are spending your time on high-end activities only you can handle.

Snapshots

- ✔ *To implement the many ideas in this book, you must leverage your activities. You can do so through technology, better use of staff, and a more disciplined approach to planning.*
- ✔ *A liberating step is to build into your business some systems that automatically take care of routine activities—putting your practice on autopilot.*
- ✔ *You can set up autopilot systems to counter the dip in communication that often occurs after a client comes on board, or for a variety of SOS activities.*
- ✔ *Staff can also be leveraged to help you communicate efficiently with your clients.*
- ✔ *It's important that financial advisers be willing to invest in their practices. The money spent should be viewed not as an expense but as an investment.*
- ✔ *Don't be over-conservative in hiring. Don't wait too long to hire, and be willing to pay for quality.*

CHAPTER 40

Planning for Success

I RECENTLY HAD THE QUINTESSENTIAL ADULT EXPERIENCE WHEN MY MOTHER called to tell me she had sold the family home to move into a condo. It was therefore time, she informed me, to clean the junk from my youth out of the basement.

So I headed to Montreal one weekend and started sorting through the boxes in the basement, hoping to find those old comic books that disappeared about 1958 and which are probably now worth millions. Naturally, I had no luck. But I was extraordinarily excited to come across a Latin text, as you no doubt would understand. Entitled *Meditationes Sacrae,* it was written in 1597 by Francis Bacon, 400 years ago. As I leafed through it, I came across his words *Nam et ipsa scienta potestas est.* If your Latin is a little rusty, let me translate: "Knowledge is power."

Many things have changed over the centuries since Bacon wrote his book. Yet until recently, that bit of sage advice was as timely as ever. Indeed, it even spawned a complementary aphorism: "Information is power."

Until about ten years ago a major problem financial advisers faced was that they didn't have enough information—they didn't have enough knowledge. That isn't the problem they face today, however. Most advisers have too much information. One of our challenges is to stop deluging our clients with more information, and more data, and more knowledge. Instead, we have to distill all that information into a few clear insights. Today, insight is power.

Linked to that is another challenge: productivity. How do advisers keep abreast of the information inundating them and distill it into insight, when they are overwhelmed with so many other activities? How do they cram into their busy work week some of the exciting ideas I've offered in this book for *Getting Clients, Keeping Clients*?

In the last chapter we looked at some possibilities for leveraging technology and staff that have provided relief for many advisers. Now I want to present another solution: the 5 Percent Equation. What would be your response to this offer of mine: "Give me 5 percent of your work week—if you work fifty hours, I'll take 2.5 of them—and I will guarantee unequivocally to increase your productivity in the remaining hours by 20 percent."

Clearly that's a no-brainer. You'd leap at the chance. And every financial adviser has the potential to increase his or her productivity by at least that much through spending 5 percent of the work week planning their time. Yet most financial advisers fail to devote time to planning on a regular basis (Figure 40.1).

Often, the most overlooked form of revenue from a client is the psychic income we receive.

Working Smarter

In the future we will witness a transition in the requirements for success. Historically, it took effort to succeed in this business. You flourished by working hard. But that's changing. In future, you will have to work smart. That's a critical transformation, requiring a fundamental shift in thinking.

I was reminded of this change when chatting with a university classmate who joined Xerox and rose to a fairly senior level in its sales organization. He was recalling how twenty years ago if a sales manager saw one of his sales reps in the office buried in paperwork or research, he would kick the rep out of the office. The operating rule was: You never make a buck sitting on your behind. If a salesperson wasn't out interacting with clients, he or she wasn't doing the job.

Today, if you're a Xerox sales manager and you see reps spending 100 percent of their time on the road, your responsibility is to haul them back and warn them, "You're working hard, you're not working smart."

Figure 40.1

Working Smart vs. Working Hard

The Planning Equation:

- 5% investment × 50 hours = 2.5 hours lost
- 20% return × 47.5 hours = 9.5 hours gained

It's the same at most large sales organizations, from IBM to Procter & Gamble. The expectation exists that salespeople will spend a significant chunk of time—maybe 5 percent, maybe even 20 percent—planning their business. And that time devoted to planning dramatically improves their sales.

I'm not suggesting that financial advisers spend 20 percent of their time planning. But I recommend at least 5 percent. And a good deal of that planning needs to be focused on clients, based on what might be called the Rule of 11—our finding, related earlier, that when we compared the results of two matched sales forces, the one that concentrated on clients achieved eleven times the returns of the one that concentrated on prospects.

In focusing on clients, it's important to be proactive. A trap many advisers slip into is responding primarily to clients who call them—the squeaky-wheel syndrome. While it's crucial that you deal appropriately with those clients who demand attention, getting snared by the squeaky wheel can leave underserviced a large number of your client base who are quieter but still substantial investors. It also might leave your less-vocal clientele vulnerable to competitors.

The Five Steps of Client Planning

To avoid that trap, you must plan how to allocate your time and what you hope to achieve (Figure 40.2). Five steps, are involved:

1. identifying priority clients;
2. setting key goals for each of those relationships;
3. developing an activity plan to achieve those goals;
4. implementing the activity plan; and
5. monitoring the effectiveness of your client planning, and readjusting as necessary.

Asking advisers to identify priority clients sometimes strikes them as contradictory. After all, isn't every client important? Aren't advisers supposed to be sensitive to every Client's 99? Definitely. I'm not preaching a program of ignoring or dismissing a chunk of clients who fail to make the cut in this search for priority. The first responsibility for a financial adviser is to provide each and every client with a solid level of service and attention. You should have developed for your operation a minimum standard of service and communication which every client receives. If somebody doesn't merit that service, he or she shouldn't be a client, and you should do both yourself and the client a favor by severing the relationship so that individual can move to an adviser who will value the assets and revenues brought to her business.

But experience shows that providing a baseline of attentive service consumes only about 50 percent of an adviser's time. With the other 50

Figure 40.2

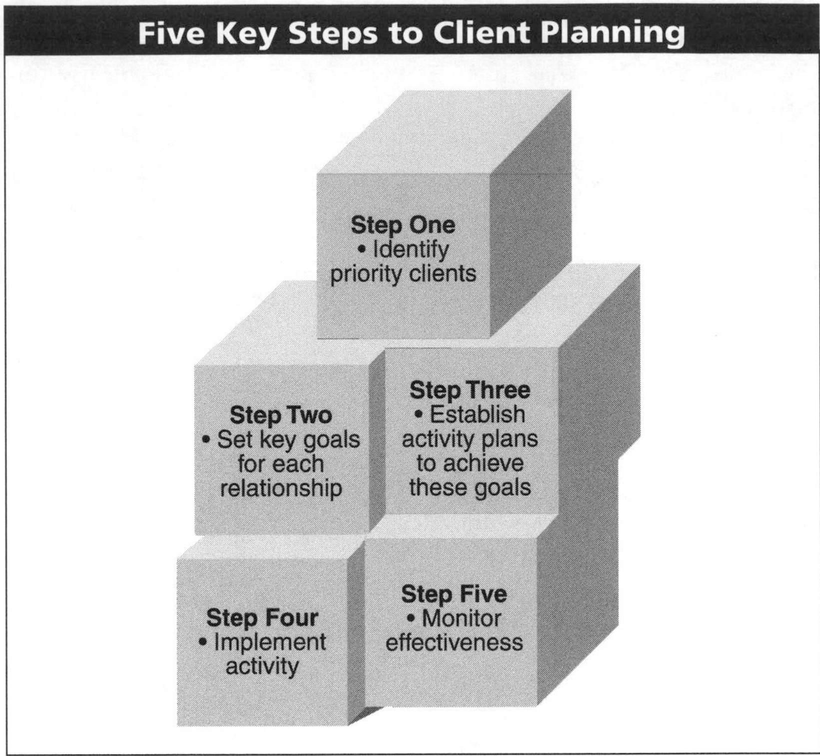
Five Key Steps to Client Planning
Step One
• Identify priority clients
Step Two
• Set key goals for each relationship
Step Three
• Establish activity plans to achieve these goals
Step Four
• Implement activity
Step Five
• Monitor effectiveness

percent, the adviser is free to improvise. And the adviser who is working smart will allocate that time to clients who offer the greatest rewards.

When advisers begin to identify priority clients, they instinctively turn to asset levels or the revenues and commissions those clients generate. But that's not the only dimension that should be considered. Indeed, several traps are common in identifying priority clients (Figure 40.3), and focusing on asset levels is only the first one to guard against.

Figure 40.3

Traps in Identifying Top Clients

- Focusing on sales or assets alone
- Ignoring profitability
- Concentrating on the present at the expense of the future
- Ignoring psychic income

The second trap is to ignore profitability. As companies have become more sophisticated in analyzing clients, they have realized that two clients with identical sales levels can represent dramatically different levels of profitability and productivity. One might beat you down on price and/or require inordinate service from you and your staff. The client will be calling every week with new demands, causing all sorts of problems for your office, while another client with the same annual sales is quite satisfied with an annual meeting and quarterly phone calls.

Another trap is forgetting the future. It's important not just to weigh the profitability that clients generate today but to consider also the profitability they will generate in future years. Again, you could have two clients with identical revenue streams today but very different levels of opportunity for the future.

Advisers also tend to forget psychic income. After our financial requirements are looked after, most of us seek some psychological rewards from our work. We like to feel good about what we do. We want to take pleasure from our work. And some clients are more enjoyable than others to work with. We look forward to meeting, helping, and sharing with them.

Rating Your Clients

In all, Marketing Solutions has identified eight components that help advisers to select priority clients (Figure 40.4).

1. It begins with the assets the client has placed under your stewardship.
2. Next is the revenues those assets have generated for you in the past twelve months.
3. Referral volume is important. Even though you may not be collecting a large amount of revenue from a client, if you're receiving referrals, that's as good as revenue.

Figure 40.4

What Makes a "Top" Client?

• Total assets with you	• Future potential
• Investments in past 12 months	• Influence
• Referrals in past 2 years	• How time-consuming
• Additional assets held elsewhere	• PITA Factor

4. The next criteria relates to additional assets held elsewhere. You may have two clients for whom you invest the same level of assets, but for one that's all her money, while for the other you are currently investing only a small fraction. That doesn't mean you demote the client when you have all her assets; but you should recognize the greater possibilities the second client might provide.
5. It's also important to assess the future potential of clients. Two clients may be of equal wealth, yet one is thirty-five and the other seventy-five. Or one is a teacher and the other a fast-rising young executive. In each case the potential for the future is different.
6. The sixth area is influence. Clients differ in their ability to help you gain access to positions on boards, introduce you to key people, and recommend you for high-profile speaking engagements. Those are important when considering whom to expend extra effort on.
7. We need to gauge how time-consuming a client is. Clients differ in terms of the demands they place on us and the energy required to keep them ecstatic.
8. The final criteria is the PITA factor. PITA stands for Pain In The Anatomy. Not all clients are equally pleasant to deal with. Clients we relish working with actually give us energy; clients that we don't like—the PITAs of this world—rob us and our staff of energy.

Figure 40.5 shows a suggested scoring system, listing each factor and offering a potential weighting. Every adviser is different, so you may want to adjust the weighting to reflect your priorities. But essentially we recommend a range of points in each category, generally from 1 to 5.

For assets, some advisers assign 1 point to a client with $50,000 in investments, and 5 points to a client with over $500,000 in investments, dividing the range between into logical segments and commensurate points. Ideally you want 20 percent of your clients at each of the five levels. But precision isn't critical; we're after broad strokes.

Referrals are one of the most important forms of income we receive from a client, so the suggested scoring system rates those up to 10 points. If a client fails to give any referrals, slot him at 0. Each referral counts for 2 points, so a client who offers 3 referrals scores 6 points.

The 1–5 scale is reversed in the category calculating the time required to serve a client. A client who needs a very high degree of attention gets 1 point, while a client who is easy to serve receives 5 points. The PITA factor works on the same principle, but this time we expand into negative numbers, since a client should lose points for

Figure 40.5

Assessing Top Clients

1. Assets — Adjustments

<$50K	1 point	____
$50K–$100K	2 points	____
$100K–250K	3 points	____
$250K–500K	4 points	____
Over $500K	5 points	____

2. Invested in past 12 months

<$5,000	1 point	____
$5,000–$10,000	2 points	____
$10,000–25,000	3 points	____
$25,000–50,000	4 points	____
Over $50,000	5 points	____

3. Referals in past 2 years

0 referrals	0 points	____
1 referral	2 points	____
2 referrals	4 points	____
3 referrals	6 points	____
4 referrals	8 points	____
5+ referrals	10 points	____

4. Additional Assets held elsewhere

<$25K	1 point	____
$25K–$50K	2 points	____
$50K–100K	3 points	____
$100K–250K	4 points	____
Over $250K	5 points	____

5. Future Potential

Very low	1 point	____
Low	2 points	____
Moderate	3 points	____
High	4 points	____
Very high	5 points	____

6. Influence

Very low	1 point	____
Low	2 points	____
Moderate	3 points	____
High	4 points	____
Very high	5 points	____

7. Time required to meet needs

Very high	1 point	____
High	2 points	____
Moderate	3 points	____
Low	4 points	____
Very low	5 points	____

8. PITA Factor

Very difficult	–10 points	____
Somewhat difficult	–5 points	____
Neither easy nor difficult	0 points	____
Fairly easy	5 points	____
Pleasure to deal with	10 points	____

being a PITA. The scale runs from –10 to +10, with the most difficult PITAs at –10 and those clients who are true pleasures at +10.

To see the value of this system, imagine you have two clients. Client A has $75,000 in assets and last year invested $2,500, while Client B has $600,000 and last year invested $40,000. Given a choice, most advisers would grab Client B because traditionally we've been motivated by assets and investments (Figure 40.6).

Now let's fill out the picture a bit more, as in Figure 40.7. Imagine Client A, who doesn't have that much in assets and investments with you, gave two quality referrals in the past year. Furthermore, he has substantial assets not yet invested with you, doesn't take up much staff time, and you really enjoy dealing with him. Client B has quite a different profile. Yes, she provides lots of assets and investments—but no referrals. She doesn't hold any assets elsewhere, she requires a lot of time, and while she's not difficult to deal with, she's not a pleasure either. Add it all up and you find that Client A is significantly more valuable than Client B and deserves greater priority.

PITA Liberation

That example demonstrates the power of this system and the productivity that can flow from employing it. Start by establishing a scoring system that reflects your own practice and values. Then apply it to your own client base. I urge you in doing so to give the task proper time. Yes, you can whip through your clients in a few hours, taking a minute for each, and then move on to the next item on your agenda. And you will have a ranking, although not a terribly thoughtful one.

Instead, try to give each client about five minutes—which allows you to rank about twelve clients an hour. With 200 clients you'll be investing about sixteen hours. Although this is a significant chunk of time, when the scorecard needs to be updated the following year it will take much less time.

One financial adviser tried a third approach. He decided it was not

Figure 40.6

Two Clients

	Client A	Client B
Assets with you	$75,000	$600,000
Invested in past year	$2,500	$40,000

only important to put this system in place but also that it should reflect the views of his staff. So he scheduled a series of twice-weekly lunch meetings with employees, and in hour-long sessions over sandwiches they went through every client and compared notes. It took a significant amount of time—they averaged only six clients per hour—but as a result he developed a better assessment of those clients as well as an appreciation for the feelings of his staff. At the same time, the staff gained a much better understanding of the clients. The result was a very effective expenditure of time.

In the process it's important to address the PITAs. These could also be described as dysfunctional or toxic clients but not, I want to stress, demanding clients. I'm not talking about clients who ask tough questions, but about that lunatic fringe of clients who are irrationally dissatisfied and troublesome.

The reality is that 5 percent of the client universe fall into this classification. No matter what you do, they won't be happy. Sometimes they're big clients, but more often they're not: small clients but big pains. I firmly believe that every year advisers should analyze their client base and search for PITAs who can be dispensed with. Few things can boost an adviser's morale—and the staff's—than picking up the phone, calling a true PITA, and saying, "Mr. Client, we've recently restructured the way we work, and as a result, I don't think we are able to meet your needs as we go forward. I think you would be best served with another adviser." Firing a PITA can be a joyful moment.

Naturally you won't eliminate all the PITAs, as other factors have to be considered. You may find you part company with only 1 or 2 percent of your client base. I'm certainly not suggesting anytime a client quibbles about something you immediately shout, "That's it! You're cut off! You're toast." Clearly, if a high-revenue client has PITA tendencies, compromises are often required. But the question is not necessarily "Can I afford to lose this client?" It's actually "Can I afford to retain this client, given the real cost?" Amid the quest for more clients, advisers shouldn't be afraid to prune the current roster of energy-sapping clients.

Identifying Goals

After identifying priority clients through this system, the next step is to identify goals. Effective goals have four elements: They are significant in impact if achieved; realistic but also stretching; quantifiable; and tied to a specific time frame (Figure 40.8).

Generally when advisers are asked about the goals they hold for a client relationship, they refer to elements related to revenue: "I want to get more of his money." "I want to obtain more referrals from her." These goals are, of course, important. But for top clients

Figure 40.7

Top Client Priority List

Client Name	Assets (1–5)	Invested in Past 12 Months (1–5)	Referrals in Past 2 Years (0–10)	Additional Assets (1–5)
Scoring	1 <$50K 2 $50–100K 3 $100–250K 4 $250–500K 5 >$500K	1 <$5K 2 $5–10K 3 $10–25K 4 $25–50K 5 >$50K	0 0 2 1 4 2 6 3 8 4 10 5	1 <$25K 2 $25–50K 3 $50–100K 4 $100–250K 5 >$250K
Client A	2	1	4	3
Client B	5	4	0	1
1.				
2.				
3.				
4.				
5.				
6.				
7.				
8.				
9.				
10.				

Future Potential (1–5)	Influence (1–5)	Time (1–5)	PITA Factor (–10 to +10)	Total (Out of 50)
1 Very Low 2 Low 3 Moderate 4 High 5 Very High	1 Very Low 2 Low 3 Moderate 4 High 5 Very High	1 Very High 2 High 3 Moderate 4 Low 5 Very Low	–10 V Difficult –5 Difficult 0 Neutral 5 Easy 10 Pleasure	
4	3	4	5	26
2	1	1	0	14

Figure 40.8

Criteria for Effective Goals

1. Significant in impact if achieved
2. Realistic but also a stretch
3. Quantifiable/Measurable
4. Time frame attached

a critical first step precedes revenue goals: consolidating the existing relationship.

Clients pass through a cycle of comfort with an adviser. At first, as prospects, they begin at the low end, being willing to take a phone call from you—or, to be more specific, if you call and they happen to pick up the phone, they won't hang up but will grant you thirty seconds. The next stage might be that if you call and leave a message, they will actually return it. Then, as they become more comfortable, they will attend a seminar, leaving the security of their home or office to hear you and your guest speak, within the safety of a crowd. Finally, they'll agree to meet one on one, and then opt to conduct business.

That isn't the end of the process. It just signals their shift from the prospect comfort spectrum to a similar one for clients. They are now sufficiently at ease to engage in business with you, but that's merely a threshold comfort level that must be intensified. At the next stage clients start to rely on you for advice—depending on you not just to complete a transaction but also to steer them. From there, they move to accepting you as their sole (or, at least, dominant) financial adviser. Finally, they become apostles who want to tell everyone they meet about the wonderful financial adviser they are lucky enough to have.

Identifying Business Goals

In goal-setting it's important to consider which of those stages each client is at and how he or she can be nudged up the spectrum. After that comes the various business goals, which divide into six different categories.

The first set are business-related. You want to increase sales. You want to diversify sales. You may want to move the client into a different product or begin to cross-sell with other products, such as insurance.

The second category contains positioning goals. You want to augment your share of the client's investments, increasing the number of financial aspects of the client's life in which you are involved until you become the single source of financial advice. Research shows a direct correlation between the quality of an adviser's relationship with a client and the number of services performed for that client. That's an obvious finding, but it again points to the importance of strengthening the relationship with the client.

The third set of financial goals relate to referrals. Maybe you have an explicit referral goal for the client geared to other members of the family, colleagues, or friends. Your goal may be nothing more complicated than obtaining names of acquaintances who might be added to your newsletter mailing list.

The fourth set of goals relate to influence. We want clients to use their influence to help us in our business by introducing us to their accountant, lawyer, friends, and associates. Perhaps the client works for a large local company and can provide an introduction to the vice-president of human resources for you to discuss establishing a pension plan at the firm. Maybe you simply want the client to bring a friend to a seminar so you can begin the prospecting process with that friend.

Your fifth goal for the client may revolve around productivity. You may simply want to reduce the time it takes to deal with that client. Maybe it's simply to persuade him or her to stop calling you on trivial matters and to deal with staff instead.

The final set of goals are defensive in nature. You want to insulate the relationship with the client from competition by heightening the defenses that exist around it.

With that framework, you will have as many different goals as you have clients. The challenge is to step back and consider each client individually with respect to those various dimensions. So for Client A, who, as we discussed earlier, is not presently a huge client but has potential, the primary goal might be to win an introduction to his accountant, and the secondary goal to bring the $25,000 in GICs maturing at the bank into the network of money you manage. For Client B, who is a large client now but doesn't appear to have much potential, the prime goal might be to strengthen the relationship while at the same time, as a secondary goal, persuading her to deal with your assistant on day-to-day matters.

Preparing Activity Plans

After establishing goals, the next step is to develop communication and activity plans to achieve them. These must be driven by the client and the nature of the goals. Maybe the goal is communications-oriented: You intend to initiate quarterly phone calls and a full financial review. Maybe it's socially driven: the client is a business owner and you intend

Figure 40.9

Client: John Client
Date Completed: December 1, 1997

SOS Activity: Subscription to *Golf Magazine*
Timing: Dec. 31

Primary Goal: Introduction to accountant
Activity:
1. Arrange for accountant to sit in on next financial review
Timing: January 31

2. Invite client & accountant to Chamber of Commerce luncheon
Timing: March 30

3. Send one referral to target accountant per quarter
Timing: First referral by March 30

Secondary Goal: Get GICs held elsewhere
Activity:
1. Get client to agree to provide statements to consolidate tracking of all investments
Timing: March 30

2. Persuade client to provide me with competitor's quotes
Timing: June 30

to spend a couple of afternoons this year golfing with him and to arrange dinner some evening with his spouse and yours. Maybe the client is a business owner and you intend to introduce a potential new client for him. Or maybe you just intend to undertake some SOS activity to strengthen your relationship.

So for John Client, a top client and a golfer, perhaps your SOS activity will be to take out a subscription for him in December to a golf magazine. At a cost of $20, this offers not just an opportunity to send a note reinforcing your friendship but also serves as a monthly reminder, when each issue arrives, of your interest in him. For $20, it's a cheap investment.

In addition, perhaps you have two key goals for that client in the coming year. The primary goal is to win an introduction to his accountant. The secondary goal is to get his GICs, which are now held elsewhere. The activity plan for that first goal might involve, by a target date of January 31, suggesting to him a financial review that would be held in conjunction with his accountant. That will occur at a time

Figure 40.10

Monitoring Progress: Top 5 Clients

Date: March 30, 1998

Clients	Primary Goal	Achieved	Secondary Goal	Achieved	SOS Activity
1. Bob & Joan Smith	Diversify investments	Moved into foreign funds	Introduction to parents	Raised—possible for later in year	Attended thank you dinner
2. Ellen Garcia	Get insurance business	Had initial conversation	Strengthen relationship	Conducted satisfaction survey	Gave subscription to *Golf Magazine*
3. Phil & June Wong	Strengthen relationship	Took to theater as thank you	—	—	Attended thank you dinner/ Sent *Guide to Disney World*
4. Roger Hebert	Get all of client's investment assets	—	Hold Money Management seminar at workplace	Discussed with VP Personnel & CFO	Sent *The Loyalty Effect*
5. Elaine Wyatt	Introduction to children	Children came to seminar	Strengthen relationship	Called once per month	Sent birthday note/gift

and place convenient to the accountant. After that session you might plan to build upon the introduction by inviting both the client and accountant to a Chamber of Commerce lunch in late March, when a well-known politician will be speaking. You might also plan, again by the end of March, to send that accountant a referral. Those three activities should serve as a springboard to forming a lasting relationship with that accountant. The vital point to remember is that those activities were driven by both the client and the goal.

You can use a blank version of Figure 40.9 to help you develop and implement your Client Activity Plans. As you begin implementing those plans, it's important to monitor progress. Too many bookshelves are filled with binders containing marvelous planning documents that were completed at great effort and have been gathering dust ever since. To avoid that, you should review progress at least monthly. The last Friday of each month is a popular time for this activity: You block it off and review your activities with your key clients, reminding yourself of the primary and secondary goals and checking what has been achieved. If you have fallen short, this is the time to figure out how to

Figure 40.11

Assessing Prospects

1. *Assets*

<$50K	1 point
$50K–$100K	3 points
$100K–$250K	5 points
$250K–$500K	7 points
Over $500K	10 points

2. *Future Potential*

Very low	1 point
Low	2 points
Moderate	3 points
High	4 points
Very high	5 points

3. *Influence*

Very low	1 point
Low	2 points
Moderate	3 points
High	4 points
Very high	5 points

4. *Satisfaction with Existing Relationship*

Very high	0 points
High	2 points
Moderate	5 points
Low	7 points
Very low	10 points

5. *Openness in Discussing Needs*

Very low	1 point
Low	2 points
Moderate	3 points
High	4 points
Very high	5 points

6. *Estimated Time Required to Meet Needs*

Very high	1 point
High	2 points
Moderate	3 points
Low	4 points
Very low	5 points

7. *PITA Factor*

Very difficult	–10 points
Somewhat difficult	–5 points
Neither easy nor difficult	0 points
Fairly easy	5 points
Pleasure to deal with	10 points

accelerate progress. Figure 40.10 provides you with a sample process for monitoring progress. A blank version will be helpful for you to use with your clients.

When we talk to financial advisers who have adopted this system, they affirm that their effectiveness has improved markedly. Just by identifying priority clients and setting specific goals, they have increased the likelihood that they will be successful.

This model can also be applied to prospects, since the same principles apply. You will weigh them according to seven similar factors, beginning with assets, future potential, influence, and their satisfaction with their existing relationship. The next element is the extent to which the prospect is open to discussing his or her needs. You also want to estimate how much time is required to meet with the prospect.

Finally, you want to rate the relationship's chemistry. How easy will it be to work with the prospect? Is this a potential PITA? Once you've identified your top prospects, you develop goals and activities to attain those goals, moving the prospects down the prospecting pipeline. Figures 40.11 to 40.16 provide some ideas to review and implement your prospecting efforts. (Figures 40.12 to 40.16 follow the Snapshots.)

In today's busy world it's easy to overlook or skimp on planning. We're all so busy hurrying from one activity to the next that we figure we don't have time to plan. But many advisers have found that it is possible to carve out time for planning, and through the 5 Percent Equation they gain extraordinary benefits. By working smarter—not just running aimlessly but developing specific client-oriented goals—they make their business far more productive.

Snapshots

✔ *In the quest for enhanced productivity, try the 5 Percent Equation. Devote 5 percent of your work week to planning, and you will gain 20 percent productivity in the remaining time.*

✔ *With clients, it's important to avoid the squeaky-wheel syndrome.*

✔ *The five steps of client planning are: identifying priority clients; setting key goals for each of those relationships; developing an activity plan to achieve those goals; implementing the activity plan; monitoring the effectiveness of your client planning; and readjusting as necessary.*

✔ *Several traps are common in identifying priority clients: concentrating on current revenue, ignoring profitability, forgetting the future, and overlooking psychic income.*

✔ *Use the following features to help you select priority clients: the assets the client has placed under your stewardship; the revenues generated in the past twelve months; referral volume; additional assets held elsewhere; future potential; influence; amount of time consumed by the client; and the PITA factor.*

✔ *Analyze your client base annually and search for PITAs who can be dispensed with.*

✔ *After you've identified priority clients, your next step is to identify goals. Those goals should begin with intensifying the relationship with the client.*

✔ *The business-oriented goals involve six facets: increasing and diversifying sales; positioning yourself to augment your share of the*

(continued on page 356)

Figure 40.12

Prospect Priority List

Prospect Name	Assets (1–10)	Future Potential (1–6)	Influence (1–5)	Satisfaction with Existing Relationship (0–10)
Scoring	1 <$50K 3 $50–100K 5 $100–250K 7 $250–500K 10 >$500K	1 Very Low 2 Low 3 Moderate 4 High 5 Very High	1 Very Low 2 Low 3 Moderate 4 High 5 Very High	0 Very High 2 High 5 Moderate 7 Low 10 Very Low
1.				
2.				
3.				
4.				
5.				
6.				
7.				
8.				
9.				
10.				

Openness in Discussing Needs (1–5)	Time (1–5)	PITA Factor (–10 to +10)	Total (Out of 50)
1 Very Low 2 Low 3 Moderate 4 High 5 Very High	1 Very High 2 High 3 Moderate 4 Low 5 Very Low	–10 V Difficult –5 Difficult 0 Neutral 5 Easy 10 Pleasure	

Figure 40.13

Possible Business Goals for Prospects

- Come to seminar
- Come to client appreciation event
- Agree to breakfast meeting
- Provide information on needs
- Agree to financial review
- Allow to provide bond pricing/quote on insurance
- Attend function with existing clients (breakfast, golf, luncheon speaker)
- Introduce to accountant

Figure 40.14

Goals for Prospects		
Prospects	**Points**	**Goal**
Prospect A	26	Agree to meeting
Prospect B	14	Do financial review
1.		
2.		
3.		
4.		
5.		

Figure 40.15

Possible Activities

Communications level	e.g. Quarterly telephone calls Full financial review
Financially related	e.g. In-house company seminar Send articles on the market
Socially driven	e.g. Golf Attend luncheon meeting at Canadian Club
Value added	e.g. Introduction to potential new client Information not related to finances Invite to appreciation event
Relationship driven	e.g. SOS Activity ("I thought of you the other day")

Figure 40.16

1998 Prospect Plan

Prospect: ____________________
Date Completed: ____________________

Primary Goal: ____________________	Secondary Goal: ____________________
Activity: 1. ____________________	Activity: 1. ____________________
Timing: ____________________	Timing: ____________________
2. ____________________	2. ____________________
Timing: ____________________	Timing: ____________________
3. ____________________	3. ____________________
Timing: ____________________	Timing: ____________________

client's investments; obtaining referrals; benefiting from the client's influence; improving productivity in dealing with the client; and insulating the relationship.

- ✔ *After establishing goals, the next step is to develop communication and activity plans to achieve them.*
- ✔ *As you begin implementing those action plans, it is vital to monitor progress.*
- ✔ *Apply the same techniques to prospects, as in the following charts.*

CHAPTER 41

Running an Efficient Practice

MANY OF US WHO GREW UP IN THE 1950S RETAIN FOND MEMORIES OF THE *Ed Sullivan Show*. Every Sunday evening for one hour starting at 8 o'clock, Ed Sullivan would bring together a broad range of top entertainers. He'd present comedians like Wayne and Shuster and Rich Little, singers and dancers from around the world, and novelty acts like the famous Italian mouse, Topo Gigio.

Everybody had their favorites. Mine were the jugglers. I never ceased to be amazed by the guy who came out with just a pile of long sticks and stack of plates. He'd place one stick on its end, start it spinning, and then sit a plate on top of it and set that plate twirling as well. He'd repeat this feat with a second stick, at the same time giving the first plate a slight twist to keep it going. Then he'd continue with a third, fourth and fifth plate, until there were twenty sticks spinning with twenty plates whirling on top. At that point the juggler would be frantically running around keeping all of them rotating, to avert a major calamity.

For me that epitomizes how many successful financial advisers run their practices. When they start, they have a small number of sticks and plates to keep spinning. As their practice grows, the number increases, until they're madly dashing around, trying to avoid major crashes. Unlike the *Ed Sullivan Show*, however, nobody is wildly applauding them.

The Adviser Conundrum

I've dubbed that frustrating juggling act the Adviser Conundrum. It's a vicious circle resulting from overwhelming external and internal pressures. The external pressures include rapidly expanding client bases, populated with more demanding clients, and an environment in which top clients are increasingly being prospected by direct competitors. Indeed, on a regular basis, competing financial planners, investment advisers, and various other money counsellors are launching full frontal initiatives on our best clients. And that attack will only get more intense.

You can thrive by delegating, putting practices on autopilot and attaining maximum leverage from your activities.

The pressures don't end there. In addition to external pressures, we face internal sources of stress—rising costs of doing business, delays on seeing paybacks in our investments in staff and technology, and a severe time crunch because of the rigors of the job. Even if we wanted to work harder, which we don't, it wouldn't be very productive, because most of us have bumped up against the point of diminishing returns. The only solution is to focus on running a highly efficient practice. In future, for many advisers the main challenge won't be to grow a bigger practice but to shape a more effective one.

That in turn will require concentrating on the four principles that underlie an efficient operation. We discussed the first principle earlier: segmenting our client base to focus on our highest-value clients. Beyond that, advisers must take advantage of three other opportunities to enhance efficiency: We must delegate effectively, we must develop systems to put routine activity on autopilot, and we must focus on doing a small number of things well with maximum impact.

I'll begin with effective delegation, which is more complicated and difficult than it might seem at first blush. In fact, effective delegation involves five elements: Broadening decision-making across the team, expanding access points for clients, building on the strength of the team, increasing the overall level of expertise offered to clients, and, finally, freeing up adviser time.

It's important to remember that from our clients' point of view the key in any delegation is to improve their overall experience of dealing with their adviser. From the adviser's standpoint, of course, effective delegation is intended to significantly free up time while in a transparent way improving clients' experience.

In doing so it's vital to avoid the Delegation Trap. This occurs when advisers, in growing their practice, add assistant after assistant, each time assigning the newcomer specific tasks but retaining responsibility for themselves. Tasks are delegated down but responsibility remains up, with the adviser. The result? The adviser's productivity fails to increase.

Consider the alternative scenario, in which the adviser sits down with each assistant and clearly identifies tasks which are his or her responsibility. Whether that involves setting up appointments, pulling paper work for client meetings, responding to client requests and calls, organizing a client-appreciation dinner, overseeing a seminar, or proactively contacting less important clients, the assistant has clearly defined responsibilities.

If the team has several members, delegation may involve broad functions. The adviser may assign marketing responsibility to one assistant, client responsibility to another, and operational responsibility to a third. As a result the adviser is liberated to focus time on the highest-valued functions which cannot be easily completed by anyone else and which provide the greatest overall impact to the practice.

Transfer Authority

This transfer of authority is the essence of delegation. To make it work the adviser must provide clear ownership for key tasks, within defined parameters. It is critical as well to encourage team members to take responsibility for maximizing their productivity, thinking beyond narrowly defined areas.

In travelling down this path it's helpful to start the journey by preparing two lists. The first details the key uses of your time during a typical week—activities that consume the bulk of your hours. The second list catalogues key time-wasters—those things that eat up time without providing clear and apparent value.

Return to the first list, and for each item contemplate possible delegation opportunities. Identify components you can strip out and delegate on an ongoing basis. Financial plans are an obvious example. Many financial advisers historically have met with new clients to review their needs and provide such plans. That has involved a multistep process, beginning with gathering all the relevant information. Afterwards, advisers would analyze that data and prepare a plan. Finally, they would meet with clients to explain their recommendations and discuss next steps.

Of those four steps, which are essential that the adviser participate in? Arguably, the adviser needs to be present in steps one and four, to explain the process and meet with the client to review overall recommendations. But the fact-finding and plan-preparation stages can be completely delegated. Beyond that, when the adviser meets with the client, if the intention is to have another member of the advisery team provide ongoing contact, that person should obviously participate in the meeting.

In essence this approach applies the same principles to an adviser's practice that we see in other professions such as dentistry. Twenty years ago most dentists would have had a single chair and perhaps shared their receptionist with two or three other dentists. That format has become less common because the economics of running a dentistry practice don't permit it. Increasingly, dentists have two or three chairs, with a staff performing functions such as cleaning teeth and taking x-rays, while the dentist participates only at crucial stages.

Those two lists analyzing your time help to apply the same principles to your practice. After reviewing each "key use of time" for delegation opportunities, move on to "key time-wasters," which, as the title suggests, is an even more critical area for this delegatory triage. By time-wasters, I should stress, we are talking not about activities that can be eliminated but rather low-value matters that must be completed by someone, but not necessarily by the adviser.

An example is reviewing voice-mail messages. It's not uncommon for an adviser who has been out of the office for half a day to return to at least a dozen voice-mail messages. If each one averages thirty seconds, an adviser can easily spend ten minutes sitting by the phone, taking notes on the messages and replaying them for missed phone numbers or key points.

Consider an alternative system: Whenever an adviser is out of the office for a stipulated period of time, say, two hours or longer, it's the responsibility of one of her team to pick up those voice-mail messages. They are then transcribed, with two copies on the adviser's desk when she returns. The adviser can take the first copy and immediately delegate those calls that can logically be returned by somebody else. That copy is divided among the appropriate team members. The second copy stays with the adviser, who can use it to identify priorities for return calls.

Follow-up letters after client meetings offer another example of delegation. Sending a quick note after those meetings signals your professionalism, organization, and commitment to the relationship. For most advisers, however, the time required to send such notes puts this activity out of the question.

Consider the alternative of a hand-held dictating machine. In a minute or less an adviser can dictate a quick follow-up note, perhaps in the car returning from the meeting. At day's end that tape is sent to one of the team members for transcription, with the letter appearing on the adviser's desk the next day for approval and signing. The amount of time required to produce those letters hasn't decreased, but delegating the bulk of the task to another team member has now made it manageable for the adviser. Sending follow-up notes can be a high-value activity, but it doesn't have to drain advisers of their high-value time.

The Autopilot Experience

So the first principle of running an efficient practice is to delegate at every opportunity—but delegate intelligently. Another delegation trap is that advisers can become so jealous of their time that they become inaccessible. Clients must pass through a gauntlet of interrogation to determine whether they'll be allowed to talk to their now well-shielded adviser. Obviously no client likes having to undergo the third degree to reach his adviser. That may be delegation, but it's not transparent, and it doesn't improve client service and value. It's a trap you must avoid.

A second principle for developing an efficient practice is to put activities on autopilot. As I've indicated, the idea is to establish automatic processes in which you have little or no day-to-day involvement. This involves three steps. First, the adviser must identify the key trigger points to make that activity happen. Second, a process must be established detailing specifically what happens and when. Finally, the adviser must assign clear responsibility.

We talked earlier about the adviser who, after losing a key client because of lack of contact, initiated a process of short telephone reviews with clients, investing two afternoons a week. One of the elements that allowed this to happen was that the adviser carefully broke down the key steps in the process, as in Figure 41.1.

His assistant identified priority clients who hadn't received contact in sixty days, and together the assistant and adviser identified which clients to approach. After drafting the letter, the adviser delegated to

Figure 41.1

Process: Telephone Review
Identify priority clients who have not received contact in 60 days
Responsibility: Assistant
Select clients to approach
Responsibility: Adviser/ Assistant
Send letter
Responsibility: Assistant
One week
Follow up call to book appointment
Responsibility: Assistant
Set schedule/pull files for review
Responsibility: Assistant
Set next appointment
Responsibility: Adviser
Send confirming follow up letter
Responsibility: Assistant

his assistant the responsibility for sending letters out, booking appointments, setting a schedule for meetings, and pulling files for the adviser to review.

Each Monday morning the adviser found on his desk a list of clients with whom he had scheduled phone appointments, along with their files to review prior to the conversation. As part of the call, the adviser set a date for the next appointment. Again, the parallel is with a well-run dentist's office, where the last thing that happens during an appointment is that the next appointment is arranged by the receptionist. To close the circle for the adviser, after the meeting the assistant is responsible for sending a confirming letter with the date, recording it in the calendar, and reminding the client a few days beforehand by phone.

In our work many activities occur that can be transformed into an autopilot process in your office. The client review is a natural opening. In fact, you could arrange an automatic process for both the period leading up to the review and the one afterward. Other opportunities appear after the introduction of a new client or a referral from an existing client.

Figure 41.2 outlines the steps leading to a client meeting. It begins with a client telephone conversation, handled either by the adviser or an assistant. They discuss the topics to be covered in the upcoming

Figure 41.2

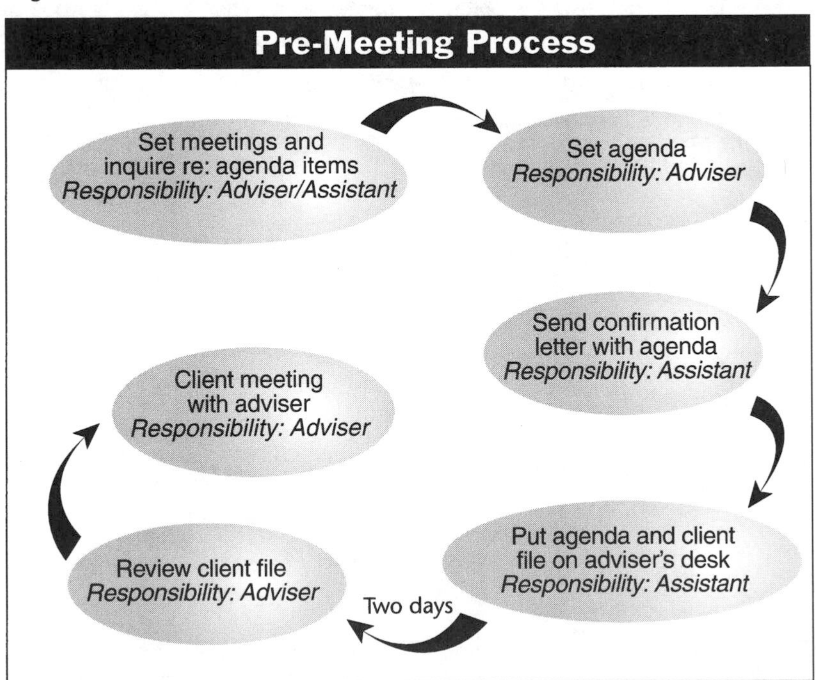
Pre-Meeting Process
Set meetings and inquire re: agenda items
Responsibility: Adviser/Assistant
Set agenda
Responsibility: Adviser
Send confirmation letter with agenda
Responsibility: Assistant
Put agenda and client file on adviser's desk
Responsibility: Assistant
Two days
Review client file
Responsibility: Adviser
Client meeting with adviser
Responsibility: Adviser

meeting, effectively setting an agenda for that session. In particular, the client is canvassed about items she would specifically like covered. After the adviser uses that information to set the agenda, the assistant sends the client a confirmation letter, along with the prospective agenda. That plan is placed in the client's file so that before the meeting the adviser can study all the appropriate background.

Some advisers like to begin meetings by reconfirming that agenda. "We talked previously about what we would be discussing today," the adviser will say. "This is the agenda we agreed to, but I thought that before starting I should check whether there's anything we've missed or that has recently come up that should be included. In fact, you'll note the first item on the agenda is blank, so that we can add any other matters you want to talk about."

With this kind of preparation the chances for a successful outcome to the meeting have increased dramatically. But what's important is that little of the work has actually involved the adviser's time. Much of it has been delegated, yet the adviser-client bond has been strengthened.

A parallel post-meeting process can also be implemented. At the conclusion of the session the adviser and client agree to next steps. At that time the next meeting is scheduled. A follow-up note is sent to the client summarizing the items that were discussed and confirming the next steps.

Here again that dictating machine comes in handy. Most advisers, if they had to type or handwrite a note after each meeting, would simply not find time. Dictating that note, on the other hand, can be squeezed in more easily. And the beauty of the system is that even though the adviser dictates the note, the assistant takes charge of ensuring everything happens, including overseeing transcription and sending out the card confirming the next meeting or phone appointment. As well, the assistant monitors completion of the next steps agreed to with the client and takes responsibility for reminding the client of the follow-up meeting. Once again an important process has been steered on autopilot, with relatively low levels of adviser time and attention but enhanced efficiency as far as the client is concerned.

Autopilot for New Clients

Autopilot processes can also be employed to ease new clients into your practice, leaving them with a highly positive feeling about the experience. We've talked previously about gestures that can help to smooth entry. Those all turn out to be perfect for autopilot systems.

One adviser, after the initial paperwork has been completed, sends a note welcoming the client, with a copy of a popular book on financial planning. In fact he has no real role in sending that letter and book out, except for signing the letter. His assistant takes responsibility for automatically generating the letter, putting it on his desk and then mailing it.

A week or ten days later, in the pattern we've discussed earlier, the assistant will call the new client, saying: "John Adviser asked me to touch base. You should have received the confirmation of your investment by now. He wanted me to make sure it has been received and to go through it with you to answer any questions you might have."

After the first statement is received, again the autopilot system is triggered. The assistant calls to check the statement has arrived and to offer to clarify anything that seems confusing. Those two phone calls, which don't take a great deal of staff time and, more importantly, none of the adviser's (unless a problem is uncovered that the assistant can't handle), leave the client with a feeling her adviser really cares about her.

This adviser adds another autopilot element to demonstrate his commitment to clients. Three months after they come on board, he sends a note asking for feedback on how he and his team are doing. Attached is a simple one-page questionnaire that serves as an interim report card on the relationship and an early warning of any problems. Of course, the adviser includes a postage-return envelope making it easy for the client to return that report card. It's rare for anything negative to crop up at this stage; after all, the client has already heard from the adviser's assistant twice. But if something emerges, the adviser or his assistant follows up with the client directly.

Referrals on Autopilot

Advisers can also apply an autopilot process to referrals, aimed at both the new prospect and the generous client who supplied the referral. When that referral arrives, your paramount objective is to start differentiating yourself, offering that prospect ample reason to carry out business with you rather than with the other financial advisers almost certainly also being considered.

In a well-oiled autopilot system the adviser will call immediately to set up an appointment. A confirming letter is at once sent out, with the type of background information we outlined earlier: biographical information, client testimonials, and perhaps an intriguing article from a reputable publication to help build an image of professionalism.

The clients—let's assume they're a couple—then receive a call from the adviser's assistant confirming their appointment. When they eventually arrive at the office and tell the receptionist they have an appointment, she asks: "Are you Mr. and Mrs. Prospect?" When they reply affirmatively, the receptionist says, "Mr. Adviser told me he's expecting you and to let him know as soon as you are here."

That couple have yet to lay eyes on the adviser but they are already receiving strong positive signals about his commitment, discipline, and professionalism: the confirming letter, the background information, the call to confirm the appointment, and the warm, personal greeting from the receptionist. Yet the adviser essentially did not have to participate in any of it. None of those routines making him shine required his precious time. They were all part of an automatic process that he originally established but his assistant has managed ever since.

The same principle can be applied to those clients who provided the invaluable referrals. Given the propensity of future referrals to flow from clients who have previously offered them, advisers can't let their response to that gift be determined by whim or the pressures of that day.

After the client provides the referral, you might send a handwritten thank-you note the same day or, at most, within twenty-four hours. Again, even though you write the note yourself, it might be initiated by your assistant, who puts it on your desk with a reminder of the recipient.

After meeting with the prospect, the outcome will generally not be determined right away. It may take multiple meetings, spanning weeks or even months, before the client makes a final decision. Afterwards, you have a second opportunity to thank the original client, sending a note that updates her on the situation with her friend or relative.

Even if the prospect decides not to become a client at this point, the opportunity to cement yourself further with the original client remains. A note can be sent: "You may recall that recently you were good enough to introduce me to your friend, Joe Prospect. I've met with Joe, and while Joe has not yet become a client, I did want to let you know how much I appreciated your confidence in introducing us." If the prospect does opt to become a client, and your office has introduced an interim report card after three to six months, you have another opportunity for automatically thanking the person who provided the original referral. If the new client is feeling good about the process, you can express your delight to him and then ask if he minds if you let his friend know. That gives you another chance to thank that original client, validating that she made the right decision in offering the introduction and increasing the likelihood that she'll think of you in the future when an acquaintance needs a financial adviser. Again, the key is to delegate as much of this process—both mechanics and oversight —to another team member, in a way consistent with your style.

Gift-Giving on Autopilot

The final opportunity for autopilot activities in the referral process that I want to highlight comes with gift-giving. Again, you have to set up a process to make it happen, like the adviser who every December sends half-bottles of ice wine to clients who provided quality referrals (leading, he has found, to a doubling of referrals in January by clients who appreciate his appreciation). In your office that would mean deciding every December to acknowledge all such referrals with ice wine or some other appropriate gift, and then turning the task over to your assistant, who tracks clients and can handle the details.

The same setup can be applied to magazine subscriptions. These are one of my five best ways of thanking people, since when you send a subscription that relates to their interests you get a chance—at a cost of $30—to remind your clients twelve times a year not only of your gratitude but that you're open for business. The assistant of one adviser I know maintains a computer file of subscription information for a variety of publications. All the adviser has to do is say "sailing," and the subscription order is generated, a card is put on her desk to sign, and the gift is on its way.

In all these situations the adviser must identify the key trigger point. What is the catalyst for action: A specific event? A time of year? The gifts may occur immediately after the referral, for example, or at a certain time each year. Then the adviser must design a workable process, in conjunction with her staff. Then she delegates.

Less Is More

The final step to running an effective practice is to ensure you're doing a few things well and receiving maximum benefit from those activities. Rather than slipping into a scattershot approach, study your operations, or the new ideas you've gleaned from this book, and calculate how to gain maximum leverage from them.

As an example, imagine what can be leveraged from a client-satisfaction survey. These are useful tools for you to gain feedback on your work and pick up early-warning signals of clients who are losing faith. But the process shouldn't stop there.

You can extend the survey's benefits by sending the results back to the clients to further nurture the relationship. When you meet with prospects, you can show them the survey results to add beef to your claims about your high commitment to service (particularly if the survey was carried out by someone unbiased, such as your accountant, and the summary of results is on her letterhead). Or if you're trying to develop a professional referral relationship with an accountant or lawyer, you can quickly allay any concerns about your abilities by giving them a copy of the survey results.

After developing a process—in this case, a client-feedback survey—the effective adviser will stand back and look at every possible way to gain leverage from that activity. This avoids diluting your efforts by rushing off madly in all directions, like that juggler on *Ed Sullivan*. Instead, study the activity and look at every possible way to derive benefit (Figure 41.3).

Newsletters are an excellent opportunity for applying this philosophy. However, preparing articles and designing each page can involve a lot of work, even in these days of desktop publishing, and the cost can be considerable, from the professional help you may want to seek in editing and design, to printing. So ask yourself: How do I maximize the benefits from my client newsletter?

One way, obviously, is to not limit it to clients (Figure 41.4). Your newsletters can be sent to prospects in your pipeline, to keep you top of mind. They can be included in the introductory package you send to new referrals, showing the kind of ongoing communication they can expect to receive.

Newsletters can also be used to spark more referrals from existing clients. Start by selecting one client who has referred a friend or acquaintance recently. Call the client and say that as a thank you, you are sending a gift certificate for a dinner out with that couple's friends (now, presumably, your clients) at one of the better restaurants in town.

Then, in your next newsletter, include an article on the back page with the headline, "Welcome and Thank You." It could read something like this:

"A special welcome to all of the new clients who have joined us since our last newsletter. Thanks in particular to those clients who have mentioned our name to people they know. As a small sign of our gratitude, four times a year we randomly select for special acknowl-

Figure 41.3

Areas to Leverage an Activity

Clients:	Prospects:	People You Know:
Centers of Influence:	Community Profile:	Other:

Figure 41.4

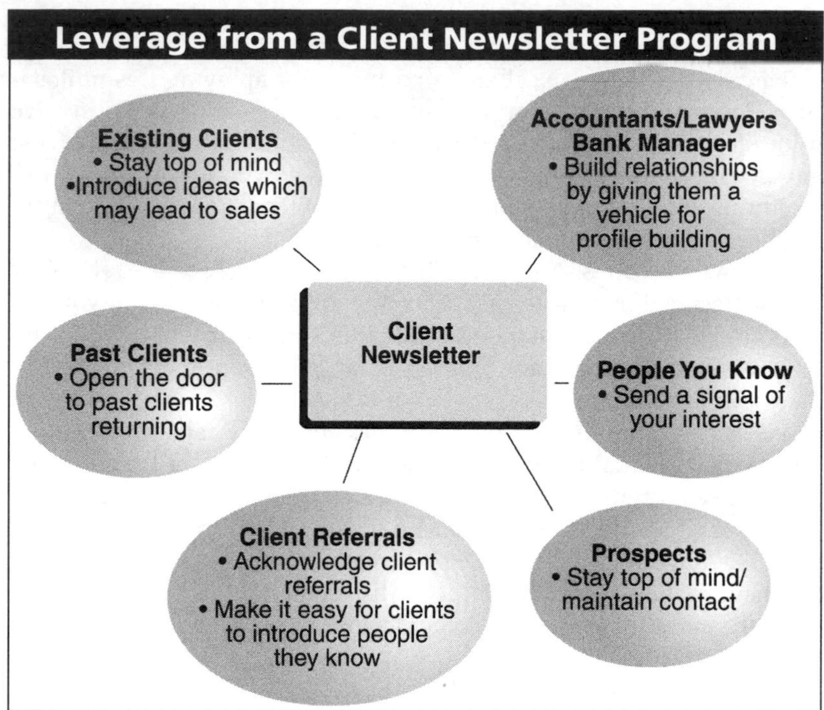
Leverage from a Client Newsletter Program
Existing Clients
• Stay top of mind
•Introduce ideas which may lead to sales
Accountants/Lawyers
Bank Manager
• Build relationships by giving them a vehicle for profile building
Client Newsletter
Past Clients
• Open the door to past clients returning
People You Know
• Send a signal of your interest
Client Referrals
• Acknowledge client referrals
• Make it easy for clients to introduce people they know
Prospects
• Stay top of mind/ maintain contact

edgment a client who has introduced our services to a friend. Receiving dinner for four this month at the XYZ restaurant are Mr. and Mrs. Existing Client and their friends, Mr. and Mrs. New Client."

Repeat this every newsletter (first ensuring, of course, that you have your clients' permission to use their names). After two or three issues chances are that you'll see referrals start to climb. Simply by rewarding one client every few months and telling people about it through the newsletter you were already producing, you've reminded all your clients of your interest in referrals, as well as showing your appreciation.

Another way to increase referrals through the newsletter is to encourage clients to suggest additions for your newsletter mailing list. The next time you have a review with a client you're confident is satisfied, send a note the week before your appointment, along with a copy of the newsletter: "I look forward to meeting with you next Wednesday at 11. In addition to reviewing your portfolio, I'd like to ask a favor. I am hoping to add to the distribution list for my newsletter people who might find the information in it of value. If you have one or two friends you think this newsletter would interest, I'd be delighted to add them to my mailing list."

At the end of your meeting, mention the note you sent. Ask your client whether she's had "a chance to think about one or two people who might find my newsletter of value." Positioned this way, you're much more likely to get a positive response, since you've focused your client's attention on the issue in a non-threatening, low-key fashion. You've given your client time to think about it, instead of launching it as a surprise. You've also appealed for something most clients will find achievable—identifying just one or two names. And again, your newsletter has served as the vehicle for gaining those precious names.

Newsletters can also be used to develop professional referrals, as we've discussed. By asking accountants or lawyers to contribute articles to your newsletter, you edge past their initial distrust and encourage them to sit down and talk about other things you can tackle together. This might even lead to an accountant purchasing your newsletter to send to some of her clients, automatically increasing the number of potential referrals for you.

Finally, newsletters can be used to stay in touch with past clients who have left for pastures that may have proven not to be greener. They may have discovered that the promises made to them by the competing adviser were exactly that—promises, without much substance. Often, however, those clients are embarrassed about returning to the adviser they left behind.

You can help by taking the first step. And one of the best ways is by sending a copy of your most recent newsletter with a low-key note (Figure 41.5). That's often all it takes to break the ice and make it easy for clients having second thoughts to give you a call and get the relationship back on track.

Developing a first-rate newsletter takes time and effort. As with everything you undertake, therefore, you should look for ways to gain maximum leverage from it. In these busy times, there are three guiding rules: Limit what you do. Do a few things well. Build from it.

Meeting the Future

Every financial adviser is familiar with the time-worn phrase, "Past performance is not an indicator for future performance." It's absolutely true of investment products. It's equally true of financial advisers. When it comes to this business, past success by a financial adviser is not an indication of future success.

Many advisers today are successful because they came into the business at a fortuitous time, when consumers were less knowledgeable and competition was less intense. Others were able to identify and take advantage of tactics such as direct mail or mass seminars before they proliferated.

Figure 41.5

Dear Any:

It's been a while since we spoke. I thought that you might find a copy of my recent newsletter interesting reading—NAME OF TOPIC on page 3 is something that is especially important these days.

I hope that things are going well for you. Please don't hesitate to call if there's ever a question I can answer or anything I can do for you.

Best regards,

Any Adviser

P.S. I have taken the liberty of adding you to my newsletter mailing list—please give my assistant, NAME OF ASSISTANT, a call if you'd like to be taken off the list for any reason.

Going forward, financial advisers must operate in a very different reality, defined by the dramatically more knowledgeable, discerning investor and the more intense, competitive environment. As a result, in the future, there will be three categories of financial advisers—the thrivers, the survivors, and the goners. Where financial advisers fall among those three categories will essentially be determined by the level of value they provide to clients and their effectiveness in achieving a distinct and unique position in the competitive marketplace.

I teach an MBA course in Advanced Marketing Strategy at the University of Toronto. In that course I have a theme borrowed from the motto of the French Foreign Legion. Their motto is: "March or Die." Ours is: "Change or Die." And there's no business for which that's more applicable than ours.

In the future, value will be the watchword defining an adviser's success. Those advisers who are order-takers—who don't provide particular value—will be goners. No matter how successful they may appear today, that success can evaporate if clients believe they can attain more value elsewhere.

The survivors (also a category you don't want to fall into) will be financial advisers who provide adequate value—enough value to prevent someone from actively looking for an alternative, but not sufficient to stand out in attracting new clients.

The thrivers, on the other hand, will be those financial advisers who provide truly superior value.

We talked earlier in this book about the components of value—the quality of the financial plan you construct, the advice you provide, your commitment to regular communication and education, and, above all, the depth of the relationship you construct with clients and prospects. The hard reality is that the competitive environment in the future will be dramatically tougher than in the past. The things that once worked successfully will not always work in the future.

One competitive assault is coming from information increasingly available on the Internet. More and more clients who are so disposed can obtain up-to-the minute information, or find asset-allocation and financial-planning models and a myriad of other information they never could have found until now. This technology fundamentally threatens the role of any intermediary, whether a real estate agent, travel agent, or financial adviser who has positioned herself merely as providing access to a transaction.

A second competitive assault is emerging from financial institutions. Banks in the past have not represented a competitive threat for the typical financial adviser. Five years ago banks didn't see themselves in the business of providing financial advice. In most branches there was typically no access to anyone with even a modicum of knowledge. Even if somebody happened to be knowledgeable, little motivation existed to pursue the client and ask for the order.

Today we have witnessed a sweeping change. All banks are moving toward structured fact-finding questionnaires to identify the client's risk orientation and help to recommend mutual fund portfolios. Speaking two years ago to the annual meeting of the Canadian Association of Financial Planners, I asked the audience to fill out the questionnaire Canada Trust was then using to identify client profiles. A number of financial advisers told me afterwards that the rigor and quality of the fact-finding process Canada Trust was employing to identify client-risk levels was superior to what they were utilizing. And it will only get better, as banks refine those techniques for their clientele.

Banks have also improved the range of mutual funds they provide. In some cases they offer the same independent funds as independent financial advisers. In other cases they have sought out top-rated investment managers from all around the world to work on a sub-adviser basis, lending their expertise.

As well, banks are moving away from investment generalists to investment specialists. Unlike circumstances five years ago when a financial adviser in a bank—if you found one—would be selling mortgages one minute, credit cards the next, and investments a little later, all the banks are moving toward dedicated specialists. More and more of these people are highly qualified with the appropriate educational designations. Beyond that, a number of banks are moving toward variable compensation, creating motivation for their investment specialists to actively pursue clients and seek their business—motivation that was lacking in the past.

Still, opportunities for financial advisers have never been greater. The market for our work has been steadily expanding and will continue to expand. Those financial advisers who truly provide outstanding value will attract a quality and quantity of clients they never imagined possible. In this book I hope I have laid out a road map to ensure you will be among those financial advisers who thrive in the period ahead. That being said, writing this book has been the easy part. Now with implementation the hard work begins.

I hope this book has given you the insights and foundation to take advantage of the many changes and opportunities swirling around us, to ensure that you will continue Getting Clients and Keeping Clients in the years ahead. In the movie *The Empire Strikes Back*, when Luke Skywalker agrees to try one of Yoda's exercises, the Master Jedi makes clear to Luke: "Do or not do. There is no try." That's the same challenge faced by the reader of this book: Act on some of the ideas contained here or fail to receive value—there is nothing in between.

Snapshots

✔ *Too many advisers are like the jugglers on* Ed Sullivan*: as their practice grows, the number of sticks and plates increases until they're madly dashing around trying to avoid major crashes. I call this the Adviser Conundrum.*

✔ *In future the main challenge for many advisers won't be growing bigger practices but shaping more effective, efficient ones.*

✔ *Rule One in running an efficient practice is: Delegate efficiently.*

✔ *It's vital to avoid the Delegation Trap that occurs when advisers add assistant after assistant to their growing practices, each time assigning specific tasks but retaining responsibility.*

✔ *Instead, the adviser must clearly identify with each assistant which tasks are his or her responsibility.*

✔ *Start the journey to effective delegation by preparing two lists: the key uses of your time during a typical week, and the key time-wasters.*

Use these to determine what has to be done by you and what can be delegated to an assistant.

- ✔ *Rule Two in developing an efficient practice is: Put activities on autopilot.*
- ✔ *In autopilot activities the adviser has to identify the key trigger points. What is the catalyst for action: A specific event? A time of year?*
- ✔ *Rule Three in running an effective practice is: Ensure you're doing a few things well and receiving maximum benefit from those activities.*
- ✔ *The future will see three categories of financial advisers—thrivers, survivors, and goners. Where financial advisers fall among those categories will be determined by the level of value they provide to their clients, and their effectiveness in achieving a distinct, unique position in the competitive marketplace.*
- ✔ *Despite increased competition, opportunities for financial advisers have never been greater. The market for our work has been expanding. Those financial advisers who truly provide outstanding value will attract a quality and quantity of clients they never believed possible.*

INDEX